D1624994

Contents

Illustrations

Maps and Charts

Preface to the Second Edition

The first edition of this book, which appeared in 1970, covered the years from 1559 to 1689. In this revised version the closing date has been moved forward to 1715. The death of Louis XIV is a more generally accepted dividing point in European history than the Glorious Revolution, and extension of the time span permits a wider view of the whole period. In an expanded Introduction I endeavor to set the stage for the narrative by describing European society in 1559. In a new concluding chapter I survey the international wars of 1683–1721 and the reign of Peter the Great, and assess European society as of 1715. In addition, I have taken the opportunity to revise Chapter 3 extensively, to make corrections and alterations throughout the other chapters, to add new maps and illustrations, and to expand the bibliography. I am very grateful to all the readers who suggested revisions, and hope they find the book improved as a result.

September, 1978   R.S.D.

The Age of Religious Wars
1559-1715

Introduction

DURING the century and a half between 1559 and 1715, Europe was in a nearly constant state of war. There were fewer than thirty years of international peace, and more than a hundred years of major combat, in which all or most of the leading European states were simultaneously engaged. Warfare has of course been endemic throughout European history, but the fighting in these years had its distinctive features. For nearly a century, from 1559 to 1648, the common denominator was Protestant-Catholic religious strife. This confessional conflict was passionate and highly disruptive. After the mid-seventeenth century, combat reverted to a more secular and orderly pattern. Thus our period marks the apogee and the decline of religious warfare in Europe.

The battles fought between Protestants and Catholics in the late sixteenth and early seventeenth centuries were tumultuous and anarchic because they characteristically took the form of civil war and rebellion. Luther had inaugurated the ideological controversy in 1517, but Luther was not a political activist. Confessional conflict intensified in the mid-sixteenth century when a new breed of militant Protestant and Catholic champions came to the fore. The French civil wars of 1562–1598, the Dutch revolt against Philip II, the Scottish rebellion against Mary Stuart, the Spanish attack on England in 1588, the Thirty Years' War in Germany between 1618 and 1648, and the Puritan Revolution of 1640–1660 and the Glorious Revolution of 1688–1689 in England were all religious conflicts, though of course they had other causes as well. This was an age of crusaders and martyrs, of plots and assassinations, of fanatic mobs and psalm-singing armies. The most militant crusaders proved to be the disciples of John Calvin and of St. Ignatius of Loyola. The Calvinists gained control of Scotland and the Dutch republic, temporarily seized power in England, and tried to take over in France, Germany, Poland, and Hungary. The Catholics, revitalized in the mid-sixteenth century, kept trying until the late seventeenth century to restore the seamless unity of the Christian Church. In France, Flanders, Austria, and Bohemia, at least,

1

Symbol of a new era—the Protestant Archbishop Cranmer burned at the stake in 1556 by the Catholic Queen Mary of England. *This woodcut is from John Foxe's* Book of Martyrs *(1563), the most popular English book—next to the Bible—for a century, and the Protestant counterpart to a Catholic* Lives of the Saints.

they successfully suppressed Protestantism. Both sides in this extraordinary contest were able to attract a high percentage of articulate, prosperous, and socially powerful people into their ranks. Both sides gradually lost their crusading zeal.

After 1648, and particularly after 1689, religion was no longer the common denominator—though it remained a disruptive factor—in European international conflict. The great wars that wracked western Europe from 1688 to 1713 and eastern Europe from 1683 to 1721 were larger in scale than the earlier civil wars and rebellions, but they were far less alarming to the established order, because they were managed from above by kings and generals rather than plotted from below by rebels and crusaders. The effect of these wars at the close of our period was to repudiate the confessional turmoil of 1559–1648 and to restore a more stable balance of power among the chief European states.

Such is the bald outline of the story that follows. But there is far more to it. The period from 1559 to 1715 is remembered for a wide array of political, economic, social, and intellectual developments, subject to sharply conflicting interpretations. Some historians label this period the age of absolutism; some call it the age of mercantilism; others focus on the growth of bourgeois enterprise or the rise of constitutional, representative government. For intellectual historians, this is preeminently a time of scientific revolution; for art historians it is the era of the Baroque; for literary historians, the golden age of the drama. Social historians, on the other hand, are inclined to find the years between the Reformation and the Enlightenment a dark time of famine, plague, poverty, slavery, and belief in witchcraft. The diversity of opinion recalls the story of the blind men who encountered an elephant and disagreed about what they had found. But the analogy is faulty, for those who study early modern Europe are neither blind nor wrongheaded. Interpretations are necessarily diverse because sixteenth- and seventeenth-century developments were so richly complex. To make sense out of the events between 1559 and 1715, we must observe the continuous interaction between contradictory forces: confessional strife, political absolutism, bourgeois enterprise, mercantilist regulation, peasant malaise, cultural innovation, and social repression. We can then appreciate the way in which the age of religious wars left a permanent impress upon nearly every aspect of European life: on concepts of liberty and toleration, on party politics, the art of kingship, business enterprise, the social structure, science, philosophy, and the arts.

EUROPE IN 1559

What were the most distinctive features of European society in the mid-sixteenth century?

Examination of the map of Europe in 1559 shows a state system that looks partly familiar and partly strange to the modern eye. Politically, Europe was divided into three zones—western, central, and eastern—and this division remained a basic fact of political life for the next century or more. The section of the map showing the eastern zone, where the Ottoman Empire, Poland-Lithuania, and Muscovite Russia were the chief states, looks unfamiliar because the Polish-Russian border stood much farther eastward than it does today and the Ottoman Empire embraced all of the Balkans. The Ottoman Turks and the Muscovites were isolated from the rest of Europe by religion and culture, and the whole eastern region was hobbled by a primitive economy, thinly dispersed population, loose political organization (except for the Ottomans), and deep internal ethnic divisions. In the central zone, by contrast, the Italians and Germans had long been the business and cultural leaders of Europe. But events in the early sixteenth century had devastated the central European political structure. The Italian state system had been wrecked by French, Spanish, and German invaders between the 1490's and the 1520's, and the Holy Roman Empire had been paralyzed by civil war, lasting from 1520 to 1555 and unresolved by the Augsburg peace settlement of 1555. The sec-

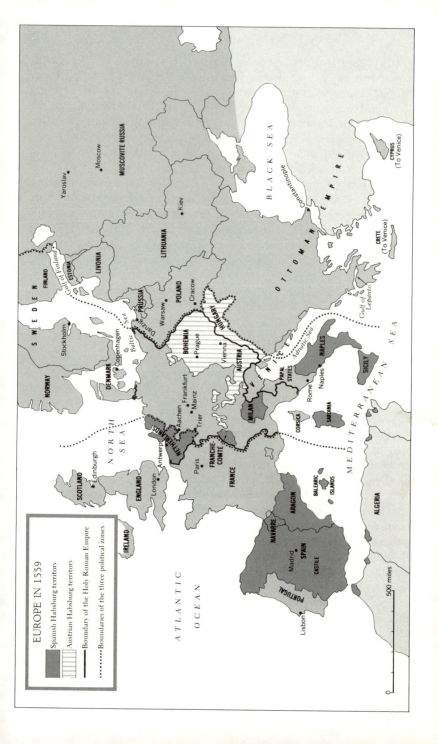

EUROPE IN 1559

- Spanish Habsburg territory
- Austrian Habsburg territory
- ▬▬ Boundary of the Holy Roman Empire
- ⋯⋯ Boundaries of the three political zones

500 miles

ATLANTIC OCEAN

NORTH SEA

BALTIC Sea

BLACK SEA

MEDITERRANEAN SEA

Adriatic Sea

Gulf of Finland

Gulf of Lepanto

IRELAND

SCOTLAND
•Edinburgh

ENGLAND
•London

NORWAY

SWEDEN
•Stockholm

DENMARK
•Copenhagen

FINLAND

ESTONIA

LIVONIA

MUSCOVITE RUSSIA
•Moscow
•Yaroslav

LITHUANIA
•Kiev

PRUSSIA
•Danzig

POLAND
•Warsaw
•Cracow

HUNGARY

BOHEMIA
•Prague

AUSTRIA
•Vienna

OTTOMAN EMPIRE
•Constantinople

CYPRUS
(To Venice)

CRETE
(To Venice)

FRANCE
•Paris

NETHERLANDS
•Antwerp

•Aachen
•Frankfurt
•Mainz
•Trier

FRANCHE-COMTÉ

MILAN

PAPAL STATES
•Rome

Naples
NAPLES

SARDINIA

CORSICA

SICILY

SPAIN
•Madrid

CASTILE

ARAGON

NAVARRE

PORTUGAL
•Lisbon

BALEARIC ISLANDS

ALGERIA

tion of the map showing central Europe in 1559 looks especially strange because the Holy Roman Empire incorporated what is now West and East Germany, Switzerland, Austria, and much of Czechoslovakia, Poland, and Italy, as well as the Low Countries in the western zone. This empire was not a cohesive state; it consisted of three hundred separate political units, none of them very large, joined by a system of alliances. Thus central Europe was politically particularistic and divided. In the western zone, however, the leading Atlantic states—Spain, France, and England—had gained notably in cohesion and power during the preceding century. The section of the map showing this region appears much as it does today, except that France's eastern border is more circumscribed, and the Netherlands have not yet been divided into modern Holland, Belgium, and Luxemburg. By 1559 the Atlantic states had developed considerable national identity; they were political units in which kings had sovereign authority over extensive, populous territories, with coherent linguistic or ethnic consciousness.

The significance of this three-zone division is that the political center of gravity lay in western Europe. Spain and France were the two most powerful states, by far, in 1559. And during the ensuing religious wars the English and the Dutch developed new political effectiveness, while the chief central and eastern empires and kingdoms remained disorganized and weak. Economically, too, the Atlantic states occupied the first rank. Their merchants were by far the most successful businessmen of the day, developing a prosperous and expanding commercial capitalist economy, while the older trade and industrial centers of Germany and Italy atrophied, and the agriculture of eastern Europe stagnated. Success in politics and economics was mirrored in artistic and intellectual expression; here too the Atlantic peoples became the cultural leaders of Europe. Inevitably, therefore, our focus must be on western Europe.

Even the most prosperous regions of western Europe were shackled in 1559 by primitive production techniques. There was far from enough wealth for all to share. In consequence, society was everywhere organized along profoundly undemocratic lines. The disparity between the upper and the lower classes, the propertied and the propertyless, was tremendous. At the top of the social scale, a small number of aristocratic landlords monopolized most of the political power, social privileges, and wealth. At the bottom of the social scale (the submerged six sevenths of the iceberg, so to speak), millions of peasants eked out a bare subsistence, excluded from schools, skilled jobs, property ownership, and creature comforts. But this hierarchical system was not immobile. In the populous cities and towns of western and central Europe, the merchants and lawyers competed with the landed elite for wealth and position, while the humbler shopkeepers and artisans scrabbled for smaller stakes. As we shall see, in most of the Atlantic states these urban classes gained appreciably in numbers and strength during the late sixteenth and seventeenth centuries. In Germany and Italy they lost ground. In eastern Europe they remained inconsequential. But even in western Europe the social gulf between an upwardly mobile merchant and an established landed gentleman was very striking. A gentleman did not work. He had numerous servants to work for him. He spent his time at play, fighting, or hunting. He spent his money on ostentatious luxuries. Everything about his life style differed so radically from that of the lower orders that he seemed to represent a higher biological species. Since land was everywhere scarce and especially valuable, the gentleman landowner deliberately squandered part of his acreage on a deer park and pleasure gardens. And he sustained his privileged status by bequeathing hereditary titles and possessions to his children.

The hereditary hierarchical principle was equally conspicuous in politics. Aristocrats almost everywhere dominated the political scene and passed their power from generation to generation. In every large state, a divinely ordained prince, king, or emperor presided over the aristocratic establishment. In three monarchies—the Holy Roman Empire, the papacy, and Poland—the ruler was elected by lesser princes. Elsewhere, royal titles were hereditary—a species of property, to be conveyed by the reigning family from one generation to the next. Obviously this system did not guarantee continuous talent: a strong king might be succeeded by his strong son, as happened in Spain in 1556; or an inept queen might be succeeded by her brilliant sister, as happened in England in 1558; or a mediocre king might be succeeded by his even feebler son, as happened in France in 1559.

There was also another significant political tendency, illustrated by the most prominent princely family of the day, the house of Habsburg. A conspicuous feature of the 1559 map is the extraordinarily diverse collection of territories governed by the Habsburgs. Philip II, of the Spanish Habsburgs, was hereditary ruler of twelve separate European territories, several North African outposts, and a vast New World empire. His uncle Ferdinand I, of the Austrian Habsburgs, was hereditary ruler of thirteen territories, besides being the elected Holy Roman emperor. Between them, Philip and Ferdinand ruled possessions incorporated today into fourteen European and three North African nations. The Habsburgs were dynastic princes par excellence; they aimed at family power more than state power, and their style of rule inhibited national development. Collecting their princely titles like pearls on a necklace through inheritance, marriage, war, and diplomacy, they handled each possession independently, mainly through deputies. The other chief princely families—Valois, Guise, Bourbon, Orange, Tudor, Stuart, Wittelsbach, Hohenzollern, Vasa, and

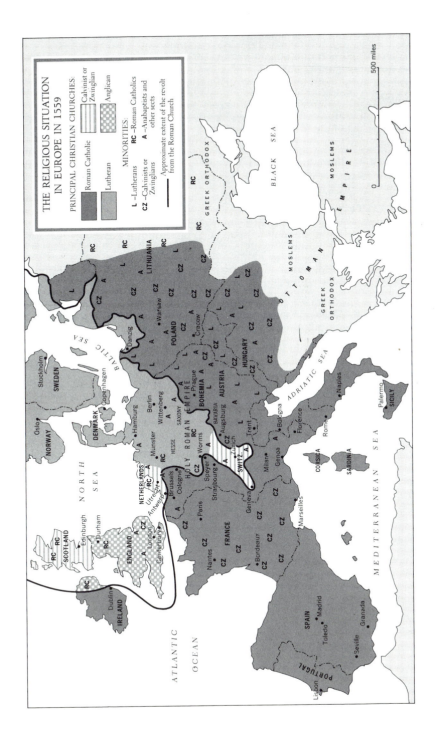

THE RELIGIOUS SITUATION
IN EUROPE IN 1559

PRINCIPAL CHRISTIAN CHURCHES:

Roman Catholic   Calvinist or Zwinglian

Lutheran   Anglican

MINORITIES:
L —Lutherans   RC —Roman Catholics
CZ —Calvinists or Zwinglians
A —Anabaptists and other sects

—— Approximate extent of the revolt from the Roman Church

500 miles

Romanov—followed the Habsburg model, pursuing dynastic ambitions and staging dynastic wars that often held no benefit for the peoples they ruled. In the political system of early modern Europe, there was constant unresolved tension between state building and family building.

The old familiar political problems were compounded by strange new religious problems. In the forty years since Martin Luther had launched his revolt, the people of western and central Europe had gradually arrayed themselves into warring Protestant and Catholic camps. Furthermore, the Protestants were themselves split into rival denominations—Lutheran, Calvinist, Zwinglian, Anabaptist, and Anglican—which were bitterly antagonistic toward one another. By 1559 the religious map was exceedingly confused. The Catholics had firm control of Portugal, Spain, and Italy; the Protestants had firm control of Scandinavia. Everywhere else, the struggle continued. The Catholics held the upper hand in France, Ireland, the Netherlands, southern Germany, Bohemia, Hungary, and Poland, but faced a powerful Protestant challenge. The Protestants held the upper hand in England, Scotland, most of Germany, and Switzerland, but faced a powerful Catholic challenge. Fluid as the situation was, neither Protestants nor Catholics were in the least willing to compromise—or to coexist. Everyone agreed that religious toleration was intolerable. Every prince strove for religious uniformity, and insisted on the right to impose one particular interpretation of Christian faith upon every subject. But as we shall see, convinced Protestants tended to rebel against their Catholic princes, and convinced Catholics against their Protestant princes.

Nor was this the only new problem. From the mid-sixteenth century on, most regions of Europe were buffeted by population pressure, rapid inflation, and eroding living standards for the laboring poor. Overall, the population had been rising for the past century, so that by 1559 the catastrophic losses caused by the Black Death two hundred years earlier had finally been made up. The demographic expansion of 1460–1559 had stimulated agricultural expansion, industrial production, and commerce: there had been a century of general prosperity. But after 1559, the picture darkened. Population continued to climb, and with all available land under cultivation, peasants were forced to work smaller and smaller plots, while the landless were driven to seek work in the cities and towns. Unemployment increased, the supply of food fell behind the demand for it, the price of bread rose faster than the income of wage workers, and beggars proliferated. Those who lived close to the margin—the vast majority of the population—were terribly exposed to famine and plague. Famine struck with devastating effect whenever the harvest failed. The bubonic plague, endemic since the Black Death two centuries earlier, repeatedly thinned out the crowded urban slums. As we shall see, it was no accident that the great witchcraft hysteria, one of the most distinctive phenomena in the age of religious wars, began in the 1560's. For the witch-hunters of the late sixteenth century were not merely intensely religious—preoccupied with heresy and sin, and fascinated by the Devil and by black magic. They also had a desperate need for scapegoats to meliorate the impact of social disasters for which they had no remedy: poverty, disease, crime, famine, plague, wartime carnage, and revolutionary upheaval, all characteristic of the troubled society we are about to examine.

One final, ironic point. In a world full of dispute and uncertainty, there was at least one proposition that every sixteenth-century male, whether Catholic or Protestant, gentleman or peasant, could agree upon; this was the fixed inferiority of the female sex. Women were spiritually frail, physically passive, socially subordinate, economically dependent. Needless to say, they had no voice in politics. But in 1558–1561 three women assumed great political power. Elizabeth I became queen of England, Mary Stuart became queen of Scotland, and Catherine de Medici became queen mother and effectual ruler of France. John Knox summed up the male reaction in his famous pamphlet, *The First Blast of the Trumpet Against the Monstrous Regiment of Women* (1558). A female ruling over men, said Knox, is repugnant to nature and contrary to God's revealed will. In public affairs a woman's sight is blindness, her counsel foolishness, and her judgment frenzy. Despite Knox's fulminations, the three queens held center stage for the next thirty years. It was indeed a novel age!

CHAPTER 1

Calvinism Versus Catholicism
in Western Europe

IN THE SPRING of 1559, envoys from Philip II of Spain and Henry II of France met on neutral ground in the bishop's palace at Cateau-Cambrésis, a little town on the French-Netherlands border, to arrange a peace treaty between their respective masters. Philip and Henry were the two strongest princes in Europe, but they both needed peace. Their rival dynastic houses, the Habsburgs and the Valois, had been dueling inconclusively for half a century, and their treasuries were exhausted. Furthermore, the Catholic King of Spain and the Most Christian King of France had a common enemy to deal with. The Protestant heresy was spreading from central Europe into Spanish and French territory, and Philip and Henry were determined to stamp it out. Accordingly, the diplomats at Cateau-Cambrésis worked out a peace settlement which could be expected to last for many years. The French abandoned their efforts to wrest Italy and the Low Countries from Spain; the Spaniards abandoned their efforts to dismember France. The Peace of Cateau-Cambrésis was more a Habsburg than a Valois victory, since France remained encircled by Habsburg territory. But Valois France in 1559 was rich, populous, and powerful. Surely this settlement was mutually advantageous to Philip and Henry. The reconciled Habsburg and Valois monarchs would now be able to crush Protestantism within their territories and join forces to restore the seamless unity of the Christian Church.

But to their surprise and dismay, the Peace of Cateau-Cambrésis ushered in a strange new era of civil wars and rebellions which the Habsburg and Valois kings were quite unable to cope with. The religious conflict which had racked central Europe from 1517 to 1555 moved with a new revolutionary force into western Europe between 1560 and 1600. In Germany the fighting had come to a temporary halt. The truce between the Protestants and the Catholics in the Holy Roman Empire, established in 1555 by the Peace of Augsburg, lasted into the early seventeenth century. But in western Europe, Dutch Calvinists rebelled against Spanish Habsburg control of the Netherlands, while French Calvinists, or Huguenots, rebelled against the Valois monarchy and plunged France into forty years of civil war. At the same time in England and Scotland, Calvinists, Catholics, and Anglicans were vying for political mastery. In essence, western Europe became a giant battleground fought over by two crusading armies, Calvinist and Catholic.

The Calvinists employed the dogma and discipline of Geneva to challenge the political *status quo* in France, the Low Countries, and the British Isles. They proved to be effective rebels, for though few in number, they were drawn chiefly from the upper and middle classes, and were zealous and self-assured. The Catholics, led by Philip II, employed all the resources of the mighty Spanish empire to crush the· French Huguenots and restore Britain and the Netherlands to Rome. Calvinists and Catholics alike can be labeled "conservative" in the sense that they clung to the traditional medieval belief that no diversity could be tolerated within Christendom. There was just one interpretation of God's commands, just one road to salvation; only by vanquishing the forces of Satan could Christ's rule on earth be achieved. Yet what gave the Calvinists and Catholics such dynamic power was their active involvement in the world. Both sides recognized the new secular forces which were transforming western civilization—overseas expansion to Asia and America, commercial capitalism, dynastic rivalry, nationalism, and state sovereignty—and they harnessed these forces to the service of God. The Calvinist-Catholic struggle was in one sense the last medieval crusade, in another the first modern war between nation-states. Nothing like it has ever been seen before or since.

RELIGION AND POLITICS

From the day Martin Luther first posted his ninety-five theses in 1517, the religious controversy between Protestants and Catholics was embroiled in politics. This was inevitable. The spiritual crisis affected men's attitudes toward this world as well as the next. The Church possessed vast political and economic resources, and when the Protestants repudiated the basic doctrinal tenets of Rome, they necessarily also attacked the Church's existing institutional fabric. Protestant and Catholic reformers alike looked to the secular authorities for help, and kings and princes gained political and economic advantage from participating in the conflict.

At mid-century, subtle—but crucial—religious and political changes took place. With the death of John Calvin in 1564, the initial creative work of the Protestant reformers was completed. Correspondingly, with the death of St. Ignatius of Loyola in 1556, and the termination of the Council of Trent in 1563, the Catholic internal reform program was fully spelled out. The ideological battle lines became frozen. But as the Protestants and Catholics lost their initial spiritual creativity, they developed a new political creativity.

The Protestants and Catholics of the late sixteenth century quarreled over predetermined issues. The central spiritual and intellectual questions had all been explored, debated, and formulated between 1517 and 1564. No Protestant theologian remotely comparable to Luther, Zwingli, or Calvin emerged during the second half of the century. The Protestants had long since fragmented into a spectrum of mutually jealous churches and sects, each with its well-defined doctrinal, ritualistic, and institutional idiosyncrasies. On the Catholic side, the cumulative effect of the internal reform program launched in the 1530's had been to stiffen resistance to all major Protestant tenets. The Council of Trent had declared that every existing Catholic ritual or practice was spiritually efficacious. Far from decentralizing the Church, the Trentine reforms magnified the hierarchical authority of pope, cardinals, and bishops. The Jesuits, most effective of the new reforming orders, took a special vow of obedience to the pope. The Roman Inquisition and the Index of Prohibited Books helped to protect the faithful from Protestant propaganda, just as the Consistory in Geneva shielded orthodox Calvinists from wicked external influences. After 1560, Protestants and Catholics had no interest in spiritual or intellectual reconciliation, and had nothing fresh to say to each other. Each side sought to convert the other by sheer brute force.

If the religious dimension of the quarrel became frozen, the political dimension was in a state of flux. In the early days, particularly between the 1520's and the 1550's, the kings and princes of central and western Europe had been able to shape and stage-manage the Protestant-Catholic conflict to a very great degree. The German princes who protected Luther from the pope and the emperor had embraced the new religion with possessive enthusiasm. The national Protestant churches of Sweden, Denmark, and England, established in the 1520's and 1530's, had all been founded by kings who eagerly assumed most of the perquisites they stripped from the pope. "The Reformation maintained itself wherever the lay power (prince or magistrates) favoured it; it could not survive where the authorities decided to suppress it."[1] Even the Catholic rulers had profited from the crisis up to the mid-sixteenth century. The German Catholic princes, the Habsburgs in Spain, and the Valois in France all had exacted papal concessions which tightened their hold over their territorial churches. They were very suspicious of any revival of papal power. Charles V's soldiers sacked Rome, not Wittenberg, in 1527, and when the papacy belatedly sponsored a reform program, both the Habsburgs and the Valois refused to endorse much of it, rejecting especially those Trentine decrees which encroached on their sovereign authority. In refusing to cooperate with Rome, the Catholic princes checked papal ambitions to restore the Church's medieval political power. By patronizing the Protestant reformers, the Protestant princes made sure that their reforms did not go too far.

[1] G. R. Elton, "The Age of the Reformation," in *New Cambridge Modern History*, Vol. II (Cambridge, Eng., 1958) p. 5.

After 1560 the rulers of western Europe were no longer able to blunt the revolutionary force of the religious crisis. Both Calvinists and militant Catholics began to rebel against the political *status quo*. They organized effective opposition against rulers who did not share their religious convictions. In the name of God they launched a wave of civil wars and rebellions against constituted authority. Mary, Queen of Scots, lost her throne and her life. Catherine de Medici of France got caught between Huguenot and ultra-Catholic crusaders. Under her management, the Valois dynasty collapsed and the French central government crumbled. Philip II of Spain was a far more heroic figure than Mary or Catherine, and was the prime champion of the Church among sixteenth-century princes. His motives were mixed, for he hoped to extend his dynastic power by crushing the heretics, but at the same time, no other political leader risked so much for his faith. He risked too much, as events proved, and instead of gaining territory, he lost some. He provoked a Calvinist rebellion in the Netherlands which could not be suppressed; his intervention in the French religious wars backfired; and he failed to conquer Protestant England. It is instructive that the two western European rulers who best survived the religious crisis behaved much more circumspectly than Philip. Both Elizabeth I of England and Henry IV of France pursued policies of moderation and compromise which eventually disarmed their Calvinist and Catholic critics. But even Elizabeth and Henry were thrown on the defensive most of the time.

John Calvin. *This woodcut shows the stern reformer in old age.*

The Calvinists, who caused so much trouble to these princes, were never very numerous. Calvin himself had had a restricted base of operations: his little city-state of Geneva on the French border of Switzerland had only thirteen thousand inhabitants. But Calvin's teachings and his presbyterian church structure proved to be highly exportable to larger centers of population and power. Before he died in 1564, he had gained an elite following in France, the Netherlands, Scotland, and England. The movement attracted recruits from the privileged classes: noblemen, landowners, merchants, and lawyers. Persons from the unprivileged classes, peasants and urban wage laborers, were less likely to join. Today Calvinism has the reputation of being a misanthropic, repressive creed. How could it win such aristocratic and prosperous adherents, let alone fire up a crusade? The best answer, perhaps, is that it offered a harsh but immensely exhilarating challenge. One had to accept Calvin's concept of God's absolute and all-pervading power and of Man's utter depravity, which renders him incapable of fulfilling God's law as revealed in the Bible. One had also to believe that God chooses to save some few persons, not on their merits (they have none), but solely by His grace. The person who accepted these premises, who abased himself before God's will and experienced God's irresistible grace, knew that he was among the predestinated "elect" or "saints," the only true Christians. As Calvin himself explained, "when that light of divine providence has once shone upon a godly man, he is then relieved and set free not only from the extreme anxiety and fear that were pressing him before, but from every care."[2] Despite Calvin's stress on human worthlessness, his church was an exclusive brotherhood which separated the saints from the sinners, the wheat from the chaff. Far from being fatalistic, the saints were intensely active.

It has been recently argued that the sixteenth-century Calvinists organized themselves into the first modern radical political party, analogous to the Jacobins and the Bolsheviks in more recent revolutionary times.[3] Of course, their chief goal was to reach the next world, not to remake this one. Yet the saints felt stifled by their unregenerate neighbors, and supposed that God wished them to master and reconstruct their corrupt environment. Their fellowship was bound to be socially and politically disruptive, for Calvinism was a total way of life. Their social model was Geneva: a homogeneous little city, rigidly self-disciplined, zealously self-righteous, and independent of any external authority. When Calvin's disciples began proselytizing in large and complex states like France, the Netherlands, and England, they gathered the saints into communities of Genevan purity and Genevan self-sufficiency. In France, for example, the Huguenots established congregations on the Genevan model, with pastors who preached and administered the Lord's Supper,

[2]John Calvin, *Institutes of the Christian Religion*, ed. by John T. McNeill (Philadelphia, 1960), Vol. I, p. 223.

[3]Michael Walzer, *The Revolution of the Saints* (Cambridge, Mass., 1965).

teachers who educated the young, deacons who looked after the poor and unemployed, and elders who watched for immorality and disorder. The Huguenots united these congregations under a countrywide discipline, with local consistories and a national synod of the chief clergy and laymen. Every member of a Calvinist congregation swore to obey and help enforce God's law, and this covenant, or contract, to which all agreed, easily came to serve as a kind of constitution binding the Calvinists in a political or military confederation against their worldly enemies. Armed with the Genevan virtues of asceticism, industry, practical education, and moral responsibility, these people were hard to suppress or silence.

Calvin himself always preached obedience to the Christian prince. But in 1558, as we have seen in the Introduction, John Knox (1505–1572), the leading Scottish Calvinist, denounced female rulers in his *First Blast of the Trumpet*. Elizabeth I took great offense at this pamphlet, and was not mollified when Knox lamely explained to her that he objected only to Catholic queens. By the 1570's the Huguenots in France had moved well beyond Knox's position, and were arguing that resistance to tyrants, male or female, was divinely ordained. This sentiment was very attractive to the great noblemen within the Calvinist movement, who hoped by rebelling against their tyrannical kings to undermine monarchical government and restore the good old days of feudal decentralization. But significantly, many Calvinists were professional and business men or small landowners, traditional proponents of strong kingship and effective central government. These men from the middle ranks were by no means trying to turn back the clock and weaken the national sovereign power of the western European states. Quite the contrary. But they refused to tolerate ungodly kings and magistrates, and they were prepared to fight for the right to participate in or even control the state.

On the Catholic side, the Society of Jesus, an order of priests founded in 1540 by St. Ignatius of Loyola, was almost equally disruptive. Calvin spoke contemptuously of "the Jesuits and like dregs," but the resemblance between Calvinist and Jesuit is a fascinating one. Working from diametrically opposite religious principles, Loyola and Calvin each built a select, cohesive, extroverted band of zealots. St. Ignatius devised a systematic emotional and intellectual discipline for the members of his society, and a highly autocratic, semimilitaristic organization, directly responsible to the pope. There were a thousand Jesuits by the time of Loyola's death in 1556, and sixteen thousand by 1624. But their influence far transcended their numbers. They established hundreds of schools to teach boys, especially upper-class boys, how to define and defend the authoritative dogmas of the Church. They excelled as preachers, and in order to engage the secular authorities in the counterattack on heresy, they made a specialty of serving as confessors to Catholic princes. Jesuit militance, autonomy, and busy intervention in all phases of Church work aroused deep hostility among many Catholics. To the Protestants,

St. Ignatius of Loyola. *Engraving by Vosterman. This portrait romanticizes Loyola somewhat, but catches his psychological intensity and robust zeal.*

"Jesuitical" meant the same thing as "Machiavellian," a curse word for the crafty intrigues and immoral tactics sponsored by these devilish priests.

The role of the Jesuits was of particular importance because they were supporters of papal supremacy. The late sixteenth-century popes, though able and energetic men, could exert little direct pressure on the Catholic rulers of western Europe. But the Jesuits, through their schools and confessionals, exercised considerable indirect influence. Jesuit confessors excelled at casuistry, the art of resolving difficult cases of conscience. The Protestants liked to believe that they winked at evil conduct, that their credo was, the end justifies the means. In fact, the Jesuits were successful at persuading others to fight for the Church because they fought so courageously themselves. Jesuit missionaries fearlessly penetrated into Protestant England and hatched a series of plots to depose Queen Elizabeth. Jesuit pamphleteers in France boldly called for the assassination of the lukewarm Catholic Henry III and the Huguenot Henry IV. Despite these inflammatory proceedings, the Jesuits had a generally conservative concept of the social order. Cardinal Bellarmine (1542–1621), the most eminent Jesuit writer in the late sixteenth century, presented a nostalgic view of the Christian commonwealth presided over by the pope. But Bellarmine, like the Calvinists, was no friend to absolute monarchy. In his view, heretical princes were liable to deposition, and even Catholic secular authority was distinctly limited.

The Protestant rebellions and Catholic assassinations of the late sixteenth century forced the proponents of strong monarchy to develop counter arguments which would bolster the prince's absolute sovereign power and make attacks upon him sacrilegious as well as treasonable. The political theory of the past was of little use on this point. Medieval theorists had generally denied that princely power was absolute, and the Renaissance theorists, like Machiavelli, who placed the prince above the law were too nakedly secular to suit the religious tastes of the late sixteenth century. It was necessary to devise a new quasi-religious doctrine of absolutism in order to answer the Jesuits and the Calvinists. The doctrine which resulted is known as the divine-right theory of kingship. According to this theory, God appoints the secular sovereign as His earthly lieutenant and invests him with absolute power over his subjects. The king has no obligation to obey the laws and customs of his state. He is answerable to God alone. Even if he rules tyrannically, he is still God's lieutenant, for God has placed him on the throne to punish the people's sins, and their only recourse is to pray for mercy. The subject has no right to rebel against his anointed king under any circumstances. This divine-right theory, absurd as it seems today, was very comforting during the religious wars to devout people who craved peace and order. It was eagerly adopted by Catholic and Protestant rulers alike. James I of England preached it; the French kings from Henry IV to Louis XIV practiced it. So did their Habsburg rivals, and most other seventeenth-century princes.

In the years of religious conflict and political upheaval between 1559 and 1689, politicians of every stripe invoked God's will to suit their particular purposes. The aristocratic and bourgeois Calvinists found divine sanction for rebellion, constitutionalism, and limited government. The Jesuits found divine sanction for the deposition of heretical rulers and a return to papal suzerainty. The secular princes found divine sanction for absolute monarchy. Radicals found divine sanction even for republicanism, democracy, and communism. Such were the effects of religion on politics, and of politics on religion.

SPAIN UNDER PHILIP II

The sixteenth century was Spain's time of power and glory. Four great rulers shaped its destiny. Ferdinand (king of Aragon, 1479–1516) and his wife Isabella (queen of Castile, 1474–1504) were the founders of modern Spain. Their grandson Charles I (ruled 1516–1556), better known by his German imperial title of Charles V, was the mightiest European prince in the early sixteenth century. His son Philip II (ruled 1556–1598) was the mightiest European prince in the late sixteenth century.

Under Ferdinand and Isabella, the crowns of Castile and Aragon were joined, the Spanish conquered Moorish Granada, and Columbus discovered America. Under Charles V, the *conquistadores* mastered the Aztecs and Incas and began to mine Peruvian and Mexican silver, while Spanish armies drove the French out of Italy and won a reputation as the best soldiers in Europe. During his forty-year reign, Charles was able to spend only sixteen years in Spain, because of his manifold obligations in Germany, Italy, and the Low Countries. But his paternalistic style of rule suited the Spaniards, and kept them internally peaceful and stable. In 1556 he bequeathed to his son Philip the western half of his immense Habsburg patrimony: the Spanish kingdoms of Castile, Aragon, and Navarre; the Balearic Islands; several North African outposts; Sardinia, Sicily, Naples, and Milan; the Netherlands, Luxemburg, and Franche-Comté; and overseas, Mexico, Florida Central America, the West Indies, the entire coast of South America except for Brazil (held by Portugal) and lower Chile and Argentina (left to the Indians), as well as the Philippine Islands and numerous smaller Pacific islands. Philip II was really fortunate not to inherit the eastern Habsburg lands—Austria, Bohemia, and Hungary—and the Habsburg claims to the Holy Roman imperial title, which Charles passed to the Austrian branch of the family. Though Philip's domain was scarcely unified, it was much more manageable than his father's had been. It was a Spanish empire, centered in Madrid, politically absolute, fervently Catholic, shielded by unbeatable armies, and fed by an apparently boundless supply of American bullion which Philip's European rivals bitterly envied.

Sixteenth-century Spain was far from being a unified nation. Philip II was king of three distinct Spanish states—Castile, Aragon, and Navarre—each with its own separate institutions, customs, language, and culture. Philip governed each state independently, but he concentrated his attention on Castile, the biggest, richest, and most populous of them. Castile had about seven million inhabitants; Aragon and Navarre together had little more than one million. Furthermore, Castile was much easier to govern. The Castilian upper nobility were immensely rich and socially powerful, but politically harmless. The crown exempted the great magnates from taxation, and recognized their huge property holdings, and in exchange they refrained from contesting royal political authority. The lower nobility, or *hidalgos*, also exempted from taxation, were useful servants to the crown. Philip II's *corregidores*, royal officials who inspected and regulated the conduct of the sixty-six principal Castilian town councils, were drawn from the *hidalgo* class. The Castilian Cortes, or parliamentary assembly, was very weak. Only eighteen towns sent representatives, and the nobility and clergy were excluded. Philip summoned this body often, whenever he wished it to levy taxes, but did not permit the deputies to share in legislation. In Aragon, on the other hand, the nobility exercised considerable political power, and the Cortes was more independent. Philip let the Aragonese nobility alone, summoned the Aragonese Cortes rarely, and avoided asking for money. Little money could be squeezed out of Aragon in any case. Nor could Philip's Italian subjects supply much revenue; and his subjects in the Low Countries refused to contribute. The king depended heavily on silver from America, but the brunt of Philip's imperial administration was borne by the impoverished Castilian peasantry.

The sprawling Spanish empire was held together at the top by a remarkably centralized bureaucracy. The king sent viceroys, generally great Castilian noblemen, to govern his distant territories, serving as his *alter ego*. Each viceroy reported to a supervisory council in Madrid: the Council of Italy, the Council of Flanders, or the Council of the Indies. Each council was staffed by six to ten professional civil servants (again mostly Castilians) vested by the king with sweeping jurisdiction over the executive, judicial, and religious affairs of their particular territory. There was also a Council of Castile, a Council of Aragon, and councils to handle matters of state, war, finance, and the Inquisition. The king himself seldom attended any of these council sessions, but he reviewed all council decisions and often reversed them. He alone had total information—or as total as the flood of dispatches, petitions, and memoranda from all parts of his domain would permit—on every aspect of affairs. Outsiders joked about the Spanish government's grave and stately pace of operations, and it is true that Philip's elaborate system of bureaucratic checks and balances prevented quick decisions. But by playing his ministers and councillors off against one another, the king reduced the possibilities for bribery and corruption, and also preserved his personal power. As far as any one man could be, Philip II was master of his empire.

He was certainly master of Italy, though he never visited his domains there after becoming king of Spain. Philip controlled half of the peninsula directly, and most of the other Italian states indirectly. Spanish garrisons in Milan, Naples, and Sicily kept order; the sole large-scale disturbance during his reign—a Neapolitan insurrection in 1585—was easily contained. The Spaniards, it was said, nibbled in Sicily, ate in Naples, and devoured in Milan. From Philip's perspective, Milan offered the best fare. This duchy, a major manufacturing center, was the strategic pivot in his far-flung military defense system and a key recruiting ground for troops to serve in Mediterranean or northern campaigns. Naples and Sicily, which were agrarian, were much poorer, without significant trade or exports. Hence Philip paid more attention to Milan than to his south Italian possessions. In all three places the Spaniards introduced few changes in local government, ruled in partnership with the local landed nobility, and enrolled the local peasantry for Mediterranean campaigns against the Turks. Beyond his own territories, Philip built political alliances with the dukes of Savoy and Tuscany, and a business alliance with the merchants of Genoa. In Rome, the nine pontiffs who ruled successively during Philip's reign included some very able men who did all they could to rebuild papal power—and incurred Philip's hostility in the process. But these popes seldom dared to challenge the Spanish king directly. Only the Venetian republic maintained an independent course, and its status was slipping; in 1571 Venice lost the island colony of Cyprus to the Turks.

Though Spanish rule was not really burdensome, it had a generally blighting effect on Italian life. Philip's policies did little or nothing to remedy the twin Italian disasters of the early sixteenth century: the political collapse of all the chief city-states save Venice, and the shift in trade routes from the Mediterranean to the Atlantic. For the Genoese, however, partnership with the Spanish king was profitable, since they managed the trade between Italy and Spain and became Philip's principal bankers. The sumptuous palaces of the Genoese nobility were mostly built during the late sixteenth and early seventeenth centuries. In Venice there was still great wealth and culture, but as the traditional spice trade slumped, the Venetian capitalists began to withdraw much of their money from risky foreign ventures in order to invest it in safe farmland. Rome remained a mecca for pilgrims, artists, and fashionable tourists. The popes, most particularly Sixtus V (ruled 1585–1590), celebrated the Catholic reformation in stone and mortar by refurbishing their city on a heroic scale. The basilica of St. Peter's, finished in the early seventeenth century, was the largest and most majestic church in Christendom. But the traveler who ventured a few miles outside the Eternal City found the countryside infested with bandits. Florence under the Medici dukes of Tuscany had sadly lost most of its magnificent creativity, though life for the upper classes remained sophisticated and gallant. With eleven million inhabitants, Italy was a densely populated region, almost half

St. Peter's, Rome. This engraving shows the greatest and grandest architectural ensemble in early modern Europe—Michelangelo's domed basilica (built between 1546 and 1626) and Bernini's immense piazza and colonnade 1656–1667).

again as populous as Spain. Five of the twelve European cities with populations of more than 100,000 in the late sixteenth century were Italian. But these cities lacked the business vitality of the Atlantic entrepreneurial centers. Politically and economically, Italy had lost its central importance in European life.

Looking westward, Philip II's management of his New World colonies demonstrates again the powerful reach of Spanish royal government. Only a generation before he came to power, a band of tough and resourceful *conquistadores* led by Hernando Cortes (1485–1547) and Francisco Pizarro (*c.* 1470–1541) had conquered Mexico and Peru, acquired personal fortunes, and harnessed millions of docile Indians to work for them. But Charles V and Philip II managed to prevent the *conquistadores* and succeeding Spanish colonists from developing political autonomy, carving up the country into giant feudal estates, or crippling royal power in America. To control the colonists, the crown sent out Castilian grandees as viceroys of Peru and New Spain (Mexico). Lest they grow too strong, the crown encouraged the *audiencias*, or courts of justice, in the colonies to challenge the authority of the viceroys. Back in Madrid, the Council of the Indies kept tabs on both the viceroys and the *audiencias*. The Church, in partnership with the crown, protected the Indians from total enslavement by the colonists. The crown received one fifth of the bullion mined in America, and earned this royalty by protecting the treasure fleets from attack by French, English, and Dutch marauders. Philip II's military power kept his North Atlantic rivals from establishing permanent colonies in the Indies until after 1600. Sir Francis Drake could raid the Caribbean audaciously in the 1570's, when he caught the Spaniards by surprise, but in 1595 he was beaten off Puerto Rico and Panama; Spanish fortifications there were now too strong for him. No Spanish treasure fleet was captured until 1628.

The Spanish government insisted on closing its colonies to outside settlers or traders. Charles V had wanted to open the Indies to any inhabitant of his Habsburg domain, but this policy was speedily reversed. Castilians insisted that America—discovered by a Genoese—was their monopoly. All American commerce had to be funneled through the single Castilian port of Seville, where it was closely supervised by royal officials in the *Casa de Contratación* ("House of Trade"). Every merchant ship in the American fleet had to be licensed by the *Casa*. All incoming and outgoing cargo was registered with *Casa* officials, whose most important job was to receive and distribute the incoming silver and gold. Not only Italian or Flemish merchants but also Catalan merchants, from eastern Spain, were denied licenses to trade. Moors and Jews, so unwelcome in Spain that a half million or more were expelled from the Iberian peninsula between 1492 and 1609, found themselves rigorously excluded from asylum in America.

Spain's great weakness, which Philip II did nothing to correct, was its

Philip II. *Painting by Coello. The king, true to his character, looks gravely dignified and is austerely dressed in black. Museo del Prado, Madrid.*

lopsided economy. The country was, as it still is, mountainous, barren, and parched. With a rapid rise in population during the sixteenth century, Spain did not produce enough grain to feed its people and had to import wheat from the Mediterranean and Baltic areas. The nobility, who owned almost all the land, preferred raising sheep to cultivating crops, and merino wool was Spain's chief export. The Spanish exported raw wool to Flanders at a low price and imported finished Flemish cloth at a high price, giving Flemish entrepreneurs most of the profit. There were no industries to speak of in sixteenth-century Spain; most manufactured goods had to be imported. The Castilians had always valued business well below fighting and praying, and much of their commerce and banking was handled by outsiders. Within Philip's empire there were three principal trade routes: between Spain and Italy, between Spain and the Low Countries, and between Spain and the Americas. The first route was dominated by the Genoese and the second by Netherlanders; only the American trade was a closed Castilian preserve, and even here, much of the cargo shipped to America was non-Spanish in origin. In the late sixteenth century, as many as two hundred ships a year sailed between Seville and the Americas, making this far and away the busiest single route of European overseas commerce. Bullion shipments into Seville reached their peak between 1580 and 1620. In 1594, silver and gold accounted for 96 percent of the value of American exports to Spain. Unfortunately for the Spaniards, little of this treasure stayed in Spain. Because of the deficiencies in the Spanish economy, it had to be paid out to foreign farmers, manufacturers, merchants, and bankers.

Philip II's military power was handicapped by Spain's unbalanced economic and social structure. He could not raise enough money to pay for his large standing armies and his elaborate military campaigns. Throughout his reign the royal exchequer was in a virtual state of bankruptcy. Philip inherited large debts from his father, and when he suspended payment to his creditors in 1557 and again in 1575, he found it harder than ever to float new loans. He was unable to tap the wealth of his richest Spanish subjects, for the members of the nobility were exempt from taxes. Three hundred magnates owned more than half the land in Castile, and the rent-rolls of the thirteen Castilian dukes and thirteen marquises totaled nearly a million ducats a year—more than the king's annual share of American bullion until the 1580's. But this money was untouchable. Nor could Philip squeeze much from the Spanish merchant and professional class, which was notably smaller than that of other western European states. The only class which he could and did tax with impunity was the one least able to pay, the impoverished peasantry. In addition, of course, he spent his American silver as fast as it came in and even mortgaged future treasure shipments. But Philip's soldiers consumed all the American bullion and all the peasant taxes that could be scraped together. When their pay still fell into arrears, they mutinied and rioted uncontrollably. An unpaid army is worse than no army at all, as Philip found to his cost.

The Spanish ardor for fighting and praying had an old-fashioned flavor, being still largely directed against the traditional Moorish enemy. One of Philip II's major taxes was the *cruzada*, or crusade subsidy, authorized by the papacy to encourage continued Spanish warfare against Islam. Spaniards could not understand the general Catholic agitation for ecclesiastical reform, since the Spanish church had experienced its own reform movement in the fifteenth century, well before Luther. The Spanish Inquisition, dating from 1478, had been designed to root out heresy among converted Moslems and Jews. These *conversos* were generally hated and feared, and by the time of Philip II a racist campaign had been launched to bar anyone from public office whose blood was impure. The Inquisition was the one institution common to Castile, Aragon, and Navarre, and once the Protestant revolt broke out, the inquisitors went to extraordinary lengths to keep the new heresy out of Spain. Anyone deviating in the slightest particular from Catholic orthodoxy was branded a Lutheran by the Holy Office, subjected to torture and secret trial, and if found guilty and obdurate, handed over to the secular authorities for public execution at an *auto-da-fé*. Erasmus' supporters in Spain were hounded into silence. St. Ignatius of Loyola was twice imprisoned by the Spanish Inquisition on suspicion of heresy. Even the archbishop of Toledo, the primate of Spain, was held prisoner by his enemies in the Inquisition from 1559 to 1576 on trumped-up heresy charges. Despite this repressive atmosphere, two late sixteenth-century Spanish mystics, St. Teresa of Avila (1515–1582) and St. John of the Cross (1542–1591), sparked a new ardor well illustrated in the rapturous paintings of El Greco (*c.* 1548–1614). Spanish rapture did not extend to the papacy. Relations between Madrid and Rome were continually strained. Like every other prince of his day, Philip was jealous of outside interference with his territorial church, and besides, "in his heart he considered religion too serious a matter to be left to the Pope."[4]

What sort of man was Philip II? He was outwardly retiring and reserved, yet inwardly secure in his Catholic faith and his royal majesty. He was slim, sober, and dyspeptic in appearance, spoke slowly and softly, rarely smiled, was bookish and artistic rather than athletic, and was happiest when at his desk reading memoranda. He never personally led his troops on the battlefield. He disliked traveling or mingling with people, and after 1559 he never left the Iberian peninsula. But he avidly absorbed all the data his officials could collect. He was a file clerk on a heroic scale. Every day he sifted through masses of papers, many of them ludicrously trivial, and wrote voluminous marginal comments, sometimes correcting errors of grammar and spelling. The king, as some of his subjects complained, tried to govern the world from a chair. He deeply venerated his father, but he had none of Charles's cosmopolitan and ecumenical temper.

Philip II bore more than his share of private sorrows. He outlived four wives, all married for dynastic expediency, as illustrated by the fact that at the age of twenty-seven he chose a bride of thirty-eight, and when she died he married at the age of thirty-two a girl of thirteen. Six of his nine children died young. His first son, Don Carlos (1545–1568), was physically deformed and mentally unbalanced. Don Carlos passionately hated his father, and when the Dutch rebellion began, he tried to escape to the Netherlands to join the rebels. One night in 1568 the king broke into his son's bedchamber with a party of councillors, seized the startled prince's weapons and papers, and placed him under armed guard. Philip never saw Don Carlos again. Six months later, the prince died mysteriously, most likely a suicide. Philip's enemies to the north were scandalized by this episode. They called the king a cruel and secretive murderer. Ever since, Anglo-Saxon Protestant historians have generally pictured Philip in very dark colors. Spaniards, on the other hand, affectionately remember him as their Prudent King and prize his dignified, methodical, and conscientious statecraft. The Spanish view is obviously closer to the truth, yet Philip's crusade against Protestantism turned out to be far from prudent.

Philip II established his court at Madrid, in the center of Spain. But he

[4]J. H. Elliott, *Imperial Spain, 1469–1716* (New York, 1964), p. 223.

The Escorial. *Painting by an unknown artist. The isolated setting, huge bulk, gridiron design, and monastic severity of Philip II's retreat are clearly shown. Standing in the center of the complex is the domed church.*

craved a solitary retreat where he could escape from the elaborate court ceremonial and the tiresome audiences with suppliants and envoys. So he built the Escorial, a vast gray granite structure rising out of the bleak foothills of the sierras north of Madrid. The building, which took twenty years to construct, perfectly expresses Philip's taste and temper. Behind its severe facade one finds a combination of palace, church, tomb, and monastery. It is laid out in the shape of the gridiron on which the king's patron saint, Lawrence, was supposedly toasted alive. Under the great dome of the church—one of the first copies of St. Peter's in Rome—the king buried various members of his family and prepared his own grave. He found peace and privacy by going into retreat with the cloistered monks he installed in one section of the building. There are splendid public chambers in the Escorial, and a fine library and picture gallery. But Philip's favorite place was a meanly furnished little room from whose window he could peep out at the high altar of his church while Mass was being sung.

Despite his love of solitude and circumspection, the Prudent King was driven by his zeal and by the military strength at his disposal to play a strong hand in international affairs. The first half of his reign was dominated by warfare in the Mediterranean against Islam, the second half by warfare in the North Atlantic against the Protestants. On the Mediterranean front, Philip II did very well. Here he sent his army and navy against the traditional

Mohammedan foe. When the Moors in Granada rose in rebellion in 1568, royal troops crushed the revolt and forced 150,000 Moorish prisoners to resettle in other parts of Spain. Philip fought an inconclusive series of engagements against the Barbary pirates of North Africa. He could not stop their raids against the Spanish coast and Spanish shipping, but he did strengthen Spanish naval protection for commerce in the eastern Mediterranean. Behind the Barbary pirates stood the mighty Ottoman Turks. The Ottoman Empire, like the Spanish, was at its peak in the early years of Philip's reign. The Turks occupied three quarters of the Mediterranean shoreline, from the Adriatic to Algeria, and they were still on the move. They almost took Malta in 1565 and did take Cyprus in 1571. To save the situation, Philip joined Venice and the papacy in a Holy League against the terrible Turk.

In October, 1571, a fleet of three hundred ships and eighty thousand sailors and soldiers (predominantly Spanish) sailed into the Gulf of Lepanto off the Greek coast to fight an Ottoman navy which had even more ships and men. The Battle of Lepanto was the biggest naval battle of the century, a showdown between Europe's western and eastern giants. Both fleets consisted of galleys propelled by oarsmen, and they fought in the old-fashioned close-range style, the men of each galley trying to ram, grapple, and board an enemy ship. When the Christian fleet closed for action, a crucifix was displayed in every galley, and all the warriors knelt in adoration as the Turks came up screaming and trumpeting. After a few hours of ferocious hand-to-hand combat, the Turkish fleet was annihilated. Three quarters of the Turkish ships, with their crews, were sunk or captured. Cautious as always, Philip did not follow up the smashing victory by trying to storm Constantinople. But he had stopped Turkish expansion, and he had proved who was king of the Mediterranean. Among the many Spanish soldiers wounded at Lepanto was a young man named Miguel de Cervantes (1547–1616). Many years later, in the prologue to his *Exemplary Novels*, Cervantes proudly described his sacrifice: "In the naval battle of Lepanto he lost his left hand as the result of a harquebus shot, a wound which, however unsightly it may appear, he looks upon as beautiful, for the reason that it was received on the most memorable and sublime occasion that past ages have known or those to come may hope to know."[5]

Philip II's greatest success came in 1580, when he annexed Portugal and the Portuguese empire. Philip's mother had been a Portuguese princess, and when the king of Portugal died in 1580 without a direct heir, Philip had as good a claim to the vacant throne as anyone. Portugal and Castile had long been bitter political and economic rivals, and the Portuguese people were strongly anti-Castilian. But by the judicious distribution of silver and promises of future rewards, Philip's agents won the Portuguese nobility and

[5]*The Portable Cervantes*, trans. and ed. by Samuel Putnam (New York, 1951), p. 706.

upper clergy to his candidacy; and more important, the Spanish king sent in an army to secure the country. In four months his soldiers overran Portugal, and Philip was soon crowned at Lisbon. His new kingdom was a small state with only a million or so inhabitants, but by joining the crowns of Portugal, Castile, Aragon, and Navarre, Philip had seemingly completed the unification of the Iberian peninsula. Furthermore, the Portuguese empire overseas was very valuable, second only to the Spanish empire in size and importance. Philip now had possession of Brazil, the Azores and other mid-Atlantic islands, slaving stations in Africa, trading posts in India, and spice islands in Malaysia. Portugal's Asian spice trade perfectly complemented Spain's American silver mines. The Portuguese had no silver of their own, and they needed Spanish bullion in order to buy spices in Asia. The Spanish colonists in America wanted slaves from Portuguese Africa, and the Spanish home government needed Lisbon (a far better Atlantic port than Seville or Cádiz) and the Portuguese navy and merchant marine.

But the promise of 1580 was never realized. Philip's annexation of the Portuguese crown was purely personal and dynastic. To conciliate the Portuguese, he promised to preserve the country's independent institutions and independent commerce and to appoint only Portuguese officials. No effort was made to break down frontiers nor even to coordinate Spanish and Portuguese economic policy. Initially, the Portuguese accepted their new Habsburg ruler without much complaint, but as the years passed, they saw less and less advantage to the union, especially when the Spanish were unable to protect the Portuguese colonies from Dutch attack. Thus what might have been a fruitful permanent partnership lasted for only sixty years.

The annexation of Portugal helped to direct Philip II's attention west and north rather than east. Portugal, much more than Spain, faced onto the Atlantic, and for the first time Philip possessed adequate naval forces to deal with his Protestant adversaries in the North Atlantic—England and the Netherlands. Furthermore, in the 1580's, bullion imports from America suddenly doubled. Philip was now receiving two million ducats in silver ingots each year. His chronic fiscal problems seemed less pressing, and he felt that he could afford more ambitious military adventures than in the past. Now was the time to deal decisively with a situation which, from Philip's viewpoint, had been steadily deteriorating ever since 1559. As we shall see, the Spanish government had long been trying to suppress heresy and rebellion in the Netherlands. English privateers had been raiding the Spanish Indies with rising impudence. The French religious wars had entered a critical stage. Accordingly, in the 1580's Philip launched his grand design to solve all these problems by an overwhelming display of military power. His soldiers and sailors would quell the Netherlands revolt, invade and conquer England, and end the French religious wars. The Catholic-Calvinist conflict was reaching its climax.

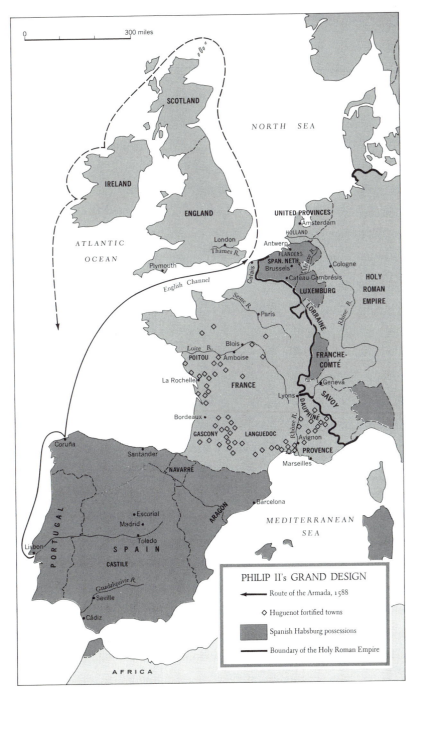

0   300 miles

SCOTLAND

NORTH SEA

IRELAND

ENGLAND

UNITED PROVINCES
• Amsterdam
HOLLAND

London
Thames R.
Antwerp
FLANDERS
SPAN. NETH.
Brussels
• Cateau-Cambrésis
Cologne
HOLY
ROMAN
EMPIRE

ATLANTIC
OCEAN

Plymouth

English Channel

Calais

Seine R.

LUXEMBURG

LORRAINE

Paris

Rhine R.

FRANCHE-
COMTÉ

Loire R.
POITOU
Blois
Amboise
La Rochelle

FRANCE

Geneva

Lyons

SAVOY

DAUPHINÉ

Bordeaux

GASCONY
LANGUEDOC

Rhône R.

Avignon

PROVENCE

Coruña

Santander

Marseilles

NAVARRE

ARAGON

Barcelona

MEDITERRANEAN
SEA

Escorial
Madrid •

SPAIN

Toledo

P O R T U G A L
Lisbon

CASTILE

Guadalquivir R.

Seville

Cádiz

AFRICA

PHILIP II's GRAND DESIGN

⬅ Route of the Armada, 1588

◇ Huguenot fortified towns

▨ Spanish Habsburg possessions

━ Boundary of the Holy Roman Empire

THE FRENCH WARS OF RELIGION, 1562–1598

In striking contrast to Spain, which enjoyed internal peace and unity during the second half of the sixteenth century, France was nearly torn apart by forty years of agonizing, destructive civil war. The French collapse was many-faceted. Huguenots battled Catholics, aristocratic factions joined together to oppose the crown, the bourgeoisie strove for new political and religious rights, the Paris mob went wild, and the outer provinces reverted to their medieval autonomy. Religion was by no means the only source of trouble, but religion triggered the crisis with explosive force. The French wars exposed all the latent flaws in sixteenth-century European civilization. The French, despite their rich cultural resources, their well-balanced economy, and their impressively centralized governmental institutions, seemed to lose all sense of social community. The trouble was partly caused by the size of the country. France was a difficult state to administer, with a population that climbed during the sixteenth century to nearly twenty million, more than double the population of Spain. Yet the French state was certainly more closely knit than the worldwide Spanish empire. A more obvious trouble in the late sixteenth century was poor royal leadership. The four Valois kings who followed Francis I (ruled 1515–1547) were all mediocre, to say the least. Between 1559 and 1589 the queen mother, Catherine de Medici, was the central figure. Catherine had political talent, but not for the situation at hand. She tried to play the Huguenots and Catholics against each other; the result was disastrous for the house of Valois and for France.

During the first half of the sixteenth century, the French state had the characteristic attributes of a "new monarchy." Francis I exercised sovereign authority through his network of royal officials, through his permanent mercenary army, through his power to levy direct and indirect taxes. The French representative assembly, the Estates-General, did not meet between 1484 and 1560. In the outer regions of the country, the crown negotiated with the provincial estates, much easier to browbeat than the Estates-General. In central France, where there were no provincial estates, royal agents annually assessed and collected the *gabelle*, or salt tax, and the *taille*, an income tax levied mainly on the peasants. The king was master of his territorial church. In the Concordat of Bologna (1516), the papacy had agreed that all French bishops and abbots were to be nominated by the crown. Ambitious members of the nobility served as officers in the royal army, fighting Francis' frequent wars against Charles V. This activity not only kept them busy but kept them out of the country as much as possible. Clearly the tendency under Francis I was toward absolute, centralized monarchy.

But the king was not all-powerful. The *parlements*, or state courts, in Paris and the provinces insisted that he obey the established laws and to some extent substituted for the Estates-General as a brake on arbitrary royal power. Border provinces such as Brittany and Burgundy, only recently annexed to the crown, enjoyed special privileges and exemptions. The great French magnates had all the rights of the Spanish nobility, including tax exemption, and they exercised considerable political control over the *lieutenants du roi*, or royal administrators, at the local level. The crown was handicapped by lack of money, despite its taxing power. One sixteenth-century money-making device, the sale of royal offices, tended to hamper the king's control over his own bureaucracy; office holding became heredi-tary and semifeudal in character. A further complication was introduced when the religious controversy began to stir men's minds and emotions. One morning in 1534, good Catholics were horrified to find placards promi-nently posted in all the chief French cities, scurrilously denouncing the sac-rament of the Mass. Some daring reformer had even nailed a placard onto the king's bedchamber door while he slept in the château of Amboise.

Opposition to centralized royal power began to mushroom during the reign of Henry II (1547–1559). This king was interested only in hunting and in his elderly mistress, Diane de Poitiers, a lady twenty years his senior. He was ashamed of his Florentine queen, Catherine de Medici, (1519–1589), because she came from a "bourgeois" family. At Henry's court three rival aristocratic factions—the Guises, the Montmorencys, and the Bourbons—began to jockey for control of royal policy. All three wanted to return to the feudal particularism of the good old days, when the great noble fami-lies ruled the various regions of France, and the king was just a figurehead. But they were bitterly jealous of each other's efforts to manipulate the king. The duke of Montmorency, constable of France, had immense landhold-ings and a personal retinue of several hundred knights. The Bourbons were princes of the blood, with the best claim to the French throne should Henry's sons leave no heirs. The Bourbon leaders were Louis, prince of Condé, and his brother King Anthony of Navarre, whose kingdom in the Pyrenees was mostly in Spanish hands. But the Guise faction was the strong-est of the three. Francis, duke of Guise, was Henry II's most brilliant gen-eral, and his brothers Charles, cardinal of Lorraine, and Louis, cardinal of Guise, led the French church. They married their niece (the future Mary, Queen of Scots) to the royal dauphin, and they persuaded Henry to continue his father's dynastic war with the Habsburgs. The heavy war taxes stirred his subjects and sent Henry deeply into debt. When he finally made peace with Spain in 1559, he had to renounce all pretensions to Italy. The nobility who had fought in this losing cause were unpaid and restless. But Henry did not have time to worry about this problem, for while jousting in a tournament during the celebrations following the Peace of Cateau-Cambrésis, he was killed when a splinter from his opponent's lance pierced his eye.

The French throne passed successively to three of Henry II's sons: Francis

II (ruled 1559–1560), Charles IX (ruled 1560–1574), and Henry III (ruled 1574–1589). All three were feeble and neurotic. All three were dominated by their mother. But though Queen Catherine de Medici could rule her sons, she could not rule France. The country dissolved into anarchy and from anarchy into downright war. The war was ignited by the spread of Calvinism into France. The Huguenots not only spread heresy but challenged the power and profits of the crown. They were well organized for political subversion. Working at first in secret, they established a network of congregations throughout France. Even when Henry II organized a special court to try Huguenots and have them burned at the stake, they continued to proliferate. In 1559 they held their first national synod. They attacked convents and desecrated Catholic churches by smashing the holy relics and statuary. In 1561 there were 2,150 Huguenot congregations worshiping openly, with roughly two million adherents—something like 10 per cent of the population. Their impact was disproportionately great, however, because most French Catholics were apathetic. Besides, the Huguenots were elite in character and strategically concentrated in the autonomous fringe provinces: Dauphiné, Languedoc, and Gascony in the south, Poitou and Britanny in the west, Normandy in the north. Merchants and lawyers, rulers of the provincial towns who were tenacious of their local privileges, joined in large numbers. Especially in the south and west, scores of walled towns became

Catherine de Medici in widow's weeds. *Painting by Clouet.*

Huguenot bastions. Even more striking was the high percentage of converts among the *noblesse*. About two fifths of all the French nobility joined the Huguenot cause. Why should so many of these proud feudal magnates become smitten with a belief in original sin and predestination? In truth, few of them had authentic conversions, but they saw a wonderful chance to reverse the trend toward absolute royal power by patronizing the new religion. They wanted an arrangement in France similar to that established in Germany by the Peace of Augsburg in 1555, with each nobleman controlling the church in his own lands. When Admiral Coligny, of the Montmorency faction, and the Bourbon prince of Condé were converted to the new religion, the Huguenots became a really dangerous political threat.

As early as 1560, Condé and Coligny hatched a plot to capture the boy king Francis II and "liberate" him from his Guise advisers. Conspirators converged on Amboise, where the king was staying. Here in the Loire Valley hunting country, the Valois kings and their courtiers spent as much time as possible, and here they built their great châteaux, fortress-palaces with massive battlements and gorgeously fanciful ornamentation in the Italian style, the finest Renaissance buildings in France. The Guises foiled the *coup d'état* at Amboise and festooned the crenellations of the château with the corpses of the conspirators. But Queen regent Catherine de Medici prevented the execution of the chief instigators, Condé and Coligny. The Guises were too powerful to suit her, and she needed the Bourbons as a counterweight.

Catherine hoped to reduce the tension in the situation by arranging a settlement which would bury the Huguenot-Catholic conflict, and in 1561 she actually got Calvinist and Catholic theologians to attend a joint conference, the Colloquy of Poissy, and tried to make them subscribe to a common body of doctrine. Having no real religious principles herself, Catherine supposed that she could paper over the dogmatic dispute. Her plan, as we shall see, was not far different from the English religious settlement which Elizabeth I was devising just at this time. But it worked much less well. In France there was no chance for a latitudinarian church or for religious toleration as long as both factions believed that they could win total victory.

The queen's overtures to the Huguenots shocked the more fervid French Catholics into taking up arms against Protestantism. The Guises had always been fiercely anti-Huguenot, and the religious crisis gave their faction a much wider popularity and a much greater driving force than it had possessed before. Under Guise leadership, the ultra-Catholics developed into a power bloc (like the Huguenots) very dangerous to the Valois monarchy and to the French state. They had the loyalty of Paris, far and away the biggest and most important city. They controlled large sections of northern and northwestern France, where they could recruit and pay for large armies. They were backed by the papacy, by the Jesuits, and by Philip II, who had no love for the Guises but welcomed the chance to exploit French factionalism to his own advantage. Correspondingly, Elizabeth I of England supported the Huguenots.

In 1562 the duke of Guise, passing the little town of Vassy with his troopers, was infuriated to see a congregation of Huguenots worshiping in a barn, and ordered his men to kill them. This incident triggered the French religious wars. Once started, the fighting was almost impossible to stop. The Huguenots formed far too small a minority to conquer France, but their armies became so expert at defensive campaigns that they could not be disbanded. Noncombatants suffered more than the soldiers: for every pitched battle there were numerous forays, sieges, lootings, and massacres. Peace treaties were repeatedly arranged only to be quickly broken. The original commanders on both sides were soon killed, not in battle but by assassins—the duke of Guise in 1563 and the Bourbon prince of Condé in 1569. These murders launched a blood feud in which the Catholic and Huguenot zealots strove for retaliation by ambushing and slaughtering the remaining leaders. Both sides were able to keep troops in the field for years at a time, their operations financed largely by tax money diverted from the royal treasury, and led by vagabond aristocrats who loved fighting and freebooting.

After ten years of inconclusive combat, the Huguenots seemed to be gaining the upper hand. In August, 1572, during an interval of peace, the cream of the Huguenot nobility gathered in Paris to celebrate the marriage of their chief, the young Bourbon prince Henry of Navarre (1553–1610), to the sister of King Charles IX. Admiral Coligny was among the celebrants. He had just about persuaded the pliable king to undertake a major shift in royal policy, to declare war against Spain and support the revolt of the Calvinists in the Netherlands against Philip II. As a French patriot, Coligny hoped by this stratagem to end the civil wars and divert the nobility into fighting their old Habsburg enemies. As a Protestant, he hoped to secure Calvinism in France and the Netherlands. But Coligny's plan was too transparently partisan to attract many non-Huguenots. Obviously young Henry, duke of Guise (1550–1588), could never agree. Nor was the plan acceptable to Catherine de Medici, who reckoned that a Franco-Spanish war would produce victory for Philip II and destroy the Valois monarchy. So Catherine felt forced to ally temporarily with the Guise faction in order to stop Coligny. Just what happened next, and why, will always be disputed, for the evidence is murky and open to diverse interpretations. Someone hired an assassin to murder the admiral. On August 22, four days after the wedding, the assassin shot Coligny but merely wounded him. The enraged Huguenots immediately threatened Charles and Catherine with reprisals, and the wounded Coligny pressed the king yet again to initiate war with Spain at once, as the only way to prevent fresh civil turmoil. But Catherine and the Guises had another solution. Someone—most likely the queen mother—convinced Charles IX

The St. Bartholomew Massacre. By François Dubois d'Amiens. This gory Parisian panorama shows the Catholics pushing Coligny (right center) out a window and then (in the street below) flaying his corpse, while Guise displays the admiral's severed head. Catherine de Medici (upper left) inspects a pile of bodies. Other Huguenot victims are seen gibbeted, stabbed, clubbed, or floating in the Seine (left), while their more fortunate colleagues escape the city through a gate on the left bank. Museum Arland, Geneva.

that Coligny and the Huguenots were about to kill him and seize power; the only escape was to ambush all the traitorous Huguenots immediately and wipe out the rebel leadership.

Shortly after midnight on August 24, St. Bartholomew's Day, armed squads broke into the houses where the Huguenots lodged. The duke of Guise personally killed Coligny, in revenge for the murder of his father. Prince Henry of Navarre managed to save his life by promising to turn Catholic. By dawn the whole hysterical city was taking up the bestial cry, "Kill! Kill!" Women and children were senselessly hacked to death and dumped into the Seine. The great scholar Petrus Ramus was cut down while he knelt at prayer, and his pupils dragged his body through the streets. Debtors murdered their creditors. Looting continued for days. Such was the St. Bartholomew massacre, in which at least three thousand Huguenots were killed in Paris. As word spread throughout the country, another ten thousand were killed in the provincial towns. Some modern historians, numbed by gas chambers for the Jews and napalm for the Vietnamese, dismiss the episode as just another atrocity. But this will hardly do. The St. Bartholomew massacre should be remembered as mass murder in Europe's greatest city, plotted by the leaders of the state, and triggered by religious hatred. When the news reached the pope, he was so delighted that he gave a hundred crowns to the messenger. Catherine de

Medici laughed exultantly when she saw Henry of Navarre attending his first Mass. Charles IX, on the other hand, sickened with guilt at having abused his royal responsibilities. Charles was wiser than his mother, for the massacre discredited the Valois monarchy without breaking the Huguenots or ending the conflict.

When Charles died in 1574, he was succeeded by his even more neurotic brother, Henry III. The new king was quickly hated for the money and affection he lavished on his *mignons*, effeminate court dandies, to say nothing of the degenerate royal ballets and masquerades, where (according to a scandalized Paris lawyer) the king "was usually dressed as a woman, with a low-cut collar which showed his throat, hung with pearls."[6] Henry's feckless extravagance was inherited from his mother, but not his sudden spasms of religiosity, during which he took up the hermit's life or walked barefoot on penitential pilgrimages. Under this last Valois king, the Catholic-Huguenot conflict reached its climax. Ultra-Catholics and Huguenots alike saw Henry as a dissembling hypocrite. They repudiated his efforts at peacemaking, and did their utmost to dismantle the French state. The Huguenots, despite their loss of many aristocratic leaders in the St. Bartholomew massacre, still held important western towns, such as La Rochelle. They were strongest in the south, and Languedoc became virtually independent. The ultra-Catholics formed a Holy League in 1576 and vowed to exterminate heresy and to seat a Catholic champion, such as Henry, duke of Guise, on the French throne. Leaders of both religions preached rebellion. In the most famous Huguenot tract, the *Vindiciae contra tyrannos*, (1578) Calvin's political theory was rewritten to show that a tyrannical king has violated his contract with the people and should be overthrown. Jesuit writers argued the League position that a king who betrays the Church must be overthrown. Both sides had strong commanders. For the League, Henry of Guise was a perfect bandit captain, brave, dashing, and arrogant, with a saber scar etched across his cheek. But the Huguenots could boast the heir apparent to the throne, Prince Henry of Navarre, who quickly renounced his forced St. Bartholomew conversion. Henry of Navarre was an easygoing extrovert with one priceless virtue: he was the only late sixteenth-century French political leader who honestly tried to serve his country as well as himself.

The turning point in the French crisis came in 1588–1589, with the War of the Three Henries: Guise versus Valois versus Navarre. The conflict began when the duke of Guise made his supreme bid to capture the monarchy. He had to move carefully, for he was in the pay of Philip II, who had his own claim to the French throne! (Philip's third wife had been a Valois princess.) In 1588 the Spanish king directed Guise to stage a revolt in

[6]*The Paris of Henry of Navarre As Seen by Pierre de l'Estoile*, ed. by Nancy Lyman Roelker (Cambridge, Mass., 1958), p. 58.

The assassination of Henry, duke of Guise, in 1588. *The pro-Guise artist shows the assassins drawing their weapons (right) as they converge on the unsuspecting duke, stab him (center), and drag his body behind a tapestry (left) as Henry III looks on.*

Paris in order to prevent Henry III from interfering with the Spanish Armada when it attacked England. Accordingly, Guise entered Paris against Henry III's express orders. He incited the city mob to disarm the king's guards and besieged him inside the Louvre palace. Before Guise could summon the nerve to assault the Louvre and kill the king, his intended victim fled the city. Nevertheless, Guise now had virtual control. He forced Henry III to make him chief minister, he dictated policy, and he managed the Estates-General which convened at Blois in 1588. The only trouble was that by this time Guise's patron, Philip II, had been badly beaten by the English and was unable to protect his French agent.

The royal château at Blois was Henry III's last retreat. This rambling palace, with its famous open staircase, myriad paneled rooms, and secret passageways, lies in the heart of the Loire Valley. Nearby are Amboise, where Henry's brother escaped conspiracy, and Chenonceaux, where his mother squandered a fortune on new construction. Catherine de Medici could no longer intervene, for she lay mortally ill. Imitating Catherine's role in the St. Bartholomew massacre, Henry III plotted to murder Guise. "He does not dare," said the duke contemptuously, but for once he underestimated the Valois. On December 23, 1588, the king's bodyguard closed in on Guise and cut him down. The old queen mother could hear the uproar as the dying duke dragged his assassins through the royal chambers above her sickbed.

Henry III now joined the Huguenots in an all-out effort to crush the Catholic League. He threw himself into an alliance with Henry of Navarre, whom he recognized as his heir, and the two men marched together against Catholic Paris. But retribution for Guise's murder came fast: in July, 1589, Henry III was himself assassinated, by a fanatical monk who had secreted a dagger in the sleeve of his habit. Only one of the three Henries was left. Could the French Catholics be induced to accept this heretical prince as King Henry IV?

The new king's strongest asset was the mounting popular revulsion against anarchy. Many Frenchmen, derisively called *politiques* because they preferred merely political goals to spiritual ones, had long craved for peace and stability. The skeptical essayist Michel de Montaigne (1533–1592) was a *politique*, disgusted with cannibalism in the name of divinity. So was the profound political theorist Jean Bodin (1530–1596), whose *Six Books of the Republic* (1576) pleaded for the establishment of centralized sovereign authority in the hands of a purposeful prince. In Henry IV, the *politiques* saw at last a French prince who could be trusted with sovereign authority, who was a statesman of humanity and honesty (unlike Catherine de Medici), with a suitably jocose, pragmatic temper. Yet it took Henry IV a full decade to end the war. With Guise dead, the Catholic champion became Philip II, who intended once he had conquered Henry IV to put a Spanish infanta on the throne. In the early 1590's, Spanish troops repeatedly swept down from Flanders and blocked Henry IV's efforts to occupy his capital city. The Parisians continued to believe their League priests, who taught that a good Catholic would eat his own children rather than submit to a heretic. In 1593, Henry concluded that he must undergo the humiliation of abjuring Protestantism. "Today I talk to the Bishops," he told his mistress. "Sunday I take the perilous leap" (that is, attend Mass). Henry's politically motivated conversion scandalized the ultra-Catholics even more than the Huguenots, but the pope felt compelled to grant him absolution. Paris opened its gates to the king who, hat in hand, saluted all the pretty ladies in the windows as he entered the city.

In 1598, Henry IV and Philip II finally made peace, restoring the terms of 1559. Spain had gained nothing. In this same year, Henry bought off the last of the Catholic League nobility with grants of money and titles and conciliated the Huguenots with the Edict of Nantes. With this edict, Henry established a lasting religious truce. He declared Catholicism the official French religion and prohibited the reformed worship within five leagues of Paris. Yet any nobleman who chose to do so could practice the reformed religion in his own household, and bourgeois and lower-class Huguenots could also worship in certain specified places. The Huguenot residents of some two hundred towns, mostly in the south and along the Bay of Biscay,

The last page of the Edict of Nantes, 1598. *Henry IV's sprawling signature is in the center.*

were granted full religious freedom, including the right to set up schools and printing presses. About half of these towns were fortified and garrisoned by the Huguenots at royal expense. In addition, Huguenots throughout the country were promised "perpetual and irrevocable" liberty of conscience, full civil rights, and eligibility for public office. The king appointed special courts (half Catholic, half Huguenot) to adjudicate breaches of his edict.

The close of the French religious wars, with the Edict of Nantes, was to some extent a Catholic victory. France was henceforth a Catholic country with a Catholic king. Yet Henry IV temporarily expelled the Jesuits and repudiated the fanaticism of the ultra-Catholic League. At the same time, his edict was to some extent a Protestant victory, since it granted the Huguenots an entrenched position within the country. Yet the Huguenots had lost their leader; toleration was a gift of the king. In most ways, the compromise of 1598 signalized the triumph of political expediency over religion. The chief lesson of the French religious wars was a political one, that strongly centralized government was the only possible alternative to rebellion and social chaos. Upon this foundation would be built the magnificent seventeenth-century absolute monarchy of Louis XIV.

THE REVOLT OF THE NETHERLANDS

In the mid-sixteenth century, the people of the Low Countries had a style of life all their own, distinctly different from both the Spanish and the French. Theirs was a business society of towns and merchants, with the highest per-capita wealth in Europe. The Netherlanders were polyglot, particularistic, and cosmopolitan. Their country was divided into seventeen autonomous provinces, of which the most important were Flanders, Brabant, and Holland. Most of the people spoke Low German (Flemish or Dutch), but the Walloons, who lived in the southern border provinces, spoke a dialect of French. The Netherlanders lived at the crossroads of northwestern Europe, where the North Sea coast is intersected by a great river system feeding into Germany and France. The chief Flemish cloth-manufacturing towns, Bruges and Ghent, were no longer as prosperous as they had been in the late Middle Ages, but by the sixteenth century the enterprising Netherlanders were cultivating a more variegated commercial and industrial pattern. Antwerp was now the biggest city in the Low Countries and the chief financial and distribution center for western Europe. English cloth merchants, Portuguese spice merchants, Spanish wool merchants, German metalware merchants, French wine merchants, Italian silk merchants, and Baltic grain merchants congregated in Antwerp to exchange northern and southern products. Antwerp and other Netherlands towns were also leading industrial centers, and sailors from Zeeland and Holland dominated the North Sea herring fishery.

The hereditary ruler of the Low Countries was the duke of Burgundy. From 1506 to 1556, the emperor Charles V had held this title. The Netherlanders had had little to complain of during Charles's long administration, for thanks to the persistence of local customs and privileges, they had been able to manage their own affairs. The emperor had drawn heavily on the wealth of his Netherlands subjects in financing his wars, but he had left the central administration (such as it was) in the hands of the high nobility, and the government of the towns in the hands of the rich merchants. These merchant oligarchs controlled the provincial estates and the States-General as well. They refused to grant taxes unless their grievances were redressed, and they did their own tax collecting, keeping any surplus for their own purposes. The Netherlands States-General was particularly hard to handle, because the delegates from all seventeen provinces had to give their consent before anything could be done. Charles V had been unable to prevent the influx of Protestantism. Netherlanders were receptive to new religious opinions; their attitude—as exemplified in their great Christian humanist, Erasmus of Rotterdam—was tolerant and latitudinarian. Starting in the 1520's, Lutheran and Anabaptist doctrines spread widely despite savage heresy-hunting by Charles's government.

When Philip II inherited the dukedom of Burgundy from his father in 1556, he regarded the Low Countries as vital to his Spanish empire. Antwerp was the chief outlet for Spanish wool and wine, and the Netherlanders supplied Spain with grain, timber, textiles, armaments, and mercury for Philip's silver mines. But Philip soon discovered that the Netherlands was much harder to govern from a long distance than Milan or Mexico. He personally disliked the place and never visited there after 1559. He could speak no Dutch, and had no trusted native advisers. And when he attempted to correct the atomistic political structure of the Netherlands, he encountered massive resistance. The people of the Low Countries had seen Charles V as a fellow Netherlander, but his son was an outsider. The high nobility found that their power was short-circuited by Castilian bureaucrats in Brussels and Madrid. Philip was so annoyed by the obstructionist tactics of the States-General that he vowed as early as 1559 never to convene it again. But the most explosive issue was religious. By the 1550's Calvinism was spreading from France into the Walloon provinces and Flanders. Antwerp became a Calvinist stronghold. When Philip found that his inquisitors could not eradicate this new heresy, he summarily reorganized the Netherlands church in 1561 by increasing the number of bishops from four to eighteen, nominating them all himself.

Philip II's Spanish absolutism had a traumatic effect upon the Netherlanders. Shopkeepers turned into soldiers; cosmopolites turned into patriots; latitudinarians turned into Calvinist fanatics. But as we shall see, in the end the revolt of the Netherlanders was only half successful. The seven northern provinces became independent and Protestant; the ten southern provinces (half Low German and half Walloon) remained loyal to Spain and to Catholicism. This division was largely accidental; in the 1560's the southern provinces were more Protestant and more rebellious against Philip II than the northern provinces. But accidental or not, the division became permanent. Between 1560 and 1600 the modern nations of Holland and Belgium were born.

The revolt against Spain was initiated by the Netherlands nobility. Three of the highest nobles, the prince of Orange and the counts of Egmont and Horn, all members of the Council of State, tried repeatedly to persuade Philip to alter his policy. When they failed, a group of the lesser nobility petitioned the king in 1566 to abolish the Inquisition in the Netherlands and to stop persecuting the Protestants. "Why be afraid of these beggars?" asked a courtier contemptuously, as several hundred gentry solemnly presented their petition to Philip's regent in Brussels. And "Long live the beggars!" suddenly became the rebel cry. Calvinist preachers sprang up everywhere in the Netherlands and whipped their excited auditors into a rage not only against the bishops but against all the outward trappings of Catholicism. In the summer of 1566 hundreds of churches were ravaged by iconoclasts. Some were converted into conventicles, or meetinghouses, of the Genevan type. This "Calvinist fury" shocked many Netherlanders and stung Philip into brutal reprisals. The duke of Alba arrived in 1567 with ten thousand picked Spanish troops, and he came very close to crushing all Netherlands resistance to Spanish absolutism. Alba executed Egmont and Horn, tortured and killed several thousand suspected heretics, and confiscated their property. He canceled all meaningful self-government and levied fantastically heavy new taxes. Only a forlorn band of exiles under the banner of the prince of Orange maintained active opposition to Philip.

From 1567 on, the Spanish maintained a formidable standing army in the Netherlands. Warfare in this region of fortified towns required disciplined, seasoned troops who could handle long sieges and surprise skirmishes. Alba and his successors mobilized 65,000 men (and sometimes more) for the campaigns; theirs was the finest fighting force of its day. Spanish and Italian infantry units were brought north along the "Spanish road"—the military corridor from Genoa and Milan through Savoy, Franche-Comté, and Lorraine—to form the core of this army. German soldiers recruited from the Tyrol, Alsace, and the Rhine Valley, along with local Netherlands troops, filled out the ranks. Alba's new taxes by no means paid for an army of this size, so Philip had to supply most of the funding from Spain. Between 1567 and 1576 the Spanish spent the equivalent of Elizabeth I's total revenue on this army every year, and still many of the soldiers were unpaid. Here was the fatal flaw in Philip's military system. Between 1572 and 1607, units within the Netherlands army staged over forty-five separate mutinies. They expelled their officers, holed up in fortified towns, lived off the surrounding countryside, and haggled for months with the Spanish authorities, until they finally got their back pay.[7] These mutinies repeatedly paralyzed Philip's battle plans and stiffened the resolve of the Netherlands rebels.

[7]For fuller details, see Geoffrey Parker, *The Army of Flanders and the Spanish Road, 1567–1659* (New York, 1972).

These rebels lacked cohesion at first. Like the French Huguenots, they were initially more destructive than constructive. They were not trying to mold a Netherlands nation-state; each of the seventeen provinces wanted to preserve its cherished autonomy. Nobility and merchants, Calvinists and moderate Catholics, could agree only in their distaste for Philip II. From 1567 to 1584 the rebel chief was Prince William of Orange (1533–1584), a man with many of the same character traits as the Huguenot chief, Henry of Navarre. Nicknamed William the Silent because of his skill at masking his intentions, Prince William was actually a gregarious extrovert who lived grandly and expensively. As a rebel leader he displayed alarming deficiencies. He was a mediocre general and so personally mired in debt that merchant creditors refused to lend him enough money. William was a religious opportunist who changed from Lutheran to Catholic to Calvinist as the circumstances warranted. In the 1560's he appeared to be a frivolous figure. But as he called upon his countrymen to stand up against Spanish tyranny, he revealed great courage and patriotism. Prince William appealed to the common people over the heads of the town oligarchs and his fellow nobles, yet scrupulously avoided grabbing dictatorial power. Almost single-handedly he strove to harmonize religious, sectional, and class differences, and weave the Netherlands into a nation. Thanks largely to

The sea beggars capture Brielle, 1572. *This was the first coastal town taken by the Dutch rebels, who are shown using artillery, musketeers, and pikemen to break in at the town gate.*

BRIELE.

William, the rebellion progressed, but it did not culminate in the achievement of his dream, a unified Netherlands nation-state. Instead, during the 1570's and 1580's the seventeen provinces split into two sections, the rebel north versus the Spanish south. Religion, which William wore so lightly, proved to be the great divider.

The decisive point came in 1572. In April of that year, fugitive rebel ships (self-styled "sea beggars") staged commando landings in the provinces of Zeeland and Holland, and captured a number of ports. These sea-beggar rebels had to overcome determined local opposition, because they were fiery Calvinists invading an area which was still predominantly Catholic. Having got possession of the territory bordering the Zuider Zee, the beggars had a permanent base of operations. The Spanish were never able to recapture Holland and Zeeland, for in this low-lying country the dikes could be opened to flood an invading army. If Coligny had brought France into the Netherlands war at this point, and if the English—who later supported the rebels—had also intervened in force, it is possible that William the Silent and the sea beggars might have expelled the Spanish from the Low Countries. But the St. Bartholomew massacre took France out of the picture, and Elizabeth I—well aware that she lacked money and soldiers—stayed cautiously on the sidelines. Within the Netherlands, religious and political refugees from the south moved into the rebel Zuider Zee area in large numbers, and Calvinism became the established religion. Here was the beginning of the partition of the Netherlands into two separate states.

In the late 1570's, William the Silent had his last real chance to unite all seventeen provinces. In 1576 the Spanish garrison in the still-loyal southern provinces ran amuck because the soldiers had been unpaid for two years. They sacked the city of Antwerp and murdered upwards of eight thousand inhabitants. This frightful "Spanish fury" persuaded the people of Brabant and Flanders that they must ally themselves with the rebel north. In 1577 all of the provinces joined the Union of Brussels, shelving religious disputes and pledging to fight Spain until Philip restored their privileges and withdrew his troops. William was recognized as their military commander. Yet the rebels were not effectively united. In 1578 a new Spanish commander, the duke of Parma, Philip II's ablest general, appeared on the scene with fresh troops and new funding based on the rapidly escalating Spanish bullion imports from America. As soon as Parma began scoring military victories in the south, he detached the French-speaking Walloon provinces from the rebel federation. Parma appealed to these southern Netherlanders not so much on linguistic as on religious grounds. How could good Catholics associate with Calvinists? In 1579 he organized the loyal south into the Union of Arras and forced William to regroup the Calvinist north into the Union of Utrecht. In 1581 the States-General of the rebel provinces deposed Philip

II as their prince and declared the independence of the United Provinces, or Dutch republic.

In the 1580's, each side tried to conquer the other, with the Spanish under Parma keeping the rebels very much on the defensive. After Parma had taken the chief Flemish towns in 1584, and Brussels and Antwerp in 1585, he held almost everything south of the Rhine River. A new wave of religious and political refugees fled north. Philip II hoped that the seven remaining rebel provinces would surrender if he could eradicate their leader. He declared William of Orange an outlaw and offered twenty-five thousand crowns as a reward for his assassination. Several efforts were made to earn this money, and in 1584 a Catholic fanatic gained entry to the prince's house in Delft, stood among a crowd of petitioners, and murdered him at point-blank pistol range.

With the death of its great founder, the Dutch republic was truly in desperate plight. The Dutch had so far received little help from Germany and France, and almost none from England. Now Queen Elizabeth grudgingly sent a small army under the incompetent earl of Leicester. For two years (1585–1587), the Anglo-Dutch force precariously held the Rhine River line against Parma. Philip II, in the Escorial, remembering his mighty naval victory against the Turks at Lepanto, calculated that another such blow could crush the Dutch, the English, and the French Huguenots. Accordingly he prepared a huge new fleet, the "Invincible Armada," designed to clear the English Channel and North Sea of Dutch and English shipping, end the revolt of the Netherlands and the Huguenots, dethrone the heretic queen of England, and eradicate North Atlantic Protestantism.

ELIZABETHAN ENGLAND

The British Isles which Philip II prepared to invade in 1588 offered three strikingly varied scenes. In England, under "good Queen Bess," there was peace and prosperity as never before. The English people, by some alchemy beyond the historian's analysis, were transforming their backwater island into a magnificently dynamic society. Scotland, by contrast, was still half wild. The Scots managed their affairs with crude abandon. This was the era of the sex-driven Mary, Queen of Scots, and the hot-gospeling John Knox. Ireland, barely on the edge of civilization, was a land of perpetual blood feuds and cattle raids, with no real government and no defense against invaders. During the late sixteenth century, the Irish slowly fell victim to English conquest and exploitation. Yet in their different styles, all three peoples experienced the western European religious crisis. Protestants and Catholics were everywhere vying for control.

When Queen Elizabeth I (ruled 1558–1603) ascended the English

The Ditchley portrait of Elizabeth I. *The queen is shown as she liked to be portrayed, in fantastic costume, standing on a map of her beloved England, impervious to thunderstorms. National Portrait Gallery, London.*

throne, religion was unquestionably the great issue. Back in the 1530's, when her father, Henry VIII (ruled 1509–1547), had so easily separated from Rome, the atmosphere had been worldly and cynical. Henry had invited the nobility and gentry who sat in Parliament to legislate the break with the papacy, giving them a larger share of power, and had then sold the confiscated Church lands to them cheap. In those days only a few Englishmen, such as Sir Thomas More, had been willing to die for the old universal Church. Only a few Englishmen, such as William Tyndale, who translated the Bible into English, had been outspoken proponents of Luther's new doctrines. But by the 1550's the atmosphere was much changed. During the reign of Elizabeth's feeble brother Edward VI (1547–1553), radical Protestants had overhauled the doctrine and ritual of the English church. In the succeeding reign, Elizabeth's fervidly Catholic sister, Queen Mary Tudor (1553–1558), had forcibly reunited the English church with Rome and burned at the stake the several hundred persons who dared to protest. This short period of violent fluctuation, reminiscent of the period of Valois rule in France, aroused deep religious passions in the English people. Would Elizabeth follow Edward's example, or Mary's?

She did neither. Queen Elizabeth I was the only ruler in western Europe in the late sixteenth century who was able to handle the religious issue. Despite the loud fulminations of Calvinists and the conspiracies of Catholics, she unerringly pursued a policy of peace and compromise, and got away with it. This achievement alone is good reason for nominating Elizabeth the ablest politician of her time. Certainly she was more attractive as a queen than as a human being. She had a temper to match her red hair and a tongue to match her sharp features. Superficially, she was vacillating, evasive, and vague, but she was willfully stubborn underneath. Her unfortunate councillors had to take the blame for whatever went wrong. She was frugal, not to say mean, in her expenditures; though she paid plenty for clothes and cosmetics, she allowed her devoted courtiers to buy her entertainment, without offering in return the royal pageantry supplied by Catherine de Medici or public monuments like Philip II's Escorial. In an age when government was reckoned to be strictly a man's job, Elizabeth refused to marry because she would not share power, but kept the bachelor princes of western Europe dangling as her suitors. In an age when women were reckoned to be fit chiefly for childbirth, and queens for the production of male heirs, Elizabeth made a virtue of her spinsterly virginity, while behaving with ever more outlandish coquetry the older she got. And yet, she was one of the greatest rulers in English history.

Elizabeth's I's first and most important work was her religious settlement, achieved between 1559 and 1563. The new queen was confronted with a church staffed by her sister Mary's Catholic appointees, with the clamors for reinstatement of her brother Edward's ousted Protestant clergy (many of whom had returned from exile in Geneva and other Calvinist centers), and with a Parliament divided between the Catholic House of Lords and a Protestant House of Commons. Queen and Parliament worked out a compromise reorganization of the Church of England so as to combine an external Catholic structure with a broadly Protestant dogma. The intention was to satisfy as wide a spectrum of religious tastes as possible. All Englishmen were required to attend public worship in the national church, but no man's inner conscience was publicly scrutinized. Under the Elizabethan system, there was no heresy-hunting, no Inquisition, no burnings, only a system of fines for those who stayed away from church. Less than 5 per cent of the clergy resigned (they were replaced, of course, by Protestants); the remainder docilely subscribed to the required Thirty-nine Articles of belief, a formula closer to Luther than to Calvin, which listed numerous "errors" in the Roman Church. The queen hand picked her bishops and sometimes kept bishoprics vacant for years in order to tap the revenues: the Elizabethan church was decidedly subordinate to the state. Men of strong conviction were of course offended by the expediency of a church which in its prayer book could describe the pivotal Communion service both as a miracle and as a memorial ceremony. But only the most radical Calvinists and the most committed Catholics refused to tolerate the dignified beauty of the Anglican liturgy, and soon many Englishmen were deeply loyal to their *via media*.

Having worked out a formula for English religious stability and peace, Elizabeth I spent the rest of her long reign trying to keep the *status quo*. She was a political conservative, and with good reason. England, after all, was a small state with a population of less than four million and a predominantly agrarian economy. The income of the royal government was very modest by Spanish or French standards. The queen could afford neither a standing army nor an elaborate civil service. She depended on the cooperation of the nobility and the landed gentry. The English nobility were less wealthy than their Spanish or French counterparts and enjoyed fewer privileges; they even paid taxes. Henry VII and Henry VIII had done a great deal to domesticate the feudal magnates who had controlled England in the late Middle Ages. But under Elizabeth the nobility still exercised great power: they commanded small armies of retainers, they sat in the House of Lords and got their adherents elected to the House of Commons, and they formed aristocratic factions at court dangerously similar to the Guise and Bourbon factions in Valois France. Like earlier Tudor monarchs, Elizabeth tried to bolster her position with respect to the nobility by patronizing the upper middle class: country squires and London merchants. She chose her two chief advisers—Sir William Cecil (1520–1598) and Sir Francis Walsingham (c. 1530–1590)—from this class, and on the local level appointed deserving squires as justices of the peace. The justice of the peace received no pay, but he had dignity, responsibility, and control over neighborhood affairs. When his interests coincided with those of the royal government, he served the queen very well.

The most obvious brake on English royal authority was Parliament. Elizabeth could neither tax nor legislate except through Parliament. Unlike the Castilian Cortes and the French Estates-General, Parliament gained power steadily throughout the sixteenth century. Henry VIII, Edward VI, Mary, and Elizabeth all worked through Parliament in their attempts to shape the English church. Much more legislation was enacted by Parliament during the Tudor era than in the Middle Ages. Parliamentary taxes were vital to the crown, and Elizabeth (unlike Philip II in Castile) had great difficulty in wheedling tax levies from Parliament even in emergencies.

In the early sixteenth century the lower house, the House of Commons, had been more tractable than the House of Lords, citadel of the nobility, but under Elizabeth, the Commons became the more independent and aggressive of the two houses. Ambitious and well-connected country gentlemen actively sought election to the Commons. Elizabethan parliamentary elections bore little resemblance to modern ones. There were no parties or platforms. Most elections were uncontested. Only candidates of high social standing, wealth, and influence presumed to stand, and they were dutifully accepted by a few hundred subservient voters. But if the electorate was subservient, the members of Parliament were not. Elizabeth was hard pressed to cope with the opinionated, self-confident gentry who crowded into the Commons chamber in St. Stephen's Chapel at Westminster, just outside the city of London, in order to question her policies and advocate their own. The queen summoned Parliament as infrequently as possible, convoking it for a session of a couple of months every three or four years. Her ministers carefully stage-managed every bit of business, but they could not prevent rude speakers in the Commons from urging Her Majesty to marry or to crush popery. Even though the government introduced legislation, members of the Commons freely debated and amended bills in committee and introduced new bills of their own. The queen became adept at seeming to surrender to Parliament, while still preserving her prerogative.

There was always a Puritan bloc in Parliament. Puritans were the English species of Calvinist. They wanted to cleanse the English church of its popish ceremonies and ritual, to abolish Elizabeth's episcopal church government, to erect a preaching ministry and a national Geneva discipline. The Puritans were less rebellious against the government than were their compeers in France and the Netherlands. Much as they disliked the queen's lukewarm Protestantism, they accepted membership in the Church of England and aimed at purifying it from within. Hence the Puritans were less easy to identify than were the Huguenots and the Dutch Calvinists. Indeed, many Anglican clergymen, including several bishops, were Puritans. The movement was attractive to articulate, educated laymen, and an increasing number of landed gentlemen and London merchants became Puritans. Cambridge University was the intellectual headquarters of the Puritans. Elizabeth intensely disliked Puritan criticism of her church. She took special pains to gag Puritan polemicists and kept the movement relatively small. But even Elizabeth could not stop the prolific Puritan pamphleteers from formulating belligerent protests against prayer books, bishops, and godless rulers, developing a line of argument which would lead—a generation after the queen's death—to the Puritan Revolution of 1640.

In the short run, the biggest challenge to the *status quo* came not from the radicals in religion, but from the conservatives. The Catholics had a very active claimant to the English throne in Mary Stuart, better known as Mary, Queen of Scots, who was everything Elizabeth was not: beautiful, alluring, passionate, and rash. Mary's reign in Scotland (1561–1567) was brief and turbulent, and suggests the chaos that might have engulfed England had she been able to take her cousin Elizabeth's place. To be sure, sixteenth-century Scotland was not an easy place to govern. The wildly beautiful countryside was economically underdeveloped. The few small towns were frequently overrun by marauders despite their grim gray stone walls. The Scots nobility were untamed tribal chieftains, continually feuding and fighting among themselves. Roughly half the people were Catholics; the other half, Calvinists. The Calvinist leader was John Knox, a brass-tongued preacher whose "Reformed Kirk" was patterned after the Genevan presbyterian system. The General Assembly of the Reformed Kirk was a more powerful body than the Scots parliament, for it was quite independent of royal control. Mary Stuart had been queen of Scotland since she was an infant, but she had spent her girlhood at the French Valois court, her mother governing Scotland as regent until she died in 1560. One foggy, dismal day in 1561 the nineteen-year-old queen returned from France to Holyrood Palace, in Edinburgh, to be greeted by a serenade of psalms sung out of tune. She was already a widow; her first husband, the boy king Francis II of France, had died the previous year. Mary established as gay a court as possible at Edinburgh and won over many of the Protestant nobility. But her charms cast no spell on John Knox. Mary reportedly told Knox, "I will defend the kirk of Rome, for it is, I think, the true kirk of God."

"Your will, madam," came the reply, "is no reason: neither doth your thought make that Roman harlot to be the true and immaculate spouse of Jesus Christ."

Mary had no desire to settle permanently in dour Scotland. She immediately pressed Elizabeth to recognize her as heir to the English throne, and when Elizabeth procrastinated, she married her cousin Henry Stewart, Lord Darnley, who had the next-best claim to the English throne. But Mary soon lost interest in the empty-headed Darnley and adopted a court musician named David Rizzio as her paramour. Early in 1566 the jealous Darnley gathered a band of conspirators who surprised Mary and Rizzio at supper in Holyrood Palace and hacked Rizzio to death as he clung to the queen's skirts. Mary shortly got her revenge. When Darnley contracted smallpox, she installed him in a lonely house outside the walls of Edinburgh, and one night someone strangled Darnley and blew up his house with gunpowder. Who did it can never be proved, but most Scotsmen at the time suspected the earl of Bothwell, Mary's latest lover. Their suspicions became firmer when Mary married Bothwell three months after Darnley's murder. The question of Mary's guilt or innocence in this lurid affair has been endlessly debated. One fact is plain. By marrying Bothwell she lost control of Scotland. The nobility revolted against the lady and forced her to abdicate. In 1568 she fled to England, and Elizabeth imprisoned her.

Mary was still young, still bewitching. In 1569 a band of Catholic lords led an abortive rebellion on her behalf in northern England. The 1570's and 1580's were marked by a series of Catholic plots to assassinate Elizabeth and enthrone Mary—all discovered (and some perhaps planted) by Elizabeth's spies. The pope had excommunicated Elizabeth, and resolute Jesuit mission-

The execution of Mary, Queen of Scots. *This contemporary drawing shows (upper left) the queen entering the great hall of Fotheringhay Castle, and then (center) standing on the execution platform by the chopping block, attended by her ladies and watched by guards and neighborhood gentry.*

aries, such as Edmund Campion and Robert Parsons, were encouraging the remaining English Catholics to stand firm in their faith. The queen and her ministers felt compelled to crack down: during Elizabeth's reign, over two hundred priests and Catholic laymen were executed on the technical charge of treason. In 1586, government spies uncovered Mary's complicity in a new assassination plot. This time she was tried and found guilty. With a great show of reluctance, partly real and partly feigned, Elizabeth signed the death warrant. In 1587, Mary Stuart was released from her nineteen years of imprisonment by the executioner's axe. Catholics naturally saw her as a martyr and denounced the Protestant Jezebel for murdering an anointed queen.

Religion was one of the causes of mounting friction between Elizabethan England and Philip II's Spain. Another was Elizabeth's support of the Dutch rebels. A third cause, perhaps the most decisive, was English intrusion into the Spanish empire in America. Until the mid-sixteenth century, English sailors had taken practically no part in the exploration and exploitation of the New World, and English merchants were perfectly content with the traditional Flemish wool trade. By the 1560's, however, even Englishmen were becoming interested in the possibility of finding wealth in the New World. Elizabeth I encouraged private investment in overseas enterprises and offered token investments herself. Sailors from Plymouth and other southwestern ports began to reconnoiter the Atlantic. Some, such as Martin Frobisher and John Davis, searched the still unclaimed North American coastline, looking fruitlessly for a passage to Cathay, and panning fruitlessly for gold. Others ventured into the Spanish Caribbean. Between 1562 and 1568 John Hawkins sold African slaves to the Spanish planters with some success. Between 1571 and 1581 Francis Drake (c. 1540–1596), a fiery Protestant, made three piratical raids on Spanish America with much greater success. On his third voyage, Drake took his ship, the *Golden Hind*, through the Strait of Magellan, captured a Spanish treasure ship off the Pacific coast of South America, then sailed up to California and from there to the South Pacific spice islands and to the Cape of Good Hope; thus, when he returned to Plymouth after an absence of three years, he had circumnavigated the globe. The queen knighted Drake in 1581, and no wonder; his cargo of Spanish treasure was worth twice Elizabeth's annual revenue. In 1585–1586, with the official backing of his government, Sir Francis took a big fleet of thirty ships once more into the Caribbean, where he vandalized the Spanish more than he plundered them. Certainly the Elizabethan sea dogs were doing all they could to provoke the Prudent King.

So it was that the two most cautious leaders in Christendom, both fearful of change and sensitive to the burdens of war, faced each other in dramatic conflict. In 1586, Philip II began to plan his invasion of England. A Spanish fleet, powerful enough to hold the English navy at bay, was to sail from Lisbon to the Flemish coast, rendezvous with Parma's army, assembled on

The defeat of the Spanish Armada. *An old English print showing the crescent-shaped Spanish fleet in flight and one struggling Spanish ship (lower left) being hunted down. The English ships display the red cross of St. George on their ensigns. The Spanish oared galley (lower right) was better suited to the Mediterranean than the Atlantic.*

barges, and cross the English Channel, landing at the mouth of the Thames. Even with the best of luck this plan would have been extremely difficult to execute, and one misfortune after another compounded the difficulty. In 1587, Sir Francis Drake daringly raided Cádiz, Spain's chief Atlantic port. He sank enough ships to delay Philip's enterprise by a year and destroyed the Spaniards' precious store of seasoned barrel staves, thereby condemning the Armada crew to a diet of stinking water and spoiled food as a result of storage in casks made of green timber. Then, on the eve of embarkation, Philip's admiral died. His replacement, the duke of Medina-Sidonia was brave but inexperienced.

The Invincible Armada that finally neared the English coast in July, 1588, was a majestic fleet of 130 ships and thirty thousand men. The English sailed out from Plymouth with an equally impressive force. They had as many ships as the Spaniards, their seamanship and their guns were better, and they had Sir Francis Drake. This was not the biggest naval showdown of the century. Twice as many ships and men had fought at Lepanto in 1571. But the Battle of Lepanto was a land battle transferred to sea, with soldiers swarming across oared galleys which had locked together. The Anglo-Spanish confrontation in 1588 was altogether·different, a mariners' duel between sailing ships armed with cannon. The Armada fight inaugurated the classical age of naval warfare, which stretched from the sixteenth into the nineteenth century, from Drake to Nelson.

The Spanish and English fleets met off Cornwall, at the southwestern tip of England. Both sides were reluctant to attack. The duke of Medina-Sidonia was dismayed to see how nimbly the English could sail around his ships. The English were baffled by the tight Spanish crescent formation, designed to force them to grapple at close quarters, to fight in the style of Mediterranean galleys, by ramming and boarding, at which the Spanish excelled. For nine days the two fleets drifted slowly up the length of the Channel, the English buzzing around the Spanish crescent, neither side doing much damage. Medina-Sidonia was approaching his rendezvous with Parma, but so far he had been continuously outmaneuvered, and he saw that if he tried to convoy Parma's men in barges from Flanders across the Channel to England, the English navy would lacerate them. He anchored off Calais, trying to think of some way to join forces with Parma. All at once, disaster struck the Armada. At midnight the English sent eight blazing fire ships into the Spanish fleet. The Spanish ships scattered to sea, their crescent formation broken. Drake and his comrades pounced on them, sank some of the ships, and pounded the rest until ammunition gave out. Then a gale swept the battered Armada into the North Sea. Medina-Sidonia had lost all hope of joining with Parma or invading England. With the English fleet chasing him north, toward Scotland, he sailed his limping, leaky galleons around the British Isles. A number of ships and thousands of men were lost off the stormy Irish coast. About half the fleet eventually straggled back to Spain. So ended the first modern naval battle. So ended Philip's plan to dethrone Elizabeth.

THE DECLINE OF SPAIN

The defeat of the Spanish Armada was a decisive event. It exposed the limitations of sixteenth-century military power. It stamped Philip II's overweening international policy with failure. It tipped the religious struggle, which underlay all western European politics during the late sixteenth century, in favor of the Protestant minority. And it closed Spain's golden century of power and glory.

After 1588, nothing went right for Philip II. The Spanish king received the news of the Armada's defeat with his customary sober stoicism—and kept on trying to conquer England and put down the Dutch rebels. In the 1590's, as has been mentioned, he took on a new opponent, invading France in an attempt to dethrone Henry of Navarre. The French, English, and Dutch formed an alliance against him, fought him to a standstill on land, and bested him at sea. The Spanish infantry was still superlative, and in northern France the duke of Parma campaigned with his usual brilliance against Henry IV. But his successes roused French patriotism against the Spanish invaders. Unwittingly, Philip II helped Henry IV to reunite his country and restore the centralized power of the French monarchy. In 1598, just a few months before his death, Philip reluctantly made peace with Henry. Though this peace treaty restored the *status quo* of 1559, psychologically it was a French victory, the first of a long series of Bourbon victories over the Habsburgs. Within a few years the agony of the French religious wars became only a memory, as Bourbon France rapidly eclipsed Habsburg Spain in political and military power.

Philip II never made peace with England. The Anglo-Spanish war continued until 1604, with the English inflicting more damage than they received. Despite the failure of the Armada, Philip doggedly kept trying to invade Britain. His last great fleet, headed for Ireland, was dispersed by storms in 1596. Through the years, the English countered by launching a series of armadas against Spain but never came close to achieving a knockout blow. In 1589, Sir Francis Drake failed to capture Lisbon; in 1596, he died while leading an abortive attack against the Spanish West Indies. The English did score some victories. In 1596, they sacked Cádiz and pillaged the surrounding Spanish countryside. Throughout the war, English privateers mercilessly plundered Spanish commercial vessels. On the whole, the long war cast a damper on the buoyant Elizabethans. They were spending too much blood and money for too little glory. Yet England emerged from this conflict in far better shape than Spain and with new ambitions for an empire of its own to rival the Spanish empire.

Philip II's bitterest legacy was the Netherlands rebellion. In the mid-1580's, Parma seemed close to reconquering the northern provinces, but his participation in the Armada fiasco and in campaigns in France against Henry IV between 1589 and 1592 killed Spanish momentum in the Neth-

The Surrender of Breda. *This famous painting by Velázquez celebrates one of Spain's few seventeenth-century victories. In 1625, after an eight-month siege, a Spanish army took the Dutch frontier town of Breda. In 1637, shortly after Velázquez commemorated this triumph, the Dutch recaptured Breda. Museo del Prado, Barcelona.*

erlands. Lack of sea power was also very damaging. When the Flemish farmers had three poor harvests in a row, the Anglo-Dutch naval blockade stopped all grain imports and triggered the worst famine of the century in the southern provinces. After 1590 every Spanish campaign was crippled by mutinies. The fighting continued until 1609, with neither side able to penetrate far beyond the Rhine River line which divided the seven Calvinist United Provinces from the ten Catholic provinces in Spanish hands. The Dutch commander, Prince Maurice of Nassau, son of William the Silent, hoped to reunite the northern and southern provinces, but many of his Calvinist supporters did not wish to join with Catholics, and the burghers of Holland and Zeeland did not wish to share their business prosperity with the towns of Flanders and Brabant. The northern provinces flourished mightily during the war; the south was in economic collapse. After Parma captured Antwerp in 1585, Amsterdam, the chief northern port, quickly became the leading entrepôt in the Low Countries. The Amsterdam businessmen did not want Antwerp's old primacy restored. Accordingly, even after the

Spanish and Dutch arranged a twelve-year truce in 1609, the Dutch insisted on blockading the Scheldt River, Antwerp's avenue to the sea. The war reopened in 1621, and this time the Dutch clearly gained the advantage. Prince Frederick Henry, the youngest son of William the Silent, was now the Dutch general, and he pushed the Spaniards well south of the Rhine. But the great Dutch successes were at sea. The purpose of the Dutch West Indies Company, founded in 1621, was to plunder Spanish America. Company ships captured the Spanish silver fleet in 1628. By 1636, they had taken 547 enemy vessels. In 1648, Spain capitulated, and after trying for eighty years to overcome the Dutch, finally recognized the independence of the United Provinces.

By this time, Spain and its empire had sadly decayed in wealth and vigor from the great days of the sixteenth century. The decay could be found at all levels of Spanish society. Philip II's successors—Philip III (ruled 1598–1621), Philip IV (ruled 1621–1665), and Charles II (ruled 1665–1700) —were feckless kings, unable or unwilling to sustain the Prudent King's grasp on the central institutions of government. The population shrank, and there was a severe slump in the production of wool, Spain's chief export. The peasants were less able than ever to pay the high taxes their government demanded. The merchant marine never recovered from the shipping losses inflicted by English and Dutch privateers. Apathy set in, extending even to the New World. American silver production fell precipitously, until by 1660, bullion shipments to Seville were only 10 per cent of what they had been in 1595. In Spanish America, the Indian population decreased, towns decayed, and the colonists fell back on a subsistence agricultural economy closely parallel to that of the mother country. Old Spain and New Spain no longer had much to contribute to each other. Though the empire remained technically closed to outsiders, the home government was helpless to prevent the intrusions of foreign traders. It is estimated that during the second half of the seventeenth century, two thirds of the European goods sold to Spanish Americans were smuggled in by Dutch, English, or French interlopers. These illicit traders did not plunder the Spanish Main as the Elizabethan sea dogs had once done. Instead, by punctiliously bribing the local Spanish officials, they gained permission to offer their wares to the colonists, who bought eagerly because the smugglers (having evaded Spanish customs taxes) undersold the Seville monopoly. Economically, the Spanish empire had disintegrated.

The Spaniards remained as proudly autocratic, devout, and introspective as ever. Indeed, as their political power evaporated, they became ever more sensitive to questions of status and honor. And war remained the chief field of honor. There were only twenty-eight years during the seventeenth century when Spain did not have armies in combat. It fought five wars with France alone. The net result of all this fighting was that Spain had to cede territory in the southern Netherlands, the Pyrenees, and Franche-Comté to the

French, and yield a number of small Caribbean islands to the English, French, and Dutch. The strain of war precipitated a chain of mid-seventeenth-century rebellions within the Spanish empire. Portugal rose up in revolt in 1640, and after long years of fighting, Spain recognized its independence in 1668. Rebellions in Catalonia, Naples, and Sicily were suppressed with difficulty. This cumulative tale of defeat and decay is not easy to explain. A formula which had worked well in the sixteenth century stopped working in the seventeenth. Philip II can be blamed for overstraining the Spanish system, but he can hardly be blamed for his people's collective loss of vitality. Spaniards were no longer swashbuckling *conquistadores*; somehow, after 1588 they lost the knack of remaking the world.

Philip II's defeat and Spain's decline signalized the collapse of the Catholic crusade against Protestantism in western Europe. The ancient unity of western Christendom had been smashed beyond redemption. Yet the Calvinist crusaders had not won an outright victory. By the time Philip died in 1598 it was apparent that neither side could conquer the other. The French religious wars resulted in a compromise: king and country remained Catholic, while the Huguenots enjoyed political autonomy and religious liberty. The Netherlands revolt also resulted in a compromise: the north became predominantly Calvinist and politically independent, while the south remained Catholic and Spanish. In England, yet another kind of compromise emerged, with both Calvinists and Catholics forced to accept a state-controlled latitudianarian church. These compromise settlements can be interpreted as moral triumphs for the Calvinists, since they had fought the Catholics, despite their far greater political and military resources, to a standstill. But the Calvinists in France and England had not achieved their Genevan ideal, and in the Dutch republic the Calvinist zeal of the 1560's was already turning by 1600 into a secular zeal for making money. Except in England, Calvinism had passed its most militant phase by the end of the century. The most effective leaders of the late sixteenth century—Henry IV, William the Silent, and Elizabeth I—were all *politiques* who did their best to bury the religious issue and keep the church subordinate to the state.

It would be a great mistake, however, to dismiss the Calvinist-Catholic conflict as unimportant because neither side won. Though the religious ideals of Calvin and of Loyola were quickly diluted in practice, the impact left by these sixteenth-century crusaders was strong and lasting. They strengthened the moral purpose and community spirit of every western European state. For the Spanish people, the sixteenth century was the golden age, illuminated by a fusion of missionary zeal, military prowess, and artistic creativity which they were never afterward able to match. For the French, Dutch, and English, the greatest days lay ahead. In the seventeenth century these three peoples would dominate Europe and give the world new definitions of individual liberty and public order, of individual prosperity and public power.

CHAPTER 2

Political Disintegration in Central and Eastern Europe

THE WARS OF RELIGION engulfed Latin Christendom, central and eastern as well as western Europe. Germany, birthplace of the Protestant Reformation, was a battleground between the 1520's and the 1640's. Switzerland, Bohemia, Poland, Hungary, and Transylvania were all religiously divided, with Catholics, Lutherans, Zwinglians, Calvinists, and Anabaptists pitted against one another. The Austrian Habsburgs, like the Spanish Habsburgs in the west, were Catholic champions; Gustavus Adolphus of Sweden was the chief Protestant leader. Yet the Protestant-Catholic conflict in Germany, and elsewhere in central and eastern Europe, took on quite a different style from the crusading ardor of the Atlantic peoples. East of the Rhine, the motives for fighting were less "religious," indeed in every sense less ideological. Protestants and Catholics exhibited less sense of moral regeneration, less missionary zeal, than did their counterparts in the west, and a stronger preoccupation with territorial aggrandizement. The Thirty Years' War, biggest of all the wars of religion, was fought for more obviously secular objectives than were the French and Dutch religious wars. It was also more destructive of life, property, and social vitality. How ironic that Luther's compatriots should suffer more damage, to less purpose, in the name of Protestant-Catholic rivalry than any other European people!

Political, social, and cultural factors help explain why the religious crisis of the sixteenth and seventeenth centuries worked out so differently east of the Rhine. In central and eastern Europe, the concept of state sovereignty at the national level had not yet developed as it had in France, England, and Spain. Political units were simultaneously larger and smaller than in the west. The Holy Roman Empire, the Ottoman Empire, Poland, and Russia were each much larger than any western national state, but within these large units the most effective authority was generally held by the local magnates—the *landgrafs, beys, szlachta,* and *boyars.* The average inhabitant owed indirect allegiance to a distant emperor or king who had no personal control over him, and direct allegiance to an aristocratic landlord whose power was real but petty. No central or eastern European prince could match

Philip II or Elizabeth I in sovereign strength. That is, no eastern European prince could expect several million reasonably cooperative subjects (like those in Castile and England) to pay burdensome taxes, obey complex instructions, perform patriotic military service, and participate intelligently in civil obligations. Only Gustavus Adolphus could muster from his people the kind of strong community spirit which animated the Spanish, English, Dutch, and French. Community spirit or national consciousness was hard to achieve in central and eastern Europe, for the population was ethnically diverse. Some fourteen major languages were spoken, as against five in western Europe, and most of the ethnic groups were intermingled. Every large eastern state was multilingual. The Holy Roman Empire alone included eight rival ethnic groups. Ethnic rivalries cut across religious rivalries. Protestants and Catholics staged their family quarrel hemmed in by alien creeds—Islam and Greek Orthodoxy south of the Danube, and Russian Orthodoxy east of the Dnieper.

Between 1559 and 1648, during the era of the religious wars, the disparity between eastern and western Europe widened steadily. In the mid-sixteenth century this disparity had been disguised by the immense size of Charles V's empire, straddling Spain and Germany. The division of Charles's empire in 1556 into Spanish and German sections symbolized the new era. In the west, as we have seen, the religious crisis stimulated the evolution of an articulate urban capitalist class, as well as the development of national spirit and of a genuine state sovereignty. In the east the effect was almost the opposite. Political organization was splintered more than ever, commerce stagnated, and only the semifeudal class of agricultural magnates emerged as the true victor. The gains of these local landlords were made at the expense of the emperors and kings above them and of the burghers and peasants below. By the close of the seventeenth century, the largest central and eastern units— the Holy Roman Empire, the Ottoman Empire, the kingdom of Poland —were in obvious decline. New power centers—the Austrian, Russian, and Prussian monarchies—were rising. But they were as yet far inferior to France and England in strength, wealth, and cultural vitality. In short, the religious wars accelerated the political disintegration of central and eastern Europe at the very time when the Atlantic states were consolidating their sovereign national power.

THE HOLY ROMAN EMPIRE, 1555–1618

When Charles V divided his Habsburg empire in 1556 between his son Philip and his brother Ferdinand, he arranged Ferdinand's election as Holy Roman emperor and gave him the family lands (known collectively as the Austrian Habsburg lands) within the southern and eastern borders of the empire: the Tyrol, Carinthia, Carniola, Styria, Austria, Bohemia, Moravia and Silesia, as well as Hungary and other territories beyond the eastern imperial border. Theoretically, Emperor Ferdinand was a very strong prince. His was an empire with a population of twenty-five million, three times the population of Philip II's Spain. Actually, his power was severely limited. The Holy Roman Empire was divided into three hundred autonomous political units, of which at least three dozen had some importance. The real rulers of Germany were the local princes. During the late sixteenth century the Habsburg emperors were only nominally in charge of the Holy Roman Empire. They were only barely able to govern their own family lands and played a far more passive role in international politics than did their Spanish cousins. However, they were spared the religious warfare which engulfed western Europe; the Religious Peace of Augsburg, which Ferdinand negotiated with the German princes in 1555, preserved an uneasy truce between German Protestants and Catholics until 1618. Peace allegedly breeds prosperity, but the late sixteenth century was a period of stagnation not only for the German Habsburgs but for their subjects within the Holy Roman Empire.

The Peace of Augsburg confirmed the sovereign authority of the local princes within the empire, its guiding principle being *cuius regio, eius religio* ("he who rules a territory determines its religion"). Catholic princes were permitted to impose Catholicism upon all their subjects, and Lutheran princes to impose Lutheranism. This recognition of territorial churches within the empire was a religious compromise, but not a political one. The German princes, Catholic and Lutheran, had in effect ganged up against the Habsburgs. They had observed, correctly enough, that Charles V had been trying not only to crush Protestantism but to increase Habsburg power and check the centrifugal tendencies within the empire. They had noticed how he confiscated Lutheran princely territory much more readily than he enlarged Catholic princely territory, and how he showed real favor only to members of his own family. The princes, both Lutheran and Catholic, had also been trying to turn the Reformation crisis to their personal advantage, by asserting new authority over their local churches, tightening ecclesiastical patronage, and squeezing more profit from church revenues. In 1552–1553 the Lutheran princes, allied with Henry II of France, had beaten the imperial forces while the Catholic princes stood by, neutral. The Habsburgs were forced to accept the Peace of Augsburg, which effectively squelched any hopes for a German state with a single religion and administration.

As a device for pacifying Protestant-Catholic strife, the Peace of Augsburg was closer in spirit to Henry IV's Edict of Nantes in France than to Elizabeth I's religious settlement in England. The Augsburg negotiators refused to let Catholics and Lutherans live together, except in those German cities where the population already included members of both groups. The sharp delineation of the two competing confessions was in strong contrast to the deliberately amorphous character of the Anglican establishment. Calvinists, Zwinglians, and Anabaptists were not recognized, though a good many

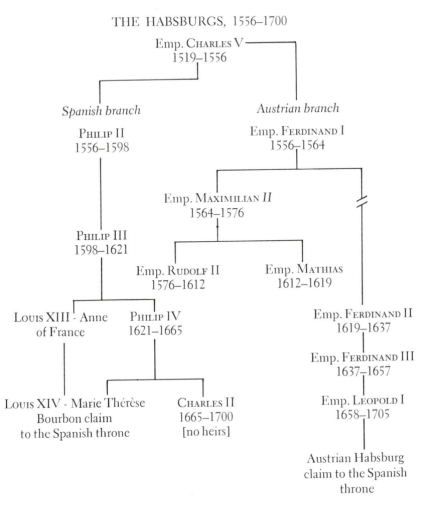

THE HABSBURGS, 1556–1700

Emp. CHARLES V
1519–1556

Spanish branch

PHILIP II
1556–1598

Austrian branch

Emp. FERDINAND I
1556–1564

Emp. MAXIMILIAN II
1564–1576

PHILIP III
1598–1621

Emp. RUDOLF II
1576–1612

Emp. MATHIAS
1612–1619

LOUIS XIII - Anne
of France

PHILIP IV
1621–1665

Emp. FERDINAND II
1619–1637

Emp. FERDINAND III
1637–1657

LOUIS XIV - Marie Thérèse
Bourbon claim
to the Spanish throne

CHARLES II
1665–1700
[no heirs]

Emp. LEOPOLD I
1658–1705

Austrian Habsburg
claim to the Spanish
throne

Germans belonged to these churches. In 1555, a large majority of the German population was Protestant, but the ruling Habsburg dynasty and four of the seven electors who chose each new emperor were Catholic. The old religion was largely confined to the western German Rhineland and to such south German states as Bavaria. Protestants controlled almost all of northern and central Germany, and Württemberg, Ansbach, and the Palatinate in the south. Even within the Habsburg family lands, Protestantism was very strong. Most Bohemians and Moravians were Protestants, as were the nobility and burghers in Austria. How long this precarious Protestant-Catholic balance would last depended very much on the princes.

The German peasantry and urban working class, scarred by memories of the debacle of the peasants' revolt in 1524–1526, were inclined to follow orders inertly on the religious issue, and switch from Lutheran to Catholic, or vice versa, as their masters required.

The emperors Ferdinand I (ruled 1556–1564), Maximilian II (ruled 1564–1576), Rudolf II (ruled 1576–1612), and Matthias (ruled 1612–1619) were all far less energetic men than Charles V or Philip II. Their highest aim was to hold off the Turks in Hungary and to administer their family holdings along the Danube. These Austrian Habsburg territories look compactly organized on the map, but they were split into a dozen distinct governments, and incorporated almost as many language groups. The greatest source of internal friction was religion. During the late sixteenth century, the Habsburg emperors' treatment of the Protestants within their Danubian lands was very gingerly, compared with Philip II's treatment of his Protestant subjects in the Netherlands. Only Rudolf II made much effort to enforce the Augsburg formula: in the Tyrol, Carinthia, Carniola, and Styria, he managed to convert or deport practically all the Protestants. Some ten thousand emigrants fled from these provinces between 1598 and 1605. In Austria the task was more difficult, because the nobility and townspeople were mainly Protestant. To enforce the Trentine reform decrees, Rudolf II appointed a Jesuit bishop of Vienna and expelled all Protestant preachers from the

Rudolf II. *Vegetable portrait of the emperor by Guiseppe Arcimboldi. Rudolf, a patron of the arts, is said to have admired this painting. Nationalmuseum, Stockholm.*

city. He could not cow the Protestant nobility and burghers, however, nor the Austrian diet or assembly. The Austrian Protestants lost some strength, but in 1609 the diet extracted a pledge guaranteeing considerable liberty of worship.

In Bohemia, the Habsburgs faced even stronger opposition. The kingdom of Bohemia was the most populous, prosperous, and cultivated possession of the Austrian Habsburgs, and like the Netherlands for the Spanish Habsburgs, the most troublesome. The Czech people were proudly Slav and overwhelmingly Protestant. They boasted two entrenched native strains of evangelical Protestantism, the Utraquists (analogous to Lutherans) and the Bohemian Brethren (somewhat analogous to Calvinists), both stemming back to the Hussite movement of the early fifteenth century and hence quite separate from the sixteenth-century Reformation. For two hundred years the Czechs had stubbornly maintained their independence from Catholic orthodoxy and German culture. Rudolf II was hardly the man to bring them into line. Melancholic and unbalanced, the king-emperor sequestered himself in the Hradschin castle in Prague, enveloped by his art collection, dabbling in science and magic. Intermittently, he tried to restore Catholicism in Bohemia by appointing Catholic officials, encouraging Jesuit missionary work among the Utraquists, and issuing edicts against the Brethren. But in 1609 the Bohemian diet rose up in rebellion. In order to conciliate the rebels, Rudolf granted his Letter of Majesty, the fullest guarantee of religious freedom to be found anywhere on the continent. Obviously the Habsburgs had not yet accomplished much in Bohemia.

In the German heart of the Holy Roman Empire, the late sixteenth century was a time of prolonged economic depression. The Hanseatic League of north German cities, which had once dominated commerce in the Baltic and North seas, was quite unable to compete against Dutch, Danish, and English merchants. The old overland route to Italy had lost its central importance. In southwestern Germany, where the cities had been especially wealthy and enterprising in the fifteenth and early sixteenth centuries, political fragmentation was most extreme, and the economy suffered as a result. Each prince, striving for sovereign power within his petty state, levied taxes and tolls which clogged commerce and reduced manufacturing output. The Fuggers of Augsburg, the leading bankers in Europe in the mid-sixteenth century, with control of Tyrolese silver and Hungarian copper production, overstrained themselves with loans to the Habsburgs toward the end of the century, and their business empire rapidly fell apart. As the Fuggers and the other leading German entrepreneurs lost their wealth and the German cities declined in population, the princes dominated the scene more than ever.

The princes, both Protestant and Catholic, were growing dissatisfied with the religious truce they had worked out in 1555. One source of trouble was Calvinist expansion. In 1559 Elector Frederick III of the Palatinate

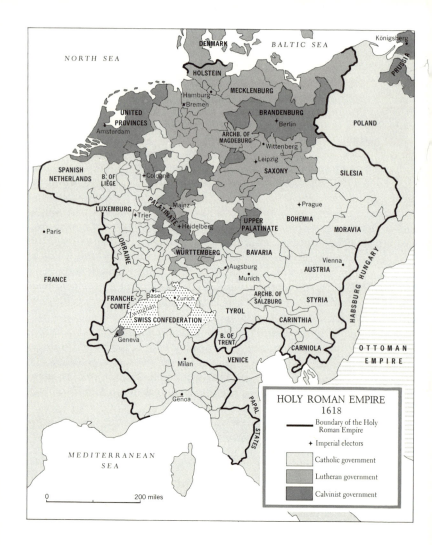

HOLY ROMAN EMPIRE
1618

— Boundary of the Holy
    Roman Empire

+ Imperial electors

   Catholic government

   Lutheran government

   Calvinist government

0   200 miles

(1515–1576) had introduced a modified version of Calvin's church organization into his central Rhineland territory. The elector's fellow princes, Catholic and Lutheran, vainly protested this clear violation of the Augsburg treaty. Heidelberg, the Palatine capital, became the Geneva of Germany. Scholars at the university formulated the Heidelberg Catechism in 1563 as a creed for the German Reformed (or Calvinist) churches. Within a generation the princes of Nassau, Hesse, and Anhalt had swung their central German states from Lutheranism to the German Reformed church. In 1613 the elector of Brandenburg announced his conversion also, though he abandoned the *cuius regio, eius religio* formula of Augsburg by letting his Lutheran subjects retain their religion. Two of the three Protestant imperial electors were now Calvinists; only the elector of Saxony remained Lutheran.

The German Reformed princes acted more aggressively than their Lutheran colleagues, because they were not included in the Lutheran-Catholic compromise of 1555. Frederick III and his Palatine successors assumed leadership of the Protestant cause within the empire, and finding the other German Protestant princes to be torpid or hostile, looked abroad to the French Huguenots and Dutch Calvinists for help in times of crisis. Yet the German Reformed church lacked dynamism. Unlike the Calvinism of western Europe it was not a spontaneous force among German merchants and gentry; it depended upon princely sponsors and was state controlled. Its growth was strictly limited. Although it made inroads into Lutheranism, it had little impact among Catholics, and it could not by itself re-ignite religious warfare.

A second, and more important, source of rising tension was the spread of the Catholic reformation within the empire. The south German state of Bavaria became the nucleus of renewed Catholic zeal and political power. Duke Albert V of Bavaria (ruled 1550–1579) enthusiastically enforced the reform decrees of the Council of Trent. He stamped out all traces of Protestant heresy by having his ecclesiastical agents inspect every Bavarian church annually, revamp the schools systematically, and censor all books. Jesuits were invited to take charge of the Bavarian schools and universities, and the duke's subjects were forbidden to study abroad. The new style of dogmatic Catholicism facilitated political autocracy in Bavaria. When Protestant nobles and burghers tried to protest, Albert excluded them from the Bavarian diet, thereby effectively emasculating that assembly. By the close of the sixteenth century, the duke of Bavaria was governing in a more absolute fashion than any other German prince.

Elsewhere in Germany, the Catholics began to win back converts. Between 1580 and 1610, Protestants were driven out of a whole series of cities, among them Cologne, Aachen, Strasbourg, Würzberg, Bamberg, Münster, Paderborn, and Osnabrück. Everywhere, the Jesuits were in the forefront of the campaign. They established schools and universities in key German cities and made a specialty of educating young Catholic princes. Peter Canisius (1521–1597) is the best known of these sixteenth-century German Jesuit missionaries. The striking Jesuit Michaelskirche (Church of St. Michael) in Munich, built by the dukes of Bavaria, is a symbol of the Catholic reformation. This church was erected in the 1580's, when St. Peter's was nearing completion in Rome, and it introduced to Germany the sumptuous classical architecture of the reformed papacy. The Munich tourist today need only visit two churches a block apart, built a century apart—the fifteenth-century Frauenkirche (Church of Our Lady) and the sixteenth-century Michaelskirche—to catch the immense psychological distance between pre- and post-reformation German Catholicism. The Gothic Frauenkirche rises in awkward vertical bulk, austere and homely, her round capped towers reflecting the native Bavarian style, and her soaring nave expressing a questing spirit. By contrast, the Michaelskirche is international in style, harmonious

St. Michaelskirche, Munich. *The architect has boldly employed Renaissance statuary, arches, columns, and entablatures to achieve a vigorous yet balanced ensemble. This is the Mannerist style, prefiguring the Baroque. In the right rear is seen one of the Gothic Frauenkirche's capped towers.*

in scale and proportion, and lavishly decorated to proclaim the certitude, symmetry, and power of the new Church Militant.

By 1609 all signs pointed to the end of the Augsburg truce. The imperial Diet, the one vestige of collective German government, collapsed in 1608 when the Protestant representatives boycotted its proceedings. In 1609 the most aggressive German Protestant states formed a Protestant Union for self-defense, headed by the Elector Palatine, whereupon the most aggressive Catholic states immediately formed a rival Catholic League, headed by the duke of Bavaria. Yet it must be emphasized that the German princes in their two armed camps still dreaded Armageddon. The Protestant Union was ineffectual because the Lutheran elector of Saxony would not ally himself with the Calvinist Elector Palatine. Nor was the Catholic League much stronger, thanks to hostility between the Austrian Habsburgs and the Bavarian Wittelsbachs. Both sides had pretext for war in 1609 when two Rhenish principalities, Jülich and Cleve, were contested by rival Protestant and Catholic claimants. Eventually, in 1614, a compromise was worked out by which Jülich went to the Catholic claimant and Cleve to the Protestant. But when the next crisis came in Bohemia in 1618, it could not be patched up.

The problems of these years become easier to visualize if we think of the Holy Roman Empire as being something like the mid-twentieth-century world in microcosm. The inhabitants of the empire were culture-bound to

Service in a German Reformed Church. *Note the disciplined Calvinist austerity of this scene, set in a bare hall, with the women (center) segregated from the men (right and left), the elders seated forward by the communion table, and all attention riveted onto the open Bible and the preacher in his pulpit.* Germanisches Nationalmuseum, Nuremberg.

their own cities or provinces as modern man is culture-bound to his own nation. People refused to admit, then as now, that their fate depended upon cooperation with strangers who spoke and thought differently, but lived uncomfortably close by. Politicians waged ideological cold war, their motivation ostensibly religious instead of political or economic. Protestant and Catholic imperial states formed alliance systems to maintain the balance of power. Whenever a Lutheran prince converted to Catholicism or vice versa, diplomacy was required to keep the conflict local. When delegates from the various states convened in the imperial Diet, the only institution effectively embracing their whole community, they raised issues without attempting to solve them, just as the members of the United Nations do today. Gradually even this meager spirit of imperial community disappeared. The cold war grew inexorably warmer. Leaders on both sides, sick of the stalemate, began supposing that they could solve issues simply by unilateral action. And when they did take unilateral action, in 1618, they plunged the empire into thirty years of civil war.

EASTERN BORDERLANDS: THE OTTOMAN EMPIRE, POLAND, RUSSIA, AND SWEDEN

To the east of the Holy Roman Empire, in the late sixteenth century, three extremely large states filled the map—the Ottoman Empire, Poland, and Russia. North of the Baltic Sea lay the extensive kingdom of Sweden. These states, particularly the Ottoman Empire and Muscovite Russia, seemed profoundly alien to western and central Europeans. Travelers found the Turks and Russians almost as barbaric and exotic as the Indians of America, and infinitely more dangerous because of their large armies, equipped with modern weapons. English merchants, venturing to trade with the Turks and Russians in the late sixteenth century, wrote home to describe the amazing Mohammedan and Greek Orthodox religious practices they had witnessed, the bizarre architecture, food, and dress, the stark contrast between an opulent ruling caste and an impoverished peasantry, the vast extent of these eastern lands and the herculean scale of their armies. "We arrived at the great and most stately city of Constantinople," one traveler reported, "which for the situation and proud seat thereof, for the beautiful and commodious haven, for the great and sumptuous buildings of their Temples, which they call Mosques, is to be preferred before all the cities of Europe. And there the Emperor of the Turks kept his Court and residence, at least two miles in compass." Yet no westerner forgot that the Turks were infidels. Their lavish oriental ceremonies seemed tedious and empty. Their eunuchs and seraglios

Palm Sunday in Moscow. *This seventeenth-century engraving shows a religious procession emerging from the Kremlin. St. Basil's Cathedral, with its spectacular display of nine onion domes, is to the left.*

evoked incredulous contempt. Turkish warriors had an unrivaled reputation for cruelty and deceit.

As for Muscovy, the few westerners who penetrated into this land told tales of a climate too extreme for civilized man to endure. In the sub-zero Russian winter, "you shall see many drop down in the streets, many travelers brought into the towns sitting stiff and dead in their sleds. The bears and wolves issue by troops out of the woods driven by hunger, and enter the villages, tearing and ravening all they can find." The Russians, it was said, besot themselves with kvass and mead. They had strange smoky complexions because they took too many steam baths. Their primitive wooden buildings were constantly burning down. When the invading Tartars set fire to Moscow in 1571, they largely wiped out Russia's chief city within four hours. The Muscovite tsar, for all his jewels and ornate skirted garments and his giant feasts on plates of gold, seemed semicivilized at best. An English poet who visited Moscow in 1568 summed up in jogging verse the westerner's easy disdain for these eastern borderlands of European civilization:

> The cold is rare, the people rude, the prince so full of pride,
> The realm so stored with monks and nuns, and priests on every side,
> The manners are so Turkey like, the men so full of guile,
> The women wanton, Temples stuft with idols that defile
> The seats that sacred ought to be, the customs are so quaint,
> As if I would describe the whole, I fear my pen would faint.
> Wild Irish are as civil as the Russies in their kind,
> Hard choice which is the best of both, each bloody, rude and blind.

Fortunately for the west, the Turks, Poles, and Russians were all politically weak in the late sixteenth and early seventeenth centuries. Size was deceptive in these sprawling eastern states. The Turkish sultan, the Polish king, and the Muscovite tsar were all less effectual rulers than western observers supposed. Their armies were much smaller than westerners thought them to be, and in any case generally faced east in order to cope with the Persians and Tartars. Hence, despite the near paralysis of the Holy Roman Empire, its eastern neighbors did not intervene effectively in German affairs between 1555 and 1618. Nor (except for Sweden) did they participate in the Thirty Years' War. How is this uniform political softness in eastern Europe to be explained?

The Ottoman Empire

The Ottoman Empire had been anything but soft before the middle of the sixteenth century. Suleiman the Magnificent (ruled 1520–1566), the last of the great Turkish warrior sultans, held the whole Balkan peninsula and most of Hungary. He had thirty million subjects, a revenue greater than that of Charles V, and a much more efficient military system, including a permanent standing army of over ten thousand infantry (janissaries), over ten thousand cavalry (spahis), and at least a hundred thousand auxiliary cavalry available for annual campaigns. The janissaries were Moslem converts, mainly drawn from the conquered Greek Orthodox peoples of the Balkans. Taken captive as boys by the sultan's forces, they were rigorously trained to fight for Islam and to administer the Ottoman Empire. They formed an enslaved elite, permanently dependent on the sultan, given a professional schooling, never allowed to marry or to inherit lands and titles, yet freely promoted on the basis of talent and merit to the highest imperial posts. They made superb soldiers.

After the death of Suleiman the Magnificent, the Turkish fighting machine lost much of its fearsome power and its expansive drive. In 1571 the Spanish Habsburgs smashed the Turkish fleet at Lepanto. In the 1590's the Austrian Habsburgs tried to capture Hungary and Transylvania, and did keep the Ottoman armies mostly on the defensive, though the peace terms of 1606 left the Balkan frontier unchanged. Ottoman passivity gave the Habsburgs freedom to concentrate on German affairs after 1618, and when the Thirty Years' War went badly for the Habsburgs, the Turks failed to capitalize on a golden opportunity for further western expansion.

The key to Turkish success had always been strong military leadership by the sultan. After Suleiman came a long line of feckless sultans who abandoned Mars for Venus. They ceased to conduct military campaigns, ceased even to emerge from the Constantinople harem. Back in the days of tough, ruthless leadership, each new Ottoman sultan had stabilized his accession by killing his younger brothers (they were strangled with a silken bowstring so as not to shed exalted blood). Now, with the sultans' amorous proclivities resulting in numerous progeny, this custom was turning the seraglio into a slaughterhouse. In 1595 the new sultan had forty-six brothers and sisters, and he thought it necessary to strangle his nineteen brothers and fifteen pregnant harem women. In the seventeenth century this systematic fratricide was stopped, but by then the sultan himself had become a puppet, frequently deposed in palace revolutions. With no new lands to conquer and little war booty to enjoy, the Turkish soldiery became preoccupied with status and intrigue. The janissaries changed radically, becoming in the seventeenth century a closed, self-perpetuating caste. They now married, passed their jobs on to their sons, agitated for new perquisites, and engineered palace coups. As the economy stagnated and tax levies dwindled, bribery and corruption greatly increased.

In the 1650's, a drastic administrative shake-up in Constantinople temporarily revived the old militancy and efficiency. In the 1660's the Turks captured the island of Crete from Venice. They tightened their grip over Hungary and resumed their drive up the Danube into Austria. In 1683 they laid siege to Vienna. But in the closing decades of the seventeenth century, Ottoman expansion was once again stopped, this time decisively. The Turks were forced to surrender Hungary in 1699, and their huge empire began to shrink. This shrinkage continued for nearly 250 years. In the early nineteenth century the Turks still held half of Suleiman's European territory and all of his North African and Near Eastern possessions. The First World War marked the final stage: the Turks were confined at last to Anatolia, and the Ottoman Empire was dissolved. Seldom, if ever, has a decaying state disintegrated so slowly. In the seventeenth century, the Ottoman Empire had by no means yet become the Sick Man of Europe. Buttressed by total intellectual isolation from the new currents in European culture, the Turks still retained their profound contempt for the West. "Do I not know," the grand vizier told the French ambassador in 1666, "that you are a Giaour [nonbeliever], that you are a hog, a dog, a turd eater?"

Ottoman Europe—that is, the Balkan peninsula—was something of a cultural no-man's-land in the sixteenth and seventeenth centuries: only superficially Turkish, cut off from Latin Christendom, and with a very rudimentary native peasant style of life. The Turks had wiped out the native ruling class when they conquered the Balkans, but they never migrated into the area in large numbers, nor did they try to assimilate the local peasantry, which they preferred to keep as permanently unprivileged agricultural laborers. From the Turkish viewpoint, the Balkan peasants were fairly easy to subjugate as long as they remained divided into six rival language groups: Greeks, Albanians, Bulgarians, Serbo-Croatians, Rumanians, and Magyars.

Christian boys levied into the Janissaries. *This contemporary drawing shows a company of preadolescents in Turkish costume, drilled by their Moslem instructors.*

Instead of imposing Mohammedanism upon the subject peoples, the Turks encouraged the perpetuation of the Greek Orthodox Church, largely to keep the Balkan population hostile to western Christianity. This Ottoman policy did indeed effectively curb Balkan defection to the Catholic Habsburgs or Poles. The Orthodox patriarch in Constantinople repaid his Turkish patrons by teaching his people to submit docilely to Ottoman rule. Certainly the Ottoman Empire was more tolerant of all sorts of alien cultures and customs than any contemporaneous state in western Europe. French, English, and Dutch merchants were granted their own trading enclaves in Turkey, governed by western law. Jews flocked from Spain to enjoy Turkish freedom. The few towns in the Balkans were inhabited mainly by Turks and Jews; minarets and bazaars gave these towns an oriental atmosphere. In the Balkan countryside, the Christian peasants were confined to the lowest rung of the Ottoman social ladder; illiterate, ignorant, and silent, they paid extortionate taxes and tributes. In the sixteenth century their young sons were frequently levied as janissaries, and in the seventeenth century their farms were often pillaged by brigands. Even so, they probably fared no worse than any other peasants in eastern Europe.

Poland

North of the Ottoman Empire and east of the Holy Roman Empire lay the extensive kingdom of Poland, stretching from the Oder to the Dnieper River and from the Baltic almost to the Black Sea. Poland had no natural frontiers except for the Baltic coast to the north and the Carpathian Mountains to the south. Its six million widely scattered inhabitants raised grain and cattle. In the eastern part of the kingdom agricultural development was hindered by the attacks of wild Cossack raiders and by vast stretches of marshland. Cracow and Danzig, both on the western border, were the two chief towns. Poland did possess considerable human and natural resources, yet in the sixteenth and seventeenth centuries it played only a feeble international role, and in the eighteenth century the Polish state completely disappeared. There were ethnic and religious reasons for Poland's failure, but by far the biggest problem was political disorganization.

The dominant Polish social class was the *szlachta*, the landed gentry. Its members—like twelfth-century feudal knights in the west—were absolute masters of their rural domains; they forced the peasantry into serfdom, extracted unpaid labor from the serfs, disdained the burghers who huddled behind the town walls, and frustrated every effort by the Polish kings to consolidate power. The *szlachta* formed a numerous class—8 per cent of the total population. A typical sixteenth-century Polish landlord owned a village and its surrounding grain fields. His serfs labored for him two or three days a week, and loaded his harvested grain into river barges to be shipped to the Baltic for export west. He tried and punished his serfs in his own court, without fear of appeal to the king, for the *szlachta* had virtual immunity from arrest and trial. The landlord paid few taxes, saw occasional military service, sat in the local *seym*, or diet, sent delegates to the national Diet, and helped to elect the king. Poland was called a royal republic because the gentry voted their king into office and handcuffed him with constitutional limitations. It is said that fifty thousand *szlachta* assembled at Warsaw in 1573 to elect as king the French prince Henry of Valois—this was an unusually bad choice, and the Poles were lucky that he skipped the country after six months in order to take the French throne as Henry III (see p. 36). The Polish gentry were so suspicious of dynastic power that they almost always elected foreigners. Between 1548 and 1668 the winning candidates were Lithuanian, French, Hungarian, and Swedish. These kings lacked the royal lands, budget, army, and bureaucracy of western monarchs. The Polish serfs had less individual freedom than the Balkan peasantry under Turkish rule. When romantic Polish historians talk of their country's sixteenth-century "gentry democracy," one should remember that they are using a pretty special definition of democracy.

Like other eastern European states, Poland was ethnically divided, a situation which compounded its political difficulties. Poles occupied the west, Lithuanians the northeast, White Russians the east, and Ruthenians the south, and Germans and Jews congregated in the towns. Of all these peoples, only Poles and Lithuanians were admitted to the ruling landlord class. Since 1386, the members of the Lithuanian nobility had shared a common king with the Polish gentry but in most ways had run their own affairs. In 1569 the Lithuanian nobility became so frightened by Tsar Ivan the Terrible of Russia that they surrendered their autonomy and in the Union of Lublin merged with the Polish ruling caste. Henceforth the Polish-Lithuanian landlords had a single king, a single Diet (meeting at Warsaw, near the Polish-Lithuanian border), and a single foreign policy. But the union was always superficial, for the Lithuanians continued to manage their White Russian peasants in their own fashion and kept their own laws and language. Indeed, each ethnic group had its own language. Since the *szlachta* sneered at the Polish dialect spoken by their serfs, they adopted Latin as the religious, political, and literary language of the ruling class. The *szlachta* sneered also at the German-speaking townspeople, who were excluded from the Diet and from political power. The Yiddish-speaking Jewish community was despised by everyone.

The Christians in Poland were doubly divided in the mid-sixteenth century. The people were predominantly Latin Christians, except in the south and east, where they were largely Greek Orthodox; this division was only papered over in 1596, when the Ruthenian Orthodox church agreed to obey the pope and accept the Roman dogma while retaining its Slavonic rites and practices. The second religious division was among Latin Christians—Catholic versus Protestant. In the 1550's, Polish Catholics found themselves in a very precarious majority, for about half the *szlachta* were

Calvinist, and the German burghers were largely Lutheran. Even Unitarian, or anti-Trinitarian, ideas were circulating, possibly inspired by contact with Jewish and Moslem teachings. In 1555 King Sigismund Augustus (ruled 1548–1572) and the Polish Diet agreed to allow individual freedom of worship to Protestants. The heresy-hunting power of Catholic church courts was suspended. More than the contemporaneous Augsburg formula in Germany, this Polish policy weakened ecclesiastical discipline and sapped what little cultural unity there was. But the Protestant Reformation was not well rooted in Poland. The *szlachta* had adopted Calvinism as a weapon against centralized monarchy, and once assured of political victory, they lost interest in the new doctrine. During the late sixteenth century the Catholics—their efforts spearheaded by Jesuit upper-class missionary work—regained control. Numerous Jesuit schools were opened for the sons of the gentry. By the mid-seventeenth century, with Catholicism securely reestablished, education stagnated even for the upper class. Proud and touchy, the Polish gentry cultivated long mustachios and oriental sashed costumes as their badge of immunity from Italian or French standards of civility. Poland in the seventeenth century became almost as isolated as Ottoman Turkey from the intellectual currents of western Europe.

Between 1559 and 1715, Poland faced east and north rather than west in all its wars and diplomacy. It fought the Turks intermittently without permanently winning or losing any territory. It fought the Swedes constantly and generally got beaten. In 1629 it ceded the province of Livonia to Sweden, and had to accept Swedish control of the Baltic. Poland's most menacing neighbor was Russia, and the Poles were lucky that internal Muscovite turmoil in the late sixteenth and early seventeenth centuries delayed effective Russian westward expansion. In 1667 Poland ceded Smolensk, Kiev, and the eastern Ukraine to Russia.

These sizable territorial losses were less alarming than Poland's rising political anarchy, which paralyzed the state and invited further foreign encroachment. The gentry were so suspicious of centralized royal power that in the Diet legislation could not pass without the unanimous consent of the *szlachta* deputies. In the sixteenth century the majority of deputies could generally persuade or coerce the minority into accepting a policy. But in 1652, for the first time, an individual deputy declared his total opposition, his *liberum veto* against the legislative proceedings, and left the chamber—forcing the Diet to disband. Henceforth, 90 percent of the Polish Diets were "exploded" in this way, by use of the individual *liberum veto*. It became possible for the French, Prussians, or other foreign powers, by bribing refractory members of the gentry, to veto Polish tax laws or stymie Polish military preparations. To many observers, Poland's "gentry democracy" proved the folly of constitutional self-government ·and the necessity for absolute monarchy. To the Russians, Prussians, and Austrians, Poland's governmental paralysis offered an excellent excuse for partitioning the state in the eighteenth century.

Russia

East of Poland lay the vast tsardom of Muscovy, or Russia. In the sixteenth and seventeenth centuries it was an open question whether Russia was part of European civilization, for in scale and temper, life there differed profoundly from life in the rest of Europe. To begin with, the country was gigantic. In 1533, when Ivan the Terrible inherited the throne, Muscovy stretched 1,200 miles, from Smolensk to the Ural Mountains, and covered five times the area of France. Ivan nearly doubled his European holdings by annexing the Don and Volga river basins to the south, and launched the Russian eastward trek across the Urals into Siberia. By the time Peter the Great became tsar in 1682, the Russians had annexed further European land along the Dnieper and Ural rivers, and their Asian settlements were strung along the Siberian river system for five thousand miles, right to the Pacific. Russia then covered thirty times the area of France.

The climate throughout this continental sweep of territory was savage by European standards, with arctic winters, blazing summers, and a short growing season. Population estimates for sixteenth- and seventeenth-century Russia are pure guesswork, but whether one accepts the lowest, four million inhabitants, or the highest, seventeen million, it is evident that settlement was far less dense than in western and central Europe. The huge reservoir of empty land encouraged hit-and-run agricultural techniques. The peasants were extremely mobile, sometimes voluntarily migrating long distances to find better land and working conditions, sometimes forcibly transported by their landlords or the tsar. In contrast with western Europe, where people habitually tilled the same ancestral land, lived in the same village, and even occupied the same buildings for centuries, no human enterprise seemed lasting in Russia. The average wooden peasant's hut was built to last four years. An English traveler between Yaroslavl and Moscow in 1553 was impressed by the numerous villages he passed through; thirty-five years later another English visitor found the same region deserted and gone back to forest. Tartar raiders periodically swept into Muscovy from the Crimea, as Viking, Saracen, and Magyar raiders had pillaged western and central Europe in the ninth century. The Tartars carried hundreds of thousands of Russians off into slavery. Belief in the individual dignity of man—fragile enough in the sixteenth-century west—was an unobtainable luxury for Muscovites. Tsars, nobles, priests, and peasants all accepted physical brutality—flogging and torture—as staple features of society.

Russia's contact with western Europe was minimal between 1559 and 1682. Blocked by Sweden from an outlet on the Baltic during most of these years, and by Turkey from an outlet on the Black Sea, Russia had only one port—Archangel, on the White Sea—from which to trade directly with western Europe. Its commerce with the Middle East was more important. Strange as it seems, western Europeans had built closer commercial and diplomatic contact with Russia in the eleventh and twelfth centuries than they did in the sixteenth and seventeenth centuries. The Muscovites found it far easier to spread eastward into empty Siberia than to reconquer from Poland the White Russian and Ukrainian lands which had once belonged to their ancestors. Not until the reign of Peter the Great did the Russians learn how to beat a crack European army.

Russia's most meaningful tie with the west was Christianity. Yet the Russian Orthodox clergy viewed Latin Christendom with the darkest suspicion. For centuries they had accepted as spiritual overlord the Greek Orthodox patriarch at Constantinople, and when Byzantium fell to the Ottomans, the Russian Orthodox naturally supposed that the metropolitan of Moscow had inherited the role of the patriarch of Constantinople as the leader of true Christianity. In 1588 the patriarch of Constantinople grudgingly accepted the metropolitan's elevation to patriarch of Moscow. The Russians called Moscow the third Rome. They believed that Old Rome had fallen into heresy under the popes, and that New Rome (Constantinople) had become a pawn of the infidel Turks; Moscow was the third and greatest capital of the Christian world. Because of their hostility to the papacy, the Muscovites were better disposed toward Protestant merchants and diplomats from England, the Netherlands, Scandinavia, and Germany than toward Catholics. But the Russians wanted no Reformation in their own church, nor even any discussion over the smallest details of Orthodox belief and practice.

The Russians settled Tobolsk, beyond the Urals, in 1587, two years after Sir Walter Raleigh first tried to found an English plantation at Roanoke Island, North Carolina. The Russians reached the Pacific in 1643, a few years after the English Puritans had founded Massachusetts. It would be hard to find a stronger social contrast than that between the Russian folk movement across Eurasia and the contemporaneous English folk movement into North America. Both peoples held an enormous reservoir of empty land, but while the Americans methodically inched their way inland, taking nearly three centuries to span the continent, the Russians lightly spanned Siberia in two generations. Frontier America was a paradise for the self-reliant, egalitarian free farmer, disdainful of government, unencumbered by taxes. But in Russia, frontier expansion fostered the sharpest possible social stratification, and Europe's most autocratic, oppressive government. The members of the Muscovite nobility, who held great estates in European Russia, were determined not to let their agricultural laborers move off to free land in Siberia. So they introduced new regulations which tied the laborer and his descendants to his master's soil or (better yet) to his master's person—in short, turned the peasant into a serf, virtually indistinguishable from a slave. At the same time, the tsars were determined not to let their nobility carve up the land into autonomous feudal principalities, or perpetrate political anarchy in the fashion of the Polish *szlachta*. So they ruthlessly killed all aristocratic troublemakers, confiscated their large properties, and divided them into smaller parcels suitable for the *pomeshchik*, a loyal dependent employed in the royal army or administration. Since the members of this service nobility could not own land outright, but held it from the tsar only as long as they served him, they tended to squeeze the peasants hard in order to make short-run profits. Peasants ran away from *pomeshchik* estates with special frequency. By the seventeenth century, the landlords and the tsar had reached a tacit understanding. The landlords accepted the principle that they must serve the tsar, and in return the tsar agreed that the peasants—90 per cent of the population—were legally defined as serfs, bound to their master and subject to his will.

Ivan IV (ruled 1533–1584), better known as Ivan the Terrible, was the principal author of the Muscovite formula: absolute power for the tsar, state service for the nobility, thralldom for the peasantry. Far less evidence has survived about the details of Ivan's reign than about the reigns of his western contemporaries, Philip II and Elizabeth I, but we know enough to tell that his style of rule differed utterly from theirs. As a young prince, Ivan amused himself by tossing animals from the palace tower and watched them die in agony. In 1547 he had himself crowned Tsar (that is, "Caesar") of All the Russians, the first Muscovite ruler to do so. His behavior toward his subjects could be described as *mad* in a half dozen distinct senses—raging, frantic, foolish, visionary, giddy, lunatic. He decimated the *boyar* class, the hereditary Russian aristocracy, by killing hundreds, probably even thousands, of its members. He pitilessly sacked Novgorod, the second city in his realm, because of a rumor of disloyalty.

Ivan the Terrible. *This old print presents evidence that the prince was well named.*

His deep piety did not prevent him from flogging and torturing priests or killing his victims in church during Mass. He once had an archbishop sewn into a bearskin and tossed to the dogs. He struck his oldest son and heir so hard with a pointed stick that he killed him, and it is supposed that his melancholic brooding over this crime hastened his own demise. Most of the time there was method in Ivan's madness. His wholesale confiscation and redistribution of land was economically catastrophic, depopulating much of central Russia, but it broke the *boyar* power and bolstered that of the new service nobility. The more Ivan bullied the Russian Orthodox Church, the more the clergy preached abject reverence to God's lieutenant, the tsar. Uncivilized Ivan certainly was, but he magnetized the Russian landlords and peasants alike with his awesome God-given power. The tsar of Russia had far greater psychological appeal for the mass of the people than did the elected monarchs of Poland or the seraglio sultans of Turkey.

Ivan the Terrible's successor, Fedor (ruled 1584–1598), was mad in a less complicated way than his father; he was a simpleton who chiefly delighted in ringing church bells. Fedor's reign inaugurated Muscovy's "Time of Troubles," the period of aristocratic rebellion against tsarist autocracy, which lasted from 1584 to 1613. Among the tsars in this anarchic period was Boris Godunov (ruled 1598–1605), more famous thanks to Mussorgsky's opera than his statecraft deserves. During these years the Russian landlords tried to run the country as the *szlachta* ran Poland. A national assembly, the *zemsky sobor*, assumed the authority to choose each new tsar. Marauding armies, led by would-be tsars, ransacked the countryside. During the Time of Troubles, the church was the one institution which held Russia together. People gathered in the fortresslike monasteries for protection, and left their land and wealth to the church. Gradually, the political role of the clergy became stronger than it had been under Ivan IV.

In 1613, the *zemsky sobor* chose Michael Romanov (ruled 1613–1645) as the new tsar because he was a youthful mediocrity—dubious accreditation for the dynasty which would rule Russia for the next three hundred years. But this first Romanov had other assets. He was a grandnephew of Ivan the Terrible, and the son of an able priest-politician named Philaret, who became patriarch of Moscow soon after Michael ascended the throne. Philaret made himself the real ruler of Russia, and the patriarchs who succeeded him after his death in 1633 were equally ambitious for secular power. The church's obtrusive political role during this period distressed many Russian clergy and laity. A crisis developed during the patriarchate of Nikon (1652–1666), for Nikon not only ruled in the name of the tsar but claimed a theoretical supremacy over the tsar, since the spiritual realm is higher than the temporal. Nikon was deposed, and the tsars regained control over the Russian church. But Nikon's policies left a bitter legacy. In order to bring Russian Orthodoxy into closer conformity with Greek Orthodoxy,

Nikon had introduced certain technical revisions in ecclesiastical practice, such as making the sign of the Cross with three fingers rather than two, and spelling Christ's name *Iisus* rather than *Isus*. Many Russians supposed that these innovations blasphemed God and imperiled their immortal souls. These people, styled the Old Believers, felt that Nikon had disastrously corrupted the third Rome. We are told that twenty thousand Old Believers burned themselves alive in despair at the impending end of the world.

The first Romanov tsars, those ruling between 1613 and 1682, were much less forceful monarchs than Ivan the Terrible. But they maintained the partnership with the church and they won the cooperation of the landlords. The *zemsky sobor* faded away, though not before it ratified the final codification of serfdom. The great problem now was how to stop the serfs from running away. A decree of 1664 required that any serf owner who was caught receiving a fugitive serf must compensate the master with four peasant families of his own. Tsar and landlord aided each other in taking away the peasant's freedom and in saddling him with taxes. The cost of warfare and of government-sponsored colonization fell squarely on the people least able to pay. It is estimated that the peasant tax rate in 1640 was a hundred times what it had been in 1540![1] In the mid-seventeenth century a major epidemic drastically depleted the Russian labor force, making the tsar and the landlords more eager than ever to exact taxes and work from the serfs, and making the serfs more eager than ever to join the floating population of runaways and bandits. Many serfs yearned to join the Cossacks on the southern frontier, and take up a nomadic life as hunters, fishermen, and guerrilla warriors against the Tartars, Turks, and Persians.

Between 1667 and 1671 Russia was the scene of the largest European folk rising of the century, a peasant rebellion led by Stephen Razin in the Volga basin. Razin was a Cossack who had operated as a river pirate on the Volga and then had sailed into the Caspian Sea to raid the Persians. Word spread that when he returned with his Persian loot to Astrakhan, he passed through the bazaars, dressed in oriental magnificence, distributing silks and jewels among the people. Suddenly he was a liberating folk hero to the Russian masses, a Robin Hood with the magical powers of the tsar. As disciples flocked to him, Stephen Razin moved along the Don and the Volga, proclaiming that he was rescuing the tsar from the wicked *boyars* so that all could live in freedom and equality. In villages and towns throughout the middle Volga region, huge numbers of serfs rose against their lords and formed into rebel bands. But Razin had no organization, and his followers had no military discipline. The tsar's soldiers beat Razin in pitched battle and chased him into the Don marshes. His magical authority evaporated. He was captured and executed.

[1]Jerome Blum, *Lord and Peasant in Russia* (Princeton, N.J., 1961), pp. 229–230.

Meanwhile, the tsar and the nobility smashed one rebel band after another, and terrorized the peasantry into submission by dismembering the rebels they caught alive, or impaling them on stakes, or nailing them onto gibbets. Razin's rebellion accomplished nothing. A hundred thousand serfs may have died in their vain struggle for liberty. Such was the starkly stratified and deeply insular society on which Peter the Great forcibly imposed western technology and cultural mores in the years following 1682.

Sweden

West of Russia and north of Poland lay the kingdom of Sweden. Seventeenth-century Sweden was a Baltic empire, double its twentieth-century size; it incorporated modern Finland, Estonia, and Latvia, and extensive Russian, Polish, and German coastal land. Sweden held 2,500 miles of Baltic shoreline. Nonetheless, its resources were puny compared with those of Turkey, Poland, or Russia. Sweden's was a simple society of a million or so peasants, who subsisted on porridge, turnips, coarse bread, and home-brewed beer. Stockholm was the one town of any size; commerce was mainly conducted by foreigners; and specie was so scarce that wages, taxes, and debts were paid in kind. The king of Sweden was the only European monarch who found it necessary to build warehouses to store his revenue of butter, fish, and hops. Sweden had always been on Europe's cultural periphery: it boasted a medieval university, but the Renaissance had scarcely touched its shores. Swedish political structure was rudimentary by western standards. Yet Sweden was the only one of the borderland states to play a vigorous international hand in the years between 1559 and 1700.

Under the leadership of a young nobleman named Gustavus Vasa, Sweden had secured independence from Denmark in the early sixteenth century. Gustavus Vasa established himself as king of Sweden and ruled purposefully from 1523 to 1560. But his three sons, who reigned between 1560 and 1611, squabbled among themselves and alienated their subjects. When sixteen-year-old Gustavus Adolphus inherited the throne in 1611, Sweden was in acute crisis. It was at war with Denmark, and the war was going so poorly that the Danes appeared likely to reconquer the country.

Gustavus Adolphus (ruled 1611–1632) shaped Sweden almost overnight into a major power. He had some good material to work with. For one thing, the Protestant Reformation had infused the early seventeenth-century Swedes with crusading ardor. As in England, the Swedish Reformation had begun in the 1520's and 1530's as a cynical maneuver to grab Church land and wealth, and only slowly did Luther's gospel cry stir the people. By the 1620's, however, Sweden's warfare with Catholic Poland and Orthodox Russia for control of the Baltic was having much the same galvanizing effect as Elizabethan England's warfare with Catholic Spain. Calvinism made small headway in Sweden; the country was solidly Lutheran. Gustavus

Gustavus Adolphus. *Pencil sketch by Strauch, drawn in the year of the Swedish king's death. Nationalmuseum, Stockholm.*

Adolphus' clergy were more truculent than their brethren in Germany. The king's chaplain dared to reprove him publicly for his sexual laxity, whereupon Gustavus Adolphus (who deserved this reproof far less than most contemporary monarchs) gave the chaplain the next vacant bishopric—surely a commendable way to avoid hearing further sermons. Another Swedish asset was the sturdy independence of the peasant farmers. In Sweden, society was not polarized into a landlord master class and an enserfed peasantry, as in Turkey, Poland, and Russia. There were no serfs in Sweden. The peasants owned 50 per cent of the arable land. They had their own chamber in the *Riksdag*, or national assembly. The nobility were correspondingly less rich and privileged than in the great eastern European states. To be sure, they assumed political leadership, possessed large farms, hired tenant laborers, and exhibited family pride. But in style of life the Swedish noblemen were none too distant from the peasants. From this comparatively undifferentiated, homespun, God-fearing society, Gustavus Adolphus drew a peerless army of self-reliant soldiers, militant chaplains, and officers eager to invade and plunder Sweden's wealthier neighbors.

Gustavus Adolphus is best known as a warrior, the Protestant hero in the Thirty Years' War. He began his reign by making peace with Denmark, but he soon took advantage of the internal weakness of his neighbors, wresting territory along the Gulf of Finland (the future site of St. Petersburg) from the Russians and Livonia (modern Latvia) from the Poles. The tolls he levied upon captured southern Baltic ports enabled him to finance further military operations without overtaxing the Swedish people. Swedish copper and iron mines supplied added revenue and metal for armaments. But Gustavus Adolphus was much else besides a soldier. He was easily the most creative administrator in Swedish history. Paunchy, jocose, explosive, this roughhewn Nordic figure with big blue eyes and blond Vandyke beard obviously bulged with manly energy, but he had deep reserves of religion and culture as well. He recruited the Swedish nobility, led by the extremely able Chancellor Axel Oxenstierna (1583–1654), into administrative service. He charmed the burghers and peasants in the *Riksdag*. He bolstered his doughty Lutheran clergy, and they in turn mixed patriotism with religion, performing such thankless civil jobs as collecting the local taxes. Ashamed of Sweden's backward school system, the king founded many new schools and reorganized the faltering University of Upsala.

Not being a magician, Gustavus Adolphus failed to transform Sweden into a lasting great power. When he led his army into Germany in 1630, to battle the Catholic Habsburgs, he committed his country to aims beyond its resources. After Gustavus Adolphus was killed in 1632, the crown passed to his five-year-old daughter Christina (ruled 1632–1654). During her minority, Chancellor Oxenstierna doggedly kept Sweden in the endless German war. Swedish armies won more often than they lost, and by peace treaties in 1645, 1648, and 1658 the Swedes gained considerable Danish and German territory. Internally, however, the country lost its cohesion. Queen Christina was partly responsible, for she was a selfish lady who grew bored with statecraft, abdicated her throne, and shocked her people by converting to Catholicism. The late seventeenth century saw a swift eclipse of Sweden's great-power status. Between 1700 and 1809 it lost the whole of its Baltic empire to Russia. Sweden's age of greatness was thus short—but decisive. To see how pivotal Gustavus Adolphus' Lutheran crusade was in the 1630's, let us return to the Holy Roman Empire and the international power struggle which devastated Germany.

THE THIRTY YEARS' WAR, 1618–1648

Other wars have lasted as long, have caused as much damage, and have settled as little. But the Thirty Years' War, which opened in Bohemia in 1618 and convulsed central Europe for a generation, had one peculiar feature. The chief combatants (after the first few years) were non-German, yet their combat took place almost entirely on German soil. The most populous provinces of the Holy Roman Empire became a playground for the invading armies of Spain, Denmark, Sweden, and France. How and why did the German people suffer this indignity?

In 1618, the Habsburg heir apparent to the imperial throne was Ferdinand of Styria (1578–1637), a cheerful, bustling little man of forty. Ferdinand was a rabid Catholic, educated and counseled by the Jesuits. He was frankly unwilling to tolerate Protestantism among his subjects. Clearly, this man was going to make a more energetic Holy Roman emperor than anyone since Charles V, but the Protestant imperial princes were none too alarmed. Not even the great Charles V had been able to exercise much power as emperor. Within the Austrian and Bohemian provinces held directly by the Habsburgs, however, the situation was different. Here Ferdinand did have real power. As soon as he was crowned king of Bohemia in 1617, he began to rescind the religious toleration guaranteed to the Bohemian Protestants by his cousin, Rudolf II, in 1609. The Bohemians were in much the same predicament as the Netherlanders had been in the 1560's—alienated from their autocratic Habsburg prince by language, custom, and religion. As in the Netherlands, the nobility engineered rebellion. On May 23, 1618, a hundred armed Bohemian noblemen cornered Ferdinand's two most hated Catholic advisers in the council room of the Hradschin castle, in Prague, and tossed them out the window into the castle ditch some fifty feet below. The victims survived the fall, perhaps (according to the Catholic view) because they were rescued in mid-flight by guardian angels, or perhaps (according to the Protestant view) because they landed on a dung heap. At any rate this "defenestration of Prague" put the rebels in charge of the Bohemian capital. Their announced aim was to preserve ancient Bohemian privileges and to rescue King Ferdinand from the wicked Jesuits. But they were really repudiating Habsburg rule.

The crisis quickly spread from Bohemia to the entire empire. The aged emperor, Matthias, died in 1619, giving the German Protestant princes a golden chance to join the rebellion against Habsburg rule. Seven electors had the exclusive right to choose Matthias' successor: the three Catholic archbishops of Mainz, Trier, and Cologne; the three Protestant princes of Saxony, Brandenburg, and the Palatinate; and the king of Bohemia. If the Protestant electors denied Ferdinand's right to vote as king of Bohemia, they could block his election as Holy Roman emperor. But only Elector Frederick V of the Palatinate (1596–1632) turned out to be willing to do this, and he backed down. On August 28, 1619, at Frankfurt, the electors unanimously cast their votes for Emperor Ferdinand II. A few hours after his election, Ferdinand learned that the Bohemian rebels in Prague had deposed him as their king and elected Frederick of the Palatinate in his place! Frederick accepted the Bohemian crown. A general war was now inevitable. Emperor Ferdinand prepared to crush his rebel subjects and to punish the German prince who had dared to usurp his hereditary Habsburg lands.

The Bohemian rebellion was poorly conceived from the start. The rebels sorely missed a folk hero equivalent to John Huss (*c.* 1369–1415) who had led the great Bohemian religious revolt two centuries before. The members of the Bohemian nobility did not trust one another. The Bohemian assembly hesitated to levy special taxes or build an army. Having no native candidate to replace Ferdinand, the rebels had turned to the German Calvinist Elector Palatine. But Frederick was a very poor choice. A simple young fellow of twenty-three, he had no feeling for the Slavic evangelical religion he was being asked to champion, nor could he supply men and money with which to fight the Habsburgs. The Bohemians counted on the other German princes to support King Frederick's cause, but very few did so. Frederick's foreign friends, such as his father-in-law, James I of England, also stayed neutral.

The rebels' best hope lay in the weakness of Ferdinand II. The emperor had no army of his own and little means of raising one; in the Austrian Habsburg lands, most of the nobility and the provincial estates were in league with the rebel Bohemians. But Ferdinand was able to buy the services of three allies. Maximilian (1573–1651), duke of Bavaria and the most powerful German Catholic prince, sent an army into Bohemia on the promise that the emperor would cede him Frederick's electoral dignity and some of his Palatine land. Philip III of Spain likewise sent his Habsburg cousin an army, in return for the promised cession of the remaining Palatine land. More surprising, the Lutheran elector of Saxony also helped reconquer Bohemia, his reward being the Habsburg province of Lusatia. The result of these shabby bargains was a quick military campaign (1620–1622) in which the rebels were utterly defeated. The Bavarian army easily routed the Bohemians at the Battle of White Mountain in 1620. From the Alps to the Oder, throughout the Habsburg lands, the rebels capitulated and were left to Ferdinand's tender mercies. The Bavarian and the Spanish armies next conquered the Palatinate. Foolish Frederick was dubbed the *Winterkönig* ("king of one winter"). By 1622, he had lost not merely his Bohemian crown but all his German territories as well.

The war did not end in 1622, though the original issues had now been resolved. One cause of continuing conflict was the emergence of private armies led by soldiers of fortune. Ernst von Mansfeld (1580–1626) was at first the most prominent of these mercenary captains. By birth a Belgian Catholic, Mansfeld had fought for the Spanish before turning Calvinist and selling his services to Frederick and the Bohemians. He subsequently switched sides several times, always working for the highest bidder. Since Mansfeld supported his army by looting the towns and villages through which he passed, he preferred to keep moving into fresh territory. After Frederick's defeat in 1622, Mansfeld—a law unto himself, less bent on fighting than on plundering—took his army into northwestern Germany. Maximilian of Bavaria kept his army in the field against Mansfeld. His troops did not subdue the captain, but they harried the German Protestant civilian population of the area ruthlessly. Maximilian was doing well from the war: he had snatched much of Frederick's land, and his seat as an elector, and the emperor owed him large sums of money; so Maximilian was none too anxious for peace. Foreign Protestant princes, who had stayed neutral in 1618–1619, now started to intervene in imperial affairs. In 1625, King Christian IV of Denmark (ruled 1588–1648), whose province of Holstein was within the Holy Roman Empire, entered the war as protector of the Protestants in northern Germany. Christian was anxious to prevent a total Catholic conquest of the empire, but he also hoped to profit as Maximilian had done from the fluid situation. He was an abler leader than Frederick and had a better army, but he could find no German allies. The Protestant electors of Saxony and Brandenburg wanted the war to end, and they declined to join the Protestant cause. In 1626 Maximilian's veterans crushed Christian at the Battle of Lutter and drove him back into Denmark.

So far, Emperor Ferdinand II had gained the most from the war. The capitulation of the Bohemian rebels gave him a free hand to suppress Protestantism, redistribute land, and revamp the administration of his dynastic Habsburg possessions. The expulsion of Frederick permitted him to tinker with the imperial constitution: by shifting the Palatine electoral vote to Bavaria, Ferdinand obtained an unbreakable Catholic, pro-Habsburg majority. The spread of the war into northern Germany enabled him to eject additional rebel Protestant princes and to parcel out their territories among his family and friends. By 1626 Ferdinand envisioned what had been inconceivable in 1618, the transformation of the Holy Roman Empire into an absolute, sovereign, Catholic, Habsburg state.

Obviously, Ferdinand's war aims were not quite compatible with those of his ally Maximilian. The emperor needed a more pliant instrument than the Bavarian army. Yet he was deeply in debt to Maximilian and could not subsidize an army of his own. This situation explains his curious partnership with Albrecht von Wallenstein (1583–1634), a soldier of fortune par excellence. A Bohemian Protestant by birth, Wallenstein had sided with the Habsburgs during the Bohemian revolt, and built a fabulous private fortune in the process. Of all the leading participants in the Thirty Years' War, Wallenstein was the most enigmatic. A tall, baleful figure, he exhibited most of the unpleasant personality traits one expects in an impatient parvenu. He was unscrupulous, greedy, reckless, cruel, quarrelsome, and superstitious. A promoter on the grandest scale, Wallenstein evidently set no limits to his ambitions. All of his contemporaries feared and distrusted the man; it is impossible for a modern analyst to be sure just what he was up to. In 1625 he contracted to field an imperial army at his own expense and was authorized by Ferdinand to requisition food and shelter from the unfortunate districts he occupied. Wallenstein once asserted that he could maintain an army of fifty thousand more easily than an army of twenty thousand, because the larger force could more thoroughly squeeze the land off which it was living. For a while Wallenstein cooperated with the Bavarian general Tilly. But he preferred to campaign independently. He chased Mansfeld out of the empire, and occupied much of Denmark and much of the German Baltic coast. By 1628, he commanded 125,000 men. The emperor made him duke of Mecklenburg, one of the newly conquered Baltic provinces. Neutral princes, such as the elector of Brandenburg, were powerless to stop Wallenstein from occupying their territory. Even Maximilian, belatedly aware of the emperor's new power, pleaded with Ferdinand to dismiss his overmighty general.

By 1629, the emperor felt the time had come to issue his Edict of Restitution, perhaps his fullest expression of autocratic power. Ferdinand's edict outlawed Calvinism within the Holy Roman Empire, and required the Lutherans to disgorge all Church properties they had confiscated since 1552. Sixteen bishoprics, twenty-eight cities and towns, and over one hundred and fifty monasteries and convents scattered throughout northern and central Germany were ordered restored to Rome. Ferdinand acted unilaterally, without recourse to an imperial Diet. The Catholic princes felt almost as menaced as the Protestant princes by the Edict of Restitution, for the emperor was trampling their constitutional liberties and enhancing his centralized authority. Wallenstein's soldiers soon occupied the cities of Magdeburg, Halberstadt, Bremen, and Augsburg, which had been predominantly Protestant for many years, and forcibly converted them to Catholicism. There seemed to be no reason why, with the help of Wallenstein's army, Ferdinand could not soon abrogate the whole Augsburg formula of 1555 and transform the empire into a Catholic absolute monarchy.

Catholic reentry into Augsburg, 1629. *The Protestant cartoonist shows two devils vomiting parish priests (left) and Jesuits (right) into the city.*

Laplånder. Liff Lånder. Schotlånder.

Caricature of the Swedish army which invaded Germany in 1630. *Gustavus Adolphus' soldiers are represented as barbarians from Lapland, Livonia, and Scotland, bent on rape and plunder. The Livonian is mounted on a reindeer.*

It was at this crucial moment in 1630 that Gustavus Adolphus thrust his Swedish army into Germany. He announced that he was coming to protect German Protestantism and constitutional liberties from Ferdinand II's attacks, but he was also obviously looking for conquest and profit. The Swedish king suffered from the same handicap as the previous would-be Protestant champion, King Christian of Denmark: he was a foreigner without German allies. Luckily for Gustavus Adolphus, Ferdinand II played into his hands. Feeling securely in command of Germany, Ferdinand called upon the imperial Diet in 1630 to recognize his son as heir to the imperial throne and to help the Spanish Habsburgs against the Dutch and the French. The emperor's plans were recklessly ambitious, and he underestimated the German princes' hostility toward him. The princes refused both of his requests, even after he tried to placate them by dismissing Wallenstein from command of the imperial army. All that Ferdinand had accomplished was to remove his best general. Meanwhile, Gustavus Adolphus had a second stroke of luck. The French government, headed by Cardinal Richelieu, agreed to subsidize his invasion of Germany. Obviously, the French cardinal had no interest in Gustavus Adolphus' Protestant crusade. Nonetheless, he agreed to pay the Swedes a million livres a year to maintain an army of thirty-six thousand in Germany, because he wanted to harass the Habsburgs, paralyze the empire, and stake out French claims to Rhenish territory. All that Gustavus Adolphus now needed was enough German support so that he could play the role of avenging hero. It was no easy task, but he finally badgered the electors of Brandenburg and Saxony into signing alliances with Sweden. Now he could take action.

In 1631 Gustavus Adolphus smashed the imperial army at Breitenfeld; this was probably the most decisive battle of the Thirty Years' War, for it wiped out at a stroke most of the Catholic gains of 1618–1629. During the next year he systematically occupied the heretofore unspoiled Catholic regions in central Germany. Bavaria was sacked with special thoroughness. The Swedish king prepared to invade Habsburg Austria and acted more and more as if he intended to usurp Ferdinand's place as Holy Roman emperor.

Gustavus Adolphus' intervention was pivotal because he saved German Protestantism and defeated Habsburg imperial centralization, but his personal triumph was very brief. In 1632 Wallenstein came out of retirement to fight him. Emperor Ferdinand had already begged his general to resume command of the imperial forces, and when Wallenstein finally took the field, his army was more than ever a personal instrument. On a dark, foggy November day in 1632 the two great commanders met at Lützen, in Saxony. Their armies locked savagely, blindly. Gustavus Adolphus galloped into the fog on a cavalry charge, and shortly his horse careered back, wounded and riderless. The Swedish troops, maddened at the loss of their king, drove Wallenstein's army from the battlefield. In the darkness and the mud they finally found Gustavus Adolphus' bullet-riddled corpse, stripped to the shirt by scavengers. "O," cried one of his grieving soldiers, "would to God I had such a leader again to fight such another day; in this old quarrel!"[2]

Old quarrel indeed, by 1632—and after Lützen a hopeless deadlock. None of the combatants was strong enough to win, or weak enough to surrender. Wallenstein, once again the most feared soldier in Germany, had a brief chance to engineer a compromise peace settlement. Unencumbered by religious passion or by loyalty to the house of Habsburg, he was ready to deal with anyone who would pay handsomely for his services. In 1633 he campaigned as little as possible for the emperor, while dickering simultaneously with all of Ferdinand's enemies: the German Protestants, the Bohemian rebels, the Swedes, and the French. But Wallenstein was by now too sickly and irresolute to play this dangerous game. In February, 1634, Ferdinand II dismissed him from command, and instructed his new general to capture Wallenstein dead or alive. Wallenstein was in winter quarters at Pilsen, in Bohemia. He appealed to his officers to fight for him rather than for the emperor, but they mutinied against him. With a few companions, he

[2]Quoted by Michael Roberts, *Gustavus Adolphus, 1611–1632* (London, 1953–1958), Vol. II, p. 789.

fled from Pilsen, but they were quickly cornered. The final scene was sordid enough: an Irish mercenary captain kicked open Wallenstein's bedchamber door, speared his unarmed chieftain, rolled the bloody body in a carpet, and dragged it unceremoniously down the stairs.

For the moment, Ferdinand II scarcely missed Wallenstein's military talents. In 1634 imperial forces decimated the Swedes at Nördlingen, and the following year the emperor made peace with Sweden's German allies, Saxony and Brandenburg. Yet the war was far from over. In 1635 France under Richelieu poured fresh men and money into Germany to compensate for Swedish reverses. The combatants were now France and Sweden versus Spain and the emperor. The war had become a Habsburg-Bourbon dynastic struggle, with the original religious, ethnic, and constitutional issues laid aside. Very few Germans wanted to continue fighting after 1635; most of them tried to stay neutral. Their lands, however, continued to be the battlefields, and their property continued to be pillaged.

The final thirteen years of the war, from 1635 to 1648, were the most destructive. The Franco-Swedish armies generally maintained the upper hand, but their objective was to keep the war going rather than to strike a knockout blow against their Habsburg opponents. It is noticeable that the French and the Swedes rarely invaded Habsburg Austria and never sacked the emperor's personal lands the way they sacked central Germany and Bavaria. Troops on both sides expended far more energy in looting than in fighting. One eyewitness, Hans Jacob Christoffel von Grimmelshausen (1625–1676), drew on his own experience to write a graphic account of the closing years of combat. In *The Adventures of a Simpleton*, Grimmelshausen follows a naïve peasant boy through one disaster after another; soldiers and civilians routinely torture and kill one another, with the civilians always getting the worst of it. In this style of warfare, every army had its train of camp followers—women and children—who kept the troops comfortable enough so that they were willing to campaign indefinitely. Except for the plague epidemics at many campsites, military life in mid-seventeenth-century Germany was definitely more safe and pleasant than civilian life. The numerous German towns were prime targets: Marburg was occupied eleven times; Magdeburg was besieged ten times. But at least town dwellers could sometimes withstand sieges behind their walls or buy off a conquering army. The exposed peasantry, on the other hand, had no defense except to run away. Agricultural collapse triggered famine. The total population loss was staggering, even when one discounts the estimates of contemporaries who exaggerated their figures wildly in order to claim damages or plead tax exemption. The German cities lost one third of their population, and the rural areas two fifths of their population, during the course of the war. The empire had seven or eight million fewer inhabitants in 1648 than in 1618. Not until the

Soldiers pillaging a farmhouse. *By Callot. Some of the troopers torture the farmer over his kitchen fire to find where the money is hidden, while others rape the houshold women and steal food.*

twentieth century could any other European conflict boast such human butchery.

Peace negotiations opened in 1644, but four years passed before the multitude of diplomats congregated in Westphalia finally settled on terms and ended the war. After all this haggling, the Peace of Westphalia (1648) turned out to be essentially a confirmation of the long-scorned Peace of Augsburg. The Holy Roman Empire remained politically fragmented, divided into three hundred autonomous, sovereign princely states, most of them very small and weak. The emperor, now Ferdinand II's son, Ferdinand III (ruled 1637–1657), had meager executive authority beyond his own family lands. The imperial Diet, in which all the sovereign princes were represented, continued to be moribund. Thus the Habsburg hope of welding the empire into a single, absolute state was dashed once again, this time permanently. The Peace of Westphalia also reaffirmed the Augsburg formula of territorial churches. Each prince kept the right to establish Catholicism, Lutheranism, or Calvinism (prohibited in 1555) within his state. A greater effort was made now than in 1555 to guarantee private liberty of conscience to Catholics living in Protestant states and vice versa, but in fact most Germans docilely accepted the creed of their ruler. Anabaptists and members of other sects excluded from the Westphalia formula continued to suffer persecution. Thousands of them emigrated to America, especially to Pennsylvania, in the eighteenth century. After 1648 the northern half of the empire was pretty solidly Lutheran, and the southern half pretty solidly Catholic, with important pockets of Calvinism along the Rhine. In no other part of Europe did Protestants and Catholics achieve such a state of balanced deadlock.

Almost all of the major combatants in the Thirty Years' War gained some territory at the Peace of Westphalia. France annexed parts of Alsace and

Lorraine. Sweden annexed western Pomerania, on the Baltic coast. Bavaria kept part of the Palatine territory and the electoral seat it had grabbed at the beginning of the war. Saxony kept Lusatia. Brandenburg, considering its passive role in the war, did exceptionally well in annexing eastern Pomerania and Magdeburg. Even the son of Frederick V, the would-be king of Bohemia, was taken care of: he was restored to his father's Palatinate (considerably reduced in size) and given a new eighth seat in the electoral college. The Swiss Confederation and the Dutch republic were recognized as independent of the Holy Roman Empire. Neither the Spanish nor the Austrian Habsburgs gained any territory in 1648, but the Austrian Habsburgs still had much the largest bloc of imperial land, and Ferdinand III exercised far firmer political and religious control over Austria and Bohemia than had his father before the Bohemian rebellion. It is hard to argue that anyone gained enough at the Peace of Westphalia to justify thirty years of fighting. But the settlement of 1648 did prove to be unusually stable. Except for some details, the intricate German political boundaries were not redrawn thereafter until the time of Napoleon. The religious boundaries lasted into the twentieth century.

The Treaty of Munster in 1648 between Spain and the Netherlands. *Painting by Ter Borch. This treaty, in which Spain finally recognized the independence of the Dutch Republic, was part of the general peace settlement of 1648. In the painting, the Dutch delegates swear the oath of ratification with hands upraised, while the Spanish delegates (right center) place their hands on a Bible.*

The Peace of Westphalia ended the wars of religion in central Europe and left Germany a mere geographical expression. Ever since 1648, the Thirty Years' War has had a continuously bad reputation. Statesmen of the late seventeenth and eighteenth centuries looked back on it as a model of how *not* to conduct warfare. In their view, the Thirty Years' War demonstrated the dangers of religious passion, and of amateur armies led by soldiers of fortune. The philosophers and kings of the age of reason, having discovered a controlled style of warfare with armies professional enough to reduce brigandage and defection, and objectives limited enough to negotiate with minimum bloodshed, scorned the uncivilized, inefficient seventeenth-century wars of religion. To observers in the nineteenth century, the Thirty Years' War seemed calamitous for a different reason: because it blocked for so long the national unification of Germany. Twentieth-century observers may no longer feel so certain of the virtues of national unification, but they still criticize the Thirty Years' War for its ideological posturing and civilian atrocities. One historian has summed up her feelings about this conflict as follows: "Morally subversive, economically destructive, socially degrading, confused in its causes, devious in its course, futile in its result, it is the outstanding example in European history of meaningless conflict."[3] This judgment may be unduly harsh. But for most Germans the war must indeed have been a miserable, profitless experience.

THE RISE OF AUSTRIA AND BRANDENBURG-PRUSSIA

During the second half of the seventeenth century, the Holy Roman Empire was a phantom state, a much revered and very elaborate constitutional mechanism which no longer worked. The princes' final victory over the emperor at Westphalia confirmed the imperial government's inability to enforce orders, pass laws, raise taxes, mount armies, or conduct foreign policy. Sovereignty could be found only at the local level, in the three hundred princely states and imperial cities. In these petty states (the average population was only forty thousand), there was a prevailing late seventeenth-century tendency toward political absolutism. Each prince wanted to have his own small standing army, in case another general war should break out. Many princes suppressed or restricted their representative assemblies. Many built expensive Baroque palaces, gaudy symbols of power, and surrounded themselves with courtiers and ceremonial functionaries in conscious imitation of Louis XIV at Versailles. Armies and courts cost money, which the imperial princes collected through a variety of crude taxes—excises, tariffs, and river tolls. These taxes impaired commerce. A cargo shipped four hundred miles down the Rhine from Basel to Cologne had to pass through thirty political jurisdictions and was subject to so many tariffs and tolls that

[3]C. V. Wedgwood, *The Thirty Years War* (London, 1944), p. 526.

the shipment was impractical. Because of the handicaps imposed upon business, German towns suffered continuing losses in population, wealth, and importance. Just as the princes exercised sovereign power in regulating (or overregulating) domestic commerce, so they exercised sovereign power in conducting international relations. The treaty of 1648 recognized their right to make alliances with foreign states. In the latter half of the seventeenth century, France was always able to buy allies among the imperial princes while she was attacking imperial territory. Thus in the 1670's, when Louis XIV invaded the Rhineland, twenty thousand Germans served in his army. Though the emperor induced the imperial Diet to declare war against France, many west German states refused to contribute to the imperial war effort, and six of the eight electors remained clients of Louis XIV.

With the empire a hollow facade, interest focuses on the several German states which were large enough after 1648 to function in the international power structure. Two German states, Austria and Brandenburg, developed vigorously during the second half of the century. The Habsburgs transformed their dynastic Austrian possessions into a great new Danubian monarchy, while in northern Germany the Hohenzollerns of Brandenburg laid the foundations for another great new state, the eighteenth-century kingdom of Prussia. Three other German states, Bavaria, Saxony, and the Palatinate, seemingly had as much chance as Brandenburg to build their strength during the late seventeenth century, but all three failed to do so. The Elector Palatine was peculiarly unlucky, for no sooner did his people begin to recover from the Thirty Years' War than the Palatinate was twice overrun and devastated by Louis XIV. The elector of Saxony dissipated his energy and his country's wealth in trying to secure election as king of Poland. The elector of Bavaria, who had earlier played a key role in the Catholic reformation and in the Thirty Years' War, now poured all his resources into his Munich court; in international affairs, Bavaria became a French satellite. The relative failure of these western and central German states, and the success of Austria and Brandenburg, meant among other things that German and imperial leadership would henceforth come from east of the Elbe. Both the Habsburgs and the Hohenzollerns ruled over territories situated on the eastern border of the empire; both faced east during the late seventeenth century and built their new states at the expense of the Ottoman Turks, Poland, and Sweden.

Austria

The rise of Austria was the most striking phenomenon in eastern Europe during the late seventeenth century. It was a story of luck as much as skill. The Habsburg dynasty which built the new Danubian monarchy—Ferdinand II (ruled 1619–1637), Ferdinand III (ruled 1637–1657), and Leopold I (ruled 1658–1705)—was not remarkable for talent. Habsburg Austria was a unique creation, a crossbreed between a centralized western nation-state

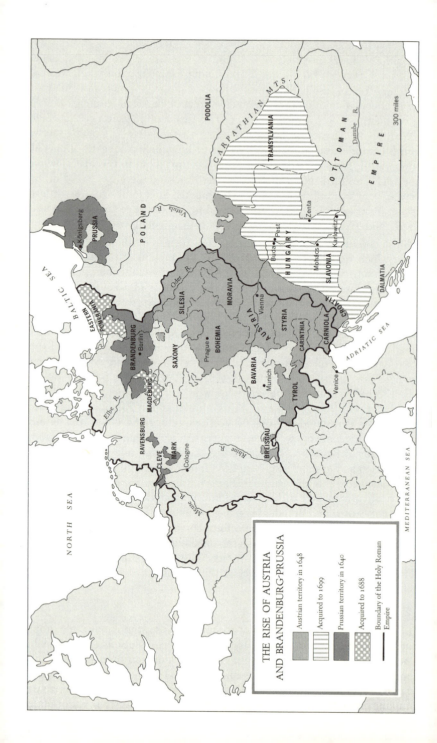

THE RISE OF AUSTRIA
AND BRANDENBURG-PRUSSIA

Austrian territory in 1648
Acquired to 1699
Prussian territory in 1640
Acquired to 1688
Boundary of the Holy Roman
Empire

like France and an old-style dynastic empire like Charles V's miscellaneous collection of territories. The reigning Habsburg prince, besides being Holy Roman emperor, was simultaneously archduke of Upper and Lower Austria, margrave of Styria, duke of Carinthia and Carniola, count of Tyrol, king of Bohemia, margrave of Moravia, duke of Upper and Lower Silesia, king of Hungary, Croatia, Slavonia, and Dalmatia, and prince of Transylvania—though in fact the last five of these territories were mainly possessed by the Turks until the end of the century. The Habsburgs managed each of these provinces separately. Every province had its individual native customs and institutional patterns. Several, notably Bohemia and Hungary, boasted long, proud histories of resistance to foreign rule. The Habsburgs' subjects spoke some ten languages and practiced at least eight religious creeds. No part of Europe was more heterogeneous ethnically and culturally. Though the Habsburg lands were physically contiguous, their peoples shared little except the accident of common allegiance to one ruling dynasty. It was the Habsburg ambition to secure absolute control over each and every province, to chase the Turks out of Hungary and adjoining areas, and to cultivate certain cultural and social uniformities which would make their subjects easier to handle. But the Habsburgs did *not* want to weld these diverse peoples into a single political unit equivalent to France or England. On the contrary, they preferred to play one province against another. The Danubian monarchy was an atomistic congeries, each province separate from its neighbors, each province bound as tightly as possible to the Habsburg crown.

This new Danubian monarchy began to take shape as early as the 1620's, when Ferdinand II reorganized Bohemia, Moravia, and Austria in the wake of the abortive Bohemian rebellion. Since the rebellion had been initiated by the nobility in these provinces, Ferdinand confiscated the huge estates of the rebel nobles and redistributed the forfeited lands among loyal Habsburg supporters. Many mercenary captains of the Thirty Years' War (Wallenstein was among them) became members of an acquisitive new landlord class in Bohemia and Moravia. Ferdinand also expelled all Protestant clergymen and school teachers, replacing them as far as possible with Jesuit missionaries. He had remarkable success in making almost all the Bohemian people rejoin the Catholic Church. Bohemia, bastion of the Hussite movement for more than two centuries, was the only thoroughly Protestantized community to be reconverted to Rome during the wars of religion.

The Austrian Habsburgs held rather fixed ideas about the good society. Devotion to the dynasty and to the Virgin Mary was supposed to give their subjects spiritual and moral strength. A big standing army provided the muscle. A small educated class provided the priests and civil servants. The German language was considered superior to the Slavic languages; hence German culture was mandatory for the ruling elite. Yet the Habsburgs were cosmopolitan enough to attract men of every European nationality into their employ. Agricultural landlords were encouraged to exploit the peasantry but

Leopold I of Austria. *Engraving by van Dryweghen. This Habsburg emperor looks less than handsome because of his protruding jaw, a common trait in his family, caused by generations of inbreeding within the Habsburg dynasty.*

were discouraged from taking active part in governmental administration or legislation. Thus in Bohemia and Moravia the once-powerful estates met seldom in the middle and late seventeenth century, and did little except to legislate the imposition of serfdom on the peasant population. The new landlords, perhaps more businesslike than their rebel predecessors, saw that they could farm very profitably if they could get free agricultural labor. Despite peasant revolts, the Habsburg government required of each Bohemian peasant three days of unpaid compulsory service (*robota*) for his lord every week. Like the Polish landlords, the Bohemian and Austrian agricultural magnates produced for export. They raised grain and timber for the western European market, and meat, grain, and fish (bred in elaborate fishponds) for the Habsburg army. In this overwhelmingly rural, stratified society the Czech and Austrian towns served few functions, and during the seventeenth century they decayed even more completely than the towns of western Germany.

The Habsburgs needed outside help in order to reconquer Bohemia in the 1620's, and again to regain control of Hungary in the 1680's and 1690's. The Habsburg-Turkish demarcation line in Hungary had been fairly stable since the mid-sixteenth century. The Turkish frontier garrisons were only eighty miles east of Vienna, the Habsburg capital. In the 1660's, the Turks renewed their efforts to conquer Austria. Though the Habsburgs beat back an invading Ottoman army in 1664, Leopold I was so alarmed at the Turks' military strength that he paid the sultan a tribute of 200,000 florins in order to secure a truce. As soon as the truce expired in 1683, another huge Turkish army advanced through Hungary, crossed the Austrian border, and laid siege to Vienna. Leopold fled his capital. For two months the Viennese hung on desperately. In the nick of time a relief army of Austrians, Germans, and Poles commanded by King John Sobieski of Poland (ruled 1674–1696) routed the Ottomans, and sent the dreaded janissaries reeling back down the Danube. This great victory opened Hungary to reconquest. In sixteen years of hard fighting, the forces of the Austrian Habsburgs, the papacy, Poland, and Venice, in a coalition known as the Holy League, drove the Turks south of the Danube and east of the Carpathians. The League armies were led at various times by Polish, Italian, Rhenish, Bavarian, and Saxon commanders. At the Peace of Karlowitz in 1699, the Turks surrendered a huge belt of territory to the Habsburgs: Hungary, Transylvania, Slavonia, and Croatia. The Danubian monarchy had doubled in size since 1648.

The Habsburgs' efforts at reorganization were not quite so successful in Hungary as they had been in Bohemia. The Hungarians, or Magyars, had long resented Habsburg overlordship, partly because the dynasty was foreign, partly because the Habsburgs had done little to rescue Hungary from the Turks, and partly because the Habsburgs' absolutist, Catholic program encroached upon Hungarian "liberties." These liberties were strictly confined to the nobility. Like their counterparts everywhere in eastern Europe, the Magyar landlords kept their serfs in thralldom while demanding total freedom for themselves. In Royal Hungary, the western strip which the Turks had never conquered, the nobility counted among their liberties the right to elect their king (as in Poland) and to govern themselves through their estates. In Transylvania, the eastern province which the Turks had only nominally conquered, the nobility operated an independent republic, which was staunchly Calvinist to boot. The Habsburgs had their best chance to reshape the society in central and southern Hungary, the area which had been directly under Turkish rule for 150 years. When they expelled the Turks in the 1680's and 1690's, the Habsburgs sold or gave as much as possible of the newly acquired land to their army officers and to others presumably dependent on the crown. But these new landlords quickly melted into the Magyar nobility. It was quite impossible for the Habsburgs to govern this frontier country without the cooperation of the local magnates. Because they had to convince the Magyar nobility that Austrian rule was at the very least preferable to Turkish, they dared not impose absolutism or Catholicism too nakedly. In 1687 Leopold did get the Magyars to surrender their elective monarchy; thereafter, the Hungarian crown was a hereditary Habsburg possession. But the Hungarian estates retained real power, and the Protestant nobility kept their religion. As commercial farming developed in Hungary, the peasants (many of whom were Slovaks and Croats) sank deeper into serfdom. They had to fulfill heavy obligations to their Magyar masters and pay heavy taxes to the Austrian government as well—taxes from which the landlord class was exempt. Habsburg Hungary, with its autocratic Austrian ruler, its selfish Magyar aristocracy, its downtrodden Slavic peasantry, its few small towns inhabited by Germans and Jews, was a melting pot in which nothing melted.

Brandenburg-Prussia

Compared with the growth of Habsburg Austria, the development of Hohenzollern Brandenburg during the late seventeenth century was modest. The key figure here was Frederick William, elector of Brandenburg from 1640 to 1688, who is known as the Great Elector. Frederick William was the shrewdest ruler of his day in eastern Europe, but his contemporaries may be pardoned for failing to notice his ability, since he governed a small state and did nothing spectacular during his reign. The Great Elector was an institutional innovator whose policies bore fruit long after his death. Because the later Hohenzollern princes followed his recipe in building the eighteenth-century kingdom of Prussia and the nineteenth-century German empire, the Great Elector's reign is of special historical interest.

In 1640 Frederick William inherited the Hohenzollern family's scattered collection of underdeveloped north German territories, devastated by the Thirty Years' War. He was a Calvinist; his subjects were mainly Lutherans. Brandenburg was his chief possession, a flat country with unproductive sandy soil, cut off from the Baltic coast, whose several hundred thousand inhabitants raised grain and brewed beer. Berlin, the chief town in Brandenburg, was a small place. More than a hundred miles east of Brandenburg, beyond the imperial border and enveloped by Poland, lay Prussia, the Elector's second most important province. Here was a region of forests and lakes, its chief center the commercial town of Königsberg. More than a hundred miles west of Brandenburg, near the Dutch frontier, lay the Elector's remaining small outposts, Cleve, Mark, and Ravensburg. These provinces all had their own autonomous estates, and being widely separated from each other and only recently joined under the Hohenzollern dynasty, they shared no common interests. Brandenburg and Prussia were both completely dominated by the *Junkers,* the noble landlords. Like the landed gentry in England and the *szlachta* in Poland, the *Junkers* had climbed to power and prosperity by extracting concessions from the ruler above them while squeezing the peasantry below. The *Junkers* had a reputation for being shrewd, tough, and boorish. During the period of rapid inflation in the late sixteenth century, they had pushed the sale price of their rye up 247 per cent while paying their laborers wages which had risen only 86 per cent. But by 1640 even the *Junkers* were in poor shape, for their Baltic grain trade was disrupted by the Thirty Years' War.

Frederick William set out to build an effective state with these un-promising materials. His basic decision was to create a permanent stand-ing army. All his other political, social, and economic innovations stemmed from the army's role in centralizing the Hohenzollern state. Dur-ing the closing stage of the Thirty Years' War, Frederick William fielded eight thousand efficient troops, a lilliputian display by great-power stan-dards, but enough to clear the foreign soldiers from his land and to give him a voice at the peace conference at Westphalia. In 1648 the Great Elector rather surprisingly gained more territory than any other German prince: eastern Pomerania and several secularized bishoprics, including Magdeburg. So far so good. Naturally, the several estates of Brandenburg, Prussia, and Cleve-Mark wanted the army disbanded once the war was over, but instead Frederick William kept on fighting. In the 1650's he first joined Sweden against Poland and then joined Poland against Sweden. He fought for purely opportunistic reasons and changed sides whenever he seemed likely to benefit as a result. In the 1670's and 1680's he outdid himself by switching between the Dutch and the French three times. Frederick William was at war about half the time during his long reign. By 1688 he had thirty thousand professional troops.

Who was going to pay for this army? The Elector knew that he could not let his soldiers live off the land in the manner of Wallenstein's mercenaries. Nor could he pay for them himself, though his large private landholdings produced enough income to cover the ordinary expenses of civil government. Foreign subsidies would help, but the cost would have to be met chiefly through taxes, which the several estates adamantly refused to approve. In 1653 the Elector worked out a compromise with the Bran-denburg estates whereby he recognized the special economic and social privileges of the *Junker* landlords in return for what turned out to be a permanent tax to maintain his army. The Elector acknowledged that only *Junkers* could own land, that *Junkers* could freely evict peasants (who were all assumed to be serfs) from lands they occupied, and that *Junkers* were immune from taxation. On the other hand, he severely curtailed the political privileges of the Brandenburg *Junkers*. After the army tax expired, he kept right on collecting it and soon imposed an additional excise tax on the towns, without the consent of the estates. In his Rhineland territories, the Elector bullied the estates into levying army taxes by threatening to send his soldiers to collect the money by force. In Prussia, resistance was stouter. To force the estates to levy his taxes, Frederick William imprisoned the two chief leaders of the opposition and executed one of them; he billeted his troops in Königsberg until the taxes were collected.

Frederick William's subjects paid twice as much per capita in taxes as

The Prussians swearing homage to the Great Elector at Königsberg, 1663. *The Prussian estates long refused to admit that the Elector had sovereign power over them, but finally in 1663 he persuaded them to pledge allegiance to him as overlord.*

Louis XIV's much richer subjects; in a state with little surplus wealth, and with the only affluent class—the *Junkers*—exempted from taxation, the burden of supporting the army was truly crushing. However, the Elector's military exactions did produce some side benefits. To collect his army taxes, Frederick William created a new bureaucratic institution, the *Generalkriegskommissariat*, or military commissariat, which also disbursed army pay and equipment, and soon supervised all phases of the state economy. The commissariat officials, zealous servants of the Elector, worked hard to promote new state-supported industry, especially the manufacture of military supplies. Some twenty thousand persecuted Calvinist textile workers from France and the Palatinate emigrated to Brandenburg, to the great benefit of the Elector's uniform-manufacturing industry. By the close of the century, the Hohenzollern lands had recovered economically from the terrible damage of the Thirty Years' War, and the population had climbed back to its early seventeenth-century level of about 1.5 million persons.

The Great Elector's standing army could not make Brandenburg-Prussia into a great power overnight. His wars brought him one paltry acquisition after 1648, a thirty-mile sliver of Pomeranian territory. But Frederick William built. enduring strength into his north German society. The Elector's army gave him and his heirs absolute political control. It encouraged the people in habits of discipline and obedience. It contributed to the unity of the state, for peasants from all the Hohenzollern provinces were recruited into the rank and file, while *Junkers* from Brandenburg and Prussia staffed the officer corps. It facilitated the growth of an efficient bureaucracy. And it enabled Frederick William to capitalize upon the existing rigid social stratification, the separation between privileged *Junkers* and unprivileged serfs. To the aspiring *Junker* squire, an officer's commission became the proudest badge of his membership in the master class. The Elector's whole policy rested on partnership with the landlords. As for the serfs, a clergyman observed in 1684, "the peasants are indeed human beings," but he went on to advise that they be treated like the stockfish, which is "best when beaten well and soft."[4]

The Great Elector's son, Frederick III (ruled 1688–1713), was a much less effective ruler. He acquired the royal title of King in Prussia (considered less honorific than King *of* Prussia) in 1701, but played a secondary role in the great wars that filled his reign. The first Hohenzollern ruler to take center stage in European affairs was Frederick the Great, in the mid-eighteenth century. Eventually, under Bismarck's guidance, the Hohenzollerns would annex all the territory between Cologne and Königsberg, and they would rule after 1871 as emperors of Germany. Compared with Frederick the Great or Bismarck, the Great Elector is a small-scale figure. But he started the fateful process by which Germany became politically united.

At the close of the seventeenth century, Brandenburg-Prussia and Austria were obviously organized along somewhat differing lines. The Great Elector had worked to make his state homogeneous; the Habsburgs cultivated heterogeneity. Brandenburg-Prussia was the more militaristic and bureaucratic. Austria could not, or did not, extract from its subjects as much money and service per capita as did Brandenburg-Prussia, but since the Austrian population was much larger, Austria was nevertheless a far greater power. Brandenburg-Prussia was Protestant, Austria was Catholic— but this difference was decidedly less significant than it once would have been. The two states gradually turned into strategic rivals, because both were headed by German dynasties hoping to expand eastward. But this Austro-Prussian rivalry should not obscure the fact that the two societies exhibited some striking similarities in their parallel climbs to power in the seventeenth century.

For one thing, both Austria and Prussia (as Brandenburg-Prussia came

---

[4]Quoted by F. L. Carsten, "The Empire after the Thirty Years War," in *New Cambridge Modern History*, Vol. V (Cambridge, Eng., 1961), p. 438.

CHAPTER 3

The Psychology of Limited Wealth

EUROPEAN BUSINESSMEN in the years between 1559 and 1715 faced problems and developed policies characteristic of a society quite well off but very far from affluent. No longer did everyone have to concentrate on the struggle for bare survival, as in the agrarian subsistence economy of the early Middle Ages. The so-called commercial revolution was in full swing, with the merchant the key figure, distributing more goods than ever before to a worldwide market. The putting-out system of domestic manufacturing was producing a rising volume and variety of consumer commodities, especially textiles. A dramatic sixteenth-century increase in the circulation of bullion spurred purchasing power. Refinements in credit facilitated international commerce. Innovations in banking encouraged private investment and public loans. The development of specialized commercial agriculture, combined with improvements in the long-distance shipment of bulk cargo, made it possible for big cities and densely populated regions to be fed from distant farmlands. On the other hand, Europe did not yet have the economic techniques to produce as much as its people needed for comfort, to say nothing of abundance. Agriculture was still by far the largest occupation, and farming methods were crude; the agrarian populace still had to expend most of its energy in meeting its own needs rather than producing for the market. Manufacturing was still done by hand rather than by machine. Transportation remained slow and difficult. Commerce was extremely risky. Business enterprises were typically small-scale. After about 1590, the population stopped growing. Small wonder that in this era of rising yet limited wealth many Europeans clung to the attitudes appropriate in a subsistence economy.

Europe's wealth, such as it was, was unevenly distributed geographically. The commercial west held a vastly larger share than the agrarian east. Within western Europe, the Atlantic ports were the chief capitalist centers. Wealth was also very unevenly distributed among the various social classes; indeed it was scarcely distributed at all. Everywhere in Europe the distance between the propertied and the propertyless was widening. Great property holders such as kings and landed magnates luxuriated in unprecedented conspicuous consumption. Small and middling property holders, independ-

103

ent farmers, artisans, shopkeepers, members of the learned professions, and the like, typically got only a taste of wealth but hoped to acquire more by copying the habits of the beaver and the squirrel. The propertyless bottom half (or more) of society, the wage laborers, serfs, unemployed, and unemployables, got nothing—and were told to expect nothing—beyond bare survival. In most of Europe the laboring classes had somewhat harder working conditions and lower living standards in 1715 than in 1559.

Also noteworthy is the fact that in this period the politically consolidated national state clearly replaced the city-state as the most effective business unit. The mercantilist policies of Spain, France, and England—politically belligerent, but economically conservative and protectionist—most fully express the sixteenth- and seventeenth-century European psychology of limited wealth.

POPULATION

Our understanding of the most fundamental aspect of life in the sixteenth and seventeenth centuries—the population pattern—is sadly deficient and likely to remain so. No government in this era took a comprehensive census of its inhabitants. In some western states the local clergy kept parish registers of baptisms, marriages, and deaths. Tax collectors occasionally enumerated households. But statistical data of this sort is spotty, inexact, and difficult to interpret, and for much of Europe—the eastern regions in particular—there is really no quantifiable information at all. Such fragmentary evidence as we do have indicates that Europe's population, which had been severely depressed for a century after the Black Death, began to grow in the mid-fifteenth century and continued on a strong upward curve for more than a hundred years. By the late sixteenth century the total count was probably somewhat over a hundred million—or about a sixth of the present figure. Around 1590 the population seems to have stopped growing in most parts of Europe. Throughout the seventeenth century the overall picture is one of demographic oscillation. Most states experienced sudden, sharp population losses, followed (though not always) by gradual recovery. The pattern varied significantly from place to place. Germany, as we have seen, lost close to 40 per cent of its population during the Thirty Years' War, but recovered rapidly in the late seventeenth century. The Spanish population dropped about 25 per cent between 1590 and 1665, and then leveled off. The French population fell and rose irregularly without much net loss or gain between 1590 and 1715. In England, the population grew some 30 per cent during this time. But overall, as far as we can tell, Europe's population in 1715 was no larger, and probably somewhat smaller, than it had been in 1590.

Why did the population grow in the sixteenth century? Why did it stop growing around 1590? Why did it fluctuate during the seventeenth century? Demographers have no agreed-upon answers to these questions, but the key variable they point to is the death rate, which rose and fell wildly during our period. The birthrate was much more regular. Wherever it has been measured in the sixteenth and seventeenth centuries, the rate of births was high: 35 to 40 per thousand, far above the modern western rate. In "good" times, without demographic crisis, the birthrate in early modern Europe was sufficiently higher than the death rate to double the population every century. Through the 1580's, though growth was frequently checked by war, pestilence, and famine, it was not stopped. Thereafter, demographic catastrophe struck frequently and massively.

The 1590's mark a watershed. From Scandinavia to Spain, and from Hungary to Ireland, harvests were poor all through this decade. We can pinpoint weather conditions with surprising precision. In the Alpine valleys the glaciers advanced rapidly in the 1590's, a sign of very cold winters. During the years 1591–1597, French winegrowers harvested their grapes very late, a sign of wet, cold summers.[1] In western Europe, wartime conditions intensified the famine by blocking emergency food distribution. The Dutch and English fleets stopped grain shipments to the Spanish Netherlands. Henry IV's army stopped grain shipments to Paris. The price of wheat rose fivefold in France between 1590 and 1593. It is estimated that the French population suddenly dropped by three million—a 15-per-cent loss.

Comparable demographic crises occurred in the 1620's, the 1640's, the 1690's, and the 1710's. We know the most about the French harvest failure and famine of 1693–1694. Parish registers for this time are much fuller than those for the earlier years, so it is possible to measure the impact of the famine in striking detail. For example, the parish registers for villages in the region of Beauvais, in northwestern France, show two to four times the usual number of deaths in the twelve months following this harvest failure. Furthermore, whereas in a normal year two thirds of those dying were young children or old people, the registers show that in 1693–1694 over half were adults of prime working age. In other words, the subsistence crisis crippled the labor force, maimed family structure, and impeded procreation. If we check the registers for babies conceived during the famine year, we find less than half the usual number.[2] There are several reasons for this sudden drop in fertility. Some sex partners died, some were too weak to procreate, and some may have aborted their children in despair. It is also probable that the semistarved women who survived the famine experienced such extreme nutritional losses that they

[1] Emmanuel Le Roy Ladurie, *Times of Feast, Times of Famine: A History of Climate since the Year 1000* (London, 1972), pp. 58, 67, 140–143, 235, 367.
[2] Pierre Goubert, *Beauvais et le Beauvaisis de 1600 à 1730* (Paris, 1960), Vol. I, pp. 45–58; Vol. II, pp. 44–61.

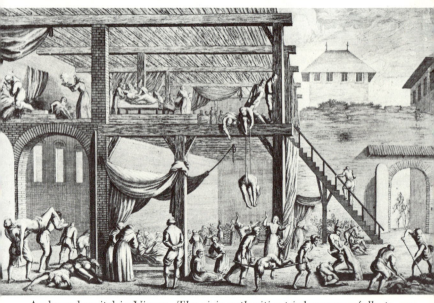

A plague hospital in Vienna. *The civic authorities tried unsuccessfully to contain plague epidemics by congregating the sick and burying the dead in pest-houses such as this.*

were temporarily unable to menstruate or ovulate. This sort of famine-induced infecundity has been observed among slave women on West Indian plantations in the eighteenth century, and among both civilians and concentration-camp inmates during the Second World War. In the case of the seventeenth-century French peasant women, recovery of fertility was rapid. The registers show that in 1695–1696 they bore more children than in a normal year. Yet the demographic impact of this famine obviously lingered for years.

Even in times of desperate hunger people seldom literally starve to death. More generally they become too weak to resist common diseases such as influenza or dysentery. In the sixteenth and seventeenth centuries, there were the added perils of typhus and the bubonic plague—diseases that killed the strong as well as the weak and struck the crowded, unsanitary cities with special frequency and force. Every European city was repeatedly thinned by the plague. To cite a few extreme examples, Hamburg lost one quarter of its population in 1565, Venice one third in 1575–1577, Naples nearly half in 1656. In London, some deaths were attributed to the plague every year, and nine major episodes killed approximately 200,000 people between 1563 and 1665. Like all urban centers at the time, London had a well-deserved reputation as an unhealthy place. Yet London kept growing rapidly. Population pressure in the countryside continually pushed landless, rootless, and adventurous migrants into the cities. In consequence, Europe was considerably more urbanized in 1715 than in 1559.

By the late seventeenth century the plague had nearly disappeared. Why this happened was not understood at the time, and is still a subject of dispute by medical experts. The key may have been a revolution among the rodents that infested all urban areas. The long-established black rat, whose fleas transmit the plague bacillus to humans, was ousted during the course of the century by the brown rat, whose fleas do not spread the disease. At any rate, the last major plague epidemics in western Europe took place in Marseilles in 1720 and in Messina in 1743.

Plague and famine acted as crude safety valves to release excessive population pressure. In most regions of Europe, inelastic production and rudimentary distribution made it impossible to feed or employ the whole population when it rose above a certain ceiling. The western and central regions could support much denser populations than the eastern or northern regions, but nearly every state reached its tolerable maximum during the late sixteenth century. In France this maximum seems to have been around twenty million, in Italy around eleven million. Except in times of unusually bountiful harvests, the French and Italians were certain to encounter subsistence crises whenever their populations climbed far beyond these limits. Once the population dropped, the high birthrate soon built it back up again. Just why the Spanish experienced a net population loss in the seventeenth century, rather than the kind of demographic oscillation found in France and Italy, is not clear. It appears that the Spaniards so mismanaged their economic resources that population density was forced downward. The German population pattern was also exceptional. The Thirty Years' War—with deaths resulting not only from combat but from pestilence and from agricultural cutbacks, transportation breakdowns, and consequent famine—had the demographic impact of the Black Death. But in Germany, as in France and Italy, the high birthrate acted to restore population losses; a strong demographic upswing occurred here after 1648.

In a few places there was net population growth during the seventeenth century. It is not surprising that England's population increased, for density was not as great here as in sixteenth-century France, Germany, or Italy, and the English had the resources to feed and employ more people. The Dutch case is more instructive. The Dutch had no apparent room for population growth, yet they did expand, supported by the highest per-capita agricultural and industrial output and the most vigorous commercial system in Europe. This development pointed the way to the future. Overall, significant changes were beginning to take place that would make possible a new demographic pattern. Though Europe's total population was not growing in the seventeenth century, productive capacity was certainly rising. A shrinking farm population was raising enough food to sustain a rising urban population. After 1715, the birthrate continued high, the plague ended, a long series of good harvests ensued, and people were living longer; they had broken through the seventeenth-century population ceiling. And in the late eighteenth century, Europeans revolutionized their whole production system by introducing scientific livestock breeding, soil chemistry, steam power, and manufacturing by machine. In consequence, they could afford to abandon traditional psychological restraints.

But during our period, people were closely hemmed in by demographic restrictions. They had to accept extreme brevity of life. One quarter of their newborn babies died within the first year. One half died before reaching adulthood. Peasant couples in the region of Beauvais produced five living children on average, yet the population level was only barely sustained. The poets of the day feasted on the bittersweet theme of brief young love, embellished by fading roses, drying dewdrops, and passing spring. In the most popular English lyric of the seventeenth century, Robert Herrick's song "To the Virgins, to Make Much of Time," the poet urges shy maidens to

> Gather ye rosebuds while ye may,
>   Old Time is still a-flying;
> And this same flower that smiles today,
>   Tomorrow will be dying.

In actual fact, the young people tended to gather their rosebuds at a surprisingly slow pace. There is very little evidence of bastardy or of premarital intercourse. The women in seventeenth-century France and England married in their mid-twenties, the men in their late twenties. When life was so short, why this delay in procreation and marriage? Few young people had much practical choice. A couple could scarcely marry until one or both drew a living wage, and most adolescents and post-adolescents in the sixteenth and seventeenth centuries labored for ten years or more after puberty as dependent servants or apprentices, learning their jobs but receiving little or no income. To understand why such a system developed, we must look more closely into the economic and social structure of early modern Europe.

AGRICULTURE AND INDUSTRY

Basic production methods remained throughout our period much as they had been in 1500—indeed, as they had been in 1300. To be sure, the Dutch made some important changes in farming practices, and the English developed some new techniques for heavy industry, but these could not begin to compare with the innovations of the agricultural and industrial revolutions of the eighteenth century. In the age of religious wars, *manufacture* still retained its Latin meaning: "to make by hand." Economic enterprise was still shackled by manual labor.

Coinmaking. *This sixteenth-century print shows the primitive character of early modern industrialism. Workers equipped with rudimentary tools pound metal into thin sheets, cut the sheets into coins, and stamp and mill the coins—all by hand. Metropolitan Museum of Art.*

It is not easy to generalize about developments in agriculture. Broadly speaking, European food production became more commercial and capitalistic between 1559 and 1715. Farmers grew cash crops for the urban market on land they owned or rented. In western Europe, landlords could make money in several ways. They might cultivate their estates with wage labor, or lease out small plots to peasants, or take half of the tenant's crop in lieu of rent—this sharecropping system was called *métayage* in France. Sharecropping was also common on the great Italian *latifundia*, or estates, and on the *latifundios* of Spain. In Poland, Bohemia, Hungary, and Prussia, landlords were less likely to bother with money wages or rent; generally they required their serfs to farm their estates three days a week without pay. The expanding agricultural market thus turned some western European peasants into wage laborers, some into tenant farmers, and others into small free farmers, while the eastern European peasants were driven deeper into serfdom. Everywhere, the market economy was eroding traditional agrarian habits of local self-sufficiency and cooperation within a close-knit community.

Many legacies from medieval agriculture nevertheless remained. Villagers still divided their arable land into three great fields to be planted with different crops in successive years. For example, the English village of Wigston Magna was surrounded by three fields of some nine hundred acres each, called Mucklow, Goldhill, and Thythorn Hill. In a given year, Mucklow might be planted with peas and beans, and Goldhill with

The Harvesters. *Painting by Pieter Brueghel (the Elder). Note the total reliance on hand labor, the employment of women and children, and the noontime picnic to speed the field work. The harvesters are cutting and stacking the ripe grain as fast as they can, to prevent spoilage by rain. Metropolitan Museum of Art.*

barley, wheat, and rye, while Thythorn Hill was left fallow. These open fields were subdivided into hundreds of individual holdings: narrow strips of land, identifiable to their owners by the plow ridges along the edges. As in the Middle Ages, each Wigston farmer held a number of these strips, but by the seventeenth century some held many more than others. A half dozen entrepreneurs had accumulated a hundred acres or more. The majority worked ten to thirty acres, just enough to support a family. The poorest cottagers had no land and hired out to their propertied neighbors. Yet these Wigston farmers, great and small, still plowed and harvested in the communal rhythm of the open-field system, as their forebears had been doing for a thousand years.[3]

Wigston Magna's time-honored but wasteful three-field system of crop rotation prevailed through much of England, France, and Germany. Plowing and harvesting techniques had not improved much since the twelfth century. The yield per bushel of seed remained wretchedly low. The traditional, undiversified crops were grown, mainly cereals and legumes, with

[3]W. G. Hoskins, *The Midland Peasant* (London, 1957), ch. 6–7.

little in the way of meat, dairy produce, fruit, or leafy vegetables. The staples were still bread and beer in the north, bread and wine in the south. Corn and potatoes had been introduced from the New World, but were not yet widely cultivated in Europe. Consumers were very grateful for the spices, sugar, tea, and coffee which were imported from Asia and America.

It is interesting to compare conditions in Spain, where agricultural production declined during the sixteenth and seventeenth centuries, with conditions in England, where production increased. In both Spain and England, large-scale wool raisers were converting grain fields into sheep runs. In Spain, an estimated 3 per cent of the population held 97 per cent of the land, so it was comparatively easy for the landlord class to increase the percentage of land devoted to sheep pasturage. The members of the *Mesta*, or sheep ranchers' association, owned some three million Merino sheep in the early sixteenth century. To graze this many animals, a tremendous proportion of Castile's barren land was required. The Spanish government granted the *Mesta* special privileges; in 1501, their migratory flocks were given exclusive possession of huge belts of pasture land which had formerly been used to raise grain for the Castilian towns. In consequence, the countryside was depopulated as the dispossessed farmers moved to the towns, wheat production fell, and Spain was faced with famine. Ironically, in the seventeenth century the *Mesta* flocks dwindled in size and value. During the same period, aggressive English landlords evicted their tenants from a half million acres of land and "enclosed" much of this land into great sheep pastures. But the English enclosure movement did not assume major proportions until the eighteenth and nineteenth centuries. In England the aristocracy and gentry controlled less of the land than in Spain. At the close of the seventeenth century, nearly half of the English rural population consisted of small farmers who either owned their own land or held it on long leases. A more important difference between England and Spain was that the English farmers, large and small, worked their land more efficiently. Some enterprising farmers created rich new farmland during the seventeenth century by draining the fen district near Cambridge. Others cut down large forest tracts and learned how to till areas which had hitherto been wasteland. Not only did wool production rise in seventeenth-century England, but grain and cattle production more than kept pace with the expanding population. By the close of the century, the English farmers exported a good deal of wheat.

The Dutch were probably the most enterprising agriculturists in Europe. They had to be, for they had very little farmland on which to support a dense population. Their low-lying fields were periodically inundated by the North Sea, and the soil was soggy. During the sixteenth and seventeenth centuries, the Dutch reclaimed huge tracts, known as polders, from the sea. They built dikes and drainage canals to keep the water out, and windmills to pump the land dry. They farmed the new lands intensively, planting orchards and truck gardens as well as grainfields and pasture. Raising tulips—the colorful bulbs were introduced from Turkey in the sixteenth century—became a Dutch specialty. They experimented with clover and turnips, which improved the soil yield and fattened the cattle. The Dutch were able to produce butter and cheese for export, whereas the English dairy farmers were hampered by their practice of slaughtering most of their animals every fall for lack of winter fodder. Spain, with its parched and rocky soil, badly needed some Dutch-style agricultural experiments. But all efforts to irrigate the Spanish fields were blocked by inertia. In the seventeenth century, Spanish clerics rejected a canal project which was designed to improve inland transport; if God had wanted Spain's waterways to be navigable, they reasoned, He would have made them so.

A good example of seventeenth-century agrarian enterprise is the development by grape growers in the French county of Champagne of a method for making superlative sparkling wine. French wines were already well established as the best in Europe, but Champagne was not among the great wine-producing regions. Its chalky soil grew stunted vines with small quantities of particularly sweet white and black grapes. Its northerly climate delayed the harvest season and slowed the crucial fermentation process by which the grape juice was converted into alcohol. The standard method of making wine was (and is) to harvest the grapes in September or October and press them into a mush, which fermented. Before the fermented liquid turned into vinegar, it was poured into great wooden casks. The liquid was then piped from cask to cask in order to remove the sediment and filtered to achieve a clear color. The standard seventeenth-century practice was to drink wine young, but it could be casked for several years, until it matured into old wine. A blind monk named Dom Pierre Pérignon (1638–1715), the cellarer of a Benedictine abbey, is supposed to have been the man who invented a new vintage process which turned the still red wine of Champagne into a sparkling white wine. First, Dom Pierre achieved a perfect blend by combining in the winepress grapes from various different vines (he had a famous nose for the bouquet of the grapes). Next, before the mush had completed its fermentation, Dom Pierre poured the liquid into bottles instead of casks, and stored it in the cool chalk cellars of Reims, the chief town in Champagne. The fermentation process continued inside the bottles, giving the wine a bubbly effervescence. Dom Pierre needed very strong bottles; in the early days of champagne making, a great many of the bottles exploded. He needed strongly wired cork stoppers instead of the oil-soaked wads of hemp which people had been using for bottle stoppers. The development of a foolproof technique took many years. Since bottled wine could not be piped or filtered, the producers of champagne had to find another way of removing the sediment from their wine. They set the bottles upside down in racks, and slightly twisted each bottle every day for many months, until the sediment had settled on the cork. Then they had to open each bottle, wipe off the sediment, hastily insert a pinch of sugar to give the wine its sweet-dry flavor, and recork it before the effervescence was lost. Seventeenth-century champagne may not have tasted very much like the modern beverage, but it was already the toast of kings. Louis XIV drank it copiously, and Charles II was so pleased with the bubbly stuff when he visited France as a young man that he introduced it into England.

Turning from food and drink to manufacturing, we once again find regional divergences and a prevailing tendency toward the large-scale capitalistic organization of production. In the seventeenth century, industrial production was geared to elementary consumer needs. Cloth is the most basic manufactured commodity, and in seventeenth-century Europe, as in the Middle Ages, textile manufacturing was by far the largest industry. Textile-production techniques had not changed since the early sixteenth century. Utilitarian wool cloth, from which most garments were made, was produced all over western Europe by the rural putting-out system. Large-scale clothiers hired peasants to spin, weave, and finish their cloth. Many clothiers did not attempt to dye the cloth, for dyeing required skill; half the price of the finished cloth was in its color. Dutch clothiers had the best formulas for wool dyeing (which they kept as secret as possible), and they imported much "white" cloth from England and dyed it. The enterprising clothier might buy raw wool from various strains of sheep, and experiment with various mixtures and various weaves to get a cloth which struck the public's fancy. He might employ hundreds of men and women, and when he controlled every stage by which the raw wool was converted into finished cloth, his organization of production resembled that of the modern assembly-line factory. But the actual work was performed under extremely primitive conditions, by semiskilled hand labor.

Luxury fabrics, such as silk, were produced in towns rather than in the countryside, because the work required a delicate coalition between highly skilled laborers, costly materials, and rather elaborate machinery. Only the rich could afford to buy silks and velvets, and the silk merchant strove for quality rather than quantity. Lucca had been the biggest Italian silk center since the thirteenth century; cities farther north, such as Lyons and Amsterdam, developed the craft in the sixteenth and seventeenth centuries. Naturally, the skilled silk weavers and dyers of Lucca were better organized and better paid than the semiskilled wool weavers and dyers of an English village. But they too were pieceworkers in a large-scale enterprise.

The tailors who sewed the finished cloth into garments were the most tradition bound of the textile workers. These small, self-employed craftsmen were to be found in every European town. They were organized, as they had been for centuries, into guilds. The tailor sewed his garments according to prescribed guild standards and offered his wares to the consumer at prescribed guild prices. The wool clothier and the silk merchant abominated such protectionist, restrictive business procedures. Yet the clothier himself expected the state to protect and promote all phases of his textile production. The English government, like other governments, obligingly prohibited English farmers from selling their wool abroad. It laid heavy duties on all imported woolens. It bought domestic worsteds and serges for military uniforms, and required that every English corpse be buried in a woolen shroud. Actually, the seventeenth-century woolen industry had more in common with the medieval tailoring craft than with the cotton industry which was going to develop in England during the eighteenth cntury. Not only would cotton be cheaper and more practical than wool, not only would cotton cloth be made by machine rather than by hand, not only would cotton textile production be concentrated in great factories rather than scattered in rural cottages, but the cotton magnates would be so self-reliant that they could disdain all regulation and protection, national as well as local. The textile manufacturers of the seventeenth century, for all their aggressive organization, did not dare to risk free competition. They thought they were living in a subsistence world.

There was not much spare capital or labor, or much technical skill, for heavy industry. England was the most industrialized society during the late sixteenth and seventeenth centuries. The coal mines along the Tyne River in northern England were big affairs, with elaborate machinery for draining the shafts, though not for cutting the coal. The colliers mined and carted the coal by hand. English coal production increased from approximately 200,000 tons a year in the 1550's to 3,000,000 tons by the 1680's. During the same span of years English iron production rose fivefold. Because of these impressive gains, Professor John Nef, the chief authority on the early British coal industry, argues that the English achieved an "industrial revolution" between 1540 and 1640 comparable in importance to the better-known machine age which began after 1760.[4] But "revolution" seems too strong a term for the industrial developments in Tudor and Stuart England. The volume of seventeenth-century English coal and iron output remained very modest, so modest that it could not greatly affect techniques of production. The English did use coal fires in their dyehouses, brick and glass kilns—and breweries, despite the cry that the smell of coke gas tainted the beer. But they had not yet discovered how to smelt iron ore with coal; this was still done by charcoal. Londoners consumed much of the new coal in place of wood to heat their houses; the new iron supply was turned into pots, grates, knives, pins, and other domestic articles. England in the 1640's produced 1/250 as much coal as the United States in the 1950's, and 1/2500 as much iron and steel. The English did not yet produce enough coal and iron to substitute coal-powered, iron machinery for handicraft manufacturing—as they would start doing in the cotton mills of the late eighteenth century.

Whether or not England experienced an industrial revolution in the seventeenth century, continental Europe certainly did not. The overall

---

[4]John U. Nef, *War and Human Progress* (Cambridge, Mass., 1950), pp. 10, 35, 80–81, 291.

European output of iron and steel remained pretty steadily at the low figure of 150,000 tons a year from the 1530's into the early eighteenth century. While English production was rising during these years, iron and steel production in Germany, Bohemia, and Hungary was declining. War is supposed to stimulate heavy industry, but the wars of religion probably had the opposite effect. They disrupted mining and metalworking more than they encouraged new enterprises. Weapons were still simple enough to be largely handmade. The muskets and cannon which Gustavus Adolphus used in the Thirty Years' War were manufactured in Swedish state factories, but the gunpowder was made in peasants' cottages.

Transportation improved somewhat, facilitating the distribution of market commodities from one European region to another. Horse-drawn carriages and wagons were equipped for the first time with spoked wheels and springs, which greatly eased overland travel and transport. The pony-express postal couriers of the elector of Brandenburg carried mail the six hundred miles from Königsberg to Cleve in only a week. But the narrow, rutted, muddy roads hindered the overland conveyance of bulk cargo, as did the prevalence of highwaymen and toll collectors. It was calculated in 1675 that coal could be shipped three hundred miles by water as cheaply as fifteen miles by road. Merchant ships were not much bigger or faster in 1715 than in 1559, but there were many more of them. The cheaply built, easily handled Dutch *flute*, or flyboat, was particularly well designed for carrying awkward cargoes like coal, timber, salt, or grain. Thus seaports and riverports received goods from many parts of the world, while interior villages still had to be nearly self-sufficient. The peasant who depended upon country fairs and itinerant peddlars to supply his wants had to have modest tastes indeed.

By and large, the seventeenth-century economy suffered from chronic problems of underproduction, as our own economy now suffers from chronic problems of overproduction. Almost the entire seventeenth-century labor force was tied up in inefficient manual labor, required to provide the bare necessities of life—food, clothing, shelter. Seven or eight out of every ten members of the labor force were agricultural workers, yet the people of seventeenth-century Europe were none too well fed or dressed. Now, less than one out of ten members of the late twentieth-century American labor force is an agricultural or textile worker, yet our farms and mills glut the market. Of the 450 occupational categories listed by the United States Bureau of the Census in 1970, at least two hundred (mostly of the white-collar type) did not exist in any form three hundred years ago. A seventeenth-century entrepreneur would hardly believe that in our mechanized society almost as many laborers are engaged in transportation as in agriculture.[5] Or that we have to create consumer "wants" by sales and advertising, and persuade customers to discard merchandise long before it wears

[5]U.S. Bureau of the Census, *Historical Statistics of the United States, Colonial Times to 1970* (Washington, D.C., 1975), pp. 127, 140–145, 467, 670–671, 709.

out. The seventeenth-century bourgeois virtues of thrift, abstinence, and restraint have become vices in our era of built-in obsolescence.

DUTCH COMMERCIAL CAPITALISM

The Dutch were the most enterprising businessmen in seventeenth-century Europe. Their success did not stem from their superiority in agricultural and industrial production, though they were indeed good farmers and skilled manufacturers. Primarily, they were middlemen: they bought, sold, and carried other people's products. They bought great quantities of spices, tea, china, and cotton in Asia, and of sugar, tobacco, and furs in America. They bought even greater quantities of lumber, grain, cattle, and copper in northern Europe, and of wool, wine, silk, and silver in southern Europe. With their ample fleet of merchant ships, the Dutch transported all these commodities to Amsterdam and other Dutch towns, and sold them to the buyers from all over Europe who congregated there. Whenever possible, they enhanced their profits as middlemen by converting the raw materials they imported into finished goods. The Dutch textile mills, dyehouses, breweries, distilleries, tanneries, sugar and salt refineries, tobacco-cutting factories, and soap works all depended on imported materials. By gearing

The Dutch East India Company warehouse and timber wharf in Amsterdam. *This engraving by Muider shows a company ship under construction, and lumber stockpiled for future shipbuilding.*

their whole society to foreign trade, the Dutch overcame their lack of natural resources, manpower, and military strength. As Dutch prosperity proved, the merchant middleman was the prime catalyst in the seventeenth-century economy.

The rise of Dutch commercial capitalism is a remarkable story. When the Netherlanders began their revolt against Philip II in the 1560's, the northern provinces (the future Dutch republic) were decidedly less prosperous than the southern provinces. Amsterdam stood far behind Antwerp as a commercial entrepôt. But the inhabitants of Holland and Zeeland, the two northern provinces bordering on the North Sea, had long been seafaring folk and possessed many ships of all sizes. They already dominated the North Sea fisheries and the Baltic grain and timber trade. Once the "sea beggars" had captured ports in Holland and Zeeland in 1572, the Dutch could ward off the Spanish army by opening the dikes when necessary; and they could outsail the Spanish fleet and plunder the Spanish merchant marine. All through the years between the Dutch declaration of independence in 1581 and the final peace settlement with Spain in 1648, Dutch commerce boomed. Dutch merchants aggressively developed old avenues of trade and opened new ones. Despite the war, they kept on buying Spanish wool and selling grain to the Spaniards. They even sold military stores to the Spanish army! They capitalized on Portugal's weakness during the Portuguese union with Spain (1580–1640) by seizing the most valuable Portuguese colonies and trading posts. When the duke of Parma captured Antwerp in 1585, Amsterdam quickly replaced that city as Europe's greatest shipping center, commodity market, and financial exchange. The Dutch insisted on blockading the mouth of the Scheldt River, Antwerp's entrance to the North Sea, to guarantee that Antwerp could never regain her old commercial primacy.

The Dutch republic in the mid-seventeenth century was very small, with an area about the size of the state of Maryland and a population of two million. The eighty-year war with Spain had not caused any appreciable modernization of its particularistic political structure. The seven sovereign provinces—Holland, Zeeland, Utrecht, Gelderland, Groningen, Overyssel, and Friesland—continued to cherish their separate identities. Cynics called them the Disunited Provinces. Wealthy, crowded, cosmopolitan Holland had few economic, social, or cultural bonds with backwater, feudal, cattle-raising Gelderland. The central government, such as it was, functioned by means of negotiations among the seven autonomous provinces. Each province sent ambassadors to The Hague to meet in the States-General, a body which rarely acted energetically because its decisions required the consent of all seven constituencies. But in a crisis the other six provinces deferred to Holland, since the Hollanders contributed over half the union's financial support. Political control in Holland was vested in the merchant oligarchs who ruled Amsterdam and the other towns. There was no central executive in the Dutch republic, though William the Silent's house of Orange developed some of the attributes of a ruling dynasty. The prince of Orange was normally the commander of the federal army and navy, and *stadholder*, or chief administrator, in five of the seven provinces. The Dutch federation looked fragile and impractical—but it worked. Dutch politics became a tug of war between the house of Orange and the merchant oligarchs in Holland. Except in times of acute military emergency, the merchant oligarchs prevailed. They wanted international peace, which would facilitate the development of Dutch trade throughout the world.

Seventeenth-century Dutch commercial capitalism produced no individual titans to compare with Jacques Coeur, Cosimo de Medici, or Jakob Fugger. Nevertheless, by pooling their resources the Dutch merchants were able to undertake ventures which would have been too expensive and risky for the solitary giants of the past. Great numbers of investors, big and small, organized themselves into companies chartered by the state, in order to tackle large commercial projects. The grandest of these companies, the Dutch East India Company, was founded in 1602 with an initial capital of 6,500,000 florins. It was a joint-stock enterprise; hundreds of investors from all over the Dutch republic pooled their money to give the company working capital. The seventeen directors who operated the East India Company were drawn from among the biggest shareholders, but the small shareholders had little to complain about. The pepper, cloves, and nutmeg which the company brought to Amsterdam netted an average annual dividend of 18 per cent.

By the mid-seventeenth century, the Dutch had created a worldwide empire which differed in every way from the Spanish empire. It was a trading network owned and operated by private enterprise, with minimal government supervision. Two joint-stock companies, the East India Company and the West India Company (founded in 1621), divided the globe between them. Each of these companies had sovereign authority to possess and govern overseas territory, to negotiate treaties, and to wage war. The East India Company was the more important. In the early seventeenth century the company's soldiers and sailors drove the Portuguese out of the spice islands, the Malay Archipelago, and Ceylon, and kept the English from moving into these places. The Dutch thus secured virtually complete control over Sumatran pepper, Ceylonese cinnamon, and Moluccan nutmeg, mace, and cloves. The company also maintained a post on an island off Nagasaki, where the suspicious Japanese government gave the Dutch a monopoly on all European trade with Japan. The company shipped home tea and porcelain from its Chinese trading posts, cotton from its Indian trading posts, silk from Persia, and coffee from Arabia. In 1652 the company established a way station at the Cape of Good Hope to break the long sea voyage between Amsterdam and Asia. The Dutch West India Company, operating in the western hemisphere, had less success because other European states were too well entrenched there. It could not capture any major Spanish colonies, and in the 1640's and 1650's the Portuguese reconquered Brazil and Angola from the Dutch. In North America, the Dutch never got much profit out of their fur-trading posts at Manhattan and Albany, and lost them to the English in 1664. However, the West India Company did get good returns from the lucrative African slave trade, and its island outposts of Curaçao and St. Eustatius proved to be useful bases for raiding and trading in the Caribbean.

The East India and West India companies were dazzling symbols of Dutch commercial capitalism, but they were actually less vital to the Dutch economy than the North Sea fishing industry and the western European carrying trade. The fisheries employed several hundred thousand Dutchmen. Many workers were needed to build, equip, and repair the fishing smacks. Others manned the North Sea fleets which fished for herring, haddock, and cod. Others manned the Arctic whaling fleets. Others pickled, smoked, and barreled the catch for export. Still others fetched from Portugal and France the salt needed to cure the herring, and from Norway the timber needed in constructing the ships and the barrels. Despite the fact that they had to import all their lumber, the Dutch built a great fleet of merchant ships. Contemporaries guessed that the Dutch possessed sixteen thousand merchant vessels in the mid-seventeenth century, something like half the European total. Danish toll records indicate that two thirds of the ships which entered the Baltic Sea during this period were Dutch. At times there were more Dutch than Spanish ships off Spanish America, and more Dutch than English ships off English America. In 1619, the first cargo of Negro slaves to Virginia was carried in a Dutch ship. This carrying fleet enabled the Dutch to collect middleman profits on nearly every branch of waterborne commerce, and caused Amsterdam to develop into the busiest trading center in Europe.

During the century following the outbreak of the Dutch revolt in 1566, the population of Amsterdam climbed from 30,000 to 200,000. The harbor was shallow and inconveniently inland from the North Sea, but the city was the most northerly and the most defensible of the Dutch ports, and was therefore safe from the Spanish. Amsterdam lay athwart the Baltic Sea, Rhine River, and English Channel shipping routes. Nobody but nobody could undersell the Amsterdam merchants because they dealt in volume. They would sail a fleet of flyboats into the Baltic laden with herring (which Dutch fishermen had caught off the English coast) and return with all of the grain surplus from a Danish island, or with twenty thousand head of lean cattle to be fattened in the Holland polders. They would buy a standing forest in Norway for timber, or contract before the grapes were harvested for the vintage of a whole French district. They would buy shiploads of undyed cloth, crude Barbados sugar, and Virginia leaf in England; have the cloth dyed, the sugar refined, and the tobacco cut and wrapped by Amsterdam craftsmen; and sell the finished commodities all over northern Europe at prices the English could not match. Foreign merchants found it worth their time to shop in Amsterdam because there they could buy anything from a precision lens to muskets for an army of five thousand. The exchange bank

Amsterdam harbor in 1663. *Engraving by Dapper, showing dozens of merchant ships moored outside the city because the interior docks are jammed to capacity. Note the church steeples and windmills silhouetted against the flat Holland countryside. Scheepvart Museum, Amsterdam.*

eased credit; marine insurance policies safeguarded transport. And no merchant could feel a stranger in a city where the presses printed books in every European tongue, and the French- and English-language newspapers were more lively and informative than the gazettes printed back home.

The Dutch republic was a Calvinist state, but John Calvin would not have felt at home in mid-seventeenth-century Amsterdam. The great Dutch merchants did not permit the Dutch Reformed clergy to interfere in politics or business. Catholics, Anabaptists, Jews, and unbelievers were tolerated in Amsterdam. The religious zeal which had stirred the Dutch into rebellion against Philip II, and nerved them into continuing the fight in the 1580's when all seemed hopeless, had turned into a secular zeal for making money. Indeed, the Dutch had lost more of their mid-sixteenth-century crusading impetus than had their old adversaries, the Spaniards. This loss of Dutch religious zeal is particularly evident if one compares seventeenth-century Dutch and Spanish mission work among the heathen overseas. Thousands of Spanish priests and monks proselytized vigorously in the Philippines, India, Siam, and China, and maintained an elaborate network of Catholic churches, schools, seminaries, and universities. The Dutch East India Company sent a good many Calvinist ministers and schoolteachers into Asia, but their missionary efforts were singularly feeble. "Nay," lamented a Dutch Calvinist in 1683, "while the Jesuits and other locusts of the whore of Babylon apply so patiently their blind zeal to promote the Kingdom of Darkness, we do so little to make the Kingdom of Mercy come!"[6]

[6]Quoted by Peter Geyl, *The Netherlands in the Seventeenth Century* (London, 1961–1964), Vol. II, p. 188.

The moneymaking ethos was certainly more pervasive and powerful in Amsterdam than it had been in such earlier capitalist centers as Florence, Venice, Augsburg, and Antwerp. We should not, however, exaggerate the modernity of seventeenth-century Dutch commercial enterprise. Amsterdam's business structure—its bank, exchange, insurance companies, and joint-stock companies—was based on sixteenth-century models. The characteristic Amsterdam business firm continued to be a simple partnership. The Dutch joint-stock companies resembled medieval guilds in their protectionist policies. The East India Company had a monopoly on the eastern trade and forbade any Dutch merchant not a shareholder from trading in the spice islands. The company did more than just resist external competition; it deliberately destroyed some of its own Sumatran pepper plantations and Molucca nutmeg cargoes in order to keep the supply limited and the price high. Furthermore, Dutch commercial prosperity was strictly limited to the upper and middle classes. The paintings of Jan Vermeer and Pieter de Hooch, with their scenes of well-fed, well-dressed burghers living in spotlessly clean, comfortably furnished brick houses, illustrate only one side of seventeenth-century Dutch life. Half the inhabitants of Amsterdam lived under slum conditions, in squalid shanties or cellars. The Dutch wage laborer worked twelve to fourteen hours a day when he was lucky enough to have a job and subsisted on a diet of beans, peas, and rye bread. For all their enterprise, not even the Dutch could achieve an economy of abundance in the seventeenth century.

PROPERTY AND PRIVILEGE

Europe's relatively low productivity during the sixteenth and seventeenth centuries helped keep its social structure sharply stratified. Class lines were formalized to an extent hard for us to credit. While there was more social mobility than in the Middle Ages, people were no less self-conscious about their proper station in life. Every rank in the social order, from princes and aristocrats at the top to serfs and beggars at the bottom, had its own distinct style of dress, diet, habitation, and entertainment; its own training, customs, and mental attitudes. The value systems of the aristocrat, the bourgeois, and the peasant differed profoundly. A person's vocabulary and accent, even his physical posture, instantly identified his social station, which helps explain why it was still exceptional for anyone born into a given rank (especially at the bottom or top of the scale) to climb up or down. Hierarchy was considered a measure of civilization. Social gradations might be rough and ready in frontier areas, such as Ireland, Sweden, Russia, and America, but in France, the center of civility, they were elaborated to the fullest extent. Ulysses' oft-quoted soliloquy in Shakespeare's *Troilus and Cressida* perfectly expresses the prevailing contemporary belief that social hierarchy preserves political order and economic well-being.

The heavens themselves, the planets, and this centre,
Observe degree, priority, and place,
Insisture, course, proportion, season, form,
Office, and custom, in all line of order: . . .
Take but degree away, untune that string,
And, hark, what discord follows! . . .
Then every thing includes itself in power,
Power into will, will into appetite;
And appetite, an universal wolf,
So doubly seconded with will and power,
Must make perforce an universal prey,
And last eat up himself.

A nobleman's kitchen and a peasant's kitchen. *For the aristocratic diners (top), a squadron of liveried servants and cooks assembles a multicourse feast. For the scrawny peasants (bottom), there is nothing to eat except bread and vegetables.*

Shakespeare evidently expected the growing spirit of capitalism to dissolve traditional hierarchical patterns, but in some ways it intensified them. To be sure, men of talent and enterprise now had a better chance to improve themselves. But the economic disparities between the upper, middle, and lower classes grew sharper. Had Europeans during the sixteenth and seventeenth centuries experienced an economy of abundance and of mechanized production, such as our own, no doubt the expectations of the very poor would have been leveled up and the tastes of the very rich leveled down. But an economy based on hand production and offering only limited wealth had a contrary psychological effect. For the people at the top of the social scale, the increase in wealth and income made possible an extravagant style of life undreamed of by medieval kings and lords. Luxury and waste became the necessary badges of high social status. The people at the bottom of the scale, on the other hand, remained as poorly off as they had been for centuries, prevented (by the economy's chronic underproduction) from achieving any improvement in their standard of living. In short, Europe in the era of the religious wars was divided as never before "haves" and "have nots"— the rich and middle classes, with their total monopoly on wealth and comfort, and the servile classes who knew that they would never have anything beyond bare subsistence.

This psychological division between "haves" and "have nots" is well illustrated by a survey of English society drawn up in 1696 by an ingenious statistician named Gregory King. Using figures obtained through personal observation during extensive tours of the country, and through his analysis of tax returns and of birth, death, and marriage records, King calculated that England's total population was 5.5 million, a guess which modern demographers support. The interesting thing is the way King divided the people included in this total into two categories: 2.7 million were persons "increasing the wealth of the kingdom," and 2.8 million were persons "decreasing the wealth of the kingdom." His first category included everyone who held some stake in society—land, office, or a profession or craft. Among these were the aristocracy, country gentlemen, royal officials, merchants, military officers, lawyers, teachers, clergymen, shopkeepers, artisans, and farmers. All of these occupational groups, according to Gregory King, had some share in the country's surplus wealth. Obviously, a noble lord with ten thousand acres had a far greater share than a yeoman with fifty acres, but even the artisan or small farmer produced more than enough from his labor to support a family. For the great majority of persons in this category, land was the chief and most valued form of property. The 2.8 million persons in King's second category formed the unpropertied, submerged half of the population, having no share in the country's wealth. Among these "have nots" were agricultural wage laborers, domestic servants, soldiers, sailors, paupers, and vagabonds. Notice the remarkably low standing of seventeenth-century soldiers and sailors, recruited from the dregs of society.

In King's opinion, the wage laborers were almost as great a drain on the economy as the paupers. Their wages ate into the wealth of the kingdom, and since they generally earned too little to cover necessary living expenses, they had to be partially subsidized by public charity. The wage laborers could scarcely afford to marry. King calculated that they produced one or two fewer children per capita than their social superiors in the first category.[7] Property owners felt little compassion for the oppressed workers, better known as "the poor," because their plight seemed irremediable. There was simply not enough wealth to go around. Thus half the people in England were categorized as a necessary evil at best. If this was the situation in relatively affluent England, the psychological division was certainly even sharper east of the Elbe, where a small landlord class enjoyed all the surplus wealth and an immense servile class was excluded from possession of any property or comfort.

A society which labeled half or more of the population as hapless and burdensome was hardly geared for social or political democracy. Everywhere in Europe the property-owning upper classes had a monopoly on political participation as well as on wealth and comfort. Even words like "liberty" and "freedom" had much less egalitarian connotations than they do today. "Liberty" in the sixteenth and seventeenth centuries referred to the enjoyment of special advantages not open to other men. For example, in Venice a closed circle of two thousand noblemen possessed the liberty of governing their state: they had an oligarchic monopoly on administration which prevented the Venetian middle and lower classes from choosing their legislators or holding office. When the Dutch burghers defended their ancient liberties against Philip II, they were not proclaiming the birthright of all Dutchmen to govern themselves, but rather protecting the vested interests of a privileged caste. Likewise, "freedom" meant exemption from restrictions which unprivileged persons had to observe. A cobbler's apprentice who served out his indentures for seven years obtained the freedom of his craft: he could now make shoes for his own profit instead of laboring for his master without pay. He was initiated into a privileged group with a monopoly on shoemaking, for no cobbler was allowed to set up shop without having first served his apprenticeship and won his freedom. Thus "liberty" and "freedom," far from conveying the modern notion of the right of all men to act as they see fit, were both expressions referring to special privileges. Property and privilege went hand in hand. The "haves" and "have nots" are perhaps better defined as the "privileged" and the "unprivileged" classes. There is no social concept today equivalent to "*un*privileged." The term "*under*privileged" is quite different, for we define underprivileged persons as those members of society who have been denied economic, social, or political rights properly belonging to all men. The *un*privileged members of seventeenth-century society could claim no such rights.

To keep the unprivileged classes in their place, every government employed repressive measures. Beggars were whipped and pilloried. Since long

---

[7]Gregory King's tabulations are conveniently reproduced in Charles Wilson, *England's Apprenticeship, 1603–1763* (London, 1965), p. 239.

Whipping a vagrant. *Bystanders watch as a wandering beggar is expelled from town. This vagrant, flogged through the streets and ordered on to the next town, is at least luckier than the malefactor being cut down from the gallows outside the town gate.*

imprisonment was too expensive, convicted criminals were either summarily executed or maimed—the tongue bored, the nose slashed, the cheeks branded, a hand or foot lopped off—and then released. In England, convicts were sometimes transported to the colonies. In France they were put to forced labor in the royal galleys. Crimes against property were punished as savagely as crimes against persons. The most trifling theft might bring a penalty of death. Public executions rivaled bearbaiting and cockfighting as popular spectacles. The authorities customarily exhibited the decaying heads of executed criminals on pikes over bridges and gateways as a grim warning to would-be malefactors. One seventeenth-century traveler counted some 150 rotting carcasses of robbers and murderers swinging from gibbets along the highway between Dresden and Prague. Despite this harsh criminal code, in the absence of police forces most crimes went unpunished. But by quartering troops in the large towns, governments could at least overawe the mobs and keep rudimentary order. It is striking to see, in an overcrowded city like seventeenth-century Paris, how much space was allocated to military display: massive forts, such as the Bastille; huge army barracks and hospitals, such as the Invalides; and suburban parade grounds, such as the Champ de Mars. Even more striking is the space consumed by royal palaces and aristocratic pleasure gardens. In Paris, the connecting Louvre and Tuileries palaces opened onto a mile-long garden bordering the Seine, designed for the use of the court nobility, and in addition, during the seventeenth century two more palaces were built within the city—the Palais du Luxembourg and the Palais-Royal, both surrounded by extensive formal gardens where a privileged few could take the air.

Hanging Thieves. *Painting by Callot. This grim scene illustrates seventeenth-century techniques of criminal justice: troops stand guard and priests shrive hastily, as two dozen condemned men are executed at once.*

It is against this background of domestic stratification, exploitation, and repression that one must assess the institution of chattel slavery in Europe's overseas colonies. In the sixteenth and seventeenth centuries, Europeans enslaved millions of Negroes and Indians. Whenever any European—whether Portuguese, Spanish, Dutch, English, or French—first came into contact with African Negroes, Indonesians, or American Indians, he instinctively and automatically ranked these people several notches lower in the social order than the unprivileged servile classes at home. The reasons are obvious. These dark-skinned peoples lacked both the Christian culture which Europeans considered essential for salvation, and the technology to resist European mastery. When even the Turks were scorned as infidels despite their military prowess and political organization, it is small wonder that Cortes and Pizarro failed to appreciate the cultural attainments of the Aztecs and Incas whom they conquered with absurd ease. A few stay-at-home savants like Sir Thomas More might picture the New World as Utopia, or like Michel de Montaigne, suggest that cultural differences between the New World and the Old were only relative. Who are we, Montaigne asked in the 1570's, in the midst of the French religious wars, to judge the cannibals of Brazil? But the rough and energetic adventurers who staked out claims to America and trafficked with Asia and Africa felt no such inhibitions. To them, the native peoples were all barbarians, to be Christianized if possible, handled like vermin when necessary, and put to work for their white masters.

As early as 1443 the Portuguese were sending home African slaves. In 1493 Columbus brought back to Spain some Arawak Indian slaves. But slave labor was needed in America, not in Europe. In the first decades of the sixteenth century the Spaniards required unskilled manpower for their West Indian mines and plantations, the sort of brute labor done by the unprivileged classes at home, which the *conquistadores* refused to undertake themselves. They soon discovered that West Indians made very poor slaves. Forced labor killed off the gentle Arawaks, and the fierce Caribs were untrainable. The problem was solved by importing from the Guinea coast Negroes inured to hard work in tropical conditions. In 1511 the first recorded slave ship to reach Spanish America sold her black cargo, unwilling pioneers in an epic folk migration.

One estimate is that 240,000 African slaves were shipped to America during the sixteenth century, and 1.3 million during the seventeenth century.[8] However inaccurate such figures may be, there can be no doubt that many more Africans than Europeans came to America in these years. Though the slave trade did not reach its peak until the eighteenth and early nineteenth centuries, it was already a roaring business in the seventeenth— highly dangerous, brutalizing, and lucrative to the slaver. The slave traders exploited and encouraged the endless political anarchy within West Africa. Hundreds of small tribes incessantly warred against one another, and any chieftain who could put together a string of prisoners eagerly sold them to the white man in return for firearms and trinkets. The trade was dominated by the Portuguese throughout the sixteenth century, by the Dutch in the mid-seventeenth century, and by the English in the later seventeenth century, but the French, Spanish, Swedish, Danish, and Germans were active also. A big problem for any slaver was how to transport his captives economically without losing too many of them. Packed like sardines into small, stinking ships, chained to the decks without air or exercise, many Negroes died before they could be sold in America. Records of the Royal African Company in England show that in the 1680's, when the slaver could buy Negroes for £3 apiece on the Guinea coast, 23 per cent of the slaves died during the Atlantic crossing. But by the early eighteenth century, when the initial investment in an African captive had climbed to £10, mortality during the crossing dropped to 10 per cent.[9] The slaver handled his cargo like any perishable produce, calculating to a nicety the ratio between cost per item and tolerable spoilage.

To some extent the lot of the American slave depended on his master's nationality, but geographical location—whether he lived on the mainland or in the islands—was really more important. Slaves in Portuguese Brazil and in the Spanish colonies had roughly the same status as serfs in eastern Europe. The Spaniards and Portuguese were accustomed to holding Moors and Jews in slavery, and accorded the African a position equivalent to that held by their other slaves. They recognized him as a moral person, insisted on his active membership in the Catholic Church, and gave him legal protection against his master's mistreatment. Brazilian slaves, in particular, could earn wages and buy their freedom. However, Brazilian slaves also

---

[8] Philip D. Curtin, *The Atlantic Slave Trade* (Madison, Wis., 1969), pp. 116, 119, 268.

[9] K. G. Davies, *The Royal African Company* (London, 1957), pp. 292–293.

died in epic numbers from disease and ill use. For the English in America, slaveholding was a novelty. Suddenly confronted with a large force of exotic, restive, and menacing black laborers, they developed repressive law codes which froze the Negroes permanently into a subhuman category as chattel slaves without moral or legal standing or hope of manumission. English-style slavery created an agonizing psychological distinction between black and white. Furthermore, the English Protestant clergy made little effort to convert or instruct the Negroes lest they stir up notions of egalitarianism and rebellion. In most practical respects, however, slaves in an English mainland colony like Virginia fared better than slaves in Brazil. They worked less hard, ate better, lived longer, formed families, and multiplied at roughly the same rate as their white masters. For slaves in the English Caribbean sugar colonies, the picture was far different. On these overcrowded little islands, the slaves were fed so skimpily and worked so hard that their death rate far exceeded their birthrate. On one Barbados plantation for which we have records, six Negroes died for every one born. The managers of this plantation reckoned that it was cheaper and more efficient to restock regularly with fresh slaves from Africa than to raise living standards to the point where the existing slave population would maintain itself. Horses and cattle were managed on a different principle, receiving enough care to keep them healthy and fertile.

In recounting the establishment of Negro slavery it is hard to refrain from moralizing. But we must remember that an unprivileged, servile class seemed as necessary then as refrigerators and washing machines do today. When sixteenth- and seventeenth-century writers envisioned the ideal society, they found room in it for slaves and servants. Sir Thomas More's *Utopia* (1516) depicts an economically egalitarian, communistic society with a class of bondsmen to do the dirty work. Francis Bacon's *New Atlantis* (1627) portrays a cooperative community of research scientists and technologists, well served by flunkies. Some social critics, notably the Spanish priest Bartolomé de Las Casas (1474–1566), protested strenuously and successfully against the enslavement of American Indians. But almost no one (including Quakers who visited the sugar islands) protested openly against the enslavement of African Negroes. The serfdom east of the Elbe and the slavery in America were ugly but natural by-products of Europe's strenuous search for wealth in an era of primitive productive techniques.

WOMEN AND WITCHCRAFT

When the French political theorist Jean Bodin laid out the principles of social order in his *Six Books of the Republic* (1576), he was one of the few to criticize the Spanish and Portuguese sharply for their enslavement of Negroes and Indians in America. In Bodin's view, slavery endangers order, for the slave will always try to rebel and regain his freedom. On the

Struggle for the breeches. *This French engraving of 1690 satirizes bossy women who dare to challenge male rule.*

other hand, Bodin insisted that the male half of the population must control the female half. Any tendency toward female egalitarianism is highly dangerous, for man is rational and woman emotional, and reason must rule affection. Bodin concedes that a family, the basic social unit, has to have a wife/mother. But the husband must have authoritative power over his wife, and the father authoritative power over his children. Hence when a man marries, he transfers his bride from her father's family into his; he takes over her property; he prohibits her from any independent public action. Bodin dislikes wife-beating, but he says that the husband should chastise his wife freely for her domestic faults. The Romans, he notes approvingly, permitted a husband to kill his wife without public trial for the crime of drinking wine.[10] Liquor releases the female's disordered desires, and tempts her into adultery, which Bodin seems to find the most heinous of all social acts. The adulteress perverts love into lust, ruins the family, and subverts order.

Here is the traditional male view of the eternal Eve—man's necessary companion, a useful person when kept in her place, yet always weak,

[10]Jean Bodin, *The Six Bookes of a Commonweale* (London, 1606), pp. 9, 14–20, 38, 44.

tempted and tempting. It will be noted that Bodin—like Shakespeare—was intent on preserving social degree, priority, and place. In fact, the role of women in European society changed markedly during his lifetime. Women had new political prominence. They had new economic functions. They had new religious choices. And they were alarmingly exposed to new social predicaments.

In politics, female prominence turned out to be transitory. The remarkable queens of the late sixteenth century—Elizabeth I, Mary, Queen of Scots, and Catherine de Medici—were followed by female rulers of much less talent and vigor. Queen Mother Marie de Medici in France, Queen Mary II and Queen Anne in England, and Queen Christina in Sweden were the chief public actresses between 1603 and 1714, and they played modest roles. Royal mistresses, such as Louis XIV's Madame de Maintenon, could exercise considerable behind-the-scenes power, but no one advocated appointive or elective offices for women. The Levellers, who campaigned ardently for political democracy during the Puritan Revolution in England, were conspicuously silent about the female suffrage. Politics remained very definitely a man's game.

In the economic sphere, female role changes were more far-reaching and long-lasting. Broadly speaking, women during the sixteenth and seventeenth centuries performed more sex-segregated jobs than in the past. They spent less time working with the men in the fields or at cottage looms, and more time working with other females as domestic servants and housewives. Women had always done the cooking and washing, but these tasks became more complex and labor-consuming as the standard of living rose for those in the upper and middle ranks of the social order. Architectural changes during our period made the domestic residence more attractive, comfortable, and important to its occupants. In England, for example, the "housing revolution," or "great rebuilding," that took place between 1575 and 1690 affected all social classes. The nobility built palatial country houses and London mansions. The gentry built or remodeled their manor houses, the yeomen their farmhouses, the artisans their town houses. They replaced timber, thatch, and dirt with brick, stone, and tile. They added new rooms, new stories, new staircases, fireplaces, and windows. They made their houses more comfortable by bringing in additional furniture.

Obviously a nobleman required a large staff of liveried servants to operate his new great house. But the ordinary yeoman farmer also needed more domestic labor than in the past. Before the sixteenth century, the typical English farmhouse was a very simple structure, often one large all-purpose room with an open hearth where the family cooked, ate, slept, and entertained. When remodeled by the Tudor farmer, this house was divided into rooms with special functions: bedchambers upstairs, a kitchen and parlor downstairs. It was still small, but it absorbed a lot of labor, especially as standards of housewifery improved. To cook, wash, spin, sew, and clean for her household, the yeoman's wife needed the help of her daughters, or a servant girl. The English housing revolution did not penetrate far into the propertyless lower half of society; farm laborers still lived in primitive little one-room cottages. But females from this sector of society were increasingly drawn out of field labor and into domestic drudgery. Adolescent girls from the middling classes worked for their mothers, or took jobs as servants in other households, until they married.

With this new domesticity, women had pleasanter work and more sharply defined responsibilities—especially as the trainers of young children —but at a significant cost. They were changing from basic producers into service laborers, and in an increasingly capitalistic society their new jobs often yielded no income. More than before, "women's work" was work that men could not and would not do, and that men deemed to be marginal. It also appears that women, despite high mortality during the child-bearing years, were more likely than men to live beyond the age of productive labor, into their sixties, seventies, and eighties. The village

The aristocratic lady and the country woman. *These charming engravings by Wenceslaus Hollar show the functional range in female dress, c. 1640. The country woman's cap, thick dress, and clogs protect her from dirt and enable her to work in rain, cold, and mud. The lady's ornate costume makes any physical activity whatsoever impossible.*

censuses show more widows than widowers. And as population pressure brought rising rates of unemployment, poverty, and crime, and the costs of poor relief increased, people complained about the socially superfluous, and they noticed the numerous old women in every community. It is in the sixteenth century that there emerges the stereotype of the village widow: elderly, impoverished, unemployable, lonely, and highly vulnerable.

Nor was this all. For women of all ages and most ranks, the Protestant-Catholic confessional conflict opened up promising new sex roles and challenged valuable old ones. Women who converted to Protestantism, who experienced Luther's spiritual regeneration through God-given grace, achieved a gratifying new sense of equality with male believers. Though female literacy was generally very low, Protestant women learned to read in order to study the Bible. Though female activism was exceedingly rare, Protestant women stood up conspicuously for their faith. A quarter of the Huguenots arrested at a Paris demonstration in 1557 were women. More than fifty of the 282 Protestant martyrs who were burned at the stake in England during the 1550's were women. Protestant churches often attracted more female than male members. In the radical sects, women held office, prophesied, and preached. The Quakers, the most radical of the new seventeenth-century sects, practiced sexual equality, and in the early days of Quakerism the women were just as active as the men.

But it must be stressed that the clergy in the main-line Protestant churches—Lutheran, Calvinist, and Anglican—were deeply suspicious of female activism. They held that Protestant women had only one acceptable vocation—that of dutiful wife/mother—for as St. Paul explained (1 Cor. 14:34–35), women should keep silence in the churches, and if they desired to know anything they should ask their husbands at home. It is also worth remembering that a woman who remained Catholic had career options and spiritual models unavailable to Protestants. She could undertake a lifelong religious vocation as a nun. She could imitate the holy lives of the saints, female as well as male. She could venerate the Virgin Mary —unlike Protestants, who prayed only to the Father and the Son. A Geneva nun named Jeanne de Jussie recorded her bitterness in the 1530's when a Protestant ex-abbess came to the convent and urged the sisters to escape as she had and marry handsome husbands. Sister Jeanne says she spat on this lady, for in her view Protestant holy marriage was no new freedom but an old domestic tyranny, the rule of husbands over wives.

It is against this background that we must consider the role of women in the great witchcraft hysteria, which lasted for about a century, from the 1560's to the 1660's. Belief in witchcraft is of course a widespread phenomenon, but systematic prosecution of witches is much rarer. In the Middle Ages and the Renaissance, there were learned sorcerers and village cunning folk. Religious deviants—heretics—were accused of Devil-worship.

Yet relatively few people were brought to trial as witches. Even during the first half of the sixteenth century, though Luther and Calvin on the Protestant side and the Spanish and Italian inquisitors on the Catholic side all condemned black magic and hunted down Devil-worshipers, witch trials remained relatively infrequent. Then in the 1560's the tempo picked up. Because the surviving records are very incomplete, we can only guess at the number of so-called witches tried, and burned or hanged, in our period. Possibly as many as a hundred thousand witch trials took place. We know that witch-hunts were organized from Spain to Poland under both Catholic and Protestant auspices. In southwestern Germany alone, 3,229 witches are known to have been executed between 1561 and 1670. In the Swiss canton of Vaud, 3,371 were executed between 1591 and 1680. These were areas where mass trials were staged, with heavy use of torture and high rates of conviction. In England, on the other hand, witch suspects were tried individually, they were not tortured, and most of them escaped execution.

In one crucial respect witch trials everywhere followed the same pattern. The accused were overwhelmingly female. In Castile, 71 per cent were women; in Geneva, 76 per cent; in Venice, 78 per cent; in Finland, 78 per cent; in Germany, 82 per cent; in England, 92 per cent.[11] Why was witch-hunting so extensive in the late sixteenth and early seventeenth centuries? And why were so many of the witches female?

No single explanation seems to be sufficient. The most obvious factor is the intense religious reawakening of the sixteenth century. Protestants and Catholics alike believed very actively in the prevalence of human sin, and believed that the Devil intervened in human affairs (Catholics thought he backed the Protestants, and vice versa). They supposed that evildoers could enter into compact with the Devil and receive supernatural power, enabling them to practice black magic and perform secret crimes. Sin, heresy, magic, and demonology were all conflated into witchcraft, which had to be rooted out. But this is only part of the picture. It must be remembered that the society was without protection against famine, plague, poverty, and crime. Sixteenth-century science could neither explain, predict, nor control the weather. Sixteenth-century medicine was unable to diagnose or cure most illnesses. Hence there was an intense craving for supernatural explanations and cures, and when the Reformation called into doubt the miraculous comforts of the traditional Christian church, people turned more readily to astrologers and cunning folk for help in their troubles. Correspondingly, when personal disaster suddenly struck, people were inclined to suspect that black magicians must be at work against them. But this too is only part of the picture. Examination of the witch

[11]E. William Monter, *Witchcraft in France and Switzerland* (Ithaca, N.Y., 1976), p. 119.

trials shows that accusers and accused generally knew each other well. They were neighbors who had quarreled. Often the trouble started when someone begged for food. In France and Switzerland, beggars who were denied charity were likely to accuse their ungenerous neighbors of witch-craft. In England, where begging seems to have been more frowned upon, it worked the other way round: beggars rejected by their neighbors were blamed for local calamities and charged with witchcraft. In both cases, the witch trials show that there was a breakdown in neighborly relations when people were desperately poor and hungry.

While witchcraft could be practised by both sexes, women were more likely targets for suspicion than men, for several reasons. First and fore-most, they were spiritually weaker. It was Eve, not Adam, who committed the original sin. It was Eve, not Adam, who was lured by the Devil. In the sixteenth and seventeenth centuries, demonology was conceived of in explicitly sexual terms: female witches fornicated with the Devil. Then too, the women identified as suspects were often socially objectionable—old, mumbling, and ugly. Our image of the witch as a wrinkled hag doubt-less developed during the sixteenth century. These women were often so poor and hungry that they were forced into beggary: they were local nuisances. And if women in these circumstances were pressed by authorita-tive male judges and clergy to "confess" their crimes or were tortured into identifying their accomplices, they were more likely to name other women of their acquaintance than to dare to implicate men. Doubtless a good many of these downtrodden women *were* witches, in the sense that they craved magical powers, or even an alliance with the Devil, in order to better their sad fortunes and redress their grievances. It is important to recognize that everyone involved—the learned magistrates and priests, the complaining neighbors, the suspects themselves—entered actively into the witch-hunt. In this fashion one accusation easily led to many more.

Finally, witch-hunting was politically and socially safe. Very few people from the upper end of the social hierarchy were implicated. King James I of England wrote a book about demonology, but those who regarded themselves as the victims of witches, like the witches themselves, tended to be poor and ignorant. Peaks in the amount of witch-hunting sometimes coincided with periods of famine, pestilence, extreme religious tension, wartime carnage, or revolutionary upheaval. The fit is seldom exact, but the point is plain that Europeans in the age of religious wars had desperate need of demons and scapegoats, and they satisfied this need by victimizing the old and the weak.

THE PRICE REVOLUTION

The people of Europe during the sixteenth and seventeenth centuries became more money conscious than they had ever been before. Between

1521 and 1660 the Spanish brought home from their Mexican and Peruvian mines eighteen thousand tons of bullion, enough to treble the existing European silver supply and to enlarge the European gold supply by 20 per cent. Over half of this precious metal flooded in during the forty years of peak production, 1580–1620. Great pains were taken to funnel all of the treasure into Spain. Every spring a Spanish fleet, convoyed by warships, carried a year's production of silver ingots from the Caribbean to Seville. Yet relatively little of the precious metal remained permanently in Spanish hands. A small quantity was captured by English and Dutch pirates in their raids on the Spanish treasure fleets. Quite a bit was smuggled into western Europe by the Spanish colonists, who thus evaded paying their king his royalty, or *quinto real* ("royal fifth"). The Spanish king did actually receive more than 25 per cent of the bullion which landed at Seville, but he could not keep it, since he had to pay his foreign creditors and his armies in the Low Countries, France, and Germany. Most of the remaining bullion which landed at Seville went to foreign merchants. It is estimated that in 1600 nearly a third of the Seville bullion was used to pay for French imports alone. In all these ways Spain's treasure circulated throughout western Europe. It was fluid wealth: some was hoarded; some was fashioned into goblets, plate, cutlery, and similar articles of luxury; but a great deal of it was minted into coins—Spanish gold escudos and silver reals, French gold louis and silver livres, Dutch gold ducats and silver florins, English gold guineas and silver shillings.

Between the beginning of the sixteenth century and the middle of the seventeenth, Europe experienced a long and startling inflationary spiral. Spain was hit first and hit hardest; the Spanish paid four times as much for their commodities in 1600 as in 1500. In the twentieth century we have grown accustomed to a higher inflation rate than this, but sixteenth-century Europeans were not accustomed to it. For them, the price rise was a veritable price revolution. What caused it? In the view of Earl J. Hamilton, the inflation was directly related to the flood of American bullion. He has calculated that Spain's annual bullion imports and price levels correlated very closely throughout the sixteenth century. As soon as bullion imports declined in the seventeenth century, prices stabilized. Hamilton's neat picture has been disputed by other economic historians, who contend that Spanish prices rose most steeply before 1565, whereas bullion imports reached their peak between 1580 and 1620.[12] Population pressure in the sixteenth century, it is now argued, had a substantial effect on the inflation rate. There was not only more money to spend on any given commodity but more demand for that commodity. The relaxation

[12]Earl J. Hamilton, *American Treasure and the Price Revolution in Spain, 1501–1650* (Cambridge, Mass., 1934), p. 301. For a criticism of Hamilton, see J. H. Elliott, *Imperial Spain, 1469–1716* (New York, 1964), pp. 183–187.

of population pressure after the 1590's probably helps to explain why prices stabilized again in the mid-seventeenth century.

In every state in western Europe the price of goods seems to have doubled or trebled between 1500 and 1650. In England the inflation was almost as severe as in Spain. What the price revolution meant in concrete terms is suggested by the following table, compiled from the ancient account books of Winchester College, a school attended by the sons of English aristocrats and country gentlemen. The figures are all in shillings, and show the rising prices the school purchasing agents had to pay for several representative commodities.[13]

	1500	1580	1630	1700
wine for the school chapel				
per 12 gallons	8		64	96
cloth for students' uniforms				
per piece	40	80	120	120
parchment				
per dozen	3	5	6	18
candles				
per 12 dozen	1	2	4	5
beef				
per 14 pounds		1	2	2
rabbits				
per 12 pair		9	12	18

As this table shows, the price rise was not uniform, but it was general. Winchester College paid three or four times as much for staples in 1700 as in 1500. The rise in the cost of chapel wine was particularly steep, perhaps because the boys were developing champagne tastes, but more likely because all wine had to be imported from the Continent and became subject to new customs and excise taxes in the seventeenth century. As a result, Englishmen tended to drink more home-brewed beer and less French wine. It is interesting to note that Winchester beef (unfortunately we lack a figure for 1500) seems to have become cheaper in real money. English cattle breeding had improved somewhat not only in quantity but in quality during the period; cooks in the Winchester kitchens and elsewhere no longer found it necessary to spice their meat dishes heavily in order to cover the taste.

No doubt the families of the Winchester boys could afford to pay the mounting bills. But many persons were profoundly distressed by the price revolution. Wages for day laborers in Spain, England, and other western states climbed more slowly than consumer prices; in other words, real wages for farm laborers and artisans fell during the late sixteenth century. Landlords and entrepreneurs naturally wanted to avoid paying higher wages if possible, and they badgered their governments into fixing wage controls. In

[13] My figures are extracted from the detailed Winchester tables in Sir William Beveridge, *Prices and Wages in England* (London, 1939), Vol. I, pp. 81–90.

the late sixteenth century, unskilled laborers in Spain, England, France, and Germany must often have exhausted their entire wages in paying for minimum requirements of bread and drink. Elderly people living on savings, and those with fixed incomes, such as clergymen, teachers, and government clerks, also tended to suffer. There is a heated historical debate as to whether the large landowners were helped or hindered by the price revolution. If the landowner rented out his land on long leases, his income remained fixed and he suffered. If, on the other hand, he hired wage laborers to produce cash crops, he was more likely to prosper. It is safe to conclude that large-scale farmers, if they were energetic, efficient, and a bit ruthless, could more than keep pace with the rising prices. It is also evident that landed property, traditionally the only honorable form of wealth, was not in the sixteenth and seventeenth centuries the best source for quick profits.

Among the most important effects of the price revolution was the strain it placed upon government budgets. Traditionally, taxation had been closely tied to agriculture. Princes drew a considerable percentage of their revenue from their own private lands; the rest came largely from taxes on farms and crops. As the inflationary spiral developed, these agricultural taxes proved to be hopelessly inelastic and inadequate. The peasants, who bore the brunt of customary tax levies, were hard hit by the price rise, and their income rose more slowly than government expenses. In France, for instance, the principal source of royal revenue was the *taille*, a relatively low-yield tax on the peasants' income. It did not occur to the sixteenth-century French government that commerce offered a far more buoyant supply of capital than agriculture, and that the most effective way to increase state revenues was to encourage economic growth. On the contrary, the Valois kings imposed so many new tolls and tariffs on French commerce that they hindered business expansion—and lost additional revenue. Whenever French tax yields proved inadequate, the government borrowed money at exorbitant interest rates from the great international banking houses in Italy, Germany, and Flanders. The Valois kings were notorious spendthrifts, but even Elizabeth I of England, remarkable among sixteenth-century monarchs for her frugality, was forced by the expenses of her war with Spain to sell royal lands valued at £800,000 (equivalent to three years' peacetime revenues) and to contract large debts.

Elizabeth's great enemy, Philip II of Spain, was in a better position than any other sixteenth-century monarch to tap the new fluid capital effectively. Yet even Philip got into terrible fiscal difficulties as soon as he undertook expensive wars. The situation he inherited in 1556 was alarming. Charles V left him a Spanish revenue of less than two million ducats a year, and a debt of more than twenty million. Twice during the early years of his reign, in 1557 and again in 1575, Philip was forced to declare bankruptcy, suspending all payments to the Fuggers and his other creditors. No wonder he felt less enthusiasm than his father had for military adventures. Yet as we have seen, the last thirty years of his reign were filled with campaigns against the Moors, the Turks, the Dutch, the French, and the English. Philip seems to have supposed that American silver would pay for all these wars. Actually, however, American silver was never his main source of income. By the 1580's he was receiving two million ducats in every treasure fleet, but this was a small sum compared with the six million annually extracted from the Castilian peasantry. Philip's subjects paid a wide range of taxes, including a sales tax (the *alcabala*) of 14 per cent on every transaction. Total Spanish revenues reached nearly ten million ducats by the 1590's. Thanks to his extortionate tax policy, the Prudent King managed to keep ahead of the price rise. But he still failed to meet the skyrocketing costs of war. All of Philip's revenues were mortgaged far in advance, and in the 1590's he was spending twelve million ducats annually. The Armada alone cost him ten million. He borrowed wildly, as his father had done, and in 1596 came another declaration of bankruptcy. When Philip died two years later, perhaps his chief legacy was a debt in the neighborhood of a hundred million ducats. Another legacy was the ruin of the house of Fugger, which went out of business shortly after 1600.

The era of inflation and fiscal crisis continued into the first half of the seventeenth century. Many of the German princes' difficulties during the Thirty Years' War were attributable to their outmoded tax systems. Even a solvent prince like Maximilian of Bavaria quickly exhausted his treasury in trying to finance his army, and once the soldiers of fortune got control, no German prince had the means to stop them from wrecking the country. But by mid-century the situation had changed radically. After 1630, silver imports declined, population pressure relaxed, and the price structure stabilized. Real wages in France, England, and the Netherlands regained or surpassed their early sixteenth-century levels. While Spain had irretrievably lost its former economic and political vitality and sank to the position of a second-rate power, the French, English, and Dutch prospered as never before, and their governments displayed unprecedented fiscal strength. In 1678 Louis XIV could pay for an army of some 270,000 men—at least three times the size of Philip II's army at its peak. Even backwater Brandenburg-Prussia maintained through tax levies an army of thirty thousand—as large as Philip's Armada force. This remarkable growth in state-supported armies was symptomatic of the vitality of governmental enterprise toward the end of the seventeenth century. What advantages did Louis XIV and the Great Elector have that Philip II lacked?

The answer lies in a combination of several factors. First, there was a general seventeenth-century rise in living standards among property holders and in the accumulation of surplus wealth, especially in the three chief Atlantic states. Second, there was a wider circulation of specie and an increased reliance on credit, both of which facilitated the use of Europe's wealth as working capital. Third, governments were devising better tech-

One of the 1,400 fountains in Louis XIV's gardens at Versailles. *Engraving by Mercy. This scene suggests the enormous size of Louis XIV's pleasure garden for the privileged French aristocracy and the crushing strain such building projects imposed on the state budget.*

niques for tapping this wealth by taxing the consumer more and the producer less.

Unlike the sixteenth-century Valois and Habsburg kings, the seventeenth-century Bourbon kings of France attempted to increase tax revenues by promoting industry and commerce. But in other respects the seventeenth-century French fiscal system, despite its ability to support Louis XIV's heroic army, was rather old-fashioned, and its yield was low by English and Dutch standards. The *taille* still brought in the greatest returns. Some regions of France were much more heavily rated than others, but everywhere the aristocrats and the bourgeoisie were in large part exempted. Jean Baptiste Colbert, Louis XIV's great minister of finance, tried without success to change the *taille* from an income tax on peasants into a real-estate tax on all property owners. He did manage to increase the *aides*, indirect liquor taxes which almost everyone had to pay. But French taxes were still collected principally from the poor. Colbert was unable to shake the French upper- and middle-class notion that tax payments were a badge of dishonor. It cannot be said that the Dutch and English embraced a "soak-the-rich" policy, but they did tax the propertied as well as the propertyless.

The English government in the 1680's tried abandoning land taxes altogether and drew 50 per cent of the royal revenues from customs duties on international and colonial trade. English overseas commerce suffered somewhat under this tax burden, but the Stuart monarchs drew enough money from customs levies to free them from dependence on the country gentlemen who sat in Parliament—with results which we shall observe in the next chapter. Since the Dutch depended even more heavily than the English on foreign trade, they refrained from imposing such heavy customs duties. Instead, they taxed domestic commerce, placing excise levies (similar to the French *aides*) on a wide range of staple market goods. The excise was intended, like the English customs duties, to siphon off surplus purchasing power without strangling business. It was a burdensome but practicable tax. Brandenburg-Prussia and England also made heavy use of the excise.

None of these states could survive on taxes alone; public borrowing was essential for covering the expenses of wars and other emergencies. Here again, the Dutch managed better than the French. While Louis XIV had to pay interest of 8 per cent or more, and consumed much of his budget in debt service, the Dutch were successfully floating government loans at 3 or 4 per cent. Thousands of Dutch citizens, including very humble people, subscribed to these loans to their government in the belief that they constituted a safe investment. Not so many years earlier, the Fuggers had been gambling their money on Philip II at extortionate rates in the hope of making a quick killing before the king defaulted.

England and the Dutch republic were fiscally the most effective seventeenth-century states because they were the most commercialized. In the era of the price revolution, commercial profits proved to be much more elastic than agricultural or industrial profits. The Dutch and English governments developed fruitful partnerships with the merchants of Amsterdam and London. In each instance, the state granted commercial privileges and protection to the mercantile community, and in return received excise and customs revenues, and was able to secure public loans at tolerable rates of interest. The vigorous Dutch and English traffic in domestic and foreign goods produced greater wealth than the mines of America. Merchants, traditionally disdained by the priests as moral parasites and by the knights as moral cowards, felt confident that they now formed the most dynamic social class. "Behold then the true form and worth of foreign trade," the English merchant Thomas Mun proudly wrote in the 1620's, "which is the great revenue of the king, the honor of the kingdom, the noble profession of the merchant, the school of our arts, the supply of our wants, the employment of our poor, the improvement of our lands, the nursery of our mariners, the walls of the kingdom, the means of our treasure, the sinews of our wars, the terror of our enemies."

CAPITALISM AND CALVINISM

Was there a connection between business enterprise and religious zeal? Did militant Protestantism spark capitalist expansion while reformed Catholicism discouraged it? Was it mere coincidence that the most dynamic businessmen were to be found in Protestant Holland and the most vigorous industrial growth in Protestant England, both states heavily tinctured with Calvinism? Why were the Huguenots so prominent in the business community of Catholic France? Or Protestant Brandenburg-Prussia under the Calvinist Great Elector almost the only seventeenth-century German state to exhibit increasing prosperity? Or Catholic Italy, Portugal, and Flanders, all flourishing business centers before 1559, so depressed by 1689? Or Spain, the most aggressively Catholic society of the day, the victim of startling economic collapse?

Scholars have been wrangling over these questions for the last sixty years without reaching agreement. The German sociologist Max Weber started the controversy in 1904 by publishing *The Protestant Ethic and the Spirit of Capitalism*, in which he maintained that the early Protestants—particularly Calvin and his followers—strongly influenced the beginnings of modern capitalism during the sixteenth and seventeenth centuries. Weber recognized that there had been many individual capitalists during the Middle Ages and the Renaissance, but he argued that these businessmen had not been able to instill into European society a pervasive profit-making ethos. He defined the capitalist spirit as a rationally calculated and highly systematized pursuit of profit rather than an irrational greed for gain, power, or glory. Weber did not find this rational capitalism in such pre-Reformation merchant-bankers as the Medici of Florence or the Fuggers of Augsburg. He contended that the Medici and the Fuggers exhibited irrational greed in their grandiose moneylending operations. They gambled for heroic stakes, made risky loans to kings and popes, and lavished their winnings on extraneous political projects, art patronage, or high living. Weber traced the beginnings of the modern capitalist spirit to the smaller-scale merchants of sixteenth- and seventeenth-century England and the Netherlands. These businessmen, he thought, practiced the restraint, sobriety, purposeful industry, and calculating frugality necessary for the construction of a rationally ordered profit system. And they were inspired in their business practices by the ethical teachings of Calvin. Weber made much of the Protestant idea that every man's worldly vocation or career was a "calling" assigned to him by God. If a man succeeded in his calling, this was a sign that God had predestined him for salvation. In Weber's view, Calvin's doctrine of predestination produced in his adherents character traits of inner loneliness and outer discipline, asceticism and drive. The Calvinist merchant's energy lifted him above the servile working class. His dignity was proof against the luxury and waste of aristocrats and banker princes. As Weber's supporter R. H. Tawney put it, "Calvin did for the *bourgeoisie* of the sixteenth century what Marx did for the proletariat of the nineteenth."

Weber's thesis has been challenged in a number of ways. Some critics deny his premise that there is meaningful cultural interaction between religious and economic forces. Others see little point in searching for an emerging "spirit" of capitalism. Marxists and other economic determinists generally reject Weber's contention that economic ideas and attitudes cause changes in business practice. They hold instead that business practices cause changes in economic attitudes; hence the focal point should be the economy itself and not the environmental "spirit." Still other critics object to Weber's dismissal of pre-Reformation capitalism. They point out that Renaissance Florence and Venice and sixteenth-century Antwerp employed almost all the business techniques of seventeenth-century Amsterdam and London. Many members of the Catholic bourgeoisie practiced self-discipline, frugality, and industry before Calvin came along to enshrine these virtues. Another line of attack is that Weber misconstrued the ethical teachings of Calvin. He has been accused of distorting the reformer's notion of a worldly "calling," of soft-pedaling Calvin's hostility to money and profit, and of ignoring the repressive atmosphere of Calvin's Geneva, which suffocated rather than stimulated business enterprise. Furthermore, it has been argued that the most intensely Calvinist areas of sixteenth- and seventeenth-century Europe—Scotland and the rural Netherlands—remained economically backward. In comparison with agrarian Friesland, Amsterdam was hardly Calvinist at all: it tolerated Catholics and Jews, and its Reformed preachers watered down the Founder's doctrine of predestination. Weber's more extreme critics go so far as to say that Calvinism was the enemy of capitalism.

The Weber controversy has run itself into the ground in recent years. Today most specialists in the history of the period regard Weber's thesis as far too simple. Yet however inadequately Weber formulated his proposition, it is surely naïve to doubt his premise, that the dynamic economic and religious forces of the sixteenth and seventeenth centuries had a strong mutual impact.

The exact impact of the Protestant and Catholic reformations upon the European business climate can never be determined, but there seems to be a large kernel of truth in Weber's contention that the Protestant ethic of disciplined individualism bolstered the value system of the western European merchant community. To be sure, St. Ignatius of Loyola placed as much stress on emotional and intellectual discipline as John Calvin did, but the disciplined Calvinist practiced underconsumption and hated sinful ostentation, whereas the disciplined Jesuit lavished his resources on Baroque extravagance for the greater glory of God. Baroque Rome, transformed by the reformed papacy's building program of gorgeous churches, avenues, piazzas, stairways, statues, fountains, and palaces, was a far more telling exhibit of what Weber termed irrational, anticapitalistic display than Renaissance Florence had ever been. Seventeenth-century Amsterdam, for all its commercial prosperity, was a plain town, with few prominent public buildings. Every Amsterdam canal presented the same view: a serried double row of tall, narrow, gabled houses, looking rather homely and very solid. The Dutch businessman characteristically maintained his office on the ground

The Fountain of the Four Rivers in Rome. *Designed by Bernini. A splendid example of ostentatious display in Baroque Rome.*

floor of his house, his living quarters on the middle floors, and his warehouse on the top floors. The grandest Amsterdam capitalist was not ashamed to have a pulley projecting prominently from the ridgepole of his house, by which barrels and bales were hoisted into his upper windows from barges in the canal below.

The impact of Calvinism upon capitalism can only be gauged impressionistically; the impact of capitalism upon Calvinism is easier to trace through several chronological stages. The early Calvinists were deeply suspicious of moneymaking. The saints of mid-sixteenth-century Geneva, inhabiting a small oasis in a desert of sin, took community action to control the wicked avarice of usurers and monopolists. But by the early seventeenth century, when Calvin's disciples had penetrated into all the business centers of western Europe, they could no longer segregate themselves from the carnal practices of their unrighteous neighbors. Only in backwater places like Scotland, New England, and the rural Netherlands was it possible to maintain exclusive and pristine communities of the elect. Increasingly, the Protestant activist had to rely on individual self-discipline. The Puritan merchant in London schooled himself to maintain his stewardship to God. But his God-given business success encouraged him to value worldly labor as an end in itself. Profit making became a duty. By the early eighteenth century those London and Amsterdam capitalists who had been trained in a Calvinist heritage still dedicated themselves to hard work, but the original ethical purpose of their "calling" had been secularized. The saint of 1559 had become the privileged property holder of 1715.

One way of testing the Weber thesis is to compare Protestant and Catholic attitudes toward the poor and toward poor relief in the sixteenth and seventeenth centuries. Weber and his followers contend that the Catholic philanthropist distributed alms indiscriminately among any of the poor he encountered, as a form of good work to promote his own salvation, whereas the Protestant philanthropist concentrated his efforts on social-welfare schemes for assisting the "deserving" poor to improve themselves. Evidence can certainly be found to support this proposition. In Spain, vagabondage was an accepted life style, and the mendicant orders of friars who organized charity for the wandering beggars opposed all efforts to take them off the roads and put them into workhouses. To hide the destitute from public view, the friars argued, would conceal their plight without correcting it, and would dampen the compassionate instincts of the affluent. In England and the Netherlands, vagabonds were harshly treated, while new, privately endowed philanthropic institutions—almshouses, orphanages, schools, and hospitals—were established, to help a select number of the poor and sick. But Catholic Venice had an equally elaborate range of mechanisms for the purposeful care of the poor. Religious societies in Venice gave alms to "respectable" poor men and dowries to their daughters. Hospitals isolated and treated the victims of leprosy, syphilis, and other communicable diseases. Special almshouses were set up for destitute women. Special banks were funded to loan money to the poor. Unlike the Spanish, the Venetians licensed a few professional beggars and ordered all others off the streets. Thus the contrast is not so much between Protestant and Catholic as between the businesslike and the unbusinesslike.

According to a study of English private philanthropy, the property-holding classes gave eight times as much money to charity in 1640 as in 1480. Merchants gave much more generously than anyone else, especially in the early seventeenth century, when so many of them joined the Puritan movement. Once we have made allowances for a 350-per-cent price rise and for England's commercial growth during this period, we may question whether the seventeenth-century Protestant donor was any more generous than his fifteenth-century Catholic predecessor. But there can be no doubt that his money went to a different set of charitable goals. The pre-Reformation philanthropist gave 53 per cent of his bequests to the church (half of this to subsidize prayers for the dead) and only 15 per cent to poor relief, hospitals, and social-welfare schemes. The early seventeenth-century philanthropist gave 12 per cent of his bequests to the church (none of it to

The English East India Company factory at Surat, India, early in the seventeenth century. *From an old print. The English, Dutch, and French maintained factories or trading posts similar to this one in numerous Asian cities. In this scene, the Indians in the foreground are evidently carting off goods they bought at the factory. The Englishmen in the courtyard within are identifiable by their broad-brimmed hats.*

subsidize prayers for the dead) and 55 per cent to poor relief and social welfare.[14] Of course this philanthropy provided little real help for the bottom half of society. Believers in the Protestant ethic supposed that there was no way to help the undeserving poor.

MERCANTILISM

The years between 1559 and 1715 saw the popularization of the quasi-economic, quasi-political doctrine which Adam Smith, a hundred years later, contemptuously branded as the mercantile system, or mercantilism. Historians have always sharply disagreed in their definition, interpretation, and estimation of mercantilism. Some prefer to drop the whole concept. Seventeenth-century economic thought, they contend, was too inchoate to be regarded as a system. Most governments may have adopted mercantilist

[14]W. K. Jordan, *Philanthropy in England, 1480–1660* (London, 1959), pp. 367–387.

planks, but no two built the same economic platform. Only a handful of polemicists and bureaucrats, such as Colbert in France, preached the pure mercantilist gospel. Although these objections have validity, it must nevertheless be recognized that mercantilism was pervasive and powerful. The term usefully identifies characteristic western European notions concerning the relation between business and government. The mercantilist attitude of mind was partly radical, partly conservative, and wholly consistent with the psychology of limited wealth.

Hazarding a definition, we may say that the mercantilists were those who advocated the conscious and artificial development of the sovereign state into an economic unit, for the purpose of fostering community wealth and

power. The businessmen and statesmen who groped toward this goal were exhilarated by the new abundance of fluid capital, hungry for profit, yet still convinced that the total quantity of wealth was relatively fixed. The best way to get and keep as large a share as possible of this limited wealth, they argued, was through a planned, cooperative society. Experience had shown the dangers of rugged individualism. After all, freewheeling entrepreneurs like the Fuggers lost their fortunes faster than they made them. Self-centered princes like the Valois, obsessed with dynastic politics, disastrously mortgaged themselves to foreign moneylenders. Mercantilists applauded the concept of secular sovereignty articulated by Jean Bodin and other social theorists who were sick of political anarchy and irresponsible wars. They

EUROPEAN OVERSEAS COMMERCE
IN THE SEVENTEENTH CENTURY

TERRITORIES OF EUROPEAN POWERS:

Spanish　English　Dutch

French　Portuguese

agreed with Bodin that final authority and power belonged to the state, not the reigning prince. The sovereign state could and should back up aggressive businessmen and protect their accumulated profits. This advocacy of a planned state economy was by no means new. The medieval town and the Renaissance city-state had functioned as economic units. But in the sixteenth-century political arena, the Italian and German city-states lacked the necessary size and strength. In eastern Europe, states like Austria, Poland, and Russia were certainly large enough, but they were too purely agrarian to achieve the benefits of a capitalist economy. Mercantilist attention therefore focused on Spain, Portugal, the Netherlands, Sweden, Brandenburg-Prussia, and—most particularly—on England and France.

Mercantilists tended to entertain fixed economic notions, one of which (inspired by the influx of New World treasure) was that bullion was the best measure of wealth. A state accumulated bullion by achieving a favorable balance of trade—that is, by exporting goods of more value than those imported. It followed that a state ought to be as nearly self-sufficient as possible, so as to minimize dependence on imports. Overseas colonies could assist self-sufficiency by supplying those goods which the state would otherwise import. The larger a state's industrial production and trade were, the greater its exports and profits. It is revealing to find how indifferent the sixteenth- and seventeenth-century mercantilists were to the fact that output was hampered by the crude hand methods of production. Hard work and full employment was their simple recipe for increasing productivity. Mercantilists were easily alarmed and dismayed by expanding domestic consumption and improvements in the living standard, which we regard as an index of wealth. They continually preached frugality and abstinence in order to assure a surplus of exports over imports.

Some interpreters weigh the mercantilists' political postulates more heavily than their economic assumptions. The trouble is that except for a broad endorsement of state sovereignty, the various mercantilists were not in agreement about political theory. French mercantilists, for example, tended more than their English counterparts to admire paternalistic, expensive central government. Businessmen and civil servants agreed in principle on cooperation for their mutual benefit, but they rarely saw eye to eye on tax programs, nor on the degree to which private citizens should help shape government policy. Nonetheless, mercantilists generally encouraged government stimulation, supervision, and protection of the economy. They were always patriots. If they did not care to sacrifice personal or local interests to the national interest, they could still glory in the collective power of the community. For example, Thomas Mun (quoted earlier) was a mercantilist with a strongly patriotic flair.

The sixteenth-century Spanish empire was at once the first great mercantilist state and the last great Catholic crusading state. Only the Spaniards could have achieved such a combination. Spain's bullion-centered imperial system did as much as anything else to inspire and popularize the whole mercantilist doctrine. Spain's insistence on closing its empire to outside settlers and traders was imitated by later mercantilist states. And the central administrative institutions of the Spanish empire—the Council of the Indies in Madrid, the *Casa de Contratación* in Seville, and the viceroys and *audiencias* in the New World—were also later copied by the French and to some extent by the English.

Even during its sixteenth-century boom period, however, Spain never developed a completely mercantilist system. For one thing, the Spanish empire was never an economically self-sufficient unit. Except for bullion, the colonists produced few commodities which the Spanish home consumers needed, and the colonists soon desired manufactured and even agricultural products which the mother country could not supply. Hence much of the cargo for the Seville-Indies trade had to be obtained from Flemish, French, or English merchants in exchange for bullion. Antwerp, not Seville, was the chief commercial entrepôt under Spanish rule—until Philip II's soldiers sacked it during the Dutch war. In the course of the seventeenth century, the Spanish empire became less and less mercantilist in character. Silver production fell off, and so did the Seville-Indies trade. The home government could not stop foreign interlopers from smuggling goods into Spanish America. The imperial administrative machinery was still intact, but the empire had disintegrated economically. From a mercantilist viewpoint, Spain had thrown away the grain and kept the chaff.

Of the three seventeenth-century Atlantic states which vied for the economic leadership abdicated by Spain, the United Provinces diverged most markedly from Spanish-style mercantilism. This was no accident. The Dutch rebelled against Philip II's business methods as well as against his Catholicism and his absolutism. They rejected, for both political and economic reasons, the mercantilist concept of the sovereign state as an economic unit. It was pointless to dream mercantilist dreams of achieving wealth through state power in a small country with only two million inhabitants. It was absurd to aim for economic self-sufficiency when the chief native products were tulips and cheese. Since the Dutch were the middlemen of Europe, their prosperity depended on wide-open trade. Dutch scholars wrote learned treatises to find legal justifications for freedom of the seas—possibly inspired by the fact that the United Provinces had by far the largest merchant marine in Europe. Dutch merchants flouted the most sacred mercantilist canons in order to stimulate trade. Orthodox bullionists were scandalized by the East India Company's shipment of specie to China and Japan in exchange for oriental luxury wares. To Dutch entrepreneurs, patriotism rarely seemed as alluring as profit. In 1622, in the midst of the war with Spain, the Dutch government found it necessary to prohibit brokers from insuring enemy ships and cargoes. The English and French governments were startled to discover Dutch investors subscribing handsomely to the English and French East India companies, which were intended to steal Asian trade from Amsterdam.

But if the Dutch rejected doctrinaire mercantilism, neither were they dogmatic advocates of *laissez-faire*. They simply adapted their economic views to fit changing circumstances. Thus in the late sixteenth and early seventeenth centuries, when the enemy was Spain, Dutch sailors could profitably plunder shipping and capture colonies, and Amsterdam thrived on war. But after the mid-seventeenth century the enemies became England and France, whose privateers could lacerate the huge Dutch shipping fleet and dislocate overseas trade. Accordingly, Dutch merchants then became advocates of international peace. The Dutch always insisted on free passage for their ships around the Danish islands to reach the Baltic; at the same time, in 1609 and again in 1648 they made the Spanish close the Scheldt River, in order to prevent Antwerp from ever again rivaling Amsterdam. Dutch belief in freedom of the seas stopped at Sumatra. The East India Company invested heavily in forts, warships, and soldiers to exclude interlopers from all the spice islands, including those not occupied by the Dutch. In 1623 the Dutch massacred some English traders who had dared to establish a post on the nutmeg island of Amboina. Nor would the company permit the native Indonesians to produce more spices than Dutch ships could handle. In the northern Moluccas they denuded whole islands, chopping down the clove plantations and killing any Indonesians who protested. The Dutch guarded their spice preserve every bit as jealously as the Spanish guarded their silver mines.

To the English and the French, the superb vitality of mid-seventeenth-century Dutch society was both impressive and annoying; the dry rot which vitiated the Spanish empire was both gratifying and puzzling. One overall conclusion seemed evident: if one could take Dutch business enterprise, combine it with Spanish centralized power, and shake thoroughly, the result would be a mercantilist's dream. After 1660, the English and the French coordinated public planning and private enterprise more consistently and self-consciously than the Spanish or the Dutch had ever done. These two great adversaries developed the mercantile system to its fullest extent. The story of their classic rivalry demands a separate chapter. Seventeenth-century England and France, competitors for wealth and power, antithetical in politics, religion, and social structure, were the two most dynamic states to emerge from the era of religious warfare.

The Spanish and the Dutch were another great pair of rivals, of course, and even the most summary review of business conditions in these two states will demonstrate the complexities and contradictions in the European economy during the sixteenth and seventeenth centuries. Both the Spanish and the Dutch were shackled by primitive techniques of hand production, both were strongly affected by the price revolution, both displayed energy in exploiting America and Asia. There is no simple explanation for Spain's economic disaster or for the Dutch boom prosperity. The Spaniards imported eighteen thousand tons of silver and gold only to wind up poorer in 1715 than they had been in 1559, while the Dutch had no gold mines or other natural resources, yet emerged in 1715 far richer than in 1559. In Spain the population shrank, farm production fell, sheep ranching declined, and the textile industry collapsed. In the Dutch republic the population grew, farm production rose, stock breeding improved, and the textile industry flourished. In Spain the government's oppressive tax policy and rigid trade regulations strangled private enterprise. The Dutch government taxed business without killing it, and Dutch merchants pooled their resources in joint-stock companies, built fleets of flyboats, developed techniques for banking, exchanging, investing, and insuring capital, and became the middlemen of Europe. Both states were at war most of the time, but while the costs of Philip II's armies drove Spain into irredeemable bankruptcy, the Dutch thrived on war until the mid-seventeenth century and could still float low-interest government loans to cover military expenses at the end of the century. Perhaps part of the answer lies in the differences between Spanish Catholicism and Dutch Calvinism. At any rate, the Spaniards and the Dutch did share three traits. Both societies were internally divided into privileged and unprivileged classes. Both readily enslaved the Negroes and Indians they encountered. And both in their own fashion expressed the psychology of limited wealth.

CHAPTER 4

Absolutism Versus Constitutionalism

SEVENTEENTH-CENTURY EUROPE saw the evolution of two strikingly effective forms of state power—absolute monarchy, best exemplified by Bourbon France, and constitutional monarchy, best exemplified by Stuart England. The contrasting development of these rival states is the subject of this chapter. The contrast was indeed dramatic. In politics and religion alike, the two societies moved toward opposite goals. In France, where the sixteenth-century Valois kings had lost control of the state during the wars of religion, a masterful succession of seventeenth-century kings and ministers—Henry IV, Richelieu, Mazarin, Colbert, and Louis XIV—built royal strength to unprecedented heights. In England, where the sixteenth-century Tudor dynasty had achieved great success and popularity, their Stuart successors were twice overthrown, in the revolutions of 1640 and 1688. Representative institutions atrophied in France, while the English Parliament gained sovereign authority. In religion, the French gradually abandoned the toleration policy set forth by Henry IV in the Edict of Nantes in favor of a unitary national Catholic church, whereas the English gradually abandoned Elizabeth I's insistence on a unitary national church in favor of toleration for minority creeds. In 1684 Louis XIV revoked the Edict of Nantes; in 1689 the English Parliament passed the Toleration Act. What caused these profoundly antithetical developments?

France and England were political and religious rivals because they were so different, but economic rivals because they were so similar. Except for such specialties as French wine and English coal, both produced much the same diversified range of goods. Both espoused mercantilism, seeking economic self-sufficiency by protecting home agriculture and industry while promoting a favorable balance of foreign trade. Frenchmen and Englishmen contested for the same products in the same places all over the world. In India they competed for cotton and calico, in West Africa for slaves, in the North Atlantic for fish, and in North America for furs and deerskins. In the West Indies they staked out rival sugar plantations on islands within sight of each other and even partitioned one miniature island—St. Christopher—into French and English zones.

Striking as this rivalry was, we must remember that the two societies shared certain basic characteristics which set them apart from their neighbors, especially those east of the Rhine. Unlike the Germans, Italians, Poles, Turks, and Russians, the French and English had already achieved national sovereignty. A comparatively homogeneous linguistic, cultural, and religious experience facilitated political cohesion and community spirit in both countries. National consciousness is no political cure-all, as recent history abundantly demonstrates, but it certainly helped the French and the English to generate more large-scale corporate energy than any other seventeenth-century society. Also, particularly in England, it tended to bridge the psychological gulf between the privileged and unprivileged classes. Agrarian magnates like those who controlled eastern Europe were decidedly less potent in France and England, where a vigorous urban capitalist class held a rising share of the wealth, and centralized institutions tended to curb local autonomy and particularism. The two Atlantic rivals could boast a wider distribution of property, a broader participation in public affairs, and a higher level of education and culture than any other contemporary state except the Dutch republic. And they far outmatched the Dutch in political power.

To most contemporary observers, France looked more impressive than England. It was the French who replaced the Renaissance Italians as arbiters of civility. Their language was spoken, their books were read, and their tastes were copied by well-bred persons everywhere. The seventeenth century was also France's *grand siècle* in international politics. Having the biggest population, the biggest army, the biggest revenue, and the best bureaucracy, France more than replaced Spain as Europe's most fearsome imperialist power. Largely because of France's glittering success, the prevailing European political trend was toward absolutism, not constitutionalism. The Bourbon style of monarchy was admired and aped not merely by petty German and Italian princes, but by the leading potentates of the day: the Spanish Habsburg kings, the Austrian Habsburg emperors, the Brandenburg Hohenzollern electors, and—most pertinent—the English Stuart kings.

THE RISE OF FRENCH ABSOLUTISM, 1598–1661

During the years between the end of the French wars of religion in 1598 and Louis XIV's assumption of personal control in 1661, France triumphantly recovered its political strength. At home, the French repaired their governmental system. Abroad, they decisively defeated the Habsburgs in Germany and Spain, and emerged as unquestionably the leading power in Europe. This achievement was no miracle, for France enjoyed splendid assets: a large population (over sixteen million people in 1600), a diversified economy, and a heritage of strong government and military prowess. But its problems during the late sixteenth-century wars of religion had seemed well-nigh insuperable. Antipathy between Huguenots and Catholics, between the aristocracy and the crown, between Paris and the provinces, had very nearly shattered the country into autonomous fragments like those of the Holy Roman Empire. That the French people not merely recovered from their civil wars, but developed a more vital society than they had known before, was due in great measure to the efforts of three purposeful statesmen—King Henry IV, Cardinal Richelieu, and Cardinal Mazarin.

Very different from one another in personality and tactics, the first Bourbon king and the two cardinals all pursued the same set of goals: to weaken local particularism, to strengthen central royal authority, and to enlarge French territory by means of an aggressive foreign policy. These aims were not new. The French Renaissance monarchs of the early sixteenth century had been trying to achieve exactly these purposes before the religious crisis and the price revolution disrupted their efforts. In taking up where Francis I and Henry II had left off, Henry IV, Richelieu, and Mazarin adroitly masked their policies through compromise and prevarication, yet they could never eradicate the centrifugal tendencies latent in French society. Opposition from Huguenots, ultra-Catholics, feudal nobility, privileged officeholders, entrenched bourgeoisie, autonomous provincials, oppressed peasantry, and the Paris mob remained constant and dangerous. Periodically—most notably in 1610–1624 and 1648–1653—several of these dissident factions coalesced to reignite the old anarchic civil tumult. But each outburst was mastered, and the centripetal process was patiently resumed. Hence while neither Henry, nor Richelieu, nor Mazarin was a conscious reformer or innovator, their sixty years of management did have great cumulative effect.

Henry IV (ruled 1589–1610) has the special distinction of being the most affectionately remembered figure in the long gallery of French kings. Stylish and witty, yet a bluff man of action, he played many roles: the soldier from Navarre with a magnificent white plume in his helmet, dramatically rallying his outmanned troops in battle; the sensual courtier with curling moustache, always in pursuit of the ladies; the conscientious administrator, absorbed by a current treatise on farming techniques—Olivier de Serres' *Théâtre d'agriculture*—read to him after dinner; and the simple, garlic-scented man of the people—*le roi de la poule au pot*, saying he hoped to live long enough to see every French peasant have a chicken in his pot each Sunday. Henry cultivated an image of himself as distinct as possible from that of the last Valois kings, the neurotic and effete sons of Catherine de Medici. In a system where so much depended on the king's character, Henry's outgoing, virile personality had immediate impact and long-range symbolic value. He never allowed the bitter war experiences of his youth to sour his temper or ossify his convictions. Raised as a Huguenot, he had twice turned Catholic. The difference between Henry's expediency and Catherine de Medici's was

Henry IV. *Painting by Pourbus. The king looks characteristically skeptical and amused. Bibliothèque Publique et Universitaire, Geneva.*

not great, except that his gambits worked and hers had not. Politics, like baseball, is a game of inches.

Henry IV spent the first half of his reign, from 1589 to 1598, closing the wars of religion, and the second half, from 1598 to 1610, securing domestic peace. The obstacles he overcame in terminating the wars have been described earlier. Henry bought off all internal opposition, bribing his Catholic subjects by joining their church, his Huguenot subjects by guaranteeing them civil and religious autonomy through the Edict of Nantes, and the commanders of the ultra-Catholic League by paying them 32 million livres (a sum greater than the annual royal revenue) to disband their troops. "France and I," he remarked in 1598, "both need to catch our breath." Having yielded so often in order to win acceptance, Henry endeavored thereafter to rebuild royal authority. In his view the Estates-General, which had met four times between 1560 and 1593, was a vehicle of feudal particularism. Hence he never summoned it. He could tolerate the continuation of provincial representative assemblies in Brittany, Normandy, Burgundy, Dauphiné, Provence, and Languedoc, with their privilege of taxing themselves (very lightly), since he possessed uncontested powers of direct taxation over the rest of the country. Correspondingly, he tolerated the claim of the *parlements*, or law courts, of Paris and the outlying provinces to authorize royal edicts by registering them, as long as they did in fact register all of his decrees, including unpopular ones like the Edict of Nantes. Henry staffed his administrative posts with the tractable bourgeoisie in preference to the high nobility, and he surrounded himself with able advisers like the Huguenot duke of Sully (1560–1641). On the vexed question of religion, he kept the Huguenots content by maintaining the protection and toleration pledged them in the Edict of Nantes. Meanwhile, he shrewdly played off the Italian papacy against the Gallican clergy in order to gain a firmer control over the French Catholic church than the late Valois kings had ever enjoyed. Even the Jesuits, when they were readmitted to France in 1604, became ardent supporters of the Bourbon monarchy.

Henry IV's handling of public finance aptly illustrates the achievements and limitations of his reign. He inherited a staggering burden of war debts. In 1596 the king owed his creditors 300 million livres at exorbitant interest rates, and annual expenditures were running twice as high as the royal revenues. Unlike the Spanish government, the French government avoided declaring bankruptcy. But the duke of Sully, Henry's finance minister, did repudiate part of the royal debt and rescheduled the remainder at a lower rate of interest. By drastically retrenching once the war was over and seeking out additional sources of revenue, Sully managed to balance his budget. By 1609 he had reduced the debt by 100 million livres and scraped together a royal treasure of 12 million livres in the form of barrels of gold, stored in the Bastille cellars. Sully, however, made only a superficial effort to reform the gross inequities in the French tax structure. The impoverished peasantry continued to pay most of the taxes, while the prosperous privileged classes were exempted. Sully did indeed reduce the *taille*, but he correspondingly raised the *gabelle*, or salt tax. Both *taille* and *gabelle* continued to be assessed at far higher rates in some sections of the country than in others. And as before, most taxes were collected by tax farmers, middlemen under government contract who could make fat profits by squeezing more money from the peasants than they had contracted to deliver into the treasury. Public finance was further hamstrung by the crown's long-established policy of selling financial and judicial offices for life to aspiring bourgeoisie, more intent on social climbing than on the zealous performance of duty. Sully not merely continued to sell administrative posts, but made them hereditary in return for payment of an annual fee, the *paulette*.

By 1610, Henry IV was again ready for war. His target was the traditional French enemy, Habsburg Spain. Every strong French king since the late fifteenth century had tested his mettle against Habsburg armies, more often losing than winning. France was virtually encircled by Spanish Habsburg territory, the Pyrenees on one side and Franche-Comté, Luxembourg, and

Flanders—provinces Henry was eager to annex—on the other. Besides, he had not forgiven Philip II for prolonging the French civil wars in the 1590's by supporting the League with men and money. In May, 1610, on the eve of his campaign, as Henry was passing through a narrow Paris street, his open carriage was caught momentarily in a traffic jam and a demented monk named Ravaillac leaped up onto the wheel and stabbed the king to death. To Ravaillac, Henry was an apostate who protected heretical Huguenots and went to war against good Catholics. It was probably lucky for Henry's subsequent reputation that he was martyred before his Spanish campaign could begin. He would have found the Habsburg armies very formidable, and Sully's treasure of twelve million livres would have been quickly exhausted. Nonetheless, his sudden death plunged France into an extended crisis, alarmingly reminiscent of the situation in the 1560's, when the religious wars began.

The French crisis lasted from 1610 to 1624. The new king, Louis XIII (ruled 1610–1643), was only nine years old when his father was assassinated. Henry's widow, Marie de Medici (1573–1642), was the regent during Louis' minority. A distant cousin of Catherine de Medici, Marie shared her predecessor's taste for intrigue and opulence, though she was more pious and shallow than Catherine, and did less damage to the French monarchy. She immediately canceled Henry's plans for war against Spain, and indeed soon reversed his policy completely by contracting a marriage alliance between young Louis and the daughter of the Spanish king. During Marie's regency the high French nobility grabbed control at the provincial level, and bullied her into squandering Sully's treasure among them in the form of new pensions and offices. Marie was pressed into calling the Estates-General in 1614, but when the three estates convened, hostility between the aristocratic and the bourgeois deputies was so paralyzing that they could accomplish nothing. Evidently a national representative institution was no longer of use in France; the Estates-General did not meet again until 1789.

While the country drifted aimlessly, Marie de Medici squabbled with her son. Louis XIII was whipped at the queen mother's orders until well into adolescence. In 1617 he pushed Marie aside, but though the young king understood the need for a drastic administrative shake-up far better than his mother did, he was too morose and diffident to formulate or execute any changes himself. France had become a cipher in international affairs, taking no significant part in the opening stages of the Thirty Years' War. By the early 1620's religious warfare was beginning again in southern France. The Huguenot towns of Languedoc were in open revolt against the crown. Louis XIII urgently needed a strong new minister if any part of his father's legacy was to be salvaged.

Cardinal Richelieu (1585–1642) became Louis XIII's chief minister in 1624 and directed the French government until his death. Born Armand Jean du Plessis, the son of a minor nobleman, Richelieu started his career in the family bishopric and entered state service during the regency of Marie de Medici. The queen mother, hoping to regain control of the government through Richelieu, persuaded the pope to make him a cardinal and the king to put him on the royal council. However, Richelieu was not her pawn. He looked thin and sickly, but his iron willpower, keen intelligence, and austere elegance ideally equipped him to rule in the king's name. Marie de Medici and most other members of the royal family soon hated him for ruthlessly shattering all their court intrigues against him. Richelieu drove the queen mother and Louis XIII's younger brother into exile. Five dukes and four counts were among the noblemen arrested, sentenced (several in secret courts), and executed on treason charges for challenging the cardinal's authority. Richelieu was greedy for power, no doubt, but he did devote this power to the service of France and of his royal master. For a prince of the church, Richelieu was remarkably worshipful of the state. Indeed, his foreign policy was more Protestant than Catholic whenever royal interests required. He lived by the philosophy of *raison d'état*: any workable expedient was justifiable as long as it aided the Bourbon monarchy.

Richelieu's first task was to prevent the Huguenot rebellion from expanding into another full-scale religious war. Fortunately for him, the Huguenots

Cardinal Richelieu. *Painting by Philippe de Champaigne. The three portraits in juxtaposition adroitly exhibit Richelieu's masterful personality. National Gallery, London.*

of his day posed much less of a threat than in the preceding century. They were less numerous, less ardent, less cohesive, and less ably led. In 1628 Richelieu captured La Rochelle, the chief Huguenot stronghold on the Atlantic coast, after a siege of fourteen months. In 1629 a royal army reduced all of the remaining rebel Huguenot towns in Languedoc. Richelieu's Edict of Alais in 1629 amended the Edict of Nantes by depriving the Huguenots of all their political and military privileges, while continuing their religious liberty. The cardinal was willing to tolerate French Protestants after 1629 because he saw that they were more likely to remain politically harmless if they were not persecuted.

In most respects Richelieu evoked the spirit of Henry IV and Sully. He constantly worked to reduce feudal and regional particularism. He managed to abolish three of the six provincial representative assemblies (those of Burgundy, Dauphiné, and Provence), though when he tried to impose direct royal taxation in Languedoc as well, opposition was so intense that he gave up the idea. He sent *intendants*, agents of the royal council, into the provinces to oversee local tax collection. He appointed himself superintendent of navigation and commerce, to focus attention on France's neglected merchant marine, navy, and coastal defenses. When Richelieu came to power, the royal navy was nonexistent, the Atlantic ports were defenseless against Spanish or English attack, and the Mediterranean coast was infested by pirates. Between 1610 and 1633, some 2,500 French vessels were captured by Barbary pirates, before Richelieu launched a series of campaigns against them. One of his proudest accomplishments was the creation of effective fleets in both the Atlantic and the Mediterranean. The cardinal's program was expensive, and he constantly resorted to deficit financing, particularly after France entered the Thirty Years' War in 1635. He did manage to double the royal revenue during his term of office, mainly by raising the *taille* and thus squeezing the peasants still further. Richelieu had to suppress tax riots in many parts of France, but accepted this consequence quite cheerfully. The common people, he wrote, should not be made too comfortable, for they were like "mules, who, being accustomed to burdens, are spoiled by a long rest more than by work."[1]

The most spectacular aspect of Richelieu's administration was his foreign policy. Once he had reestablished domestic order, he picked up where Henry IV had left off in 1610 and entered into war against the Habsburgs. From Richelieu's viewpoint, the international situation in the late 1620's was thoroughly alarming. While France had stood by, neutral, during the dozen opening years of the Thirty Years' War, its Habsburg rivals had slowly gained the upper hand. Ferdinand II appeared to be well on his way to converting the Holy Roman Empire into an absolute monarchy, while his

[1]Charles W. Cole, *Colbert and a Century of French Mercantilism* (New York, 1939), Vol. I, p. 139.

Spanish cousin, Philip IV, had added part of the Palatinate to his belt of territory which stretched from Milan to Flanders, and Spanish armies were even making some small progress in their efforts to reconquer the Dutch republic. Hence, in 1630 Richelieu subsidized Gustavus Adolphus' invasion of Germany, to the scandal of orthodox Catholics, and after the Swedish king's death in 1632, he organized a new Swedish-German league against the emperor. The Habsburgs' overwhelming victory over the Swedes at Nördlingen in 1634 abruptly liquidated this league. Richelieu was now compelled to take a more active role. He declared war against Spain in 1635 and opened a three-pronged French attack in northern Italy, the Rhineland, and the Netherlands. This bold scheme very nearly boomeranged in 1636 when counterattacking Spanish and imperial forces overran Picardy and threatened Paris. But thereafter the French kept the fighting off their own soil, while the Spanish were crippled by internal crises in Portugal and Catalonia. Richelieu did not live to see his troops annihilate a larger, veteran Spanish army at Rocroi in 1643—the first total defeat inflicted on the vaunted Spanish infantry since the accession of the Habsburg dynasty in 1516. But it was Richelieu who laid the groundwork for the French diplomatic success and the Habsburg defeat at Westphalia in 1648.

It is instructive to compare Richelieu's administration with the strikingly parallel efforts of his Spanish counterpart, the count of Olivares (1587–1645), to overhaul the Habsburg monarchy of Philip IV. Like the French under Louis XIII, the Spaniards desperately needed skillful statesmanship if they were to recover their sixteenth-century heritage of effective government. There was little to choose between Louis XIII and Philip IV. Each was intelligent yet weak-willed, and each depended on a strong minister. Olivares was Philip's chief minister between 1621 and 1643. Like Richelieu, he secured control over his government by winning the confidence of his royal master and ruthlessly eliminating all rivals. He was a big man, always in a hurry, bursting with ideas and energy. He was determined to revive Spain's sixteenth-century imperial greatness by revamping its easygoing, inefficient style of rule. Like Richelieu, Olivares had to wrestle with soaring war costs, a badly unbalanced budget, and an outdated tax system which grossly overburdened the peasantry. And like Richelieu, Olivares tried to break down the entrenched regional particularism of his state. The Iberian peninsula was divided into four semiautonomous kingdoms: Castile, Aragon, Navarre, and Portugal—the latter annexed only in 1580. Under Charles V and Philip II, the Spanish empire had been the private preserve and responsibility of Castile, but Olivares wanted to broaden the responsibility and to make the outlying Iberian regions (where the taxes were comparatively light) share Castile's crushing financial and military commitments. The Portuguese and the people of Catalonia, a province in Aragon, viewed Olivares' efforts at "Castilianization" with the deepest suspicion. These people taxed themselves through their own representative assemblies, or cortes, and they repeatedly ignored Olivares' pleas for the men and money he needed in order to maintain Spanish armies in Italy, Germany, and the Netherlands. When Olivares undertook war against Richelieu's France without first making peace with the Dutch, the Swedes, and the German Protestants, he quickly met disaster. In 1640 both Portugal and Catalonia rose in rebellion and declared their independence of Habsburg rule. The Catalan revolt was at last suppressed in 1652; the Portuguese revolt was never suppressed, though the Habsburgs did not recognize Portugal's independence until 1668. Long before then, Olivares had died a broken man, and Spain's international leadership had irretrievably vanished.

The stark contrast between Richelieu's success and Olivares' failure can scarcely be accounted for by personality differences between the two men. Richelieu may have been somewhat shrewder than Olivares, or less rash. But the antithetical results from their parallel efforts at reform are better explained by fundamental differences between the two societies. Bourbon political and military effectiveness must be correlated with France's rising wealth and vigor, likewise Habsburg political and military weakness with Spain's social and economic stagnation. Seventeenth-century France was so much more prosperous and populous than Spain that Richelieu inevitably had far greater resources at his disposal. Spain was so much more particularistic and hidebound than France that Olivares' imaginative and energetic strategy shocked his people without stimulating them. In trying to arrest Spanish decay, Olivares actually hastened the process of collapse.

After Richelieu's death in 1642, France also plunged into a period of domestic turmoil, but unlike Spain, soon recovered. Louis XIII died in 1643, a few months after his great minister, leaving his five-year-old son as King Louis XIV and his widow, Anne of Austria (1601–1666), as regent. The regency was instantly unpopular, for Anne was a Habsburg princess and she entrusted the management of affairs to her paramour, a smooth and supple Italian adventurer named Guilio Mazarini (1602–1661). This Mazarin, as he was called in France, was a matchless opportunist. Starting as a papal diplomat, he entered French state service under Richelieu, was made a cardinal (though he was not a priest), collected expensive tapestries and paintings, married his beautiful Roman nieces into the high French nobility, and—what particularly galled the pamphleteers who flooded the Paris bookstalls with libels against him—became the queen's lover and very likely her secret husband. But Cardinal Mazarin did not deserve the abuse heaped on him, for he proved to be an astute administrator, entirely devoted to the continuation of Richelieu's policies and to the training of the young king. During the opening years of his administration, Mazarin kept the factious nobility occupied with the war against Spain and the Holy Roman emperor. But the mounting costs of this war strained his ingenuity. He tried various shoddy expedients for raising additional money, such as creating and selling new and useless government offices, manipulating the stock market, and levying fines on trumped-up charges. By an unhappy coincidence, the 1640's saw terrible agricultural depression and famine in France. The desperate peasants not only were unable to pay their manorial obligations to the nobility and their taxes to the crown, but were forced to surrender many of their small landholdings to their bourgeois creditors. Economic dislocation and political unrest ignited the Fronde, a series of tumults (1648–1653) directed against Mazarin's rule.

The Fronde started as a protest by royal officials against Mazarin's perverted administrative techniques; in effect, it was a protest against the whole fifty-year absolutist trend launched by Henry IV. These dissident officials felt cheated out of their rightful perquisites. Having gained privileged status by buying their posts from the crown, French officials had found over the years that Sully, Richelieu, and Mazarin in turn kept cutting back their salaries, creating rival new offices, and imposing over them *intendants* who stole away their authority. The *Parlement* of Paris, the chief law court in France, voiced these grievances in 1648, and demanded that Mazarin and the queen restore the former privileges and powers of the entrenched bureaucracy. The Paris mob rioted wildly in support of the *Parlement*—indeed, the *fronde*, which gave its name to these disorders, was a slingshot used by mischievous Paris boys to mess up the streets by flinging mud or stones. But the officials of the *Parlement* of Paris disapproved of riots and rebellions; their aim was to safeguard their own privileged status within the government, not to tear the government apart. In 1649 the *Parlement* came to terms with Mazarin. By this time the Thirty Years' War was over, and the aristocratic French army officers, itching for fresh action, marched their troops against the hated cardinal. The Fronde thus suddenly turned into a feudal rebellion led by the princes of the blood who felt excluded by Richelieu and Mazarin from their rightful station. These aristocratic *frondeurs* were much more dangerous and destructive than the officials of the *Parlement* of Paris had been. They chased Mazarin out of France, and the king and his mother out of Paris. Many of them were hoping to dismantle the central government and to cut France into a mosaic of sovereign princely states like the Holy Roman Empire. For three years their private armies roamed the country, tilting against one another as if in a gigantic tournament. At last, in 1652, the fourteen-year-old Louis XIV declared his majority and was welcomed back to Paris. By 1653 Mazarin was back also, the rebel nobles had retired to their country estates or disappeared into exile, and the Fronde was over.

Like the French crises of 1560–1598 and 1610–1624, the Fronde demonstrated that there was no palatable alternative to absolute monarchy in seventeenth-century France. The *frondeurs* had plenty to complain about, but their motives were so patently and narrowly selfish that they could not mount a constructive protest movement, let alone produce a tolerable substitute for Mazarin. Throughout the crisis the various rebellious elements in French society—the nobility, the bureaucracy, the peasantry, the Paris

An anti-Mazarin cartoon, *c.* 1652. *One of the leading* frondeurs, *Mademoiselle de Montpensier, having rallied the city of Orleans in the name of the young king, is putting the torch to the hated cardinal.*

mob—worked at cross-purposes. One traditionally rebellious group, the Huguenots, took no part in the Fronde, supposing that fulsome loyalty to the crown offered the best chance for survival. Indeed, the Fronde compelled all Frenchmen who placed much value on stability and prosperity to be ardent royalists. Certainly Louis XIV believed that such anarchy must never recur. The bitter experience of 1648–1653 made an indelible impression on the young king. His memory of rampaging Parisians, particularly of the crowd which burst into his palace bedchamber one night in 1651 to make sure that he had not escaped with Mazarin, persuaded Louis to remove the royal court from Paris to Versailles. His memory of irresponsible noblemen dividing the spoils during his minority convinced Louis that he must politically emasculate the privileged aristocracy. His memory of the Paris *Parlement* daring to criticize royal policy sharpened his resolve to assert his own majesty, based upon divine right and buttressed by a phalanx of obsequious underlings.

But Louis XIV was still too young to take personal charge. Hence, Cardinal Mazarin resumed direction of affairs from 1653 until his death in 1661. Under Mazarin, France reaped the rewards of Richelieu's ambitious foreign policy. At the Peace of Westphalia in 1648, despite his preoccupation with the Fronde, Mazarin had secured very advantageous terms. Portions of Alsace and Lorraine were ceded to France, while the permanent internal paralysis of the Holy Roman Empire permitted the French government to build a network of alliances with German princely states against the

Habsburg emperor. War against Spain continued for a decade longer, though both contestants were largely engrossed in domestic problems. In 1659 this war finally terminated in the Peace of the Pyrenees, another diplomatic success for Mazarin. France gained further territory—Artois, adjoining Flanders, and Roussillon, bordering the Pyrenees. The Bourbon-Habsburg conflict was papered over by the second intermarriage between the two families in two generations, this time between Louis XIV and his cousin Maria Theresa, the Spanish infanta. Through his new queen, Louis established a strong claim to the inheritance of all the Spanish Habsburg possessions in Europe and America. He could thus hope to create a new dynastic empire greater than that of Charles V. There seemed no limit to Bourbon ambition or success. The Sun King was staging his grand entry into European affairs.

English Civil War

THE PURITAN REVOLUTION

During the first half of the seventeenth century, while in France the Bourbons were consolidating power, in England the Stuart kings James I (ruled 1603–1625) and Charles I (ruled 1625–1649) lost control of the government. The English civil war of the 1640's, also known as the Great Rebellion or the Puritan Revolution, was a much more fundamental protest against monarchy than was the contemporaneous Fronde in France. Superficially, this English revolution is something of a puzzle. The English monarchy was immensely popular when the last Tudor sovereign, Elizabeth I, died in 1603. Elizabeth left no direct heirs, and the throne passed to James Stuart, king of Scotland. James and his son Charles were certainly inferior kings, yet they were trapped in circumstances which might well have baffled far abler rulers. England was a more cohesive community than France, less dependent on strong management from above. The country was only one quarter as large and as populous as France. Parliament was the uncontested national representative assembly, there being no regional assemblies. The nobility, gentry, and merchants, whose spokesmen sat in Parliament, were more homogeneous than in France and better able to cooperate in politics—or in opposition to their king.

After a century of Tudor paternalism, the English had grown restive during the final years of Elizabeth I's reign. The crown was handicapped by inadequate revenues, a stunted bureaucracy, and the absence of a regular army. And England was one of the few European states—the Holy Roman Empire and Sweden were the others—where religious tensions were rising rather than declining during the early seventeenth century. The Puritans formed a dissident Calvinist movement within the state church, agitating strenuously against the Catholic ceremonial and institutional elements in Anglicanism. Puritans could be found practically anywhere in England, but they were most evident in intellectual circles, among the lesser landed gentry

SUCCESSION TO THE ENGLISH CROWN, 1558–1714

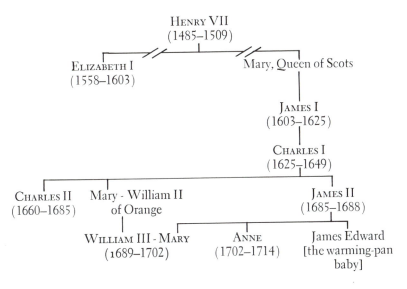

(particularly in the eastern counties of Norfolk, Suffolk, Cambridge, and Essex), in the city of London, and in Parliament. It was far from easy to cope with a movement half hidden and amorphous, yet infused with righteous zeal.

The first Stuart king, James I, was a tragicomic failure despite good intentions and real abilities. He was the son of Mary, Queen of Scots, an alarming pedigree, but James had little of his mother's reckless passion—or bewitching charm. He was an erudite scholar, and proud of it. He had ruled Scotland successfully for many years, but the overbearing tactics he had used in handling wild lairds and fanatic Presbyterians were inappropriate in England. In 1598, James had published *The Trew Law of Free Monarchies*, in which he exhorted his Scottish subjects to obey their king, who was accountable to God alone. All laws were given by the king, he asserted, and all constitutional forms and assemblies existed entirely at his pleasure. Elizabeth I had tacitly subscribed to this divine-right theory of monarchy, but she carefully avoided writing a book on the subject, nor did she lecture Parliament on her God-given powers, as James did repeatedly when he took the English throne. James did not look like God's lieutenant. His tongue was too big for his mouth, and his rolling eyes gave him a perpetually apprehensive expression. He wore his clothes heavily padded against the stilettos of would-be assassins, and while stag hunting he sometimes was tied onto his horse to keep from falling off. Even sycophantic courtiers disliked these hunting parties, during which the king might exultantly slash a fallen

James I. *In this engraving, as in most of his other portraits, James looks apprehensive. He seems to doubt whether he can stay astride his horse. National Portrait Gallery, London.*

stag's belly, shove his hands into its entrails, and slop his dogs and attendants with blood.

In the course of James's reign, the revolutionary crisis began to take clear shape. The new king quarreled publicly with the Puritans, mostly because he identified them with the Scottish Presbyterians who had tried to shackle him with Calvin's church government. "No bishop, no king," he cried out during a conference with Puritan spokesmen—a telling aphorism with which his adversaries would one day agree. "I will make them conform themselves," James warned the Puritans, "or I will harry them out of this land or else do worse." James did in fact deprive many Puritan clergy of their benefices, with the consequence that the movement spread among the laity more powerfully than before. James's fiscal policy exposed the crown to further criticism. His expenditures were double those of Elizabeth, partly because of the continuing inflationary spiral, partly because he had a wife and children to support, but mostly because he was more extravagant than the late queen. In order to increase revenue, the crown resorted to various business-damaging expedients, such as the sale of hundreds of monopolies, which artificially rigged the production, distribution, and price of such everyday commodities as soap, coal, vinegar, and pins. Elizabethan monopolists had been highly unpopular, and James's growing dependence on them greatly irked the hardheaded landowners and businessmen who sat in Parliament.

The king's relations with Parliament deteriorated steadily. He would have done well to imitate Elizabeth, who asked Parliament for as little money as possible, and saw to it that her ministers prepared programs of government proposals in advance and steered debate and legislation through both houses. James asked Parliament freely for money, without bothering to justify his needs. The initiative in debate and legislation was quickly seized by critics of the government. Ignoring the king's lectures on his divine attributes, Parliament voted him very little money and devoted a good deal of time to the formulation of statements of grievances. The House of Commons, James complained, was a body without a head—-true enough, since the king had abdicated the responsibilities of headship.

Everything went wrong for James I during the closing years of his reign. As he grew older and slacker, his previously latent homosexuality asserted itself, and he handed over the direction of affairs to his favorites, young men whose only qualifications were their physical beauty and their grace. The last and most seductive of these favorites, the scatterbrained duke of Buckingham (1592–1628), had total control over the infatuated king from 1619 until his death. James's last parliaments, in 1621 and 1624, were more openly critical of the government than the earlier ones had been. The House of Commons had a great leader in Sir Edward Coke (1552-1634), the wisest jurist of the age, who had been dismissed from judicial office by the king. In 1621 Parliament revived the medieval procedure of impeachment against Coke's bitter enemy Lord Chancellor Francis Bacon, the philosopher, on charges of bribery. Bacon's impeachment was a clear step toward parliamentary regulation of the king's ministers. Parliament also denounced the government's foreign policy, which was pro-Spanish because the king hoped to arrange a Spanish Habsburg marriage for his son Charles. In 1623 he let Charles slip off secretly to Madrid with Buckingham in a romantic effort to woo and win the infanta. The doting king wrote anxiously to his "sweet boys," as he called them—"Baby Charles" and "Steenie"—and closed his letters, "your dear dad and husband, James R." But Baby Charles came home from Madrid furious at the Spaniards' refusal to let him court or marry the infanta, and Steenie secured Parliament's consent to a war against Spain, despite the senile king's protestations. Thus, by the time James died in 1625, all his hopes had been ludicrously dashed, and the opposition to the Stuart monarchy was formidable.

Charles I was more truculent than his father, and during the opening years of his reign, 1625–1629, the political and religious critics of the Stuart monarchy began to join together in a serious rebel party. In the elegant portraits by Anthony Van Dyck, Charles cuts the perfect figure of a king: he looks handsome, reserved, abstemious, cultivated. But the new king was totally insensitive to public opinion and incapable of political give-and-take. Charles I was a stalwart High Churchman, valuing the Catholic ceremonial elements in Anglicanism, and he held his father's views on divine-right monarchy. The hated duke of Buckingham continued to be chief minister. Charles immediately quarreled more violently with Parliament than his father had ever done. The new king peremptorily demanded money, but Parliament was only interested in impeaching Buckingham. So Charles levied a forced loan, which gave him as much money as he would have obtained through Parliament. Seventy-six prominent gentlemen (including several members of Parliament) were jailed for refusing to "contribute."

When Charles I, still needing money, summoned another Parliament in 1628, he found both houses united against him. Lords and Commons cooperated closely in framing the famous Petition of Right. By bribing the king with a tax grant, they extracted his promise not to levy or borrow money without parliamentary consent, nor to imprison men without due process of law. By agreeing to these conditions, Charles acknowledged that he had violated his subjects' liberties. In time, the Petition of Right became a constitutional landmark, but its immediate effect was slight, for the king soon resumed his nonparliamentary levies and the arbitrary punishment of persons who dared to criticize his regime. One great grievance was permanently removed in 1628; the duke of Buckingham was assassinated, to the king's grief and the public's joy. Any remaining possibility of cooperation between king and Parliament disappeared in 1629, when the tempestuous Sir John Eliot (1592–1632) started the Commons on a new hue and cry against royal policy. When the king ordered the House to adjourn, two of the more athletic members held their weeping speaker in his chair to keep the meeting in session, while the excited assembly passed by acclamation Eliot's three resolutions declaring High Church innovations and the collection of customs unauthorized by Parliament to be treasonable. This dramatic gesture alienated many moderate men and permitted the king to seem more reasonable than his adversaries. Charles vowed to govern without Parliament and did so for the next eleven years.

Charles I's personal rule between 1629 and 1640 has often been compared with Richelieu's contemporaneous administration in France. But whatever his ultimate aims, Charles never came close to erecting a Bourbon-style monarchy. To be sure, his most conspicuous ministers after Buckingham's death, Archbishop William Laud (1573–1645) and Sir Thomas Wentworth (1593–1641), thought they knew better than the people what was good for them and urged "thorough" measures to achieve efficiency and order. But Laud and Wentworth were often frustrated by rivals within the royal council, and in any case Wentworth was mostly absent in northern England or Ireland, where he served as the king's deputy. No English minister could enforce decisions as Richelieu did. Charles I had no *intendants,* no standing army. Local administration continued to depend on the cooperation of unpaid justices of the peace, many of whom had sat in Parliament and criticized royal policy. The government lived from hand to mouth, a cipher in international politics. The king's advisers searched for legal loopholes by which to circumvent parliamentary control over taxation. For example, they discovered a long-forgotten requirement that any gentleman worth £40 or more a year should present himself to be knighted at the king's coronation, and this permitted Charles to collect £165,000 in fines from all the wealthy gentry who had not been knighted at his coronation in 1626! More crucial was Charles's manipulation of ship money, an impost which had customarily been levied on seaports in times of emergency to provide naval vessels for defense. Charles turned ship money into an annual national tax, levied on inland as well as coastal areas. John Hampden (1594–1643), a wealthy squire, challenged his £1 assessment in the courts on the ground that if a national emergency existed, Parliament should be called. The royal judges upheld the legality of ship money by the narrow majority of seven to five, but the tax could no longer be collected effectively. Charles's financial policy thus roused more troublesome opposition than Richelieu's. The French tax burden fell mainly on the unprivileged peasantry, but the Stuart extraparliamentary levies provoked the nobility, gentry, and merchants. These people could well afford to pay, for their collective wealth was vastly greater than the king's. But conscious of their rising prosperity, they deeply resented being excluded from power.

Religion, however, was the most explosive single issue. Charles I entrusted management of the state church to Archbishop Laud, a martinet with exceptional powers of industry and obstinacy. Where Cardinal Richelieu respected the religious liberty of the Huguenots, Archbishop Laud deliberately challenged the Puritans. His ambition was to elevate the power of the

Charles I. *Painting by Van Dyck. The portrait was painted about 1635, when the king seemed to be winning his battle against Parliament and the Puritans. Louvre, Paris.*

Anglican episcopate and the dignity of Anglican public worship. By teaching all Englishmen to revere "the beauty of holiness" as expressed in the order of worship in the Anglican prayer book, Laud hoped to foster social decorum and suppress Puritan zeal. These aims were closer in spirit to the Catholic reformation than to the Protestant and gave a new ring to James I's motto—"no bishop, no king." In fact, however, few among the bishops supported Laud, and on the parish level his wishes were freely ignored. The archbishop's efforts to bully the Puritans by prosecuting his most obnoxious Puritan critics in the royal law courts backfired painfully. In 1637, when three antiprelatical pamphleteers named Burton, Bastwick, and Prynne had their ears cropped—very mild punishment compared with the ruthless religious persecution of the sixteenth century—they were immediately hailed as martyrs. Bigger trouble came in Scotland when Charles I and Laud endeavored to impose an Anglican prayer book on the Presbyterian populace. The Scots riotously rejected the prayer book and in 1638 swore a national covenant to defend to the death their religious and political liberties. Charles tried to suppress the Scottish rebellion, but he could not raise an effective army, and by 1640 the Scots had invaded the north of England. The king was now completely cornered. With no money, no army, and no popular support, he had to summon Parliament in 1640.

The Long Parliament, so called because it remained in session from 1640 to 1653, triggered the biggest revolution in English history. Scholars have traditionally argued that the crisis of the 1640's was a contest over religious and political principles—Puritanism versus Anglicanism and parliamentary self-government versus royal absolutism. The current tendency, however, is to stress the economic and social factors underlying these religious and political issues. Marxist historians, for instance, have greatly enriched our understanding of the crisis by viewing the English revolution as an expression of class warfare, like the French and Russian revolutions. It was, they argue, the first major victory by the European bourgeoisie over the feudal class. There is considerable evidence for this argument: in the 1640's the English merchants and artisans, particularly in London, generally supported Parliament, while the aristocracy and the economically backward northern part of the country backed the king.

Yet the awkward obstacle to this class-war interpretation is the role of the gentry, or lesser landlords. These people were the chief actors in the English revolution, and they divided themselves pretty evenly between the parliamentary and the royalist camps. Whether we label the gentry as feudal or as bourgeois, how are we to explain in economic terms their prominence in the struggle and their ideological disunity? Various efforts have been made to do so. One school, adapting Marx's thesis, sees them as a rising agrarian middle class, gaining prosperity at the expense of the crown and the aristocracy between 1540 and 1640. The more prosperous and self-confident members of this class, it is argued, led the fight for Parliament and Puritanism in the 1640's in order to consolidate their power. But a contrary school insists that the most prosperous members of the gentry attached themselves to the king's court, and that those small landlords who had to live on their farm income were becoming less prosperous between 1540 and 1640. Caught by the inflation and by agricultural depression, and excluded from government patronage by the Stuarts, these declining gentry turned to Puritanism and to revolution in a desperate effort to retrieve their status. The first of these interpretations appears to fit the facts better than the second, but neither is convincing. Present evidence suggests that the gentry—like most Englishmen—were neither booming nor collapsing economically in the mid-seventeenth century.

Reacting against the Marxists, many scholars now stress the conservative social forces at work in 1640. Analyzing the membership of Parliament, they find no significant economic or social differentiation between the supporters and the critics of the king. Analyzing the network of merchants who ruled London, they find wealthy men fearful of change. Analyzing the communities of country gentry who controlled the forty counties, they find deep suspicion of any central authority. How then did a revolution take place? It appears time to revive the traditional emphasis on national political and religious issues, for an economic or social interpretation either distorts the English crisis by turning it into a French- or Russian-style cataclysm, or trivializes it by denying that any real crisis occurred. It is certain that many Englishmen *were* wildly excited over political and religious issues. Religion was the greatest single

The House of Commons in 1640. *From an old print. The Commons chamber was very small and, as this picture shows, some of the members had to stand. The Speaker of the House sits in the tall chair with two clerks before him; the sergeant-at-arms, who carries the mace (lower center), has the job of keeping out strangers.*

catalyst. The crisis of the 1640's is best called the Puritan Revolution; it constituted the last and grandest episode in Europe's age of religious wars.

The course of events in England from 1640 to 1660 is not easily summarized, for the English revolution, like all great revolutions, was a complex phenomenon with its own special heroic and tragic qualities. At the outset, in 1640, there appeared to be no possibility of civil war. Parliament had the united support of the English upper classes, and Charles I stood helplessly isolated. Exhilarated by the frenzied London atmosphere, the Lords and the Commons speedily rescued the king from the evil advisers who had perpetrated the "eleven years' tyranny" of nonparliamentary rule. Wentworth and Laud were imprisoned. Parliament sentenced Wentworth to death, and half the population of London jammed Tower Hill to watch and cheer his execution.

The members of Parliament were not conscious revolutionaries in 1640. They supposed themselves the guardians of England's ancient liberties, though in fact, under the astute management of John Pym (1584–1643), who had learned his tactics from Sir Edward Coke, Parliament circumscribed Charles I's sovereignty through a series of constitutional innovations. All of the king's recent extraparliamentary taxes were declared illegal. The royal law courts which had been used by Wentworth and Laud were abolished. Parliament was henceforth to sit every three years at least, and the present Parliament could not be dissolved without its own consent.

Having pulled down the old government, Parliament in 1641 began building a new one. Immediately, parliamentary unity dissolved. As controversial issues came to the fore—should Parliament nominate the king's ministers? control the army? reorganize the church?—many members began to ally with Charles I. The hottest question was religious: whether or not to abolish the office of bishop and eliminate the prayer book. The Puritans and the political radicals, who held a slim majority in the House of Commons, hardened into a truly revolutionary party bent on reconstructing church and state. In reaction to this, a royalist party formed, within Parliament and throughout the country, to resist further change. In January, 1642, Charles I tried to break the parliamentary radicals with a military coup. But his plan was too clumsy. When he entered the House of Commons, backed by four hundred armed men, intending to seize Pym and the other leaders, his intended victims had already escaped. Mob pressure forced Charles and his adherents to leave London. Within a few months both sides were raising troops, and the war was on.

The civil war of 1642–1646 was very modest in scale and intensity. At the peak of combat, no more than one Englishman out of every ten of fighting age was in arms (compared with one out of four in the American Civil War), and the amateurish campaigning kept damage to life and property fairly negligible. The parliamentary soldiers were nicknamed Roundheads because of the Puritan propensity for cutting the hair short; the royalists, or Cavaliers, looked swashbuckling and romantic by comparison. It was no accident that the Roundheads won the war. They held London and the wealthy and populous southeastern half of the country. Parliament collected large sums of money through excise and property taxes—far heavier levies, ironically, than Charles I had ever attempted. The Cavaliers operated out of the more sparsely populated northwestern half of England, and they were chronically short of money, manpower, and war materials. The king's troops resembled the roving bands led by soldiers of fortune in the Thirty Years' War. Prince Rupert, the most dashing Cavalier commander, could open a battle brilliantly with a madcap cavalry charge, but his undisciplined horsemen then often disappeared in search of the enemy baggage train, while the Roundheads regrouped and won the engagement. The Roundheads' greatest initial resource was their exalted moral fervor. An unprecedented torrent of pamphlets, averaging 1,500 a year throughout the 1640's, expressed in manifold ways their ardent quest for the political, religious, or social rebirth of England. John Milton's *Areopagitica* (1644), the most famous of these pamphlets, epitomized the Roundhead wartime spirit. "Methinks," the exalted Puritan poet chanted, "I see in my mind a noble and puissant nation rousing herself like a strong man after sleep, and shaking her invincible locks. Methinks I see her as an eagle mewing her mighty youth, and kindling her undazzled eyes at the full midday beam." But the parliamentary leaders were not equal to Milton's vision. For two years Charles I's troops held the upper hand, mainly because the Roundhead generals really did not want to fight and defeat their anointed king. The tide began to turn in 1643 when Pym secured a military alliance between Parliament and Presbyterian Scotland. The next year a parliamentary-Scottish army beat Prince Rupert at Marston Moor in the biggest pitched battle of the war. But even more significant in the long run was the emergence of a Puritan soldier of genius, Oliver Cromwell (1599–1658).

Nothing in Cromwell's humdrum prewar career prepares us for his preeminent role in the Puritan Revolution. When the Long Parliament convened, he was an obscure middle-aged country squire, one of the least affluent members of Commons. Few noticed this blunt, roughhewn man when he spoke out occasionally and chaotically against the Anglican bishops. Once fighting started, Cromwell enlisted in the parliamentary army and subscribed £500 (his annual income) to help defray military expenses. Some inner resource—Cromwell would have said it was God's redemptive grace—gave him the rock strength to master every problem he encountered from his first battle in 1642 until his death in 1658. He recruited in 1643 a cavalry regiment of "honest, godly men," who maintained strict discipline and sang psalms as they chased the Cavaliers. Most Puritans, believing (as Cromwell did) that God had predestined them for salvation, gathered themselves during or after the war into congregations or churches of the elect. Cromwell never joined a Puritan church. He saw his regiment as a kind of church, the Lord's humble instrument for rescuing England from popery and slavery. Cromwell's regiment, soon christened the Ironsides, won every engagement

Oliver Cromwell. *This crude engraving of the Puritan commander conveys his homely appearance and purposeful energy. National Portrait Gallery, London.*

it fought. Cromwell and his troops were chiefly responsible for the defeat of Prince Rupert's Cavaliers at Marston Moor in 1644. "God made them as stubble to our swords," wrote Cromwell in describing the battle. At his instigation, Parliament reorganized the Roundhead army, weeding out the lukewarm generals who hated to fight the king. This "New Model" parliamentary army (with Cromwell second in command) decimated Charles I's remaining forces at Naseby in 1645. The king was taken prisoner in 1646 and remained under army guard for the next two years. The Puritans seemed to have secured a stunning victory.

It was much easier to end the war than to reach a peace settlement. The Puritans had been held together only by their common hostility to bishops, the prayer book, and arbitrary monarchy, and by 1646 they were hopelessly fragmented into three factions. Most conservative were the Presbyterians, who wanted the Church of England transformed into a tightly organized national Calvinist church on the Scottish model, and believed that the king should be subordinated to parliamentary control, but advocated no further changes in the social or political order. The Presbyterians were less strong in England than in Scotland, but they held a majority in Parliament and dominated the London mercantile community. In the center, the Independents wanted more thoroughgoing changes. They rejected any sort of compulsory state church, whether Anglican or Presbyterian, and advocated religious toleration for a variety of voluntary, autonomous Puritan churches. In their view, Parliament as well as the monarchy needed to be reformed so as to respond more effectively to the needs of the common people. The Independents had spokesmen in Parliament, but their stronghold was the officer corps of the New Model Army. Oliver Cromwell was an Independent. More extreme than the Independents were numerous radical Puritan sects, most of which had not even existed before 1640. Their members called for the total regeneration of English society. Some of them were apocalyptic, as were the Fifth Monarchy Men, who supposed that Christ's second coming was imminent. Others were more secular, as were the Levellers, who drafted constitutions providing for universal male suffrage and other guarantees of popular sovereignty, democratic principles not to be realized in England or anywhere else until the nineteenth century. More extreme than the Levellers were the Diggers, or agrarian communists, who believed that God forbade the ownership of private property. Naturally, these radical sects appealed more to the poor than to the rich; they drew enthusiastic support from the rank and file of the New Model Army. Thus, in the maelstrom of the English revolution, Presbyterians, Independents, and radical sectaries had developed Calvin's precepts into a full spectrum of social attitudes, from self-righteous bigotry to compassion for the unprivileged, from repressive conservatism to visionary radicalism, from autocracy to anarchy.

Between 1646 and 1648, while trying to negotiate a settlement with the captive Charles I, the Presbyterians, Independents, and radical sectaries struggled violently among themselves for control of the revolution. The Presbyterians in Parliament made the fatal mistake of trying to disband the New Model Army without paying the soldiers. Under Cromwell's leadership, the army refused to disband. Cromwell barely managed to keep the radicals within his army under control. The shorthand notes have been preserved of a fascinating debate between army spokesmen for the Independents and the Levellers at Putney in 1647. "The poorest he that is in England hath a life to live, as the greatest he," cried one of the Levellers. "I do not find anything in the Law of God, that a lord shall choose twenty burgesses [representatives in Parliament], and a gentleman but two, or a poor man shall choose none." The Independents retorted that "the meanest man in England ought to have a voice in the election of the government he lives under—but only if he has some local interest," that is, some property to give him a stake in society. Cromwell's role in the Putney debate was to call for prayers whenever the argument grew too hot. His soldiers still shared enough spirit of common purpose to remain an invincible force. In 1648, Cromwell crushed a Presbyterian-Cavalier uprising on behalf of the king. His army entered London and executed the sort of military coup against Parliament which Charles I had failed to carry off in 1642. A certain Colonel Pride stationed his troopers around the Parliament house and permitted only those members friendly to the army—some sixty Independents—to enter. "Pride's Purge" eliminated the Presbyterian majority in Parliament and reduced the proud national assembly of 1640 to a minority "rump" session.

Now Cromwell was in a position to deal with the king. Convinced that Charles I was the chief remaining obstacle to peace, Cromwell determined that he should be killed as publicly and solemnly as possible. The "Rump"

Parliament erected a High Court of Justice which sentenced Charles to death as a tyrant, traitor, murderer, and public enemy of the people of England. On January 30, 1649, he was executed outside his banqueting hall at Whitehall. "I am a martyr of the people," Charles protested to the groaning crowd, just before the masked executioner decapitated him with a single stroke of the ax.

The king's execution was very unpopular, yet Cromwell had little choice. It was pointless to negotiate any further with a man who refused to accept a Puritan state in any form, and it was unsafe to let Charles stay in prison or retire abroad. Ironically, Cromwell had tried harder than any of his adversaries—far harder than Charles himself—to find a generous settlement. But his methods had become more extreme, more tyrannical, than Charles's had ever been. The royalists, Presbyterians, and radicals all hated Cromwell's recourse to naked military rule. Though the Independents were securely in control by 1649, their liberal aims were hopelessly compromised.

From 1649 to 1660 England was a Puritan republic. In its relations with other states, the revolutionary regime acted with impressive energy. In 1649 Cromwell conquered Ireland, slaughtering Catholics much more freely than he had killed Cavaliers during the English war. In 1650–1651 he conquered Scotland. By compelling both peoples to accept union with England, the Puritans did what no English king had been able to do; they welded Great Britain into a single political unit. In 1652–1654 the English fought a naval war with the Dutch, during which they captured 1,400 enemy ships and bolstered England's competitive position with respect to the Dutch merchant marine. In 1655–1659 they fought Spain, capturing Jamaica in the West Indies, and Dunkirk in Flanders.

Internally, however, the revolutionaries were less successful; they could find no acceptable constitutional framework. Between 1649 and 1653 the government consisted of an awkward alliance between the Rump Parliament (the sixty members who had not been purged in 1648) and the army officers. Cromwell felt increasingly frustrated by the petty spirit of his civilian partners and increasingly convinced that his all-conquering army was God's chosen instrument. "Is not this Army a lawful power," he asked, "called by God to oppose and fight against the King, and being in power, may it not oppose one name of authority as well as another?" In 1653 he disbanded Parliament in another military coup and cut his last tie with the pre-1642 constitution. Cromwell took the title of Lord Protector and operated pretty much as an absolute monarch. Most Englishmen wanted a king. Cromwell refrained from adopting the royal title only because his army officers so adamantly opposed his doing so. The Protector's standing army of fifty thousand men and his belligerent foreign policy required a budget triple the size of Charles I's in the 1630's. The gentry and merchants protested, with better reason than under Charles, that they were being overtaxed. The Protector, having ejected the Long Parliament, called three Parliaments of his own, but since he would not let these assemblies control taxation or

Death warrant of Charles I, 1649. *It was signed and sealed by fifty-nine members of the High Court of Justice which found him guilty of treason. Oliver Cromwell's signature is the third in the first column. Some of the judges signed with great reluctance, and one of them later alleged that Cromwell had forcibly guided his pen.*

question his executive powers, he got along with Parliament no better than the Stuarts had done.

Oliver Cromwell was not a conscious dictator. Religion mattered most to him, and he offered Puritans of every description, whether Independents, Presbyterians, Baptists, Fifth Monarchy Men, or even the highly inflammatory new sect of Quakers, the liberty to quest freely for spiritual grace. The doctrine of religious liberty is the Puritans' noblest legacy. Yet there was no liberty for Anglicans, to say nothing of Catholics. As far as most Englishmen were concerned, the Puritan crusade had ossified into a killjoy code of blue laws, enforced by military police. The tonic faith of the 1640's that England could be spiritually regenerated was gone. The mood of the 1650's was better captured by Thomas Hobbes's *Leviathan* (1651), the most remarkable book to come out of the English revolution. Hobbes endorsed the Protector's dictatorship, not on religious grounds (Hobbes was a cynical materialist) but because Cromwell abridged the people's individual liberty more effectively than the Stuarts had done, and thus restrained them from their natural propensity to destroy one another.

Oliver Cromwell died in 1658. In the eighteen months following his death, a series of artificial governments were set up and overthrown. None of the army officers had the stature to succeed Cromwell, but the army could not be dislodged from power, despite the bankruptcy of the revolutionary cause. Finally, in 1660, General George Monck arranged the election of a new Parliament, which promptly invited Charles I's son to return to England as Charles II. With the restoration of the Stuart monarchy, a new era began.

Some historians like to view the Puritan Revolution as part of a wider "general crisis" which swept across western Europe in the mid-seventeenth century. The revolt against Charles I in England occurred during the same period as the Fronde directed against Mazarin in France, and the Portuguese and Catalan revolts against Olivares in Spain. In each of these contemporaneous revolutions, a parliament or equivalent assembly challenged the crown on the specific issue of taxation and the general issue of expensive, paternalistic, central government. Each was triggered to some degree by economic and social malaise, resulting from the interminable Thirty Years' War, the inflationary spiral, a series of bad harvests, a severe slump in the cloth business, and dislocations in international trade.[2] The 1640's and 1650's were indeed years of depression and famine in many parts of Europe. But the English did not overthrow Charles I because they were impoverished and insecure; they acted because they were strong. The dreary image of "general crisis" scarcely suggests the dynamic creativity of the English rebels in the 1640's. Their expression of protest was not merely larger in scale and intensity than the Fronde and the Iberian revolt. It was galvanized by a religious idealism missing in the other revolts. Unlike the reactionary *frondeurs*, and the provincial Catalan and Portuguese rebels, the Puritans launched new ideas of great motor power. They could not erect a lasting republic, but no subsequent English king dared to forget the lesson of 1649. The task the Puritans started would be completed in the English revolution of 1688–1689.

FRANCE UNDER LOUIS XIV

As England's revolutionary crisis was dying down, a very different era dawned in France. In 1661, with the death of Cardinal Mazarin, Louis XIV (ruled 1643–1715) assumed personal direction of the French government. Circumstances were ideal for a grandiose reign. No radical innovations were required of the young king, for Henry IV, Richelieu, and Mazarin had

[2]For a fuller exposition of this "general crisis" thesis, see *Crisis in Europe, 1560–1660*, ed. by Trevor Aston (New York, 1965), pp. 5–116.

already laid down his guidelines. The French privileged classes were eager to be commanded by a king who acted the part. Louis' army and his revenues were much the largest in Europe. France had just defeated archrival Spain, and with Germany divided, England distracted, and the Dutch posing no military threat, French international preeminence was incontestable. Louis XIV, being but twenty-two years old in 1661, could anticipate a long future as the first gentleman in an elaborately hierarchical society, graced by sumptuous royal pageantry and the glory of fairly easy foreign conquests. Such hopes were lavishly fulfilled. For an incredible fifty-four years, Louis held the stage as the *Grand Monarque*, the archetype of absolutism, admired and feared by all other European princes. Toward the end of the reign, to be sure, Louis' style of rule created serious problems both at home and abroad. But during the years 1661–1688, with which we are here concerned, he could aptly characterize his royal performance as "grand, noble and delicious."

Louis XIV might not have succeeded in many occupations, but he was superbly equipped to be a divine-right monarch. To begin with, he appeared majestic, with his proud demeanor, robust physique, graceful carriage, opulent costumes, and perfect manners. More important, he had the stamina and concentration to act out each tiresome detail of his role as potentate before thousands of hypercritical spectators, day after day and year after year. Finally, he had the common sense to enjoy what was given to him, without overstraining his powers in trying (like the English Puritans) to remake

Louis XIV visiting the Gobelins workshop. *In this busy scene, the king (upper left) inspects tapestries, fabrics, furniture, and urns of precious metal made at the Gobelins shop. Colbert heavily subsidized this luxury craftwork. Musée de Versailles.*

France. That Louis had received a very superficial education was doubtless an advantage, since it permitted him to accept his own greatness naïvely, without having to worry about the subtleties and complexities of governing a powerful state. He hated to read, but he was a good listener and enjoyed presiding over council meetings for several hours a day. Greater brilliance or intellectuality would have handicapped Louis in his crucial position as leader of the French aristocracy, a role in which breeding and ceremony counted for more than brains. Louis moved his royal court from the Louvre to Versailles, twelve miles outside Paris, partly to escape the tumultuous citizenry and partly to provide a suitably huge yet secluded social center for the aristocracy. At Versailles he built a colossal palace, the facade a third of a mile long, the echoing marble chambers embellished with Gobelin tapestries and bravura ceiling paintings celebrating his military triumphs, the vast surrounding formal gardens decorated by 1,400 fountains, the orangery stocked with 1,200 orange trees, and the halls and grounds adorned with classical statuary—most often representations of Apollo, the sun god. Today Versailles is a huge museum. In the late seventeenth century, ten thousand noblemen, officials, and attendants lived there. Sixty per cent of the royal tax revenue was expended on Versailles and the upkeep of Louis' court.

The secret of Louis XIV's success was really very simple: he and he alone could give the French aristocracy and upper bourgeoisie what they each wanted more than anything else at the moment. The king devoted more than half of each working day to the ceremonial ballet of his court. This was time well spent, for the aristocracy had long been the most fractious and unmanageable element in French society, and would cooperate only if the king honored and glorified their exclusive world of social privilege. They alone were permitted to attend the king at Versailles. Louis shrewdly required all of the chief members of the nobility to live at court, where he could keep an eye on them. He regimented every aspect of his own daily routine, and that of his courtiers, by a strict code of palace etiquette, so as to impart order to the huge court, exalt his own person, and domesticate his semifeudal nobility. The aristocrat who might otherwise have been plotting a new Fronde at his country château was harmlessly occupied at Versailles by court scandal, his highest ambitions being to hold one sleeve of Louis' garment when he dressed, hear the king speak a few daily platitudes, and watch him eat. Louis was a hearty trencherman and preferred to dine alone, unencumbered by aristocratic attendants. By the time a guard of honor had escorted the king's dinner several blocks from the kitchens to the royal table, the food was invariably cold, but this did not stop Louis from polishing off a half dozen plates of fowl and meat at a sitting. The menu for one of his banquets included 168 distinct garnished dishes.

Only through assiduous court attendance could an aristocrat obtain favors, sinecures, and pensions. The king had numerous honorific positions in his gift; deserving aristocrats were appointed bishops, generals, provincial gover-

Central courtyard, palace of Versailles. *Painting by an unknown artist. This picture shows the way Louis XIV's enormous palace looked soon after it was built. In contrast to Philip II's Escorial, Versailles was designed as a stage for courtly pageantry on the grandest possible scale.*

nors, or foreign ambassadors. Only the highest and luckiest magnates could expect such favors. Most of the 200,000 members of the aristocracy lived in obscure exile on their country estates, but even they enjoyed the privilege of tax exemption. Overall, the aristocracy under Louis XIV enjoyed little real power. But the chief aristocrats, at least, preferred Louis' reflected glory to the feudal autonomy they had once known. They no longer wished to dismantle the French state, though by the close of Louis' reign they did wish to control it. In the eighteenth century, the aristocracy's bid for increased political power commensurate with their exalted social privilege was to be a root cause of the French Revolution.

While Louis XIV encouraged the aristocracy to become useless parasites, he invited the upper bourgeoisie to govern France under his direction. Louis took his executive responsibilities as seriously as his court pageantry. After

Mazarin's death, he made all important decisions himself, or thought he did. "*L'état, c'est moi,*" he allegedly boasted—"I am the state." Or as one of Louis' bishops put it, "all the state is in him; the will of all the people is included in his." This French concept of absolute monarchy was rather different from the contemporaneous version of absolutism in eastern Europe. Louis XIV thought he personified the French community; he identified his sovereign power with the collective will of his people, unlike Leopold I and Frederick William, whose subjects had no sense of national community, because Austria and Brandenburg-Prussia were congeries of unrelated territories. Moreover, the eastern monarchs' absolutism rested on a simple partnership with their landed magnates, whereas Louis XIV devised a double partnership with his aristocracy and his bourgeoisie. Like his Bourbon predecessors, Louis preferred middle-class men as his ministers, councillors, and *intendants*. His chief ministers, such as Colbert, a draper's son, worked under the king's direct supervision. No members of the royal family or the high aristocracy were admitted to the daily council sessions at Versailles, where the king presided over deliberations on war, diplomacy, finance, and justice. Council orders were transmitted to the provinces by the *intendants*, who supervised all phases of local administration, notably the courts, the police, and the collection of taxes. Louis effectively nullified the power of all remaining French institutions which might challenge his centralized bureaucracy. He never called the Estates-General. His *intendants* muzzled the three provincial estates still in existence by arresting and harassing all members who dared to criticize royal policy. The *parlements* offered no further resistance.

Louis XIV's centralized administrative system had its drawbacks. The king's orders could be enforced at the local level only by the more than forty thousand bourgeois officials who had bought from the crown lifelong possession of their posts. Despite all that the *intendants* could do, these officials continually ignored or evaded unpopular decrees. Yet the partnership worked well enough. The king's civil servants were more docile and efficient than noblemen would have been. The French bourgeoisie eagerly entered state service, finding the reflected power it conferred more satisfying than such "vulgar" occupations as commerce and industry. Only in the eighteenth century did the bourgeoisie, like the aristocracy, become dissatisfied with their position; their consequent bid for increased social privileges commensurate with their political and economic power was another root cause of the French Revolution.

Like every other seventeenth-century prince, Louis XIV offered little to the huge unprivileged sector at the base of his society. He did protect his peasantry from civil war and foreign invasion, at least until the closing years of his reign. But in a society where 80 per cent of the population were farmers, very little was done to stimulate increased agricultural productivity. There were terrible years of famine in France in the 1660's and again in the

1690's. Many French peasants owned their own land, but they still had to render feudal dues and services to their local lords. The poorer peasants were compelled to surrender their mortgaged plots to their bourgeois creditors, and the percentage of *métayers*, who rented land on the sharecropping principle, and of those who worked for wages was probably increasing during the late seventeenth century. The idle poor were conscripted into the Sun King's army, or put into workhouses. Taxes nearly doubled during Louis XIV's reign, increasing from 85 million livres in 1661 to 116 million in 1683, and 152 million in 1715. Many bourgeoisie managed to gain tax exemption during this period, so the burden on the peasantry was pitiless. Whenever the peasants attempted to rebel against new taxes, Louis XIV quartered soldiers in the rebel districts and hanged the ringleaders or condemned them to state service as galley slaves.

The money wrung from the French peasantry subsidized Louis' court and army, and also Colbert's mercantilist policy. Jean Baptiste Colbert (1619–1683), finance minister from 1661 to 1683, was exceptionally energetic and exceptionally doctrinaire. His energy is demonstrated by the way in which he plugged a gaping hole in the king's revenue system. On taking office, Colbert

A French peasant. *This sympathetic cartoon shows the abused farmer, gaunt and tattered, feeding his livestock, toiling in the field, and paying all of his profits to the tax collector (right rear).*

discovered that only 25 per cent of the tax money paid by the French people was reaching the royal treasury; the other 75 per cent disappeared in middleman profits to tax farmers and corrupt officials, and in interest payments on the royal debt. Colbert clamped down on the tax farmers and repudiated part of the debt. By the time he died, the treasury's net receipts had risen to 80 per cent of gross tax payments. With the same energy, Colbert pursued his mercantilist goal. He employed every stratagem at his disposal to turn France into a self-sufficient economic unit. Colbert equated wealth with bullion, and since the amount of bullion circulating was fairly stable in the late seventeenth century, he supposed that France could increase its wealth only by taking bullion from other states. He was particularly anxious to take from the Dutch, being jealous of their business enterprise. In order to introduce French exports into areas dominated by the Dutch, he organized a series of French trading companies, the most important being the East India Company, the West India Company, the Company of the North, and the Levant Company. He paid bounties to ship builders. He raised the tariffs on Dutch and English imports. He did what he could—which in truth was not much—to expedite internal French commerce: he improved the roads a little, built some canals, and eliminated some toll barriers. But shipping goods across the country still took a month, and cost more in transport charges than most cargoes were worth. Colbert put special effort into the promotion of new French industries. He sponsored the manufacture of goods which France had habitually imported, in particular luxury items such as silk, lace, fine woolens, tapestries, mirrors, and glass.

Was all this effort well spent? The limitations of Colbert's achievement are painfully obvious. He did not build a merchant marine to rival that of the Dutch, nor could he shut off foreign imports. French internal trade remained clogged by tolls and regional customs barriers. Since French merchants refused to invest in Colbert's overseas ventures, the king had to pay more than half the costs of the East India and West India companies. In any case, most of Colbert's companies collapsed within a few years. His pet industrial projects took better root, though his meticulous regulation of them choked initiative and hampered growth. He neglected heavy industry, such as iron manufacturing. And he neglected agriculture, because French food production was generally adequate. Yet there can be no doubt that French commerce and industry gained a great deal from Colbert's paternalistic prodding. In a society where businessmen were not socially respectable, it was important for the government to protect and dignify the role of commerce and industry. Furthermore, late seventeenth-century France was well suited to the application of Colbert's mercantilist doctrine. The French economy was more diversified than Spain's, and French businessmen tolerated government interference in private enterprise more readily than did their Dutch and English counterparts.

One of Colbert's accomplishments was to shape the scattered French overseas plantations founded earlier in the century into a huge colonial empire. By the 1680's, Louis XIV held trading posts in India, several island way stations in the Indian Ocean, slaving stations in Africa, and fourteen Caribbean sugar islands. By far his most imposing overseas possession was New France; fur traders and Jesuit missionaries were exploring the vast North American hinterland from Acadia and the St. Lawrence north to Hudson Bay, west to the Great Lakes, and south along the Mississippi to the Gulf of Mexico. To be sure, only a few thousand Frenchmen lived in these far-flung places. The amount of fur, fish, and tobacco exported from New France disappointed the crown. Only the sugar islands and the trading posts in India would develop into a great source of wealth for France. All in all, however, under Colbert the French had taken a long stride toward their impressive global economy of the eighteenth century.

So far, little has been said about religion. Louis XIV was troubled by the anomalous position which he occupied within the Catholic Church. He permitted Huguenot heretics to worship within his state, which scarcely any of his fellow Catholic princes would tolerate. And his country was the one Catholic state to ignore the reform decrees promulgated by the Council of Trent, because the French crown steadfastly refused to share control of the Gallican church with a pope or council. Certainly Louis had no thought of surrendering his ecclesiastical powers. On the contrary, in 1682 he encouraged his bishops to assert that the pope had no temporal authority over the French church. Still, Louis wanted to impose the equivalent of Trentine orthodoxy and discipline upon French religious practice, in order to promote the unity of his state and at the same time clear his conscience. It was not easy to unify French religious practice. Quite apart from the Huguenot problem, the Catholics were experiencing a highly variegated spiritual revival. The Catholic reformation had come to France in the seventeenth century, decidedly later than to Spain, Italy, and Germany. New orders sprang up, such as the Trappists and the Christian Brothers. St. Vincent de Paul (c. 1581–1660) founded the Sisters of Charity to care for the sick poor, foundlings, and prostitutes of Paris. Some of the reformers quarreled among themselves; in particular, three groups—the Jesuits, the Quietists, and the Jansenists—competed for support from the French ruling class. Louis favored the Jesuits. In their schools, pulpits, and confessionals, the Jesuits did an admirable job of instructing the faithful to shun schism and obey church and state. Many devout Catholics, however, were affronted by Jesuit casuistry and by the pragmatic implication in Jesuit teaching that God helps those who help themselves. The Quietists retreated into a religion of private mystical experience, in the optimistic belief that the soul could achieve perfectibility through passive union with God. The Jansenists went to the opposite theological pole. They rejected the Jesuit belief in free will and reaffirmed St. Augustine's—and Calvin's—doctrine of inherent human depravity and irresistible grace for the elect. The Quietist and Jansenist movements attracted some of the finest spirits in seventeenth-century France: François Fénelon is the best-known Quietist, and Blaise Pascal the best-known Jansenist. Nevertheless, Louis found Quietism and Jansenism intolerable, and he drove the members of both groups into surrender, prison, or exile.

If Louis XIV was so hostile to Catholic heterodoxy, his attitude toward the Huguenots may be easily guessed. Since the 1620's, when Richelieu had crushed their political and military independence, the Huguenots had been docile subjects and valuable citizens. They had changed from the warlike, aristocratic faction of the sixteenth-century religious wars into a respectable society of bourgeois officials and businessmen. But there were still upwards of a million of them in France when Louis undertook to eradicate Protestant heresy. He demolished Huguenot churches and schools, paid cash gratuities to converts, and billeted soldiers in the houses of those who refused to convert. In 1685, the king revoked Henry IV's Edict of Nantes. Henceforth, French Protestants had no civil rights, their children were to be raised as Catholics, and their clergy were exiled or sent to the galleys. Protestantism did survive in France after 1685, but very inconspicuously. The most stubborn Huguenots—estimates run as high as 200,000—fled to England, the Dutch republic, and other Protestant states. Louis willingly paid this price to achieve the kind of cohesive Catholicism found in Spain, Austria, and Bohemia. In the late seventeenth century, the Dutch and English were exceptional in permitting any degree of nonconformity. The French were perhaps no more bigotedly anti-Protestant than the English were anti-Catholic, but they did persecute minority creeds more savagely. Louis, like other absolute monarchs, claimed the right to control the consciences of his subjects. His motto was, *un roi, une loi, une foi.*

However coercive his methods, Louis XIV was far from being a modern totalitarian dictator. His autocracy was superimposed on a stratified society in which every class had its own distinct function and status. Louis had to enlarge the special privileges of the aristocracy and the bourgeoisie in order to secure their cooperation. The king rarely ventured beyond his Versailles court circle. He had no means of establishing direct contact with the great masses of unprivileged peasantry, who remained subject to their feudal lords. When the great revolution of 1789 awakened an egalitarian, national consciousness among the French people, it opened up new dimensions of state power beyond Louis' dreams. His method of governing France is most fruitfully compared with Philip II's method of governing Spain a century before. At first glance the two kings seem a world apart—the introspective, somber Philip in his tomblike Escorial versus the extroverted, worldly Louis with his gilded pageantry at Versailles. Yet these are differences between the Spanish and the French temperament. Both monarchs enjoyed the assets and endured the limitations characteristic of early modern European absolutism. Sixteenth-century Spain and seventeenth-century France were both agrarian, semifeudal societies, in which the king was as strong as his army and his bureaucracy, and as rich as peasant taxes would permit. Because Bourbon France was larger and wealthier than Habsburg Spain, Louis XIV could extract greater power out of the absolutist formula than Philip II had been able to. He raised much larger armies with which to pursue his dynastic ambitions and challenge the international balance of power. But France's rivals kept pace. Louis discovered—as had Philip before him—that war could bankrupt the mightiest absolute prince.

During the first half of his reign, from 1661 to 1688, Louis XIV's foreign

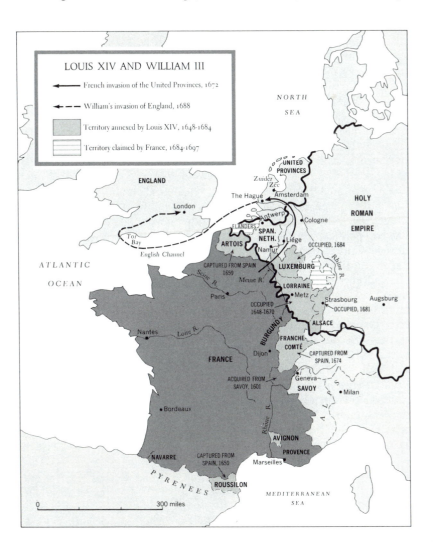

LOUIS XIV AND WILLIAM III

→ French invasion of the United Provinces, 1672

◄--- William's invasion of England, 1688

▓ Territory annexed by Louis XIV, 1648-1684

☰ Territory claimed by France, 1684-1697

policy was his most glorious achievement. Building on the conquests of Mazarin, he annexed further territory all along France's northern and eastern frontiers—in Flanders, Luxemburg, Lorraine, Alsace, and Franche-Comté. His generals defeated the Spanish and the imperial armies with ease. In 1672 they invaded and almost conquered the United Provinces. French diplomatists skillfully played Louis' enemies off against one another so as to prevent a coordinated anti-French coalition. England and Sweden were bribed by French subsidies into forming alliances with the Sun King. But after 1688, Louis' grandiose foreign policy suddenly stopped working so smoothly. France had to wage twenty-five years of grueling warfare against an international coalition which first halted Louis' expansion and then threw him on the defensive. The organizer of this anti-French coalition was one of the master politicians of the century, William of Orange. A frail little Dutchman, whose fishlike personality masked his calculating common sense and his indomitable courage, William spent his entire career fighting Louis XIV and all that he stood for.

Prince William III of Orange (1650–1702) was *stadholder*, or chief executive officer, in the United Provinces, and the great-grandson of William the Silent, the instigator of the Dutch rebellion against Philip II. Everything in William's experience made him hostile to the absolutist style, Habsburg or Bourbon. The Dutch republic over which he presided was small and loosely structured. His countrymen had no political ambition beyond maintaining the independence which they had wrested from Spain. By the mid-seventeenth century the Dutch had already reached their economic zenith. The two political factions, the Orangists and the Regents, were both well satisfied with the *status quo*. The Regents were patrician merchants in Holland, by far the most populous and important of the seven Dutch provinces. They advocated political oligarchy, religious toleration, and international peace. The Orangists, as the name implies, wanted more power for William's princely house. In times of international crisis, the military talents of the Orange dynasty were especially in demand. William the Silent and his sons had led the long war against Spain from the 1560's to 1648. During William's boyhood, the Regents controlled Dutch politics. The Regent leader, Jan de Witt (1625–1672) based his foreign policy on friendship with France; hence his position was disastrously undermined when Louis XIV invaded the United Provinces in 1672. At the height of the invasion crisis, a hysterical mob in The Hague caught de Witt in the street and hacked him to death. Young Prince William took charge. To stop the French advance, he made a truly last-ditch effort: he opened the dikes and flooded a belt of land extending from the Zuider Zee to the Rhine. The stratagem worked; Louis withdrew his army. During and after the invasion crisis, William was content to have the substance of power without the form of kingship. He recognized that monarchy was contrary to the traditions and temper of the Dutch people, so he preserved the established federal, republican framework while purging de Witt's adherents from all government posts. In any case, his obsession was foreign affairs, above all, the prevention of further French conquests.

In 1674 William organized the first of his anti-French coalitions. It consisted of the United Provinces, Austria, Spain, and several German states. To William's mortification, his allies fell apart under French military pressure and in 1679 sued for peace on Louis XIV's terms. A decade of ostensible peace followed, during which the French continued to advance inexorably toward the Rhine. Louis occupied Strasbourg in 1681, Luxemburg in 1684. By this time all of France's neighbors were thoroughly alarmed. A new and larger anti-French coalition took shape: the League of Augsburg included the partners of 1674 plus Sweden and all the major German states. William knew that in order to stop Louis the League of Augsburg needed the participation of England as well, and he knew that the English people were on the brink of revolution against their king, James II. William had a personal interest in English politics and in the fate of the English throne, for both his mother and his wife were Stuart princesses. In 1688 he undertook to direct a *coup d'état* against his father-in-law, James, and thereby bring England into his grand European alliance against France. Let us follow him across the English Channel.

THE GLORIOUS REVOLUTION

There is a refreshingly farcical touch to English events between 1660 and 1688, welcome after the heavy pomp of French absolutism. The English people had worked the Puritan crusading impulse out of their system. They were sick of Cromwell's army rule and blue laws. Hence in 1660 they joyfully welcomed the restoration of the Stuart monarchy. Charles II (ruled 1660–1685), son of the martyred Charles I, was a tall young man with black curls, sensuous lips, roving eyes, and irrepressible wit. He had spent the years from 1649 to 1660 in humiliating exile in France and the United Provinces, and this experience had given him a cynical view of politics and patriotism. Charles's restoration in 1660 was unconditional. Constitutionally, this meant a return to the situation that existed in 1642, on the eve of the civil war. The king had full executive control, but he was financially dependent on Parliament. Thus the battle for sovereignty between crown and Parliament had by no means been settled. The prewar religious situation was less fully restored. After 1660 the Church of England was again the state church, with bishops and prayer book, though without Archbishop Laud's aggressive High Church leadership. The Anglican establishment, however, no longer embraced all Englishmen. The Presbyterian, Independent, Baptist, and Quaker sects were too firmly rooted to be destroyed. The Anglican majority might despise and persecute these Puritan relicts, but English Protestants were permanently divided into conformists and nonconformists. Economically, crown and church lands were restored in 1660, but many a Roundhead landowner and merchant emerged in better shape than those Cavaliers who had lost their estates during the revolution. Intellectually, there was no restoration at all. The prewar milieu had been metaphysical, dogmatic, passionate, and ornate. The new age of John Dryden and the Royal Society was mechanistic, skeptical, clever, and urbane. The mood was new, but the basic political and religious issues were old and unresolved.

The 1660's saw the full-scale emergence of mercantilism in England, paralleling Colbert's efforts in France. English mercantilist policy was not shaped by a presiding genius; it sprang from the mutual needs of the business community and the government. Whereas Colbert supervised all aspects of the French economy, English mercantilists concentrated on the one area most in need of stimulation and protection: overseas trade. English foreign trade had grown during the first half of the century, but it remained dangerously dependent on one export—woolen cloth—and it was crippled by an inadequate merchant marine. English merchants needed protection against Dutch competition. The government needed increased customs revenues. The result was a series of Navigation Acts, passed between 1651 and 1673—initiated, it may be noted, by the Puritan republic and reinforced by Charles II's Parliament. The Navigation Acts stipulated that imports to England were to be carried there directly from the country of origin, in ships belonging either to that country or to England—thus the Dutch carrying trade would be excluded and the Amsterdam entrepôt bypassed. Such English colonial products as sugar and tobacco, for which there was a heavy European demand, had to be shipped first to England, and the colonists were required to buy on the English market any non-English commodities they desired—thus the English merchants would be encouraged to become middlemen, like the Dutch, and London's development as an entrepôt would be stimulated. The Dutch fought back, defending their free-trade principles. Three Anglo-Dutch naval wars took place in rapid succession, in 1652–1654, 1665–1667, and 1672–1674. The two commercial rivals battled each other to a standstill. But since the Dutch also had to ward off Louis XIV, they were exhausted by the struggle and nervous for the future. In the end they resigned themselves to England's new mercantile policy. By 1700 Dutch commerce, industry, and banking had stopped expanding, whereas by every index the English economy was growing fast. England's foreign and colonial trade were particularly flourishing. Between 1660 and 1700, the value of English imports and exports climbed 50 per cent, its merchant marine more than doubled in size, and customs revenues nearly trebled. The English had replaced the Dutch as the business leaders of Europe.

After 1660 the English colonial empire also took firm shape. In the sixteenth and early seventeenth centuries, English explorers and colonizers had been completely outflanked by the Spanish and the Dutch in their quest for quick profits from precious cargoes, such as bullion and spices. It took some time for the English to reconcile themselves to their role as the founders of basically agricultural colonies overseas. More than a century elapsed between the first English exploration of North America and the first permanent settlement, at Jamestown in 1607. Thereafter, the English made a substantial colonizing effort. Some eighty thousand emigrants crossed the Atlantic from England between 1607 and 1640, nearly as many as had gone from Spain to America during the entire previous century. The English emigrants were mainly young people from the middle classes, lured by free land and open air. Initially, the English government played a much more passive role than the Spanish government had done. James I and Charles I anticipated no quick profits from American agriculture, and since most of the early settlements were operated by Puritans, the crown declined to subsidize or supervise them. Thus it happened that without any overall plan or purpose, two dozen separate little English communities sprouted in America, scattered from Newfoundland to Guiana. Each colony functioned as an autonomous unit. Each developed its own identity. Some were sponsored by joint-stock companies; some were sponsored by individual proprietors; some lacked any authorization from the home government. In contrast to the Spaniards, with their epic conquest of the Aztecs and the Incas, the English hugged the Atlantic coast, hesitant to explore the vast continent at their backs, unable to make the Indians work for them or pray with them. But the English colonists possessed a self-reliance lacking among the Spanish in America. Each colony had its own representative assembly, with all the constitutional ambitions of Parliament at home.

In the 1670's Charles II launched a new policy toward English America, designed to shatter colonial autonomy and bind each plantation closer to the crown. Recognizing the rising commercial value of Caribbean sugar and Chesapeake tobacco, English mercantilists belatedly began to erect a central imperial administration for the colonies. After a generation of protest and rebellion throughout English America, the colonists by 1700 had adjusted to their new imperial status. They learned to live with the Navigation Acts, the sugar planters more willingly than the mainland colonists. But they prevented the home government from centralizing the empire in a thoroughgoing Spanish or French sense. Englishmen in America retained a larger measure of local self-determination, diversity, and democracy than could be found in any seventeenth-century European society. Meanwhile, by 1700 English merchants dominated the lucrative African slave trade. The English East India Company was doing a booming business through its trading posts at Bombay, Madras, and Calcutta. All in all, England's worldwide commercial undertakings were worth much more than the bullion and spices the English explorers had failed to find.

Though the English economy was thriving under Charles II as never before, domestic politics had seldom been so erratic. The new king greatly admired Louis XIV's absolute monarchy, and he also rather preferred

French Roman Catholicism to English Protestantism. But Charles was ill equipped to be a Sun King. His court at Whitehall was far less grandiose and glittering than Versailles. The English upper classes were less dependent on royal patronage than they had been under Elizabeth or the early Stuarts. They wanted direct political power, not reflected glory. Charles was much too foxy to risk starting another revolution, and besides, he was too lazy to work seriously at building an absolute state.

During the first fifteen years of his reign, Charles II masked his views by employing a hodgepodge of ministers: old-fashioned Cavaliers, ex-Cromwellians, and opportunistic Catholics. Of these, only the Catholics enjoyed the king's confidence. Charles's first Parliament was so enthusiastically royalist that the king figured it could never be improved upon. He kept this Cavalier Parliament in session for eighteen years, from 1661 to 1679. Even so, king and Parliament were soon pursuing divergent religious policies. The Cavalier Parliament was ardently Anglican and harassed the nonconformist sects with a series of persecuting laws known as the Clarendon Code. The king meanwhile secretly promised Louis XIV (in return for an immediate subsidy) to restore England to Rome as soon as conditions were favorable. Charles moved circumspectly. In 1672 he suspended the Clarendon Code and all other penal laws against Catholics and Protestant nonconformists. But the popular outcry was so terrific that Charles decided his pledge to Louis must be abandoned. He reinstated the persecuting laws and reorganized his ministry in support of Anglicanism. In the mid-1670's, two clearly delineated political factions emerged within the English upper classes: the Tories, who supported Charles's government, and the Whigs, who criticized it. The Tories, led by the king's chief minister, the earl of Danby (1631–1712), had much in common with the Cavaliers of 1642. They championed divine-right monarchy and the established Anglican church. The Whigs, led by an ex-minister, the earl of Shaftesbury (1621–1683), had much in common with the Roundheads of 1642. They advocated parliamentary supremacy and toleration for Protestant nonconformists. Three factors, however, kept the party division of the 1670's less fundamental than that of the 1640's. Tories and Whigs were both fearful of another civil war. Both were anti-Catholic and anti-French. And both were out of step with their willowy monarch.

In the closing years of Charles II's reign, from 1678 to 1685, the Whigs and Tories grappled furiously without resorting to arms—a notable step toward the domestication of party politics. The Whigs got their big chance in 1678, when a shifty character named Titus Oates announced to the startled world that he had uncovered a horrendous Popish Plot. According to Oates, the Jesuits (with papal blessing) were planning to assassinate Charles, massacre the English Protestants, and install the king's brother James on the throne. Englishmen high and low avidly swallowed this preposterous story. Oates had dramatized a fatal flaw in the Stuart dynasty. Charles, with his

James II in prayer. *This engraving of the pious king was made when he was in exile in France after the Glorious Revolution.* Pepysian Library, Magdalene College, Cambridge.

bevy of mistresses, had sired several bastards, but no legitimate children. The heir to the throne, his brother James, was extremely unpopular because he was a zealous Catholic convert. For two years the country was swept by anti-Catholic hysteria. Charles knew that Oates was a liar, but he dared not pooh-pooh his story, lest someone uncover the real popish plot that Charles himself had engaged in with Louis XIV. Shaftesbury, the Whig leader, also guessed that Oates was a liar, but by skillfully manipulating the popular hysteria he discredited the Tory leader, Danby, and built a Whig majority in Parliament. Between 1679 and 1681 three Whig parliaments were elected in rapid succession. Each of these, under Shaftesbury's management, had a single aim: to exclude James from the royal succession. But Charles II had the last laugh. After 1681 he ruled without Parliament. The rising customs revenues, together with Louis XIV's subsidy, permitted him to dispense with parliamentary taxation, and hence to gag the Whigs. Charles restored Tory control. Shaftesbury was charged with treason and died in exile, and the king found pretexts for executing a number of other Whig leaders. He persecuted the nonconformists more heartily than before. He remodeled a great many town constitutions and parliamentary electoral districts, so as to make local governments subservient to the crown, and future Parliaments manageable. When Charles died in 1685, there was no effective opposition to James's succession.

Superficially, Charles II appeared to have achieved Louis XIV's absolutism after all. In fact, he had scarcely affected the English trend toward constitutional monarchy. Charles was not really independent of Parliament. In any fiscal emergency, such as a war, the crown would still require taxes which only Parliament could authorize. Charles had been able to punish the Whigs, persecute the nonconformists, and remodel local governments because the Tories warmly supported these policies. The Stuart dynasty was as strong as its Tory support. Should the Tories turn against the Stuarts, their autocratic policy would easily be reversed. Charles had buried the Popish Plot, but England's fear of French power, and of popery, was by no means dead. Three years of exposure to James II touched off a new revolution against the Stuarts, the Glorious Revolution.

James II (ruled 1685–1688) attempted single-handedly to reverse a whole century of history. Few kings have failed so spectacularly. James was fooled by his easy accession to power. In 1685 royal troops quickly nipped an inept Whig rebellion. The House of Commons dutifully voted the new sovereign such generous revenues that he did not need to call Parliament after his first year. He also received money from Louis XIV. But James alienated this initial support. He dismissed his brother's Tory ministers and appointed Catholics wherever possible to all government posts down to the level of justice of the peace. Since there were very few English Catholics to draw upon, James's appointees were generally untried and inferior men. The king also stationed a standing army, largely officered by Catholics, outside London. He did his best to undermine the Anglican establishment by reviving Charles II's suspension of penal laws against Catholics and nonconformists. Unlike Charles, he frankly broadcast his motives. "We cannot but heartily wish," he told his subjects, "that all the people of our dominions were members of the Catholic church." As a result, most nonconformists distrusted his toleration policy, and Anglicans were scandalized.

The breaking point came in June, 1688. When the king ordered the Anglican clergy to read his toleration decree from their pulpits, seven bishops dared to protest. James put them in the Tower and ordered them tried for seditious libel. To his amazement, the jury returned a verdict of not guilty. In this same month, James's queen bore him a son. According to the rules of royal inheritance, this infant immediately took precedence over the king's two grown daughters, both Protestant, the offspring of a previous marriage; James had the Catholic heir his subjects had been dreading. James's elder daughter was married to William of Orange. Like many Englishmen, William wanted to believe that the royal birth was an imposture. A fantastic rumor spread that the baby had been smuggled into the queen's bed in a warming pan. There is much greater truth in the well-known nursery rhyme which describes what happened to the newborn prince and his father during the closing months of 1688:

Rock-a-bye baby, in the tree top.
When the wind blows,* the cradle will rock.
When the bough breaks, the cradle will fall,
And down will come baby, cradle and all.

By June, 1688, Tories and Whigs were allied against James II. The king was more isolated than Charles I had been in 1640. But no one wanted another full-scale upheaval. In the revolution of 1688–1689, no new Cromwell rose up to crusade against the Stuarts. Instead, a cross section of Whig and Tory aristocrats discreetly invited that cool and calculating Dutchman, William of Orange, to bring a foreign army to England and restore their religion and their liberty. Nothing was said in the invitation about overthrowing James, though everyone knew that William and his wife, Mary, were the prime Protestant candidates for the throne. William accepted the invitation, primarily because it gave him leverage for pulling England into his coalition against Louis XIV. Poor James was paralyzed by the magnitude of the conspiracy against him.

In November, 1688, William landed his army unopposed in southwestern England. Despite the king's flurry of desperate, last-minute concessions, the chief men in the country deserted to the prince's camp. Had James led his army into battle against William, he might still have rallied English patriotism against the Dutch invader. But the king was incapacitated by a severe nosebleed—about the only blood shed during the Glorious Revolution. William advanced implacably toward London. James abjectly fled to France. In February, 1689, a parliamentary assembly declared that James II had abdicated and offered the vacant throne to William and Mary. The new sovereigns accepted Parliament's Bill of Rights, the Magna Charta of 1689. The Bill of Rights enumerated the elementary civil liberties of Englishmen and declared absolutist practices like those of the last Stuart kings to be illegal. It epitomized England's evolution into a constitutional monarchy, in which the king governed by parliamentary consent and was subject to law.

Strictly speaking, the Glorious Revolution was a *coup d'état*, but in the wider sense it marked the final victory for representative self-government and religious pluralism in England. The Whig philosophy had triumphed, but only with Tory support. The revolutionary settlement of 1689 was a compromise with which almost all Englishmen could live. William and Mary still exercised great executive independence, but Parliament henceforth met annually, controlled the purse strings, and shared in the direction of public affairs. No English king after James II tried to govern without Parliament, or in defiance of Parliament. Party factionalism continued as a permanent feature of English political life, but after 1689 the Whigs and Tories

*This phrase refers to the gale which blew William of Orange's invading fleet from the Netherlands to England in November, 1688.

William of Orange landing in England, 1688. *This old print shows William, unflappable as always, seated in a rowboat, his Dutch fleet to the rear, as happy Englishmen scramble to welcome their deliverer. Actually, few English joined William when he first landed, since they disliked the prospect of a Dutch king almost as much as James's Catholicism.*

contested for power within the framework of parliamentary government. In religion, the Toleration Act of 1689 permitted nonconformists to worship publicly, though in comparison with the Anglicans they remained second-class citizens. The provisions of the Toleration Act did not apply to Roman Catholics, but Catholics in England, in the latitudinarian post-revolutionary atmosphere, suffered much less persecution than Protestants in France. Economically, the revolution cemented the partnership between business and government. Henceforth, to a much greater extent than in France, merchants and landlords underwrote the costs of government through taxes and loans. The Bank of England, founded in 1694, utilized private capital to perform public services. In France, it was still risky to lend the king money, and any deficit incurred by the French government was construed as the king's personal liability. But in England, crown and Parliament floated huge war loans in the 1690's at guaranteed interest rates. The moneyed classes invested with confidence in a government they helped to control. The king's deficit was transformed into a national debt.

The Glorious Revolution had its inglorious aspects. It was carried out by and for the propertied classes, who were determined to perpetuate their privileged status. To the unprivileged, servile sectors of English society, the revolution brought no benefits. Back in the 1640's, democratic and even communistic aspirations had been loudly voiced. Such sentiments were unheard now. Only educated and prosperous Englishmen could practice the "liberties" specified in the Bill of Rights, enjoy representation in Parliament, or take advantage of the atmosphere of religious and economic emancipation. In Ireland, the revolutionary settlement was especially inglorious. Here, the downtrodden Catholic majority naturally supported their coreligionist, James, against the Calvinist William. Once William and Mary's forces gained control of Ireland in 1691, all power and most property were given over to a small ruling caste—the Protestants from England and Scotland who had been trying for 150 years to conquer and exploit the Irish. Some members of this Protestant master class lived grandly in England as absentee landlords, spending there what little surplus wealth could be extracted from Irish subsistence agriculture. Their colleagues in Dublin developed a code of vindictive penal laws which outlawed Catholic priests and schools, excluded Catholics from public life, and hindered them from holding property or pursuing trades and professions. The purpose of this code was not to wipe out Catholicism, but to keep the native Irish in a state of peasant servility. No other people in western Europe was so brutally oppressed.

The chief international consequence of the Glorious Revolution was that William III brought England into the League of Augsburg against Louis XIV. The year 1689 marks a major turning point in Anglo-French relations. Between 1559 and 1688, England and France had been almost always at peace with each other, despite the obvious contrasts in their internal development. Between 1689 and 1815, they fought against each other in seven major wars. No pair of adversaries had ever been better equipped, for both French and English strength had been tempered by 150 years of religious conflict. A long road had been traveled since the 1560's, when the Calvinists and Catholics began their battle for the mastery of western Europe. But, as has been shown, both the Calvinist and the reformed Catholic movements had great survival power. In 1689 William III was recognizably John Calvin's heir, and he drew upon Calvinist resources in the Netherlands and England. His family had led the Dutch Calvinists against Philip II. He himself brought to a successful conclusion the English Calvinists' century-long rebellion against the Stuarts. The Calvinist ethic had left its distinctive imprint on Dutch and English business enterprise and political organization. Louis XIV drew upon a different heritage, one in which the Catholic reformation was a prime stimulus. His dynasty had restored France to Catholic unity. He himself had crushed the Huguenots. His style of rule bore many of the conservative attributes of the reformed Roman Church: it was majestic, paternalistic, tightly ordered, hostile toward disruptive new ideas, and aggressive in the defense of old ones. Thus fortified, the English and French began their eighteenth-century contest for world leadership.

CHAPTER 5

The Century of Genius

IF THERE WERE no other reason for examining the years between 1559 and 1715, the galaxy of superb artists and thinkers who flourished during this period would still command our attention. This was the age of Shakespeare, Cervantes, El Greco, Montaigne, Descartes, Galileo, Rubens, Milton, Molière, Bernini, Rembrandt, Velázquez, Hobbes, Spinoza, Newton, and Locke—all men of creative genius whose work still lives today. If the ultimate measure of genius is to produce work of timeless beauty and universal significance, these great artists and thinkers can stand comparison with any in history.

It is not easy to characterize in a few words the culture of early modern Europe. The difficulty is increased by the jagged intellectual and aesthetic crosscurrents of the period. The sixteen men just listed did not share a common platform of ideas and ideals. Six or seven of them can be identified as participants in the scientific revolution of the seventeenth century. Another five or six can be identified as Baroque artists. But since Shakespeare, Cervantes, and Rembrandt can be placed in neither category, this formulation is scarcely satisfactory. In the seventeenth century, European culture was passing through an especially iconoclastic, aggressive, experimental phase. Something in the atmosphere encouraged thinkers to question rather than to synthesize, and inspired artists to wrestle with the newest, biggest, and most variegated subjects they could find. For want of a better label, the seventeenth century is often called the century of genius.

Inevitably, all branches of art and learning reflected the wide disparity—political, economic, and social—between western and eastern Europe which was such a conspicuous feature of our period. Culturally, the years from 1559 to 1715 constituted a golden age for Spain, the Dutch republic, and England, and at least a silver age for France. But for Italy the golden age was passing, and for Germany it had not yet arrived. In Italy, which had been the artistic center of Europe for three centuries, the most significant seventeenth-century figure was a scientist—Galileo. In central Europe, too, the most eminent personages were scientists—Kepler and Leibniz. Poland and Russia, during the late sixteenth and seventeenth centuries, were more isolated from general European cultural trends than they had been during the Middle Ages and the Renaissance.

To facilitate our understanding of the western European culture of this time, let us focus upon three major themes. First, the scientific revolution from Copernicus to Newton. What effect did the new science have upon man's view of nature and of himself? Second, the Catholic-Protestant struggle for mastery of Europe. How did this conflict inspire new forms of religious art, and at the same time provoke new antireligious intellectual attitudes? Third, the social and economic disparity between rich and poor, privileged and unprivileged. How did the arts reflect this social polarity, and why did European culture grow more aristocratic in the course of the seventeenth century? We stand today in the shadow of these questions.

THE SCIENTIFIC REVOLUTION

Between the 1540's and the 1680's, a brilliant constellation of astronomers, physicists, and mathematicians, including Copernicus, Kepler, Galileo, Descartes, and Newton, accomplished a veritable revolution in science. They obliterated the traditional view of nature and established scientific practice on an impressive new footing. This great breakthrough equipped the physical scientist with new methods and new standards which worked exceedingly well throughout the eighteenth and nineteenth centuries. So total was the victory, that it requires an effort of imagination to understand how any intelligent man could have taken the pre-Copernican view of nature seriously. Yet this traditional view was scientific within its own terms. For many centuries thinking men had found it logical and empirical, as well as emotionally convincing. We must try to reconstitute this obliterated system in order to appreciate the magnitude of the scientific discoveries which swept it away.

The traditional view of the cosmos, accepted by almost every educated man until well into the seventeenth century, was a synthesis of Aristotelian mechanics, Ptolemaic astronomy, and Christian teleology. Commonsense observation demonstrated that Aristotle's theory of motion did indeed represent the way God operated the universe. All heavy bodies, said Aristotle, naturally fell toward the center of the universe and rested there, unless propelled by a mover in some other direction. It followed that the round earth, obviously solid and weighty, stood motionless in the center of the universe. Both Catholic and Protestant theologians associated the earth's heaviness with corruption and compared terrestrial mutability with the changeless purity of the firmament above. Thus the earth, divinely appointed to mortal man's use, was in effect the cesspool of the universe, with hell at its innermost core. Such teachings harmonized nicely with Ptolemaic astronomy. According to the second-century mathematician

Ptolemy, a concentric series of transparent crystalline spheres revolved in an ascending order of purity around man's corruptible habitat. The moon, the sun, the planets, the fixed stars, and the *primum mobile* (the outermost sphere, which drove the entire system) all wheeled in perfect circles, going once around the earth every twenty-four hours. Beyond the *primum mobile* lay the purest region of all, God's heavenly abode. Everything in this picture conformed to men's experience and expectations. Anyone could see that the earth stood still and that the stars were fixed. Ptolemy's theory of harmonious celestial motion coincided as well as could be expected with the crude astronomical observations which stargazers were able to collect.

Pre-Copernican science embraced a corresponding set of biological and chemical assumptions, which again suited men's experience and expectations. It was believed that God had created all living things within an immense, purposeful, and harmoniously ascending order: the great chain of being. Inanimate objects (such as liquids and metals) belonged at the lowest level of existence. Next came the subdivisions of the vegetable class, possessing life as well as existence. Next, the various gradations of dumb animals, with feeling as well as life. Next, man (the little world, or microcosm), endowed with intelligence and a soul in addition to all the lower earthly faculties. At the top of the ladder was the hierarchy of angels, purely spiritual creatures, enjoying man's understanding without his sinful and mutable nature. The angels, it was thought, dwelt in the pure ether of the spheres, beyond the realm of scientific analysis. The composition of terrestrial matter, however, was much discussed. In chemistry, the basic assumption was that all terrestrial matter was compounded of four elements: earth, water, air, and fire. Earth was the basest element, and fire the noblest, but life required all four, and health depended on keeping them in balance. Hence in *King Lear*, when Shakespeare wanted to dramatize the chaos of the storm, he had Lear cry out that all four elements were at war:

> Blow, winds, and crack your cheeks! rage! blow!
> You cataracts and hurricanoes, spout
> Till you have drencht our steeples, drown'd the cocks!
> You sulphurous and thought-executing fires,
> Vaunt-couriers to oak-cleaving thunderbolts,
> Singe my white head! And thou, all-shaking thunder,
> Strike flat the thick rotundity o' the world!

In human physiology, the four elements had their counterparts in four fluids known as humors—melancholy, phlegm, blood, and choler—which were thought to pass through the veins from the liver to the heart. During the Middle Ages and the Renaissance, the chief object of medical and psychiatric practice was to keep the patient's humors in proper balance, and thus preserve his good health and his normal temperament.

Two features of this pre-Copernican science require special emphasis. In the first place, it rested to an extraordinary degree on past authority, not merely on ancient Greek theory, but also on the results of ancient Greek experimentation. Before the mid-sixteenth century, no anatomist tried to improve upon Galen's authoritative experiments in the dissection of the human body, nor did any astronomer dare to question Ptolemy's celestial calculations, even though Galen and Ptolemy had both done their work back in the second century. In the second place, there were major mysteries unexplained by this traditional view of the world which made it difficult to draw a line between science and superstition, between experimentation and magic. Despite Aristotle's assertion that all matter preferred rest, the whole universe was in constant motion. What drove the *primum mobile*? The elements could not be artificially isolated, and the humors could not even be seen. Why were they so unpredictable? Why should a healthy man suddenly drop dead, or a thriving crop be blasted by insects, or a city be swept by the plague? What caused storms, floods, and other natural catastrophes? What made one metal precious and another dross? What did it mean when strange comets suddenly blazed in the sky? The fickleness of life seemed to show that God had delegated a large role in nature to fate, fortune, or chance. Hence astrologers, who claimed to be able to predict human events by the position of the stars, were given as much credence as astronomers. Alchemists, who claimed to be able to transmute base metals into gold, were given as much credence as chemists. Most people absorbed the folklore of fairies and pixies, small-scale supernatural beings who meddled in human affairs for good or ill. As we have seen, the late sixteenth and early seventeenth centuries marked the high point in the acceptance of witchcraft, the intercession of evil spirits (fallen angels) or the Devil himself. In short, there was no confidence that man, through the exercise of his God-given intelligence, could learn to master his physical environment.

The New View of the Universe

It is ironic that the first thinker to challenge this traditional view of nature was Nicolaus Copernicus (1473–1543), for Copernicus was a conservative and quiet Polish cleric who lived in an obscure East Prussian cathedral town. He published his revision of Ptolemy's geocentric theory of celestial motion in 1543, hoping to bring Ptolemaic astronomy up to date. Instead, he sapped the accepted foundations of science. Copernicus had no quarrel with the Ptolemaic vision of concentric crystalline spheres wheeling in perfect circles around the central point in the universe. What troubled him was the fact that Ptolemy's spheres were not perfectly circular. Even Ptolemy's own astronomical observations indicated that only the sun moved with perfect uniformity. The moon, the planets, and the fixed stars sometimes speeded up or changed direction. To plot all observable celestial motion around the earth in spherical form required an intricate network of eighty interlocking circles and epicycles. Copernicus believed that God must have designed a simpler, more harmonious pattern for His universe than this.

Copernicus' great discovery was that he could account for the irregularities in celestial motion much more simply by making a single elemental adjustment. He visualized the sun rather than the earth as the immobile center of the universe. Copernicus was something of a sun worshiper, considering the sun a nobler orb than the earth. His central hypothesis, that the earth rotated daily on her axis and revolved annually around the sun, temporarily bolstered the ancient doctrine of the spheres. Spherical motion could be plotted around the sun in thirty-four circles and epicycles, as against Ptolemy's eighty. But the heliocentric theory cast doubt on the ascending purity of the spheres. The earth was now seen as one of the planets, operating on the same physical principles as Jupiter or Saturn, which had previously been regarded as situated on a higher level. According to Copernicus, it was no longer necessary to believe that the distant fixed stars wheeled completely every twenty-four hours. But most men accepted the daily revolution of the stars more readily than the daily rotation of the earth, which contradicted common sense. And if Copernicus was correct, why did not centrifugal force tear the world to pieces? Copernicus had no satisfactory answer to this question, but he stimulated other scientists to work on it.

For a half century after Copernicus' death, his heliocentric theory gained few adherents. It was taught at only one university (Salamanca, in Spain), and it was not broadcast in layman's language to the general public. Such late sixteenth-century savants as Bodin and Montaigne lightly dismissed Copernicus. Tycho Brahe (1546–1601), the leading practical astronomer in the half century after Copernicus, clung to the geocentric theory. For, he argued, if the earth rotated and revolved, a stone dropped from a high tower would fall to the west, which in fact did not happen. In science-fiction parlance, Tycho Brahe was something of a mad scientist. On a Danish island he built and operated the fantastic castle of Uraniborg, equipped with outsize instruments, observatories, laboratories, and a team of research assistants; there he engaged in astronomical, astrological, and alchemical studies. Nevertheless, he was an important contributor to the scientific revolution. He tracked the positions of the planets more systematically than had ever been done before and compiled a mass of astronomical observations which reached the limits of naked-eye accuracy.

Tycho's ablest assistant, Johannes Kepler (1571–1630), was a Copernican. Kepler used Tycho's data to demonstrate beyond question the mathematical symmetry of Copernicus' heliocentric system. Kepler, like Tycho, fused science with pseudoscience. His undigested and unreadable books are stuffed with rhapsodic musings about the harmony of the universe and the magical geometry of the planets. For Kepler, "the music of the spheres" meant that Mars was a tenor, Mercury a falsetto, and so forth. But he was also a mathematician of genius. For years he puzzled over the apparently erratic

The castle of Uraniborg in Denmark. *The site of Tycho Brahe's scientific and pseudoscientific investigations.*

orbit of Mars. According to Tycho's observations, this planet moved in a far from perfect circle, and it traveled faster when approaching the sun than when receding from it. Kepler's efforts to find mathematical expression for Mars's orbit led him to his three descriptive laws of planetary motion. He discovered that Mars, the earth, and all the other planets orbit elliptically around the sun, and that the sun is not at the center, but at one focus of the ellipse. An ellipse is less obviously perfect in shape than a circle, but it too has abstract properties, reducible to a mathematical formula. Kepler further discovered that while the planets do not travel at uniform speed, the radius vector between the sun and a planet always sweeps over equal areas in equal times. In other words, all planetary motion can be described by a single mathematical formula. Finally, he discovered that while each planet takes a different length of time to go around the sun, the square of the planetary period of orbit is always proportional to the cube of its distance from the sun.

In other words, all planetary time periods can likewise be described by a single mathematical formula.

Kepler had done more than prove mathematically that Copernicus was right and Ptolemy wrong. His laws reconciled fact with theory. They stripped the cosmos of some of its old mystery and endowed it with a new mechanistic regularity. For all his mystical rapture, Kepler abandoned Copernicus' traditional belief in the crystalline spheres. He saw the planets as moving through immense empty spaces, held to their courses by some power beyond his investigation, yet always operating in accordance with simple, uniform, verifiable, mathematical principles.

The first Copernican scientist to gain wide public attention was a doughty Florentine, Galileo Galilei (1564–1642). Galileo was a Renaissance man, cast in the same larger-than-life mold as Leonardo da Vinci and Michelangelo before him. He was a wonderfully complete scientist: a lucid analytical thinker, an ingenious experimentalist, a masterful technologist, and a zestful writer. Kepler's laws were abstract and abstruse, but there was nothing abstract or abstruse about Galileo's frontal assault on Ptolemy and Aristotle.

In 1609 Galileo heard that a Dutchman had invented a spyglass through which distant objects could be seen as if close up. He soon constructed a telescope of his own, which magnified distant objects thirty times. In 1610 he jubilantly announced in his *Starry Messenger* the exciting new things he had seen in the heavens through this instrument. The moon, he reported, had a mountainous surface very much like the earth's, concrete evidence that it was composed of terrestrial matter rather than some purer substance, as Aristotle had supposed. Galileo was struck by the difference between the planets and the stars; when viewed through his telescope, the planets looked like solid globes, but the stars, far more numerous and less sparkling than when seen by the naked eye, were still without distinct size or shape. The stars, he realized, must be fantastically remote from the earth. Galileo was especially pleased to discover four satellites orbiting around Jupiter. Here was additional evidence against the uniqueness of the earth and her moon. Later, Galileo detected rings around Saturn, observed the moonlike phases of Venus, and noted spots on the surface of the sun. Each of these findings cast further doubt on the validity of the Ptolemaic cosmos. Each demonstrated how a seventeenth-century experimental scientist could learn far more about nature than was taught in ancient books. "Oh, my dear Kepler," wrote Galileo in 1610, "here at Padua is the principal professor of philosophy, whom I have repeatedly and urgently requested to look at the moon and planets through my glass, which he obstinately refuses to do. Why are you not here? What shouts of laughter we should have at this glorious folly!" When another professor who scorned his telescope died, Galileo was heard to hope that he would notice the new celestial phenomena on his way up to heaven.

Galileo knew that the professors denied the evidence of his telescope because it conflicted with the accepted Aristotelian concept of motion.

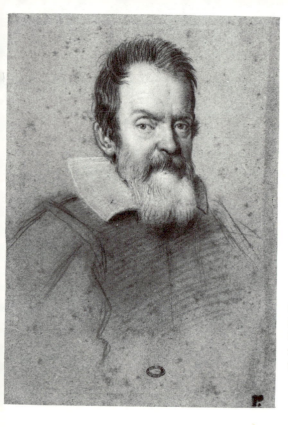

Galileo. *This drawing by Ottavio Leoni, showing Galileo at the age of sixty, nicely catches the man's truculence and verve.*

Aristotle had taught that for a body to be put into motion, a mover, either internal or external, was necessary. He distinguished between *natural* motion, the result of internal self-direction, and *violent* motion, the result of artificial propulsion by an external force. For example, heavy bodies were thought to fall naturally at an accelerating rate because they were jubilant at returning home to rest at the center of the universe. Light bodies naturally rose to their proper station. To Aristotelians, it violated nature to suppose that the moon and the planets could fly permanently through outer space if they were heavy like the earth. Surely God would not permit the earth to be violently swung in perpetuity about the incorporeal sun.

Putting aside the Aristotelian concept, Galileo developed a wholly new approach to dynamics, the study of the behavior of bodies in motion. He tried to explain not why bodies move, but how they move. In a series of experiments he demonstrated that the movement of bodies through time and space can be described by mathematical equations. For instance, having shown that a pendulum of fixed length always completed its swing in a fixed time whether it moved through a long or a short distance, Galileo could express the period of the pendulum mathematically. Similarly, having worked out the parabolic trajectory of a cannonball, he could formulate a general theory of projectiles. Perhaps Galileo did not really drop a ten-pound weight and a one-pound weight simultaneously from the top of the Leaning Tower of Pisa, but he certainly did prove that a heavy body falls with no greater velocity than a light body of the same material. The behavior of all free-falling bodies, regardless of weight, is described by Galileo's law of acceleration. This series of demonstrations vitiated the Aristotelian distinction between natural and violent motion. Galileo's experiments with rolling balls on inclined planes led him toward his most fundamental achievement, the reinterpretation of inertia. Galileo was the first to see that under ideal physical conditions, with gravity and friction eliminated, a moving ball will continue to roll infinitely unless checked or hastened or deflected by another force. All past thinkers had equated inertia with rest, and the science of mechanics had always been concerned with explaining the motion of bodies. Once Galileo equated inertia with rest *or* infinite uniform motion, he saw that only *changes* of motion required explanation. In Galileo's view, it was as easy to conceive of the earth in perpetual rotation and revolution as to conceive of it at rest. Once his principles of dynamics were established, the traditional physics became as worthless as the traditional astronomy.

It is scarcely surprising that Galileo's repudiation of Aristotle and Ptolemy got him into trouble with the Church. The old science, though pagan in origin, was deeply embedded in the Christian intellectual tradition. The new science conflicted with some passages of Scripture. Galileo argued that Scripture and nature should be treated as separate truths, but he took perverse delight in mocking the stupid scientific opinions of his clerical critics. Owing largely to pressure from the Jesuits, the Holy Office in 1616 labeled the Copernican theory as "foolish and absurd, philosophically false and formally heretical." Galileo was admonished not to accept or propound Copernicanism. Nevertheless, in 1632 he thought it safe to publish his *Dialogue Concerning the Two World Systems—Ptolemaic and Copernican.* By presenting the respective merits of the old astronomy and the new in dialogue form, Galileo could pretend to be neutral. In fact, he portrayed the champion of the old science as an ignorant clown, Simplicio, who got the worst of every argument. Pope Urban VIII (ruled 1623–1644) believed that Galileo was lampooning him as Simplicio. Galileo was brought to Rome, examined by the inquisitors, made to recant his errors, and sentenced to house arrest for the remainder of his life. The *Dialogue* was put on the Index. The legend is that when Galileo retired to his Florentine villa, he looked up at the sky, stamped his foot on the ground, and muttered, "*Eppur si muove*"—"It still moves."

Galileo's trial has perhaps received undue attention. Being a good Catholic, he accepted his punishment with better grace than have modern secular liberals. The Church did not prevent him from working or writing. In 1638 the dauntless old man published his last and greatest book, the

Discourse on Two New Sciences, in which he laid the foundation for modern physics. Yet it is not accidental that Galileo sent this manuscript to Leiden for publication. As the seventeenth century wore on, Protestant countries, particularly the United Provinces and England, provided the freest atmosphere for the exploration and discussion of the new science.

The Scientific Climate of Opinion

During the first half of the century, two influential philosophers vigorously championed the scientific revolution: Francis Bacon (1561–1626), an Englishman, and René Descartes (1596–1650), a Frenchman who settled in Holland. Both Bacon and Descartes announced their contempt for the outdated old science. Like Petrarch at the dawn of the Renaissance, they saw themselves as pioneers in a glorious new age, ending 1,500 years of intellectual stagnation. Bacon and Descartes were bolder pioneers than Petrarch, for they endeavored to emancipate themselves from *all* past intellectual authority, classical as well as medieval. Descartes felt so suffocated by the dead dogmas of Aristotle and his medieval scholastic disciples that he set himself the intellectual task of doubting all past knowledge and custom. He stripped

Descartes. *Painting by an unknown artist.*

away belief in everything except his own existence as a thinking and doubting being—"I think, therefore I am." On this naked premise he erected a brand-new metaphysics and physics. Both Bacon and Descartes believed that science, properly practiced, offered the key to unprecedented human progress. "The true goal of the sciences," wrote Bacon, "is none other than this: that human life be endowed with new discoveries and power." Although he lived in an era of very slow technological development, Bacon understood that the scientific revolution would immeasurably strengthen man's control over his physical environment. He foresaw the kind of interplay between science and technology which has indeed transformed the modern world.

Both Bacon and Descartes had valuable things to say about scientific method. In his *Novum Organum* ("The New Instrument"), published in 1620, Bacon argued that the true scientist (unlike Aristotle) worked by the inductive method, moving from the particular to the general, from specific experiments to axioms which in turn pointed the way to further experiments. Bacon urged scientists to experiment as systematically as possible, to pool their knowledge and dovetail their research projects, and above all to keep open-minded about the results. Though not himself an experimentalist, Bacon advocated the kind of empirical, inductive procedure normally followed by modern chemists and biologists. But Bacon's method was not employed by the greatest scientists of his own day. The thinking of mathematicians, astronomers, and physicists is more abstract than Bacon realized.

The most important science of the seventeenth century was deductive, as when Kepler deduced his general laws of planetary motion. Here Descartes' understanding of scientific method was much more relevant. Descartes was a great mathematician in his own right. He invented analytical geometry and perfected Galileo's law of inertia. In his *Discourse on Method* (1637), Descartes laid down rules for the abstract, deductive reasoning suitable to mathematicians. The true scientist, according to Descartes, was interested not so much in concrete phenomena as in the laws which systematized and explained nature. To uncover nature's secrets, he had to search for the simplest elements making up the physical world and deduce from these elements principles which would give meaning to concrete phenomena. Descartes' method was far closer than Bacon's to the intellectual process by which Copernicus, Kepler, and Galileo arrived at their discoveries.

Both Bacon and Descartes had their limitations as philosophers of the new science. Bacon's concept of science was too crudely utilitarian; Descartes' was too divorced from experience. Bacon's defects are more obvious. His insistence on material results blinded him to the revolution in astronomy and physics. He could not appreciate the creativity of abstract thinkers who worked by intuitive leaps of the mind. He particularly condemned Galileo for expressing the problem of motion in mathematical formulas. Bacon wanted Galileo to investigate and explain the internal tensions within particular moving bodies. Like the despised scholastics, he adhered to a concept of nature which was loaded with pseudoscientific embellishments. Descartes went to the opposite extreme. He condemned Galileo for being too experimental and insufficiently abstract! Descartes confidently asserted that his comprehensive new philosophy explained why and how the universe operated much better than Galileo's experiments could.

Descartes reduced nature to two absolutely distinct elements: mind and matter, or *res cogitans* ("thinking substance") and *res extensa* ("extended substance"). He did not presume to investigate the realm of thinking substance, which included soul and spirit, the province of theologians and the Church. But his concept of extended substance enabled him to explain every aspect of physical nature in terms of an all-inclusive, self-operating mechanism. According to Descartes, the universe was continuously and completely filled with an infinite number of particles of matter. Each particle was mathematically definable, having length, breadth, and depth. There was no room for occult forces like gravity and magnetism. Descartes explained motion on mechanistic principles as incessant whirlpool contact among invisible particles. "Give me extension and motion," he bragged, "and I will construct the universe." Cartesianism was immensely popular among seventeenth-century intellectuals who had lost faith in the old Aristotelian-Ptolemaic view of nature. It incorporated every branch of science. Descartes made a useful contribution to physiology by insisting that the human body was a machine, subject to the same laws as the cosmic machine. The trouble was that he explained too much too rigidly. He was more ingenious than Aristotle, but just as dogmatic, and no truer to nature. Before the close of the century Cartesianism had been superseded by Newton's improved version of the World Machine.

Bacon and Descartes helped to create a new climate of opinion, in which the scientist became an esteemed public figure. After 1650 scientists found it easier to get money for equipment and experiments. Their findings were more widely circulated and more quickly appreciated. Most important, scientists from various countries exchanged ideas with one another as never before. Since the universities, traditional centers of intellectual life, disdained the new learning, scientists did not feel at home within the cloistered precincts of Oxford, Paris, and Padua. Bacon urged them to form their own scientific societies, in which new ideas and experiments could be freely tested. When he envisioned an ideal commonwealth in the *New Atlantis* (1627), he lovingly described the operations of Salomon's House, where a team of scientists were busily unlocking nature's secrets. And indeed, in this century scientists did begin to form societies of their own. Galileo belonged to one of the earliest, the Accademia dei Lincei ("Academy of the Lynx-Eyed"), in Rome. By the 1650's, similar informal groups were meeting regularly in Florence, Paris, and London. During the following decade, much more powerful and permanent scientific institutions were founded in England and France under government patronage. Charles II chartered the

Pascal's calculating machine. *Pascal invented this device at the age of nineteen. One of the fifty models built under his supervision is shown. The machine adds and subtracts more efficiently than it multiplies and divides. To Pascal's dismay, it proved to be too expensive for practical use.*

Royal Society in 1662. Colbert sponsored the Académie des Sciences in 1666. Most of the great figures in late seventeenth-century science were affiliated with these bodies. The members listened to papers, shared instruments, collected specimens, conducted experiments, and reported their findings in volumes of *Transactions* or *Mémoires*—prototypes of the modern scientific journal. The membership was an odd medley of professional scientists and gentleman *virtuosi* or dilettantes. Charles II himself enjoyed working in his chemical laboratory.

The popularity of the new science among dilettantes was easy to laugh at. In *The Virtuoso*, by Thomas Shadwell, a popular English farce of 1676, a gentleman scientist named Sir Nicholas Gimcrack was portrayed as a speculative ass. Sir Nicholas transfused sheep's blood into a man (this experiment was actually performed by the Royal Society) in order to cultivate human wool. He watched armies in battle on the moon through his telescope. He read a Geneva bible by the phosphorescent glow of a putrid leg of pork. When a skeptic asked him why he lay on a table, flailing his limbs in imitation of a frog in a bowl of water, the following exchange ensued:

GIMCRACK: I swim most exquisitely on land.
SKEPTIC: Do you intend to practice in the water, Sir?
GIMCRACK: Never, Sir. I hate the water, I never come upon the water, Sir.

SKEPTIC: Then there will be no use of swimming.

GIMCRACK: I content myself with the speculative side of swimming. I care not for the practick. I seldom bring anything to use, 'tis not my way. Knowledge is my ultimate end.

Actually, the *virtuosi* tended to make the emphasis in the new scientific societies excessively utilitarian rather than speculative. Charles II and Colbert hoped for Baconian technological improvements. Much effort was spent on designs for industrial machinery, ship models, experiments with new recipes for brewing beer, and so forth. Very little was accomplished along these lines. In the second half of the seventeenth century the most fruitful scientific research continued to be highly abstract.

Sir Isaac Newton

The supreme genius of the Englishman Isaac Newton (1642–1727) brought the scientific revolution to a majestic climax. Newton was not an exceptionally interesting or attractive personality. He was very much the absentminded professor: he forgot to eat when he was working, and had to be prodded into publishing any of his findings. He suffered from paranoia, and unjustly accused his colleagues of stealing his ideas. He expended much time and energy on alchemical studies, not to mention his laborious and inaccurate calculations of the dates of biblical events. But when Newton turned to physics and astronomy, only Galileo among seventeenth-century scientists could rival his extraordinary imagination and discipline. Only Galileo shared his mastery of the whole scientific terrain from instrument making, to experimentation, to theory. And Newton was a much better mathematician than Galileo, and a more powerful abstract thinker. Like many scientists, he did his best work as a very young man. In 1665, when he was a student at Cambridge, an epidemic of bubonic plague closed the university. Newton was forced to spend nearly two years on his mother's isolated Lincolnshire farm. In this unlikely setting, he began experiments in optics which made the study of light for the first time a branch of physics. In mathematics, he invented the differential and integral calculus. In mechanics, he began to formulate his laws of universal gravitation and motion. "In those days," he later reflected, "I was in the prime of my age for invention, and minded mathematics and philosophy [science] more than at any time since."

Newton's supreme achievement was to weld Kepler's laws of planetary motion, Galileo's laws of falling bodies, the concept of inertia developed by Galileo and Descartes, and his own concept of gravitation into a single mathematical-physical system. Newton asked what inward pull kept the planets in elliptical orbits about the sun, and the moon in orbit about the earth, when according to Galileo's concept of inertia each of them should fly off in an infinite straight line. As he sat in his orchard, the thud of a falling apple startled him into thinking that the moon must be pulled toward the earth's center by the very same force which drew the apple to the ground. He deduced that gravity must be a universal force, equally affecting all celestial and terrestrial matter, and that the action and reaction between any two masses is equal and opposite. That is, the moon draws the earth with the same force with which the earth draws the moon; the pull exerted by the moon causes the oceans' tides. In the case of the falling apple, its mass is so tiny in comparison with the earth's mass that the pull of the apple has no measurable force. Twenty years passed before Newton felt satisfied with his mathematical proofs. At last, in 1687, he set forth his theory of universal gravitation and motion (and much else) in an epochal book, *The Mathematical Principles of Natural Philosophy*, always known by its abbreviated Latin title, the *Principia*. It sold for five shillings a copy.

The *Principia* is a deliberately difficult book, addressed to those few scholars who could understand Newton's mathematics and appreciate the elegance of his theory. No brief synopsis can capture its intellectual thrust. First of all, Newton brought together the mathematical, astronomical, and mechanical findings of the preceding century, effecting a synthesis which was badly needed. In particular, he correlated Kepler's celestial mechanics with Galileo's terrestrial mechanics and distilled from this material three basic laws of universal motion, which he expressed mathematically. Next, he formulated his law of universal gravitation: every particle of matter attracts every other particle with a force proportional to the product of the two masses, and inversely proportional to the square of the distance between them. The whole *Principia* is an extended demonstration of this key discovery. Newton did not pretend to understand the mysterious force of gravity. He clashed head on with Descartes, who had denied the existence of gravity and explained mechanically how and why particles move. Newton's view of nature, like Descartes', was mechanistic and mathematical, of course, but he intensely disliked Descartes' method of inventing an intellectualized picture of the world which bore no relation to empirical observation. Like Galileo, Newton believed that the scientist should describe how the universe operates, not why. He took special delight in puncturing the Cartesian balloon. Meticulously supporting his abstract reasoning with experimental evidence, Newton concluded his book with a marvelously precise description of the structure of the celestial system. This section particularly impressed and satisfied his readers. For instance, Newton detected and calculated a conical twist in the earth's axis of rotation, so slight that the cycle takes twenty-six thousand years to complete. His general description of the universe needed no correction for more than a century, and physicists continued to work within the framework of Newtonian, or classical, mechanics until the age of Einstein. The *Principia* was immediately recognized as a masterpiece, even by Cartesians who could not accept Newton's theory of gravitation. Far from being persecuted as Galileo had been, Newton was lionized. He was knighted, made master of the English royal mint, and elected president of the Royal Society. When he died, he was given a state funeral and buried in Westminster Abbey.

Biology and Chemistry

Very little has been said so far about biology and chemistry, for there was no revolution in these sciences between 1559 and 1715. Biology remained a neglected auxiliary to medical practice, chemistry an auxiliary to medicine and metallurgy. Neither science had as yet developed rational methods, standards, or objectives. However, in some areas of biology—notably in anatomy, physiology, and botany—there were important developments. For the first time the 1,500-year-old medical teachings of Galen were corrected and amplified, mainly by professors and students at the University of Padua, Europe's leading medical center. In 1543, the year in which Copernicus announced his heliocentric theory, Andreas Vesalius (1514–1564), a Flemish

The perils of seventeenth-century medicine and surgery. *Title page of* De effi-caci medicina *(1646).*

professor at Padua, published a pioneering treatise on human anatomy. Vesalius had dissected many more human cadavers than Galen, and he was able to correct many—though by no means all—of Galen's mistakes. His book was a work of art as well as science, for the text was illustrated with superb drawings of muscles and bones.

A much more fundamental advance over Galen came in 1628, when William Harvey (1578–1657), an Englishman who had studied at Padua, demonstrated the circulation of the blood. It had previously been supposed that since venous blood is tinged with blue and arterial blood is bright red, the blood in each system must ebb and flow separately. Galen had taught that venous blood distributed nutrition from the liver, and arterial blood distributed an intangible vital spirit which kept man alive. Harvey rejected these views; he proved that blood is pumped into the arteries by the heart at a massive rate, travels to the veins, and returns to the heart. Harvey was a heart worshiper as Copernicus had been a sun worshiper, and he was much influenced by the Aristotelian belief that circular motion is perfect. His great discovery undermined the traditional humoral theory of medicine, but Harvey's fellow doctors did not recognize this. Even physicians who comprehended the physiology of the circulatory system continued to suppose that the sovereign remedy for almost any internal disorder was to bleed the patient copiously.

In botany, naturalists collected a great mass of new data about the plant kingdom. In the 1540's only five hundred distinct botanical species had been classified, as against eighteen thousand by the 1680's. But there was no disposition to challenge traditional views about the fixity of species and the great chain of being. During this period the Dutchman Anton von Leeuwenhoek (1632–1723) made a microscope which magnified objects three hundred times. Through this instrument he uncovered a whole new world of one-celled organisms, invisible to the naked eye. But he never understood that the microbes he delighted to watch swimming about in human spittle might be disease carriers. That fact would remain hidden until the nineteenth century.

In chemistry, it is hard to see much purposeful development during this period. There were chemists in plenty: mining engineers who assayed ores, pharmacists who compounded drugs, alchemists who tried to transmute metals, and philosophers who speculated about the atomic structure of matter. Physicians liked to purge their patients with chemical drugs like mercury and antimony especially when trying to cure such frightening new diseases as syphilis. These chemical potions may have been no more harmful than the traditional herbal recipes, but their effects were certainly more violent. The modern chemist's concept of elements and compounds had not yet been developed. Robert Boyle (1627–1691) was the leading chemical experimentalist and theorist of his day. He discarded the Aristotelian belief in four basic elements—earth, water, air, and fire—but he had no better theory to offer concerning the structure of matter. The chemical revolution would not start until the late eighteenth century, when Lavoisier isolated oxygen and drew up the first table of chemical elements.

Nevertheless, the cumulative change in scientific thought and practice between 1559 and 1715 was immense. One measure of the revolution in science is the way in which Descartes and Newton persuaded the intellectual community to view the cosmos mechanistically. Newton's concept of nature as a kind of giant clockwork, the World Machine, was in its own way as satisfying intellectually and emotionally as the Aristotelian-Ptolemaic view had been. Instead of admiring perfect circles and the ascending order of purity, man could marvel at the perfect regularity of nature, at the way in which all inanimate objects, however great or small, were governed by the same timeless laws. There was certainly more romance in the old view of the world, more rationality in the new view. How can one weigh the loss in passion, imagination, and complexity against the gain in precision, elegance, and common sense? In educated circles there was no longer much room in 1715 for belief in myth, magic, and demonology. The Salem witch-hunt of 1692, during which twenty persons were executed in Massachusetts, was one of the last major outbursts of this particular form of public dementia.

The new philosophy forced men to reframe their religious beliefs. Both Protestant scientists like Kepler and Newton, and Catholic scientists like Galileo and Descartes, eagerly sought to harmonize their findings with Christian teleology. Nonetheless, it was hard to see any explicitly Christian purpose in the abstract mathematical design of the Newtonian World Machine. The Great Clockmaker, however perfect His handiwork, was more remote than the Creator worshiped by Calvin or Loyola. Human incentive and achievement seemed correspondingly more significant. To be sure, man no longer lived at the center of the cosmos. He occupied a second-rate planet spinning through endless empty space. But he was learning to master his physical environment. If God set the clock in motion, man could tell the time. Here was the most pervasive long-range consequence of the seventeenth-century scientific revolution, a buoyant faith in rational human progress.

RELIGIOUS ART IN THE BAROQUE AGE

In art, as in science, the years from 1559 to 1715 saw a revolt against traditional standards and values. In the late sixteenth century the Renaissance style in painting, sculpture, and architecture was vigorously challenged. In the seventeenth century it gave way to a new style, the Baroque. At first glance this artistic revolt is puzzling, since the Renaissance style reached a majestic peak during the opening three decades of the sixteenth century, the period art historians call the High Renaissance. In these years five great masters—Leonardo da Vinci, Michelangelo, Raphael, Titian, and Dürer—were expressing the Renaissance ideal of human beauty with matchless skill. No later artist could hope to surpass their harmonious, lifelike and exalted depiction of man. How could one improve upon Leonardo's psychological insight, or Michelangelo's glorification of the male body, or Raphael's idealization of women, or Titian's vibrant color, or Dürer's mastery of design? So perfect was this High Renaissance art that by the 1520's it was reaching a dead end. Michelangelo himself, having mastered all the problems inherent in the old style, began to formulate a new style known as Mannerism, which deliberately violated Renaissance conventions.

In the 1520's the Renaissance tradition was also attacked from a very different direction, by the Protestant movement. Luther denounced the religious art of the High Renaissance. He called it more pagan than Christian, and questioned the whole Catholic tradition of religious art. Protestants found it blasphemous to worship God in lavishly decorated churches, filled with statues and paintings honoring the saints, and carnal representations of the Madonna, Christ, and God the Father. Catholics, of course, rejected this protest, asserting the efficacy of religious imagery more ardently than ever. But by the mid-sixteenth century, Catholics too were finding the Renaissance style uncomfortably pat and worldly. They needed a new artistic way of expressing old truths. The moral and aesthetic issues raised in the early sixteenth century, and the crusading ardor of Protestants versus Catholics during the religious wars, gives special interest to the religious painting, sculpture, and architecture produced by Catholic and Protestant artists between 1559 and 1715.

Painting in the Sixteenth Century

Throughout the sixteenth century the Protestant Reformation had a blighting effect upon northern European art. In Germany and the Low Countries, as in Italy, painters had always supported themselves principally by filling commissions for religious works, such as altar panels and church frescoes. But the preaching of Luther, Zwingli, and Calvin incited iconoclastic riots against such symbols of popish idolatry. Protestant mobs smashed church statuary, burned altar pieces, and whitewashed frescoes. Lutheran and Calvinist churches were kept characteristically austere and undecorated. In the sixteenth century even Catholic churches in northern Europe offered fewer ecclesiastical commissions to painters, sculptors, and architects than they had in the good old days. Albrecht Dürer (1471–1528), the greatest German artist of Luther's generation, was not much affected by this crisis. Dürer earned his living by painting portraits and illustrating books. He did simplify his style in the religious engravings of his closing years and chose biblical themes compatible with the reform spirit, for Dürer greatly admired Luther although he did not actively join his movement. Dürer's colleague Hans Holbein the Younger (*c.* 1497–1543) had to abandon the painting of Madonnas, at which he excelled as a young man. Holbein moved from Germany to Switzerland and from Switzerland to England in search of work.

Massacre of the Innocents. *Painting by Brueghel. Kunsthistorisches Museum, Vienna.*

He spent the last half of his career painting portraits of Henry VIII and his courtiers. Holbein left no successor in Germany or in England, and there were few outstanding masters in sixteenth-century France or the Low Countries.

The paintings of Pieter Brueghel the Elder (*c.* 1525–1569) illustrate very well the changing temper of art in northern Europe. Brueghel was a Flemish Catholic who painted his greatest pictures in the 1560's, just as the Low Countries were starting to rebel against Philip II. He painted for private patrons in Antwerp and Brussels rather than for the Church, specializing in noncontroversial genre paintings of everyday life, scenes of peasants at work and play, artlessly rustic in appearance, yet richly detailed and ingeniously composed. Brueghel's religious paintings are in the same style as his genre paintings. For example, his "Massacre of the Innocents" is highly unconventional. The subject, of course, is a sensational one, generally represented by a theatrical tableau of twisted bodies, with knife-wielding soldiers, wailing mothers, and naked babies expiring in pools of blood. Brueghel's picture is very different. At first glance we see a wintry Flemish street scene, then notice the invading cavalry sealing off the village with their pikes, the frantic peasants milling about helplessly in the snow, the soldiers prying open the shuttered doors. Few babies can be seen, and only one pool of blood. But Brueghel's understatement gives his picture great realism and poignancy, for the viewer knows what is going to happen and feels as helpless as the rustic crowd in the street. By catching the timeless horror of soldiers preying on civilians, Brueghel found a fresh way of illustrating a very old Christian story.

In sixteenth-century Italy the artistic crisis was more complicated. Viewing the sumptuous paintings of Titian (c. 1477–1576), one might conclude that there was no crisis at all. For seventy years this Venetian master filled his spacious canvases with glowing Venuses and Virgins in stately perpetuation of the High Renaissance style. But other artists betrayed moral and aesthetic tension. The sack of Rome in 1527 by Charles V's soldiers ended the High Renaissance for the papacy if not for Venice. Temporarily, the popes suspended their patronage of artists and architects. Under the reforming popes of the mid-sixteenth century, the Roman climate became austere and antihumanist. Pope Pius IV (ruled 1559–1565) was so offended by the naked figures in Michelangelo's great fresco of the Last Judgment in the Sistine Chapel that he had loincloths painted on to cover them decently. But the Church soon recovered its old confidence. In 1563 the Council of Trent decreed that religious imagery was beneficial for instructing the faithful and stimulating piety. St. Ignatius of Loyola reasserted the Church's belief that worship demanded the Christian's full physical and psychological resources. His *Spiritual Exercises* taught the reader how to use all of his senses to achieve a vividly personal spiritual experience. Gradually, the popes resumed their building program. St. Peter's was completed at immense expense in the late sixteenth and early seventeenth centuries, and the whole city of Rome was refurbished on a very grand scale. Once the Catholic reformation was in full swing, architects and artists enjoyed unparalleled ecclesiastical patronage.

Sixteenth-century Italian artists searched for a new style appropriate to the Catholic spiritual revival. Michelangelo Buonarroti (1475–1564) altered his whole approach in the 1530's, and initiated a far-reaching rebellion against Renaissance standards and values. His two celebrated frescoes in the Sistine Chapel illustrate Michelangelo's changing concept of religious art. The ceiling fresco of scenes from Genesis, painted about 1510, retains the proportion, harmony, and restraint of classical Greek sculpture, despite the immensity of its scheme. But the wall fresco of the Last Judgment, painted in the 1530's, after the sack of Rome, erupts in violence and distortion, deliberately transgressing all classical canons. It is true, of course, that no great artist would treat a joyous subject like the creation of Adam in the same spirit as a terrible theme like the end of the world. But Michelangelo changed his style drastically over the years even when handling the same subject. In his first effort to carve a statue of the dead Christ, the "Pietà" (1499) at St. Peter's, Michelangelo managed, by means of artistic sleight of hand, to achieve an exquisitely naturalistic rendering of an implausible tableau. He wanted to convey a double vision of the Mother of God sorrowing over the crucified Christ and of the young Mary cuddling her infant Jesus. So he gave Mary the face of the young Virgin and reduced the scale of Christ's body, in order to cradle Him gracefully in Mary's arms and lap. Thanks to the sculptor's mastery of Renaissance style—the anatomical perfection and harmonious modeling of the figures—we accept this artificial composition as completely realistic. As an old man, Michelangelo returned to the same subject in his anticlassical style. His "Descent from the Cross" (1555), in the cathedral at Florence, is unfinished, but there is no mistaking the jagged, searing design of Christ's broken body, too heavy for three mourners to lift. Michelangelo elongated and exaggerated Christ's limbs, and flouted traditonal scale and proportion, in order to evoke the tortured weight of His sacrifice.

Michelangelo's late paintings and sculpture inspired a school of imitators, known as Mannerists because they worked "in the manner of" Michelangelo. It was a dangerous manner to imitate unless one had Michelangelo's genius. Mannerist artists generally manipulated classical components to achieve anticlassical effects. In late sixteenth-century Italian churches and palaces, the columns, arches, entablatures, and pediments of Greco-Roman building design are juxtaposed unconventionally in the effort to escape the old Renaissance clichés. Mannerist painters decorated walls and ceilings with complex allegorical scenes of muscle-bound athletes in contorted attitudes. Today most of this hectic art and architecture seems jejune at best, vulgar at worst, and singularly ill suited to the Catholic revival. However, two Mannerist painters produced religious art of great power and originality. One was

Left: Pietà. *Carved in 1499 by Michelangelo. St. Peter's, Rome.* *Right*: Descent from the Cross. *Carved in 1555 by Michelangelo. Cathedral, Florence.*

Tintoretto (1518–1594), of Venice, and the other was El Greco (*c.* 1548–1614), of Toledo in Spain.

It is said that Tintoretto posted this motto over his studio door: "The drawing of Michelangelo and the color of Titian." Whatever Tintoretto's coloring was originally like, his canvases are now generally much less rich than Titian's. But the electric energy and daring of his composition is still exciting. He had little interest in Titian's pagan themes, and preferred religious subjects of the sort which Protestants abominated—saints, miracles, and Madonnas. Tintoretto's output was prodigious. In emulation of Michelangelo's "Last Judgment," he painted a number of monumental panoramas, the most grandiose being his seventy-foot mural of Paradise in the Ducal Palace at Venice. In this painting, nearly five hundred figures swirl around the Virgin and Christ. For centuries Venetians bragged that they had the largest oil painting in the world until Forest Lawn Cemetery in California installed an even bigger one. Some of Tintoretto's smaller pictures are equally dramatic. His "Massacre of the Innocents" is a tumultuous avalanche of movement, the exact opposite of Brueghel's picture. He could be vulgar, as when he painted the Last Supper with the table askew and the apostles lounging and jostling like drunken louts. He could also achieve an otherworldly incandescence. In the National Gallery at Washington there is a beautiful Tintoretto painting of Christ walking on the waters with majestic yet incorporeal tread. The painter's eerie lighting and subtle rhythms recreate the miracle before our eyes.

El Greco was an even more individual artist than Tintoretto, and it is perhaps misleading to label him as a member of the Mannerist school. His real name was Domenicos Theotocopoulos; he was called "the Greek" because he came from the Greek island of Crete. He spent a long apprenticeship in Venice and Rome before moving to Spain in the 1570's. El Greco hoped to be a court painter, but Philip II did not appreciate the work of this bizarre foreigner, so utterly different from the insipid and derivative painting of sixteenth-century Spaniards. So El Greco settled down in Toledo to a busy and unspectacular career as a church painter. We think of him as the most "modern" stylist of his day; hence it is worth emphasizing that El Greco's mystical, ardent temper was entirely attuned to the sixteenth-century world, and very congenial to the Spain of Don Quixote. El Greco learned much from Tintoretto, Titian, and Michelangelo, but he was always an independent artist. Having Byzantine origins, he viewed the whole classical Renaissance tradition from the outside. He never had to strain in order to avoid the naturalistic clichés of the Renaissance style; there was no artificiality in his elongated, emaciated, sexless, two-dimensional figures, who seem to hover between heaven and earth.

El Greco called his painting of the burial of the Count of Orgaz "my sublime work," and this masterpiece does indeed epitomize his religious style. The painting commemorates a local miracle: when the pious Count of

The Burial of the Count
Orgaz. *Painting by El Greco*
Church of San Tomé, Toledo

Orgaz died in Toledo, St. Stephen and St. Augustine descended from heaven
to lay him gently in his tomb. A little boy, El Greco's son, shows us the
miracle, and the gazing priest at the right carries our attention to the dead
grandee's soul, being carried by an angel up to Christ. By subtle tricks of
color, bodily gesture and facial delineation, the painter carefully stages three
hierarchical levels of reality: the dead man in his sepulcher, the living
mourners, and the heavenly spirits. It is remarkable that such a crowded
composition should convey an exalted upward sweep. El Greco's silent
gravity precludes false sentimentality or melodrama. His painting radiates a
spirit of loving communion between Christ, the saints, and man—the
quintessence of Catholic art.

Beautiful as El Greco's painting seems to us, it was too ethereal for
contemporary Catholic taste. At the turn of the century, in Rome, the
painter Michelangelo da Caravaggio (*c.* 1565–1609) cultivated a realistic and
earthy approach at the opposite pole from that of El Greco. Caravaggio
protested very effectively against the desiccated artificiality of the Mannerist
school. He shocked people by painting Doubting Thomas as a bald and
wrinkled peasant, jabbing his finger into Christ's open wound. He set the
scene of the Virgin's death in a dingy cottage, with Mary's stiffened corpse
attended by coarse-looking common folk. Caravaggio was a highly talented

painter, and his pictures were honest and robust, but if El Greco was too rarefied for seventeenth-century sensibilities, then Caravaggio was too plebian. Art patrons, especially princes and churchmen who paid the largest commissions, craved grandeur as well as robustness. What they wanted was the Baroque, a splendiferous new style developed by seventeenth-century painters like Rubens, Van Dyck, and Velázquez, and architects like Bernini.

The Baroque

The Baroque is a notoriously difficult concept to define. Seventeenth-century Baroque art and architecture is generally characterized by magnificence, theatricality, energy, and direct emotional appeal, though as we shall see, these characteristics are more apparent in some Baroque works than in others. There is no clear dividing line between the Mannerism of the sixteenth century and the Baroque of the seventeenth; both styles are anticlassical, though Baroque artists tend to be more cheerfully extroverted and less tense than Tintoretto and El Greco. Admirers of the Baroque like to apply the label to every positive feature of European society between 1550 and 1750. They speak not only of Baroque art, music, and literature, but of Baroque thought and Baroque politics.[1] But this deprives the concept of all useful meaning. It is difficult enough to correlate with any precision the Baroque traits in seventeenth-century art and music. In music, the most obvious Baroque manifestation was the development of opera. Such seventeenth-century composers as Monteverdi in Italy, Lully in France, and Purcell in England popularized this new form of secular entertainment, which combined music, acting, dancing, and pageantry. The opera became an instant success in court circles all over Europe. In seventeenth-century church music, too, there was a new brilliance and dramatic intensity, apparent, for example, in the contrapuntal choral and organ writing of Schütz and Buxtehude. In music the Baroque style reached its fullest development considerably later than in art. Corelli and Vivaldi worked out the concerto form at the close of the seventeenth century, Scarlatti wrote his harpsichord sonatas in the eighteenth century, and the two greatest Baroque masters—Bach and Handel—composed most of their music after 1715.

Our concern is with Baroque art and architecture. This new seventeenth-century style was more class-conscious than Renaissance art had been, for Baroque artists knew how to flatter rich patrons by celebrating the pomp and luxury of upper-class life. The new style appealed far more to kings and aristocrats than to the middle classes or the peasantry. In bourgeois Holland, painters like Rembrandt, Hals, and Vermeer had little affinity for the grand manner. It was in Habsburg territory, in Italy, Spain, Belgium, Austria, and Bohemia, that the Baroque style developed most vigorously. Habsburg

[1]Carl J. Friedrich is a Baroque enthusiast. His *Age of the Baroque, 1610–1660* (New York, 1952) presents an all-embracing interpretation of the movement.

territory was Catholic territory, and Catholics liked the Baroque far more than Protestants. What better proof of renewed Catholic vigor than the splendidly assertive Baroque churches of the seventeenth century, stunningly ornamented with bravura paintings and statuary? The principal Jesuit

The Triumph of the Name of Jesus. *Ceiling fresco by Gaulli in the Church of the Gesù, Rome. Note the Baroque device of combining fresco painting with gilded stucco and statuary so as to achieve an overpowering ensemble.*

church in Rome, the Gesù, combines a sixteenth-century Mannerist exterior with a seventeenth-century Baroque interior. The Baroque decorations of this church have a lavish intensity hard to describe. The painting on the vaulted ceiling depicts ecstatic worshipers straining upward toward the mystical name of Jesus. The dazzling tomb of St. Ignatius, studded with lapis lazuli and bronze, expresses exultation rather than grief. The statue groups to either side show religion trampling on heresy and barbarians adoring the faith. No longer harking back to pagan classicism, Baroque Rome expressed the power and exuberance of reformed Catholicism. Unhappily, this vibrant style slowly degenerated into the sugar-and-gingerbread kitsch manner which has vitiated most religious art, Protestant as well as Catholic, since the eighteenth century.

Peter Paul Rubens (1577–1640) was the first full-scale Baroque artist. A Fleming trained in Italy, he established a fantastically successful studio in Antwerp. His breezy, florid pictures, crowded with heavily fleshed figures bathed in lush colors, were exhilarating to people accustomed to Pieter Brueghel's meticulous peasant scenes. Rubens was an artistic entrepreneur. He operated a picture factory, with an assembly line of assistants trained to execute his compositions, each assistant a specialist in figures, faces, animals, or backgrounds. Rubens himself would apply the finishing touches to each canvas, but often no more than that. For example, he sent one prospective customer a list of twenty-four paintings for sale, only five of which were entirely his own work. The choice included *"Prometheus Enchained on Mount Caucases*, with an eagle which devours his liver; an original work of my own hand, the eagle done by Snyders, 500 florins. *Christ on the Cross*, life-size, considered perhaps the best thing I have ever done, 500 florins. A *Last Judgment*, begun by one of my pupils after an original which I made of much larger size for the Prince of Neuberg, who paid me for it 3,500 florins in ready money. As the present piece is not quite finished, I will retouch it altogether by myself, so that it can pass for an original, 1,200 florins." [2] Rubens' mass-production technique was especially geared to heroic mural painting, where the general impact of his exuberant design is greater than the sum of the details. His decorating talents were highly prized by the crowned heads of Europe. Marie de Medici and Louis XIII of France, Charles I of England, and Philip IV of Spain all commissioned Rubens murals or tapestry designs for their royal palaces. While traveling from court to court, this man of the world also served the Habsburgs as a diplomatic agent. Rubens was a fervid Catholic, and almost half of his pictures treat religious themes. He often preaches the Catholic reformation, as when he shows St. Ignatius exorcising evil spirits from the sick. His religious paintings are generally festive and always vividly alive. A favorite subject is the adoration of the Magi. Rubens invariably crowds a horde of people around the manger,

2*Rubens: Paintings and Drawings*, ed. by R. A. M. Stevenson (New York, 1939), p. 26.

The Adoration of the Magi. *Painting by Rubens. Baroque devices here include the contorted attitudes of the spectators, to indicate their joyful amazement, and the exotic camels, which almost steal the scene from the Christ child. Royal Museum, Antwerp.*

making the stable look like rush hour at Grand Central Station. Yet all this bustle is so spontaneous, joyful, and loving that the viewer feels himself participating in the discovery and worship of the newborn Christ Child.

The two other chief Baroque painters, Van Dyck and Velázquez, were primarily court portraitists, and did much less religious work than Rubens. They exemplify the increasingly secular character of seventeenth-century art even in Catholic countries. Anthony Van Dyck (1599–1641) was a Fleming who painted in Rubens' studio for some years before establishing his own portrait business. Few society painters have excelled Van Dyck's elegant and flattering style. He endowed his aristocratic sitters with a languid pride and poise to match their fine clothes. Like Rubens, he was a mass-production artist. During the decade he spent in England, Van Dyck, with his assistants, turned out some 350 portraits, including thirty-eight of Charles I. Van Dyck's Spanish contemporary Diego Rodríguez Velázquez (1599–1660) was an even finer portraitist, indeed, one of the giants of western painting. For thirty-seven years Velázquez was court painter to Philip IV, and his genius immortalized the mediocre men and women who ruled mid-seventeenth-century Spain. His portraits of Philip IV are much more candid than Van Dyck's glamorous portraits of Charles I, yet just as appealing. He manages to convey the king's official majesty and his personal frailty all at once.

Velázquez painted every sitter, whether king, court jester, or dwarf, with the same objective sincerity. His great portrait of Pope Innocent X illustrates his remarkable integrity and immediacy. The picture seems a caricature at first: how could such a brutal man masquerade as a pope? But the longer we study this canvas, the more we admire Innocent's scrutinizing gaze and his caged energy. Velázquez was a superb technician. In this painting, every brushstroke distributes light and shadow, gives texture to the papal robes, defines the muscles of Innocent's body, imparts life to his sweat-beaded features. Although Velázquez had an eye for color and costume, he painted in a simple, grave, and static style. Even his most theatrical work, the "Surrender of Breda," celebrating a Spanish victory over the Dutch, is as stately and restrained as a High Renaissance composition, with none of El Greco's supercharged tension nor Rubens' heroic tumult. He did, however, exhibit two important Baroque traits: artistic concentration upon the royal court, and emotional repudiation of Renaissance idealism. He was an uncompromising realist and painted life exactly as it is, not as it should be. This dissociation from the classical ideal of beauty hampered Velázquez's effectiveness as a religious painter. He found no adequate flesh-and-blood models for Mary and Jesus, and he lacked Raphael's or Holbein's Renaissance vision of perfect human form. Here he suffered from the same handicap as Van Dyck. Both artists painted gently melancholy Madonnas and Crucifixions

Innocent X. *Painting by Velázquez. Galleria Doria, Rome.*

which are reverent and handsome, yet distressingly vacuous in comparison with their court portraits inspired by real people.

In Baroque sculpture and architecture, the central figure was Gianlorenzo Bernini (1598–1680), a Neapolitan who spent most of his career in Rome, building and decorating for five popes. No other seventeenth-century artist, not even Rubens, epitomized the Baroque spirit so completely. Bernini had a genius for theatrical effects. He manipulated classical building forms with much more freedom than his Mannerist predecessors had displayed. His facades, colonnades, and stairways look like stage settings. He carved a statue of David in frenzied action, slinging his shot at Goliath. Compared with Michelangelo's noble David, standing reflectively in naked majesty, Bernini's beetle-browed actor looks a bit comic. Bernini was primarily a church architect and decorator. By the time he became papal architect, the monumental basilica of St. Peter's was nearly finished. He enclosed the immense piazza in front of the church with two semicircular colonnades, a stroke of genius, since the marching columns draw worshipers toward St. Peter's while distracting their attention from the basilica's top-heavy facade. Within the church, under Michelangelo's mighty dome, he erected a flamboyant baldacchino, or altar canopy, which stands the height of an eight-story building on four bronze corkscrew columns. Bernini appealed blatantly to the senses, for he believed that the church was a stage for the physical display of divine mysteries. In one Roman chapel he dared to stage St. Teresa's vision of being pierced through the heart by a flaming arrow of heavenly love. Leaning upon clouds suspended in mid air above the altar, Teresa swoons, her face ecstatic with blissful pain, a smiling seraph poised above her with the arrow, while bronze shafts of light cascade upon the scene. Rarely has a miracle been made so tangible. Other seventeenth-century Roman architects, sculptors, and painters followed in Bernini's footsteps. The papal city became a festival of domed churches, of curved and columned facades, of flamboyant fountains, monuments, and tombs, of ceiling frescoes erupting skyward as if to dissolve earth into heaven.

Itinerant Italian architects carried the Baroque building style into central Europe and Spain during the second half of the seventeenth century. In Germany, Austria, and Bohemia, incessant warfare crippled major building projects through most of the century. The Baroque age could not begin in Bohemia until after 1648, or in Austria until the Turks were driven out of the Danube Valley in the 1680's. In Spain the new Italian fashion was initially resisted by local builders accustomed to the austere Escorial style of Philip II. Once established, Baroque architecture flourished in Austria and Spain into the 1730's. In both Austria and Spain, Baroque architecture had its own distinct character, compounded of local custom and Italianate borrowings. In Austria, Baroque churches sported onion steeples as well as

The Ecstasy of St. Teresa. *Sculpture by Bernini. Cornaro Chapel, Santa Maria della Vittoria, Rome.*

Roman domes. In Spain, Baroque churches displayed explosively ornamented facades and altar screens owing little to Bernini. In both central Europe and Spain the new building style was less sophisticated and more fanciful than Italian Baroque. Because the Germans, Slavs, and Spaniards had never really assimilated the classical building style of the Italian Renaissance, they could manipulate and multiply ornamental effects more spontaneously and innocently than Bernini, who was a self-conscious rebel against his architectural heritage.

The first notable Austrian Baroque builder, Fischer von Erlach (1656–1723), was trained in Italy and heavily influenced by Bernini. His chief clients were princes and noblemen who wanted imposing new palaces. To provide the necessary pomp and grandiloquence, Fischer developed what became a trademark of central European Baroque: the grand staircase supported not by conventional pillars, but on the shoulders of muscular, straining Atlas figures. Fischer also designed churches. Many Baroque churches and monasteries were built in newly converted Protestant areas like Bohemia. For example, in Prague, a city very rich in Baroque architecture, the Jesuit Church of St. Niklas has a nave whose rhythmically curving walls and vault achieve an extraordinary undulating effect. Spanish Baroque architecture was primarily ecclesiastical. It is called "churrigueresque," after José Churriguera (1650–1723), the leading Spanish Baroque architect. The convoluted sculpture of his church facades and the gilded richness of his altar screens is overpowering. The style even spread to Spanish America; the far-off Mexican city of Puebla could boast thirty-six domed churches in the 1680's, including the staggeringly churrigueresque Church of Santo Domingo.

French, English, and Dutch Art

The Baroque spirit did not triumph everywhere. In France, Bourbon absolutism required an artistic style emphasizing grandeur, monumentality, and power, yet the French never accepted the Baroque. They found Rubens' paintings and Bernini's buildings distastefully showy, passionate, and undignified, and clung to the classical values and standards against which Baroque artists were rebelling. Seventeenth-century French painters, sculptors, and architects prized clarity, simplicity, and harmony of design. French classicism is a rather frigid version of the High Renaissance style. The two chief seventeenth-century French painters, Nicolas Poussin (1594–1665) and Claude Lorrain (1600–1682), spent their careers in Rome, trying to recapture the aesthetic and moral values of the antique Romans. Poussin specialized in scenes from classical mythology which celebrated the dignity of the ancient republic or the grandeur of the empire. Compared with the paintings of Tintoretto, Caravaggio, or Rubens, his canvases appear calm, chaste, and congealed. Claude Lorrain had a warmer style than Poussin, but he too was far from boisterous. His dreamy landscapes of the countryside around Rome evoked the bucolic poetry of Virgil. All this was a far cry from the art of Bernini.

When Bernini visited Paris in 1665, Louis XIV rejected his plans for the rebuilding of the Louvre palace. The Sun King could not bear to imitate a style so intimately associated with the papacy and with Habsburg Europe, and he settled on a sober and massive design for the Louvre. Louis' architectural taste ran toward featureless monumentality. His great palace at Versailles is Baroque in scale but not in temper. The regimented facade is without flamboyance. The fountains and statuary in the garden served as formal backdrops for Louis' rigid court pageantry. In the arts, as in politics, Louis imposed order. His favorite painter, Charles Le Brun (1619–1690), laid down rules of composition, proportion, and perspective which court painters were expected to obey. At Versailles, Le Brun organized a team of builders and decorators who suppressed their individual eccentricities in order to achieve a blandly grandiose effect—the aim of most government architecture ever since.

In Protestant northern Europe, the impact of the Baroque style was relatively superficial. The English and the Dutch, in particular, were too bourgeois to appreciate the exuberant pomp of Baroque secular art and too puritanical to appreciate the brilliant theatricality of Baroque religious art. In seventeenth-century England, the Stuart court patronized Rubens, Van Dyck, and other far less talented society portraitists. Had they been able to afford it, Charles I and Charles II might have built Baroque palaces. But Sir Christopher Wren (1632–1723), the greatest native English artist in the seventeenth century, drew upon the High Renaissance and French classicism rather than the Baroque in shaping his elegantly classical style. Wren was a very insular Englishman, whose one trip abroad was to Paris. By accident he became the most prolific church builder in seventeenth-century Europe; in 1666 the disastrous fire of London gutted eighty medieval churches, including St. Paul's cathedral, and Wren was commissioned to rebuild the cathedral and fifty-one of the parish churches. Wren's churches were the Protestant answer to Bernini's papal architecture. The twisted, narrow London streets offered no opportunities for vistas, colonnades, and eye-catching facades. Wren had to build his churches on crowded commercial sites, squeezing the church doors between tightly packed rows of shop fronts. Wisely, he focused all external emphasis on his tall, fanciful steeples, each one different. These steeples ingeniously combine the verticality of the Gothic spire with the classical ornamentation of the Baroque cupola. To save money, he built the interiors of his churches with plastered brick rather than stone. He was no Puritan, yet his Anglican churches look like meeting halls rather than shrines. They are sparingly decorated, and designed so that the whole congregation can see the pulpit and hear the preacher. Compared with these parish churches, the rebuilt St. Paul's cathedral is elaborate and magnificent; compared with St. Peter's in Rome, however, Wren's cathedral is modest and reticent. Though Wren stole shamelessly from other archi-

Steeple of St. Bride's Church, London. *Designed by* Wren.

tects in designing St. Paul's, he achieved an original total effect. The cathedral's one great ornament is the central dome, which floats over the London skyline in simple dignity, the embodiment of Wren's classical spirit.

The Dutch were even more impervious than the English to the Baroque spirit. In art, as in business, they distrusted ostentation and extravagance, and prized common sense and discipline. They were not philistines. The seventeenth century was the golden age of Dutch painting. Every self-respecting burgher had his picture painted; every drinking club and almshouse board commissioned a group portrait; the popular demand for art was so great that peddlers hawked landscapes, seascapes, and genre scenes. Dutch painters did not travel to Italy for inspiration or training. Like Brueghel and other earlier Netherlandish artists, they found beauty and significance in the humdrum details of everyday life. Their art was both anticlassical and anti-Baroque, for they neither idealized nor dramatized the bourgeois society they recorded. Their subject matter was emphatically secular. For instance, three of the best seventeenth-century Dutch painters, Frans Hals, Pieter de Hooch, and Jan Vermeer, produced no religious pictures whatsoever.

Frans Hals (*c.* 1580–1666) was a rollicking portraitist. With rapid-fire brush strokes, he painted a gallery of artlessly casual middle-class folk, sometimes catching them laughing out loud. Hals's bluff pictures were the antithesis of Van Dyck's blue-blooded society portraits. Pieter de Hooch (1629–*c.*1683) painted quiet interior and courtyard scenes. He had none of Hals's gift for bringing people to life, but his finicky style gave charm to the spotless rooms, tiled floors, and brick walls on which he dwelt so lovingly. Jan Vermeer (1632–1675) is now reckoned a more complete artist than Hals or De Hooch, though he was unappreciated in his own day. Vermeer painted only a few small-sized pictures of trivial scenes, but in these bejeweled miniatures he created a world of timeless beauty. There is certainly nothing arresting about Vermeer's representation of a painter in his studio. The artist at the easel may be Vermeer himself, but since he turns his back to us, we look at the jumble of objects in his studio. Vermeer's technique is so flawless that the plaster cast on the table can be identified as Michelangelo's "Brutus," and the elaborate map of the Low Countries on the wall is accurate to the smallest detail—the Dutch were much the best cartographers in seventeenth-century Europe. But Vermeer is not merely a photographer in paint. He endows the studio scene with a limpid purity, as if to say that the commonest things in life have beauty and significance.

The greatest of all Dutch artists was Rembrandt van Rijn (1606–1669). He started out as a Dutch-style Rubens. Before he was thirty he was operating a fashionable studio in Amsterdam, painting opulent portraits and bombastic scenes in a richly Baroque color scheme all his own—deep browns and reds, luridly highlighted by barbaric gold. Like Rubens, he was very prolific. Over six hundred of his paintings and nearly two thousand of his etchings and drawings have survived. But Rembrandt became increasingly

The Painter in His Studio.
Painting by Vermeer. Kunst-
historisches Museum,
Vienna.

unwilling to curry public favor, and as his genius ripened, he gradually lost his popularity. His magnificent "Night Watch," depicting an Amsterdam company of musketeers going their rounds, displeased the militiamen who commissioned it, because many of their faces were obscured by the murky light and the tumbling pattern of pikes and charging figures. The proud artist's tragic decline from youthful prosperity to bankrupt old age is hauntingly recorded in his long series of self-portraits. He was a self-contained artist, who never left Holland, and fused elements of Netherlandish, Italian Renaissance, and Baroque art into his own inimitable style. Like other seventeenth-century Dutch painters, he was a realist, exploring the joys and sorrows of ordinary people. Even the works of his early Baroque phase were never theatrical, and the older he grew the more introspective his pictures became. He was a devoutly pious Mennonite, and despite the Protestant distaste for religious pictures, almost half of his paintings, etchings, and drawings illustrate biblical stories. Rembrandt was thus the one supremely great Protestant religious painter of the seventeenth century.

In his religious art, Rembrandt chose biblical themes which permitted him to dwell in Protestant fashion on the isolated individual's personal relations with God. He avoided portraying monumental scenes like the Creation, the deluge, the slaughter of the innocents, or the Last Judgment.

In his youth, Rembrandt was attracted by externally dramatic subjects like the blinding of Samson, but in later life he preferred to depict men's inward failings and sufferings. Like Shakespeare, he tried to imagine a scene from the viewpoint of every participant. Some of his most sympathetic portraits are of his Jewish neighbors in Amsterdam, and he put these men and women into his biblical pictures. He visualized the life and passion of Christ not only through the Gospel record but through the eyes of Christ's Jewish critics, which adds a fresh dimension of human tragedy to his religious art. Among his private papers are hundreds of sketches of Gospel scenes, such as his drawing of Christ's arrest by a gang sent from the chief priests, a drawing which illustrates his genius in its simplest form. A few strokes of the pen can say more than acres of painted canvas. Rembrandt has caught the full drama of the confrontation: a crowd surging angrily toward the passive Jesus, confounded by His radiance. A fuller statement of Rembrandt's religious art is the last picture he ever painted, his "Return of the Prodigal Son." This very simple picture violates all the classical rules of composition, color, perspective, and proportion. It is wholly at odds with the Renaissance concept of human dignity and self-reliance, and equally at odds with the Baroque concept of exuberant display. Rembrandt concentrates attention on the old father's compassionate forgiveness, and the tattered son's humble repentance. The solemn figures stand immobile, but inwardly deeply moved.

The Arrest of Christ. *Drawing by Rembrandt. Nationalmuseum, Stockholm.*

Return of the Prodigal Son. *Painting by Rembrandt. Hermitage, Leningrad.*

It is doubtless the aged painter's own last affirmation of faith in God's loving mercy toward weary and repentant man.

Rembrandt was the first great Protestant painter—and the last. The roll of outstanding Catholic artists during the era of the Catholic reformation is much longer. Tintoretto, El Greco, Rubens, and Bernini are only the most conspicuous figures. But the works of the Baroque age turned out to be the swan song of great Catholic as well as Protestant art. Since 1700, broadly speaking, creative artists and architects have pursued secular goals. The quality of popular Christian art, divorced from the aesthetic standards and values of the modern world, has been distressingly low during the last two and a half centuries. Catholics and Protestants alike have contented themselves with mawkishly sentimental pictures and statuary, and slavishly derivative church architecture. It is hard to think of a major painter, sculptor, or architect since 1700 who has been primarily a religious artist. It is equally hard to think of a major painter, sculptor, or architect before 1500 who was not primarily a religious artist. Nothing demonstrates more plainly the secular temper of modern society, and Europe's profound cultural transformation during the sixteenth and seventeenth centuries.

FIVE PHILOSOPHICAL WRITERS: MONTAIGNE, PASCAL, HOBBES, SPINOZA, AND LOCKE

The years from 1559 to 1715 constituted an extraordinarily fertile period in moral philosophy and political theory. The general intellectual revolt against tradition and authority during these years inspired thinking men to ask fundamental questions about human nature and social organization. Such questions were essential because the humanist moral and intellectual postulates of the early sixteenth century no longer worked. Erasmus and his fellow humanists, with their touching faith in man's rationality, had supposed that through a thorough grounding in classical literature and the teachings of the Gospel, men would acquire all necessary moral virtue and intellectual discipline. But Erasmus' effort to civilize and pacify Europe through a fusion of pagan and Christian values was smashed by the Protestant Reformation. Pico della Mirandola's complacent concept of the dignity of man was subverted by Calvin's doctrine of human depravity, and to a lesser extent by Copernicus' heliocentric theory. Even the validity of Machiavelli's coolly rational analysis of political behavior was cast in doubt by the flagrantly irrational dynastic and religious wars which shook sixteenth-century Europe. Throughout the late sixteenth and seventeenth centuries, speculative thinkers and writers invented a rich variety of new approaches to old moral and intellectual issues, but they did not reach a consensus, for they quarreled violently with each other on religious, political, and scientific grounds. Only in the eighteenth century did the *philosophes* reestablish an intellectual framework roughly comparable to the discarded humanist assumptions of the Renaissance. It is quite impossible to describe early modern Europe's chaotic compound of philosophical creativity and polemical disputation in a few pages. The best we can do is to sample the intellectual range and vitality of the period by focusing on five particularly well-known philosophical writers: Montaigne, Pascal, Hobbes, Spinoza, and Locke.

Montaigne

Michel de Montaigne (1533–1592) was a classical humanist ruefully aware that his standards and values were out of place in late sixteenth-century France. His father, a prosperous country gentleman from Perigord, gave him the sort of classical education which Erasmus had wanted for all well-born boys. Until Michel was six years old, he spoke nothing but Latin, and he always preferred Latin to French literature. "I do not take much to modern authors," he said, "because the ancient seem to me fuller and more vigorous." Montaigne spent some years as a lawyer and a royal courtier, but when the French religious wars broke out, he was ill equipped by training and temperament to participate in this ferocious struggle. In 1571, at the peak of the fighting, he withdrew from public life and shut himself up in his château. There he converted a tower storeroom into a book-lined study, and began to write his *Essays*, a series of informal musings about himself and his personal experiences. When Huguenot or Catholic troopers overran his estate, he offered no resistance, and somehow shamed them into leaving him alone. The ideological posturing of Huguenots and ultra-Catholics sickened Montaigne. Each side, he felt, was trying to obliterate the other, a cheap—but false—way of coping with the complexities of life. "Greatness of soul is not so much mounting high and pressing forward, as knowing how to put oneself in order and circumscribe oneself," he wrote. "Between ourselves, these are things that I have always seen to be in remarkable agreement: supercelestial thoughts and subterranean conduct." In his view, crusaders such as the Huguenots and ultra-Catholics were victims of self-delusion: "instead of transforming themselves into angels, they transform themselves into beasts." Montaigne was too circumspect to criticize any of the combatants in the French wars by name, but in his *Essays* he continually preached moderation and toleration. His strictures against cruelty to children, servants, and animals show how revolted he must have been by the hysterical butchery of the St. Bartholomew massacre.

Montaigne is not a systematic philosopher, but few books are richer in moral reflection than his *Essays*. "I have no other aim," he says, "but to disclose myself." He is not trying to brag, nor to confess his sins. Montaigne believes, with Socrates, that self-knowledge is the starting point for purposeful human experience, and he encourages the reader to attempt his own searching self-examination. "There is no description so hard," he assures us, "nor so profitable, as the description of oneself." Montaigne details the quirks and complexities of his personality with urbane wit and charming candor. One scarcely notices what a dronelike existence this cultivated gentleman led. He treats most topics with ironic skepticism, not only questioning the moral absolutes brandished by the Protestant and Catholic crusaders, but wondering whether "civilized" Europeans are really morally superior to the "savage" Indians of the New World. Are we not all cannibals? he asks. Montaigne is an utterly secular thinker. He can write about education, repentance, death, and immortality without reference to the Christian verities. He speaks as a weary middle-aged man who knows his own limitations, dislikes violent change of any sort, yet always accommodates himself to the necessary evils in life. In essence, he presents a chastened restatement of Erasmus' Renaissance humanism, stripped of all its buoyant optimism and Christian idealism.

Yet Montaigne was not a completely passive witness to his country's agony. He became a leading spokesman for the *politique* party, which finally brought the French religious wars to a halt. Montaigne entertained Henry of Navarre at his château and in the 1580's supported him against the Valois and Guise factions. He did not live long enough to witness Henry's expedient conversion to Catholicism or his compromise Edict of Nantes. But unquestionably Montaigne would have approved of these measures, for they exemplified his moderate and tolerant philosophy.

Pascal

To Blaise Pascal, Montaigne's brand of humanism was intellectually and spiritually inadequate. Pascal (1623–1662) is a complex and controversial figure. The blinding headaches and other debilitating illnesses which he endured throughout his short life help explain his distinctive blend of toughness and delicacy. Pascal combined razor-sharp intellectual prowess with an anguished sense of man's moral predicament. His father, a French government official, encouraged the boy's precocious aptitude for mathematics and science. While still a youth, Pascal published an essay on conic sections, conducted elaborate experiments concerning atmospheric pressure, and invented a calculating machine. He was a proud and brilliant participant in the scientific revolution. Then one night in 1654 he had an experience of religious ecstasy. "FIRE!" he wrote in white heat on emerging from this vision. "God of Abraham, God of Isaac, God of Jacob, not of the philosophers and savants. Certitude. Certitude. Feeling. Joy. Peace. God of Jesus Christ."—and so on for a pageful of exclamations inadequate to express his rapture. The short remainder of his life he dedicated to austere devotions. Both of his best-known books, the *Provincial Letters* and the *Pensées* ("Thoughts") are religious apologetics.

Pascal was drawn to Jansenism, the movement within the French Catholic church which preached a semi-Calvinist doctrine of human depravity and divine predestination of the elect. He retired periodically to the Jansenist community of Port-Royal, at the very time when the Jesuits were stigmatizing the Jansenist movement as heretical, and pressing the French government to close down Port-Royal. Pascal counterattacked with the *Provincial Letters*, an anonymous series of pamphlets which accused the Jesuits of employing immoral tactics in order to gain power. The *Provincial Letters* are sensationally effective satire, written in the mocking style of Molière. In order to expose Jesuit casuistry—that is to say, the Jesuit method of handling cases of conscience—Pascal quotes (or misquotes) from various Jesuit confessional manuals which wink at evil conduct. In one of the letters, a Jesuit proudly explains to Pascal the confessional technique of mental reservations: "After saying aloud *I swear that I have not done that*, add in a low voice, *today*; or after saying aloud *I swear*, interpose in a whisper *that I say*, and then continue aloud, *that I have done that*. This, you perceive, is telling the truth." "I grant it," replies Pascal, "though it might possibly be found to be telling the truth in a low key, and falsehood in a loud one." The Jesuits had the last laugh, however, for after Pascal's death, Port-Royal was closed and the Jansenist movement was crushed.

Pascal's chief target during his closing years was not the Jesuits, but the rationalist freethinkers in the tradition of Montaigne. Although he had learned from the *Essays* how to examine himself, Pascal was repelled by Montaigne's urbane skepticism toward new ideas and high ideals. As a practicing scientist, Pascal was keenly aware that the rational pursuit of mathematics and physics was shaping a scientific view of the world even more belligerently secular than Montaigne's. Unless the new seventeenth-century science could be wedded to revealed religion, the intellectual community would lapse into outright agnosticism. Accordingly, Pascal planned a monumental apology for the Christian religion which would convert rationalists by appealing simultaneously to their minds and their emotions. He did not live to write this book, but he did leave nearly a thousand scrappy notes, which were collected and published posthumously as his *Pensées*. The reader can appreciate Pascal's *Pensées* as finely chiseled fragments or piece them together into a unified argument. To demonstrate that the natural world is not our final home, Pascal dwells on the frailty and folly of man's earthly life. Much of his argument is compressed into one aphorism: "Man's condition: inconstancy, ennui, unrest." In another famous passage, he says, "Man is but a reed, the weakest thing in nature; but a thinking reed." He believes that this ability to think, honestly directed, will make us acutely aware of unbearable moral conflicts and spiritual hunger, which can only be assuaged by the grace of God. Pascal's argument has not perhaps converted many rationalists, but his *Pensées* are strangely unsettling. The eighteenth-century *philosophes* tried to bury Pascal, but he has had a continuous influence upon

Pascal. *Painting by an unknown artist. This portrait conveys hauntingly Pascal's keen and suffering gaze.*

subsequent moral philosophers, not least upon the existentialist thinkers of the twentieth century.

Hobbes

The English philosopher Thomas Hobbes (1588–1679) shared Pascal's pessimistic view of the human condition but not his faith in a religious solution to man's problems. Hobbes was a boldly materialistic thinker. The story that he was born prematurely when his mother was scared by the noise of the Armada guns is a little hard to credit, since his birth occurred three months before the arrival of the Spanish fleet. But it is very easy to believe that young Thomas rebelled against his environment: his father was an incompetent country parson, and his teachers at Oxford had nothing fresher to offer than medieval Aristotelian scholasticism. Hobbes gradually broadened his intellectual horizon while tutoring English aristocrats and chaperoning them on grand tours of the Continent. He became friendly with such leading scientific personages as Galileo, Bacon, Descartes, and Harvey, and he was so delighted by their experimental attitude toward physical nature that he determined to apply the new scientific method to the study of human nature as well. He sharpened his understanding of human conduct by translating Thucydides' *History of the Peloponnesian War*, the deepest and most withering analysis of political behavior by any classical writer. To Hobbes, the Puritan Revolution of the 1640's appeared to be a sickening repetition of the fratricidal agony described by Thucydides. Soon after the English revolutionary crisis began, he fled from London to Paris under the exaggerated impression that his life was in danger. In exile, he tutored the Prince of Wales, the future Charles II, with no discernible effect, and wrote the *Leviathan*, his monumental treatise on how to prevent revolutionary turmoil. Although a proponent of absolutism, Hobbes was no orthodox royal absolutist. Once Cromwell had executed Charles I in 1649, he transferred his allegiance to the Puritan absolutist state. In 1651, the *Leviathan* was published and Hobbes came home to settle down under Cromwell's dictatorship. The Restoration of 1660 renewed his apprehension, but Charles II graciously gave his old tutor a small pension. Hobbes spent his remaining years answering an avalanche of critics who found his books atheistic and depraved.

Hobbes's *Leviathan* is generally reckoned the greatest treatise on political philosophy in the English language—a special compliment, since very few readers of this remarkable book have liked its argument. Hobbes's analysis of political conduct rests on his mechanistic concept of human psychology. He sees men as animals, stimulated by appetites and aversions rather than by rational calculation or moral ideals. Hobbes's picture of mankind's desperate and continuous struggle for self-preservation anticipates by two hundred years Darwin's picture of the struggle for survival in the animal world. Hobbes says that men, stripped of all social conventions, are the most formidable and rapacious of beasts. Every man in his natural state is at war with all other men, and his life in Hobbes's pungent phrase is "solitary, poor, nasty, brutish and short." Hobbes does not deny the crucial importance of man's rational powers but argues that reason can merely regulate the passions, not conquer them. Rationality persuades men to cooperate in forming civil governments which will rescue them from their natural state of war and restrain their urge to destroy one another. Each man surrenders his right of self-government to his neighbors on condition that they all do likewise. By this mutual social contract, men form a commonwealth, which Hobbes calls "that great Leviathan (or rather, to speak more reverently, that mortal god) to which we owe . . . our peace and defense." The commonwealth vests its collective power in a sovereign, preferably one person, who becomes sole judge, legislator, and executor. The sovereign's sole purpose is to prevent war. He has absolute and unlimited power over his subjects, except that he cannot compel them to kill themselves, which would violate the primary human law of self-preservation. Subjects are obliged never to rebel, and the sovereign is obliged always to suppress rebellion. Should the sovereign fail to exercise power effectively, however, he loses his sovereignty, and his subjects shift their allegiance to a new sovereign who will protect them. In this fashion, Hobbes justified the transfer of English sovereignty from Charles I to Cromwell, and later from Cromwell to Charles II.

Ever since 1651 commentators have argued over the implications of Hobbes's political theory. Several points are generally accepted. Hobbes's effort to apply the scientific method to social analysis produced a train of thought much more corrosive than Montaigne's tolerant humanism or Pascal's appeal for divine grace. Not since Machiavelli had power politics been subjected to such an unsentimental, utilitarian analysis. Though Hobbes's approach, unlike Machiavelli's, was theoretical, both men judged politicians by their ability to stay in power, and governmental institutions by their effectiveness in protecting people against their own worst instincts. Hobbes justified absolute monarchy without recourse to the customary monarchist claims of historical legitimacy and honor; English royalists could not forgive him for repudiating the divine-right theory of monarchy. Like Machiavelli, Hobbes distinguished between the "ghostly" realm of revealed religion and the earthly realm of politics, and divorced spiritual from temporal power. Accordingly, he excoriated with equal vigor Catholic and Protestant crusaders who confused this world with the next, and he assigned to the secular sovereign total control over ecclesiastical institutions. In his concept of corporate state power, Hobbes went far beyond Machiavelli and even beyond the sixteenth-century French theorist Jean Bodin, the first to articulate a modern view of national sovereignty. Hobbes's sovereign has more coercive authority over his subjects than Louis XIV ever dreamed of. However, those who have labeled the *Leviathan* a manifesto for totalitarianism, have ignored Hobbes's basic premise that the commonwealth provides its individual members with peace and contentment. The *Leviathan* shocked both liberal constitutionalists and conservative monarchists in the seventeenth century, but it is evident now that Hobbes came closer than any other thinker of his day to envisioning the modern omnicompetent state.

Spinoza

Benedict Spinoza (1632–1677) was an even more controversial thinker than Hobbes. Unfortunately Spinoza's unorthodox opinions cannot be briefly summarized without grotesquely distorting them. His philosophical system is abstruse and intricate, and unlike Montaigne, Pascal, and Hobbes, he wrote in a style far from easy to understand or enjoy. In his Latin treatises, Spinoza sought to combine the metaphysical precision of medieval scholasticism with the mathematical precision of seventeenth-century science. His *Ethics*, for instance, is a long series of geometrical definitions, axioms, propositions, and corollaries. Spinoza lived the life of a social leper. He was born in Amsterdam, the son of a Jewish merchant. While still a boy, he rebelled against the cloistered Hebrew intellectual code of the Amsterdam Jewish community and learned Latin and several modern languages in order to master the new scientific knowledge of the seventeenth century. In 1656 his synagogue excommunicated him as a heretic. Thereafter Spinoza remained independent of any religious sect. Recurrently the Dutch Calvinist clergy branded him an atheist. He eked out a living by grinding optical lenses and turned down a professorship at the University of Heidelberg because it would infringe upon his solitude and intellectual freedom. However, he was no ivory-tower recluse. His *Tractatus Theologico-Politicus*, published in 1670, championed freedom of thought and speech in the teeth of the Dutch Calvinist clergy. He was almost lynched by a mob at The Hague, and when he prepared to publish his *Ethics* in Amsterdam, the outcry was so great that the book remained in manuscript until after Spinoza's death. Why was this solitary and difficult thinker so obnoxious to his contemporaries?

Spinoza was a deeply religious man, but his concept of God outraged orthodox Jews, Protestants, and Catholics more than the skepticism of Montaigne or the materialism of Hobbes. Spinoza was not satisfied with Descartes' and Hobbes's method of divorcing the realm of metaphysics from the realm of physical nature and exploring only the latter. On the contrary, he fused metaphysics with physics. He conceived of nature as unified and uniform, incorporating all thought and all things, embracing mind and body, and he defined philosophy as the knowledge of the mind's union with the whole of nature. To Spinoza, everything in nature is an attribute of God, nothing in nature is independent of God, and God cannot be conceived of as distinct from His creation. God determines all of man's actions, as everything else in nature. Yet Spinoza cannot be charged with fatalism. His view of human potentiality is considerably more buoyant than that of Calvin or Pascal or Hobbes. Most men are swayed by their passions, he says, but one passion can be mastered by another, and reason teaches us how to master hatred by love. Man's highest goal is the intellectual love of God, which gives us a vision of the infinite beauty of the universe and contentment beyond any vulgar notion of heavenly reward.

It is easy to see why people called the *Ethics* an atheistic book. Spinoza's God cannot be imagined anthropomorphically. In his pantheistic system there is little place for the Jewish and Christian concepts of divine revelation through the Scriptures or through miracles, and no room for belief in divine rewards and punishments, or in personal immortality. His heretical opinions were too rational for seventeenth-century sensibilities and too mystical for eighteenth-century sensibilities. Spinoza's first enthusiastic admirers were nineteenth-century romantics like Goethe and Shelley. Ever since, he has been accepted in the pantheon of great philosophers.

Locke

All four of the philosophical writers we have considered were somewhat lonely rebels. Hobbes worked out a political theory which scandalized his readers, while Montaigne, Pascal, and Spinoza agitated people by their probing moral arguments but did not win many converts. Our last philosopher, the Englishman John Locke (1632–1704), was more fortunate. His political philosophy was enshrined by the Glorious Revolution of 1688–1689; his commonsense morality comforted his late seventeenth-century audience; and his concept of human nature nicely complemented Newton's concept of physical nature. Locke was the son of a Puritan country lawyer who fought briefly in the parliamentary army during the English civil war. He was educated at Westminster School and at Oxford. In retrospect Locke shared Hobbes's opinion that English schools and universities were harmfully old-fashioned and restrictive, though his own academic experience was certainly open-ended enough. He was given a post at Oxford which required no teaching duties, joined the Royal Society, and traveled on the Continent. The turning point in Locke's career came in 1667, when the earl of Shaftesbury, the great Whig politician, invited him into his household as physician, secretary, and intellectual companion. Before he joined Shaftesbury, Locke had been a conventional Anglican royalist, suspicious of religious and political dissent. Shaftesbury thrust him into the rough and tumble of Whig party politics. Locke watched and perhaps helped the earl scheme against Charles II and his brother James during the stormy years of the Popish Plot and the attempts to exclude James from the succession. In 1683, after Shaftesbury and the Whigs had been defeated, Locke fled to Holland. This experience completed his education and molded him into a pragmatic champion of political liberalism, religious latitudinarianism, and intellectual toleration.

Locke composed all his major books during the 1680's, the heyday of strong-arm rule by Charles II and James II. The *Two Treatises on Civil*

John Locke. *Drawing by Sylvester Brownover, who was Locke's servant. National Portrait Gallery, London.*

Government, written to justify Shaftesbury's abortive rebellion against Charles II, were laid aside unpublished when the rebellion fizzled out. The *Essay Concerning Human Understanding* and the *Letter Concerning Toleration,* written during Locke's Dutch exile, were circulated in manuscript among his friends. Suddenly the Glorious Revolution transformed him from an outcast into a celebrity. In 1689 Locke hurried home to England and published his three major books. The aptness and lucidity of his common-sense philosophy were immediately recognized, and during the closing years of his life Locke enjoyed an intellectual esteem second only to Newton's.

Locke's theory of limited parliamentary government is propounded in the *Two Treatises on Civil Government.* The first of these treatises ridicules the notion that kings possess a divine right to paternal power. The second, and much more important, treatise argues that the subjects of a state are endowed with inalienable natural rights to life, liberty, and property. This theory conveniently lent sanction to the Glorious Revolution, though it was originally framed to justify Shaftesbury's activities a decade earlier. Locke was also trying to refute Hobbes's *Leviathan.* In contrast to Hobbes, Locke supposes that man is animated by reason rather than passion. When he imagines man in a state of nature, he stresses the perfect freedom and equality of precivilized life rather than the Hobbesian natural state of war. Therefore, Locke argues, man's natural liberty should be preserved as fully as possible in civil society. He wants a minimal degree of governmental regulation, in contrast to Hobbes's all-embracing sovereignty. Locke offers no empirical proof of man's natural rights, but the doctrine and its corollary of limited government proved immensely popular throughout the eighteenth century. Among man's natural rights, according to Locke, is the right to acquire private property. He recognizes that the unequal division of property undermines man's natural equality and incites crime. Hence man needs civil government to protect his life, liberty, and property. Locke insists that government should reflect the opinion of the majority, which meant, in England, a majority of the property owners represented in Parliament. Most important, he defends the people's right to resist and overthrow tyrants. His doctrines endorsed the Bill of Rights of 1689, and in a more general way commended the post-revolutionary English social pattern of representative self-government, acquisitive capitalism, and an entrenched division between the propertied and unpropertied classes. No wonder Locke's political philosophy was so popular in England. His posthumous influence in eighteenth-century France and America was even greater.

Locke's commonsense view of religion was also welcomed by many Englishmen. His *Letter Concerning Toleration* attacks the idea that Christianity can be promoted or defended by force. He sees no harm in a wide variety of religious practices, as long as the worshipers profess faith in God, obedience to God's will, and belief in an afterlife where virtue is rewarded and sin punished. Locke has a poor opinion of Protestant "enthusiasts" such as the Quakers, whose attitude of familiarity toward God seems blasphemous to him. For political reasons he is willing to deny toleration to Roman Catholics, as subversive agents of a foreign power, and to atheists, who can not be bound by oaths to fulfill civil obligations. To some critics, Locke's own latitudinarian credo verged on atheism. One Calvinist pamphleteer sneered that Locke "took Hobbes's *Leviathan* for the New Testament" and Hobbes himself "for our Saviour and the Apostles." Indeed Locke did have a Hobbesian motive for wanting to separate the church from the state, or more accurately, rescue the state from the church. His notion of religious toleration was a far cry from the Puritan religious liberty of the 1640's. John Milton had demanded the liberty to search for spiritual truth untrammeled by secular politics; John Locke wanted to liberate man's rational powers from religious restrictions. The Toleration Act of 1689 carried Locke's theory into practice.

Locke's commonsense philosophy, so lucid on the surface, is pretty muddled underneath. Much of the confusion in his thought stems from the seventeenth-century conflict between empiricism and rationalism. As we have seen, Bacon was the apostle of the inductive, empirical intellectual method, in which knowledge is obtained through observation and experimentation. Galileo and Newton, though deviating widely from Bacon's precepts, were leading exemplars of the empirical method. Descartes was the rationalist par excellence, a deductive system builder who evolved his ideas through abstract ratiocination. Hobbes and Spinoza, however much they quarreled with Descartes' ideas, were likewise rationalist thinkers, their conclusions in no sense drawn from empirical observation. John Locke was sometimes a rationalist and sometimes an empiricist. His political philosophy is strictly rationalist. His central tenet, the existence of natural rights, is a proposition incapable of empirical proof. On the other hand, Locke's *Essay Concerning Human Understanding* presents an empirical theory of the mind. In this book Locke denies that men are born with innate ideas or principles. The human mind at birth is a *tabula rasa*, or blank slate. We furnish our minds, he says, through sensate experience. Our ignorance is always infinitely larger than our knowledge; consequently we have little reason to be dogmatic in our beliefs. The *Essay*, like Locke's other books, appeals to the reader's intellect rather than to his faith or his feelings. Locke consistently eschewed the conventional Christian emphasis on original sin and moral anguish. He preferred to show, like his friend Isaac Newton, what man could accomplish by applying his reason to the study of nature. Locke was not able to discover a system of social laws as simple, uniform, and majestic as Newton's universal laws of motion. But he offered the hope of human self-improvement through education and mental discipline. The most unspectacular of great philosophers, Locke voiced his society's growing confidence in worldly progress through freedom, individualism, and hard work.

THE GOLDEN AGE OF ENGLISH, SPANISH, AND FRENCH DRAMA

We cannot close this rapid survey of early modern European culture without saying something about late sixteenth and seventeenth-century literature, the most enduring achievement of the age. In poetry the spectrum ran from such monumental epics as Tasso's *Jerusalem Delivered*, Spenser's *Faerie Queene*, and Milton's *Paradise Lost* to daringly experimental lyric verse by Donne and the other English metaphysical poets, Góngora in Spain, and Vondel in Holland. Miguel de Cervantes wrote the first great novel, *Don Quixote*. John Bunyan wrote one of the most enduring Christian allegories, *Pilgrim's Progress*. Bunyan, Bacon, Milton, Sir Thomas Browne, and many others contributed to the amazing development of English prose style. In 1559 the English language was a clumsy instrument for the conveyance of ideas or the creation of moods, but by 1715 English prose writers could generate the utmost power or shade the most delicate nuance. Correspondingly, in France, such prose stylists as Montaigne, Pascal, La Rochefoucald, and Boileau were purifying and polishing their tongue so as to exploit its elegance, precision, and wit.

Above all, this was the golden age of the theater—the age of Marlowe, Shakespeare, and Jonson in England; of Lope de Vega and Calderón in Spain; of Corneille, Molière, and Racine in France. For both the English and the Spanish stage, the peak years can be specified rather precisely—from 1580 to 1640. The heyday of the French theater came a little later, between 1630 and 1680. Seventeenth-century drama, like its twentieth-century counterpart, was as much show business as art. The circumstances of theatrical production reveal a great deal about contemporary social and economic conditions. And the plays themselves, written to please a capricious public, illustrate most of the generalizations made in this book about the religious and intellectual climate and the political structure of European society in the late sixteenth and seventeenth centuries. To the social historian, perhaps the most interesting aspect of the English, Spanish, and French theater between 1580 and 1680 is the gradually changing character of the audience. In 1580 the playwright addressed himself to the poor as well as the rich; in 1680 he wrote only for the rich. Why did the drama become more aristocratic?

England

The professional theater which suddenly emerged in the 1570's was quite unlike any previously to be found in England. In the Middle Ages, English drama had been chiefly religious. In more than a hundred towns the local guilds annually staged plays which celebrated the Christian mysteries. There were also medieval folk plays about such figures as Robin Hood and St. George. Elaborate pageants were staged in London on state occasions. By the early sixteenth century, the spread of humanist learning had led the English schools and universities to produce plays grounded on Roman comedy and tragedy. But when in 1576 the first two professional theaters operated by acting companies for paying audiences opened in London, they caught the public attention with a repertory of richly romantic plays far more exciting and entertaining than the didactic medieval religious plays or the humanist school plays.

The first two great hits of the English professional stage were Thomas Kyd's *Spanish Tragedy* and Christopher Marlowe's *Tamburlaine*, both produced in the 1580's. Kyd's *Spanish Tragedy* fascinated the Elizabethans because of its lurid story about a father, maddened with grief at his son's murder, who filled the stage with corpses in his efforts to gain revenge. The revenge theme recurred in a majority of the great Elizabethan tragedies, *Hamlet* being the most obvious example. Christopher Marlowe (1564–1593) was a much more notable literary figure than Kyd, even though his five plays are all the work of a very young man: he died at age twenty-nine. Marlowe was the first English poet to use blank verse effectively in the theater. His protagonists, notably Tamburlaine and Faustus, were larger than life, and they poured out their outrageous demands with a propulsive force which thrilled the Elizabethan audience and which is still thrilling today. Like Kyd and Marlowe, other Elizabethan dramatists packed their plays with action. Their comedies were slapstick and bawdy. Their tragedies were passionate and gory. These plays were rarely set in contemporary

England, and often set in Italy, partly because the playwrights borrowed so many plots from Italian *novelle* and partly because the Elizabethans believed that anything could happen in Italy. Since every play had to be licensed by the royal censor, most playwrights (including Shakespeare) avoided controversial issues. Historical subjects were popular. Classical history afforded a safe opportunity for moralizing, and medieval English history offered a chance for displays of patriotism, as in Shakespeare's *Henry V*. Very few Elizabethan plays touched on the question of Protestantism versus Catholicism, the most explosive issue of the day.

The Elizabethan theater was a roaring business. Between 1580 and 1640 over three hundred playwrights wrote for a hundred companies of actors. In and around London, four to six professional theaters were in operation six afternoons a week, except during plague epidemics, when the players would pack up and tour the provinces. Some of these London theaters were circular unroofed structures, like Shakespeare's Globe playhouse, holding upwards of three thousand people. Half the audience at the Globe stood in the pit for an admission charge of one or two pennies. At a time when a prostitute or an evening in the tavern cost at least sixpence, the only cheaper form of entertainment was a public hanging at Tyburn. Other London theaters, like Blackfriars, where Shakespeare's company also performed, were roofed rectangular boxes, holding no more than five hundred persons, with the price of tickets high enough to exclude the rabble. It is estimated that 10 per cent of the total population of London might be found in the theaters on any given afternoon.

The Elizabethan theatrical audience was a great audience because it was so diversified. Court nobility, lawyers, shopkeepers, apprentices, and drifters all came to demand their money's worth. They formed an audience worthy of Shakespeare, and inspired him to write plays which traverse the entire range of human experience and feeling. Not all Elizabethans joined in the applause. Puritans continually bewailed the wickedness of the London stage. The city fathers considered the theaters a public nuisance, and therefore all the London playhouses were built either outside the city walls, like the Globe across the Thames, or, like Blackfriars, on crown land, which was exempt from city jurisdiction. Elizabeth I enjoyed the theater, and she countered Puritan and civic disapproval by inviting the professional troupes to present their best plays at court. But the queen was very stingy. In the 1580's and 1590's she sponsored only six to ten court performances a year, many fewer than would occur under the Stuarts. Thus the Elizabethan theater began as unsubsidized private enterprise. To make money, Elizabethan theatrical companies had to run a grueling repertory of up to fifty plays a year, including a dozen new ones. Each new play would be acted several days consecutively; then it was entered into the repertory, and if unpopular, soon forgotten. Nearly two thousand of the plays produced between 1580 and 1640 still survive, perhaps a third of the total number.

The Swan Theater, in London. *This is the only contemporary interior view we have of an Elizabethan playhouse. The Swan, built in 1594, was an open-air arena designed for daytime performances, and probably closely resembled Shakespeare's Globe playhouse.*

William Shakespeare (1564–1616) was of course the greatest Elizabethan dramatist and also probably the most popular playwright of his day, though the audiences at the Globe and Blackfriars certainly did not appreciate how far he towered over all other English poets. Contemporaries saw Shakespeare as a complete man of the theater, author of three dozen successful plays, and actor and shareholder in the chief theatrical troupe of the period, the Lord Chamberlain's Company, later called the King's Company. Regrettably little can be discovered about Shakespeare's career. His life is better documented, however, than that of any other Elizabethan playwright except Ben Jonson. A great many people have refused to believe that a Stratford glove maker's son, with only a grammar-school education, could possibly write *Hamlet*. It makes them happier to suppose that the plays were secretly written by some aristocrat with a university education, such as Francis Bacon or the earl of Oxford. There is no way of reasoning with people who equate genius with book learning or blue blood. But it should be emphasized that the Elizabethan stage provided a suitable career for an ambitious country boy of middling birth like young Shakespeare. Players and playwrights could make a good living, even though they ranked socially just above beggars and whores.

The theatrical life could be brutal. Christopher Marlowe died in a tavern brawl, stabbed through the eye, and Ben Jonson narrowly escaped execution for killing an actor in a duel. Shakespeare was much more even tempered than Marlowe or Jonson. He worked hard in London for about twenty years, and once he had earned enough money, retired in comfort to the Warwickshire country town he loved much more. Obviously he composed his plays quickly, even if not as fast as some of the hack writers who teamed up in threes or fours to cobble together a play in a few days.

Shakespeare always carefully designed his plays for the two dozen actors in the Lord Chamberlain's Company. The protagonist in the late plays is generally older than in the early plays, because Richard Burbage, the company's leading actor, had grown older. There are never many female roles in Shakespeare's plays, since women were represented on the Elizabethan stage by boy actors, less experienced and effective than the men in the acting troupe. Shakespeare published some of his poetry, but he published none of his plays, regarding them as company property without independent literary value. Fortunately, since his plays were popular, eighteen of them printed in pirated versions during Shakespeare's lifetime. And even more fortunately, his friends (spurred on by Ben Jonson's careful edition of *his* plays in 1616) collected the plays in a folio volume in 1623, printed "according to the True Originall Copies." Actually, some of these folio texts are quite imperfect. *Macbeth*, for instance, has survived only in a shortened, doctored acting version, perhaps used for touring in the provinces.

Even before Shakespeare's retirement from the stage in 1613, London theatrical conditions were beginning to change. His younger colleague Ben Jonson (*c.* 1573–1637) was writing biting comedies set in contemporary London and bookish tragedies set in ancient Rome, which pleased the courtiers in the box seats much more than the groundlings in the pit. Francis Beaumont and John Fletcher were collaborating on a series of tragicomedies, a fancy new kind of escapist entertainment, far more frivolous than Shakespeare's tragedies and more exotic and farfetched than his most romantic comedies. Such plays did better in small enclosed theaters like Blackfriars than in big open arenas like the Globe. Playwrights were getting more daringly controversial. A sensational hit of 1624, Thomas Middleton's *A Game at Chess*, lampooned Prince Charles's expedition to Spain to woo the Infanta. This play ran at the Globe for nine consecutive days while the royal court was out of town, and grossed £1,000, with customers lined up for hours to get in, before James I heard about it and banned further performances.

As Puritan criticism of the London theater grew louder, the acting companies allied themselves with the Stuart court. James I and Charles I spent much more money on theatricals than had Elizabeth. James I employed Ben Jonson to write court masques, in which the songs, dances, scenery, and costumes greatly outweighed the libretto. Jonson dedicated his splendid anti-Puritan play *Bartholomew Fair* to James, who must have enjoyed Jonson's portrayal of the unctuous hypocrite Zeal-of-the-land Busy. In 1632 the real-live Puritan William Prynne produced a thousand-page diatribe against the stage called *Histriomastix*, written in a style very reminiscent of Zeal-of-the-land Busy. Prynne had seen only four plays, but he damned the theatrical profession wholesale, implied that Charles I's queen, Henrietta Maria, was a whore because she acted in court masques, and demanded that her royal husband close the theaters. "Do not Play-Poets and common Actors (the Devil's chiefest Factors) rake hell and earth itself," he asked, "so they may pollute the Theater with all hideous obscenities, with all the detestable matchless iniquities, which hitherto men or Devils have either actually perpetrated or fabulously divulged?" Prynne had his ears cropped for publishing this polemic, and the play-poets continued their pollution undisturbed for another decade. By the 1630's the London stage was certainly somewhat decadent. Dramatists provided their jaded audience with hectic spectacles of lust and debauchery. There is a corrosive brilliance to this Caroline drama quite different from the adolescent rampaging of Kyd and Marlowe in the 1580's and from the witty naughtiness of the Restoration stage after 1660. The Puritans quickly took their revenge. In 1642, as soon as they gained control of London, they closed the theaters, and they kept them closed for the eighteen years they remained in power.

When the London playhouses reopened after the return of Charles II in 1660, the theater was a strictly upper-class form of entertainment. Restoration drama was more sophisticated, more libertine, and more limited than Elizabethan drama had ever been. Actresses now assumed the female roles, and the plays were staged within a proscenium arch, with elaborate scenery, stage machinery, and artificial lighting. But the public theater was no longer a roaring business. An average of ten new plays a year appeared on the London stage between 1660 and 1700, as against a hundred a year between 1580 and 1640. Although the Restoration playhouses were small, the audience was not large enough to support two theaters simultaneously. Charles II was an ardent playgoer, and he honored Nell Gwyn, the most popular actress of the day, by taking her as his mistress. Great aristocrats such as the second duke of Buckingham amused themselves by writing plays. The best Restoration playwrights—Etherege, Wycherley, Congreve, Vanbrugh, and Farquhar—wrote their plays when they were very young men and quickly retired from the stage. John Dryden (1631–1700) produced a series of stately heroic dramas, but the Restoration stage is best remembered for its witty, indecent comedies of manners, which perfectly mirrored the cynical, farcical temper of the late seventeenth-century English aristocracy.

Spain

The Spanish theater enjoyed its *siglo de oro*, or golden age, during exactly those years—1580 to 1640—when the Elizabethan public stage was flourishing. As in England, medieval Spanish drama had consisted chiefly of religious plays (*autos sacramentales*), performed by the various guilds in each Spanish town to celebrate the feast of Corpus Christi. There was also a sixteenth-century humanist drama of pastoral plays performed in noble households. The first professional theaters, which opened in Madrid and Seville in the 1570's, were operated by acting companies very similar to those in England, though the plays they put on have a much different literary character from the Elizabethan drama. When the professional theaters first opened, they produced plays composed by the great novelist Cervantes, among others, modeled on Seneca and Plautus. But the Spanish public, like the English, wanted something more romantic and entertaining. Lope de Vega began writing for the Spanish stage in the 1580's, and soon established a wildly successful formula which all the other Spanish playwrights imitated.

The Spanish *comedia*, or play, was divided into three acts, interspersed with vaudeville skits, ballads, and dances, making the total effect much more of a variety show than in England, where the plays were performed straight through without any interludes or intermissions. One great advantage the Spanish theater had over the Elizabethan was that women were allowed to act in the *comedias*, as well as dance the voluptuous *zarabanda* between acts. In place of the Elizabethans' ornate blank verse, Spanish playwrights used a medley of quickstep verse forms to give their *comedias* a spontaneous and racy stamp. The *comedia* was something like a modern television script, punctuated by commercials. Its prime purpose was to show off the actors, its appeal was immediate and obvious, and like a television script, a *comedia* was seldom repeated more than a few times. Hence the Spanish theater needed an even larger supply of new plays than the Elizabethan theater. Not surprisingly, in Spain playwrights were paid relatively less than in England, and actors relatively more. There are no towering literary masterpieces among the thousands of Spanish *comedias*, though a very high percentage of those surviving have beauty and interest. The range of subject matter is immense: comedy, tragedy, history, mythology, court life, city life, peasant life, saints' lives. Romantic love is the pervasive theme, and contemporary Spain is the characteristic setting. The Spanish drama is introverted without being introspective. Even more ardently than the Elizabethan dramatists, Lope de Vega and his fellows uncritically extol their Spanish way of life.

The whole society became play-mad. Madrid was the center of theatrical activity, but being a much smaller city than London, could only support two *corrales*, or public playhouses. However, every big town had its *corral*, even Mexico City in distant America, where touring companies introduced the latest Spanish *comedias*. Bands of strolling players performed in innyards and farmyards throughout the Iberian peninsula. Some of their escapades in the remote villages read like scenes out of *Don Quixote*. When one fly-by-night troupe was playing *Lazarus*, the director, who took the part of Christ, called "Arise, Lazarus!" several times, but nothing happened. The actor playing Lazarus had managed to sneak out of his sepulcher and run away.

The director was furious because the vanished actor had stolen his costume, but the peasant audience was well satisfied, believing that Lazarus had miraculously ascended to heaven. In Madrid, the customers were much harder to please. The audience there was as variegated as in London. Philip II did nothing to encourage the popular drama, and many clergymen disapproved, but everyone else from high to low crowded into the two public theaters, which were open arenas similar in design to the Globe. If the playgoers liked the performance, they shouted "*Victor! Victor!*" If they disliked it, they whistled derisively, and the women who sat in the *cazuela* ("stewing pan") pelted the actors with fruit. Beginning playwrights were advised to write *comedias* treating saints' lives, which the audience would not hiss out of respect for the saint. Religious themes were much more conspicuous in the Spanish popular drama than in the English. The reason is obvious: the whole population was unitedly Catholic, devoted to the saints, receptive to miracles, and accustomed to seeing representations of sacred stories in the churches. The traditional *autos sacramentales*, staged at the feast of Corpus Christi, achieved their greatest magnificence and popularity in the seventeenth century. The *autos* were now written by the major dramatists, such as Lope de Vega, and produced by professional actors rather than by the amateur guilds.

Lope de Vega (1562–1635) was the Spaniards' answer to William Shakespeare. He had the same middle-class background, a better formal education, and a far more explosive temperament. He conducted a long series of passionate love affairs, generally with married women, and took up the last of these mistresses after he had become a priest. Lope de Vega was a fantastically prolific writer. In less than fifty years he turned out 1,500 *comedias*, of which nearly five hundred still survive! In his sixties he was writing two plays a week. Lope enjoyed immense celebrity and earned a fortune from his plays, but he valued them much less highly than his now-forgotten epics. "If anyone should cavil about my *comedias*," he once wrote, "and think that I wrote them for fame, undeceive him and tell him that I wrote them for money." Unlike Shakespeare, however, Lope de Vega did publish a large number of his plays. In plotting his action, he generally delayed the denouement as long as possible, for once the audience guessed it, they walked out. In a play like *The Discovery of the New World by Christopher Columbus*, Lope could not keep the audience guessing as to whether Columbus would find America, so he brought his Spaniards to the West Indies early in the second act, and concentrated thereafter on their patronizing treatment of the childlike Indians. In the third-act climax, a demon inspires the Indians to kill some of the gold-crazy Spaniards and pull down their cross. Instantly a new cross miraculously rises and the stupefied savages are converted to Christ. Other dramatists might feel impelled to explore the obvious moral issues raised by this story; Lope de Vega was content to amuse his audience with a colorful romance.

By the 1630's the Spanish stage was declining, for several reasons. No playwright after Lope de Vega had his range and universal appeal. The collapsing Spanish economy shrank box-office receipts. The clergy, like the Puritans in England, criticized the immorality of actors and actresses with mounting indignation and pressed the government to close the theaters. During the reign of Philip IV (1621–1665), such clerical agitation had small effect, for this dissolute monarch—the patron of Velázquez—was an ardent lover of plays and of actresses. Philip IV turned the Spanish drama from a popular art form into a royal hobby. He built a palace theater and spent so lavishly on court productions that the leading acting companies came to depend on his patronage. The king would disrupt public performances in the Madrid theaters by commanding certain actors and actresses to come immediately to the palace to rehearse for royal performances!

The changing character of the theater is reflected in the plays of Pedro Calderón (1600–1681), the chief Spanish dramatist after Lope de Vega. Whereas Lope wrote for the people, Calderón wrote for the court. In his youth, up to 1640, Calderón wrote comedies about lovesick grandees in pursuit of their mistresses and tragedies about jealous grandees in pursuit of their wives' lovers. His plays are more subtle and complex than Lope's, but less variegated. Everything hinges on the aristocratic code of honor, which the proud Spaniards cultivated as a substitute for their lost political power and prestige. Calderón clearly approves of the way his gentlemen fight duels at the twitch of an eyebrow and murder their adoring wives on the rumor of infidelity. During the crisis of the 1640's, with Catalonia and Portugal both in revolt, all theatrical activity ceased temporarily. Calderón himself took holy orders, and for the last thirty years of his life wrote only *autos sacramentales* and operatic court masques. He left no successors. By the close of the century, the professional theater in Spain was dying; it was in worse plight than in England, where the court circle kept the London stage alive.

France

In France, the great theatrical age began about 1630, just as it was drawing to a close in England and Spain. The first French professional acting companies had begun operating in the late sixteenth century, but they put on crude shows for uncultivated audiences and did better in the provinces than in Paris. In these early years, no Frenchman remotely comparable to Marlowe, Shakespeare, or Lope de Vega wrote for the stage. The political turmoil during the sixteenth-century wars of religion and again during Marie de Medici's regency certainly delayed the development of the French public theater. Finally, Richelieu's administration gave France the self-confident stability which England and Spain had achieved fifty years earlier. In 1629 two auspicious events occurred: an accomplished troupe of actors established fixed residence in a Paris theater, and an immensely talented dramatist, Pierre Corneille, produced his first play. When the French theater began to flourish in the 1630's under Richelieu's patronage, it provided entertainment

The Imaginary Invalid. *A performance of Molière's play before Louis XIV at Versailles in 1674. Musée de Versailles.*

for the elite, like the English theater of the same period, patronized by Charles I, and the Spanish theater patronized by Philip IV. The French drama remained closely tied to the royal court throughout its period of greatness, 1630–1680. Corneille, Racine, and Molière never wrote for the kind of huge and diversified audience which had thronged to the Elizabethan and Spanish playhouses at the turn of the century. Their audience was sophisticated but limited. In seventeenth-century Paris there were never more than three theaters, playing three evenings a week. Playwrights and actors could not make ends meet without royal patronage. Richelieu opened the finest theater in Paris, pensioned dramatists, and subsidized actors. Mazarin was less generous, but Louis XIV in his youth was extremely fond of the theater, and his support kept afloat five acting companies: three French, one Italian, and one Spanish. Molière's company, for example, was not only subsidized by Louis XIV, but given the use of a royal theater. In addition, Molière held a court appointment as the king's bedmaker. Many of his plays were commissioned by the king for production at Versailles. Louis also pensioned Racine, without quite appreciating what he was paying for. The royal pension list for 1664 includes the following entries:[3]

[3]W. H. Lewis, *The Splendid Century: Life in the France of Louis XIV* (New York, 1953), pp. 23–24.

| To the Sieur Racine, a French poet | 40 louis d'or |
| To the Sieur Chapelain, the greatest French poet who ever lived | 150 louis d'or |

In the drama, as in art and literature, the Bourbon monarchy wished to cultivate a pure and dignified classical style. Court patronage helped to steer seventeenth-century French playwrights away from the exuberant romanticism of the Elizabethan and Spanish stage. In the time of Richelieu, French critics adopted the Aristotelian rules for dramatic composition. Seventeenth-century French playwrights generally observed the three unities of time, place, and action, and avoided Shakespeare's rambling plots and his mixture of high tragedy and low comedy. The spectator is spared the sight of murders, duels, and similar violent acts which are instead decorously reported by messengers. This classical influence is particularly evident in seventeenth-century French tragic drama, whose themes and plots are largely derived from Greek and Roman sources. French tragedies tend to be more literary and less stageworthy than the romantic tragedies of Elizabethan England and Habsburg Spain. But the French neoclassical tragedians were not blind copyists. They always reworked ancient history and myth to suit seventeenth-century taste, expanding the love interest and expunging the pagan religious element. Racine's Greek heroines and Corneille's Roman heroes are always recognizably ladies and gentlemen of the Bourbon court.

Pierre Corneille (1606–1684), the first great French dramatist, wrote a number of effective comedies but is best remembered as a neoclassical tragedian. In 1636 his *Cid* caused a sensation. Corneille's mastery of dramatic verse, his fiery lyricism, his characterization and plot structure, thrilled and shocked his audience as Marlowe's *Tamburlaine* had hit the Elizabethans, only more so, for *Le Cid* is a much finer play. It tells a tale of star-crossed lovers, kept from each other by a feud between their families. When the boy kills the girl's father, her love conquers her sense of filial honor, and she agrees to marry him. This ending scandalized the moralists, and the resulting furor had a somewhat unhappy effect on Corneille. In his subsequent plays he tried to please the critics with safer themes, extolling family honor, patriotism, monarchy, and Christianity. His favorite setting was imperial Rome, which gave him abundant opportunity to moralize on the virtues of benevolent despotism. Corneille never recaptured the verve, passion, and warmth of *Le Cid*. By the 1660's he had woefully lost his touch, and in a pitiful effort to outdo his young rival, Racine, he produced in his late years a series of grotesquely contrived melodramas.

Jean Baptiste Racine (1639–1699) was a poet of surer taste and control than Corneille, and he perfected the French neoclassical tragic style. At the age of four Racine was sent to school at the Jansenist stronghold of Port-Royal, and he emerged with an austere piety akin to Pascal's, and a deep love of the classics. He quickly established his reputation at court with a play about Alexander the Great, tactfully dedicated to Louis XIV. His next play,

Andromaque (1667), was a great success. It told the story of Hector's widow after the fall of Troy, forced to choose between marrying her Greek captor and seeing him kill her child; in other words, here once again was Corneille's theme of love versus honor—in a presentation graced by an exquisitely euphonious and precise verse style. In later plays, Racine reworked the tragic themes of his favorite Greek poets. *Phèdre*, perhaps his best play, follows Euripides' *Hippolytus* so closely that some scenes read like translations from the Greek. Suddenly, at age thirty-seven, Racine retired from the secular stage. His last two plays are biblical dramas designed for private performance by schoolgirls, in reversion to the early sixteenth-century amateur theatrical tradition.

The great comic master of the seventeenth-century French stage was of course Molière (1622–1673), whose real name was Jean Baptiste Poquelin. His father, a prosperous Paris furniture maker, sent the boy to a Jesuit school for the sort of classical education which Descartes, Calderón, Corneille, and thousands of other Jesuit pupils had received. Young Poquelin was determined to be an actor, and he endured a strenuous apprenticeship to prove himself. In 1643, taking the stage name of Molière, he helped to organize a Paris troupe, which rapidly went bankrupt. Molière and his companions toured the provinces for twelve years before they felt ready to attempt another assault on the capital. While touring, Molière wrote his first plays. In 1658 his troupe reappeared in Paris, performed successfully before the young king, and received the use of a theater in the Louvre palace. During the remaining fifteen years of his life, Molière wrote and produced a brilliant constellation of farces, parodies, and satires for his company. He generally took the lead role of valet or comic marquis himself, for Molière was a wonderfully accomplished comic actor. He made the Paris bourgeoisie and the Versailles aristocracy laugh at themselves. He mocked bourgeois greed in *The Miser*, and social climbing in *The Bourgeois Gentleman*. He mocked the rottenness of court society in *The Misanthrope*, and the hypocrisy of canting clerical bigots in *Tartuffe*. He mocked medical quackery in *The Imaginary Invalid*, and overly educated women in *The Female Savants*. Unlike Corneille and Racine, Molière was a total man of the theater. His plays read well, but they act better, and they remain more vibrantly alive than any other seventeenth-century plays except Shakespeare's. Molière's humor is realistic and hard-hitting, like Ben Jonson's but more universal and humane. His style is witty and urbane, like that of English Restoration comedy, but less smutty and trivial. Naturally he stepped on many toes. The clergy were so incensed by *Tartuffe* that the play was banned for five years, and only the king's patronage shielded Molière from heavier punishment. No doubt Molière was lucky that he wrote *Tartuffe* before Louis XIV had become pious and persecuting. No doubt he would have been silenced fast enough had he ventured to mock Bourbon absolutism or to ask his royal patron to laugh at himself. Nevertheless, it remains ironic that the best social satire of the century was sponsored by the most complacent and authoritarian monarch in Europe.

With Molière's death, Racine's retirement, and Louis XIV's growing preoccupation with international war, the great age of the French theater drew to a close. To compare the art of Molière and Racine with that of Lope de Vega and Shakespeare is to see once again the bewildering diversity of European culture in the early modern period. Artists and intellectuals lived in closer proximity than ever before, yet the international cultural community established during the Middle Ages and the Renaissance had been shattered. Scientists, to be sure, cooperated with unprecedented fruitfulness, sharing discoveries and building on one another's experiments and theories. Painters, sculptors, and architects congregated in Italy and in a few of the large northern cities for their training and roved over Europe in search of commissions. This helps explain the spread of the Baroque style from Italy to Spain, Belgium, and Austria. But the Baroque was not all-conquering. In philosophy, as in theology, there was no consensus, scarcely even a dialogue. The art and thought of the seventeenth century has a deeply fragmented quality which reflects the loss of traditional religious unity and the rise of autonomous sovereign states. Catholics and Protestants evolved distinctly different responses to art. Literature, always the most chauvinistic art form, acquired a self-consciously national style in each vernacular language. At the close of the century, sophisticated persons everywhere wanted to copy French taste, but this attitude was symptomatic of the coming era, the Enlightenment. The seventeenth century was intellectually disorderly, contentious, intolerant. Audiences were easily unsettled by shocking ideas. Iconoclasts like Galileo and Spinoza were muzzled. Even poets like Milton and Molière risked persecution for their polemical art. Yet no censor or inquisitor could suppress the general intellectual revolt against authority, the richest legacy of the age.

CHAPTER 6

Toward a New Balance of Power

THE YEARS 1688–1715 saw massive power realignments throughout Europe. In a generation of warfare and diplomacy, the map was redrawn, the most divisive issues of the seventeenth century were resolved, and the stage was set for a new era, the eighteenth-century age of Enlightenment. During these eventful years, Louis XIV—who threatened in the 1680's to overrun all of his neighbors—was contained. The English, who had withdrawn from continental politics for much of the seventeenth century, established their position as leaders in European affairs. The Spanish empire, which had nearly dissolved by the close of the seventeenth century, received fresh leadership. The Austrian Habsburgs built a new and very extensive Danubian monarchy. The Russians, led by Peter the Great, entered actively for the first time into European politics. Above all, the chief European states worked out among themselves a new balance of power that stabilized international relations.

These changes were brought about through a series of interlocking wars, fought on a very extensive, expensive, and bloody scale. These wars marked the culmination of powerful trends that had been gathering force for a long time. In western Europe, the Nine Years' War of 1688–1697 and the War of the Spanish Succession of 1702–1713 constituted in effect a twenty-five-year combat between Louis XIV of France and a "Grand Alliance" of his adversaries headed by England, the Dutch republic, and Austria. Louis' long-standing ambition to dominate Europe was frustrated by his aroused neighbors. In eastern Europe, the Ottoman Turks battled from 1683 to 1699 against another alliance, one that included Austria, the papacy, Venice, Poland, and Russia, and then staged further wars against Russia, Venice, and Austria between 1711 and 1718. These Turkish wars resolved the long Ottoman-Habsburg struggle, dating back to the 1520's, for control of the middle Danube. And in the Baltic region, Sweden fought against Russia, Poland, and Denmark in the Great Northern War of 1700–1721. This war closed Sweden's brief season as a great power and signaled the emergence of Russia as a major European state.

These wars of 1683–1721 differed strikingly from the military operations examined earlier—the French civil wars of 1562–1598, the Dutch and English wars of 1566–1609 against Spain, the Thirty Years' War of 1618–

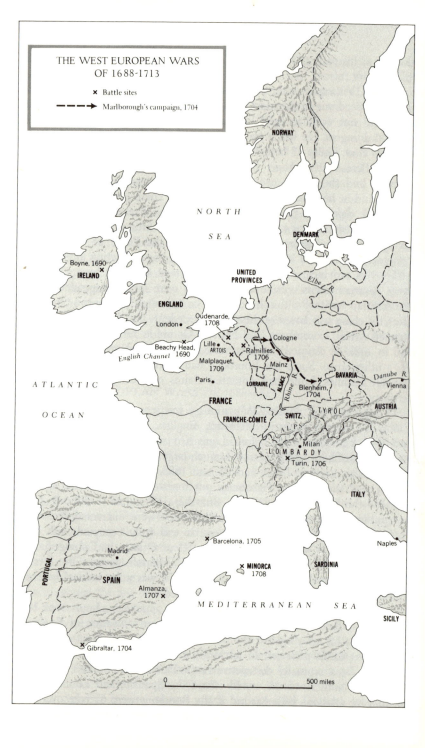

THE WEST EUROPEAN WARS
OF 1688-1713

× Battle sites
■ ■ ■ ➤ Marlborough's campaign, 1704

NORWAY

NORTH
SEA

DENMARK

Elbe R.

UNITED
PROVINCES

Boyne, 1690 ×
IRELAND

ENGLAND

London •

Oudenarde,
1708

Cologne

Beachy Head,
1690

Lille •
ARTOIS ×
Malplaquet,
1709

Ramillies,
1706

Mainz •

English Channel

ALSACE

Rhine R.

BAVARIA

Danube R.

ATLANTIC

Paris •

LORRAINE

Blenheim,
1704

Vienna •

OCEAN

FRANCE

SWITZ.

TYROL

AUSTRIA

FRANCHE-COMTÉ

ALPS

Milan •

LOMBARDY

Turin, 1706

ITALY

Barcelona, 1705 ×

Madrid •

× MINORCA
1708

SARDINIA

Naples •

PORTUGAL

SPAIN

Almanza,
1707 ×

MEDITERRANEAN   SEA

SICILY

× Gibraltar, 1704

0   500 miles

expansion into the Rhineland, and he decided to move quickly, before Leopold and his German allies—who had just captured Belgrade from the Turks—could regroup their armies on their western front. So in September, 1688, Louis occupied Cologne and the Palatinate. But the French king miscalculated. The German princes mustered enough military strength so that he felt forced to withdraw across the Rhine. William ascended James II's throne without bloodshed and brought England into the coalition. By 1690 Spain also was persuaded to join the Grand Alliance. Thus Louis' quick campaign turned into a major war.

The Nine Years' War

The war between Louis XIV and the Grand Alliance, fought from 1688 to 1697, was an exhausting defensive struggle, staged mainly in the Netherlands, an arena for siege warfare. The French were very good at this style of fighting. Marshal Vauban was renowned for the art with which he had conducted fifty-three sieges, and everyone sought to copy his techniques for attacking and defending fortified bastions. Many of the troops on both sides were foreign mercenaries; in peak years as many as thirty thousand Swiss were hired by either the French or the allies. Altogether, nearly 250,000 troops were put into the Netherlands theater for the 1693 campaign—and these big armies were not very mobile. The fighting grounds were filled with fortresses, strongpoints, and siege lines. Soldiers were segregated as much as possible from civilians, and kept close to their magazines to prevent looting and desertion. Battle drill was so formal that commanders took hours to deploy their men for action, thus removing any element of surprise. Since soldiers were expensive and battlefield casualties ran very high, commanders were reluctant to engage in pitched battles. The infantry were beginning to use flintlock muskets, quicker and easier to fire than the old matchlocks, and for close combat they had the newly designed ring bayonet. Infantry who were disciplined to stand their ground proved to be far more lethal than the cavalry and pikemen who had dominated the wars of the mid-century. At Fleurus, in 1690, 20 per cent of the seventy thousand combatants were killed or wounded in a few hours of fighting.

If Louis XIV had been willing to concentrate all of his troops in one theater—to risk an all-out assault on England, the Netherlands, or the Rhineland—he might have forced an early settlement in 1689 or 1690. William was tied up in Ireland, where James II had launched a counterattack, the Spanish were too weak to defend their Netherlands barrier forts, and Leopold's forces in Germany were poorly coordinated. In 1690 the French navy defeated an Anglo-Dutch fleet at Beachy Head, on the English Channel, opening the possibility of an invasion of England. But Louis was not the man to gamble everything in one throw. By 1692 the

Capture of Cambrai by Louis XIV. This old print shows the style of siege warfare favored by Louis. The French took this Spanish Netherlands town in 1677 by breaching the city walls (left center) with their siege guns. The king himself (lower center) is reciving an obsequious emissary from Cambrai.

English and Dutch were in clear command of the sea, and he had lost his chance. Meanwhile, William defeated James at the Battle of the Boyne in 1690 and chased him out of Ireland. For the rest of the war William campaigned in Flanders. Leopold stayed in Vienna, and Louis paid only occasional visits to the combat zone, but William was an active warrior-king in the tradition of Henry IV and Gustavus Adolphus. Though he won very few battles against the French, he did hold the allied coalition together.

By 1694 Louis was feeling the strain. He now had 400,000 soldiers in pay, absorbing about 74 per cent of France's public revenues. Even in the peacetime era of Colbert, Louis' fiscal system had been inelastic. To meet the new war costs, the French resorted to old and dubious tactics: they levied enlarged direct taxes on the peasantry, they negotiated high-interest loans, and they sold newly created bureaucratic offices. Then in 1693–1694, after two disastrous harvests, came the worst French subsistence crisis of the century. At least one tenth of the French population died during this famine year. Louis was forced to cut back his military operations, and French diplomats explored the possibilities of peace. But the allies, each hopeful of gaining something, kept on fighting until every participant finally recognized that the war was a hopeless stalemate. The Peace of Ryswick in 1697 basically restored the situation of 1679, when Louis, William, and Leopold had negotiated their last settlement. Louis dropped his claims to Cologne and the Palatinate, surrendered Luxemburg and Lorraine and some of the Alsatian territory he had annexed in 1679–1681, and recognized William as king of England. Ryswick canceled most of Louis' territorial gains of the last two decades. But it did not cancel his belief in his property rights as king of France and head of the house of Bourbon.

The Ryswick settlement was only an armistice because it did not resolve the chief diplomatic question of the day: who would succeed the childless Charles II as king of Spain? Charles, who had reigned since 1665, was the pathetic end product of six generations of Habsburg inbreeding (since his parents were uncle and niece, Charles's mother was also his first cousin).

Charles II. *The last—and least— of the Habsburg kings of Spain. Kunsthistorisches Museum, Vienna.*

A backward child, he was neither weaned nor able to walk when he ascended the Spanish throne at the age of four. As he grew up, Charles bore the Habsburg genetic trademark, a lower jaw so protrudent that his teeth did not meet and he could not masticate his food. More important, he was mentally retarded and sexually infertile. When Charles's first wife, a French princess, and his second, a German princess, both failed to conceive, the poor king supposed that he must be bewitched, and his priests exorcised him to drive the devils out. Meanwhile, two of his cousins—Louis XIV (who had married Charles's elder sister) and Leopold I (who had married Charles's second sister)—were maneuvering to secure the Spanish inheritance. The Spaniards naturally were determined to keep their empire intact, while the Dutch and English hated to see either Louis or Leopold gain so much. In particular, they would not tolerate a French take-over of the Spanish Netherlands or of trade with Spain's overseas colonies. Louis, for his part, had damaged his chances by attacking Spain in the Nine Years' War, so he made generous amends at Ryswick by restoring all the Spanish territory that he had taken since 1679. In 1698, he even joined William III in a diplomatic compromise: the two monarchs agreed to a treaty by which Spain and most of its possessions would go to a neutral candidate—the six-year-old Joseph Ferdinand of Bavaria, who was Charles II's grandnephew—with Bourbon and Austrian Habsburg princes dividing the rest. This compromise was angrily received in Madrid and Vienna, but it might well have worked, except that Joseph Ferdinand died in 1699.

By now the likelihood of another general war, triggered by the Bourbon-Habsburg dynastic rivalry, was very great. Louis XIV played his cards more boldly than Leopold I. The French king did not want another big war, nor did he expect to obtain the entire Spanish inheritance, but he was ready to fight if necessary for his Bourbon rights, and he intended to start any fighting on his own terms. Knowing that England and the United Provinces had little enthusiasm for another war in which they had no territorial stake, Louis worked out a second partition treaty with William III. This time the two arbiters allotted most of the Spanish inheritance to Archduke Charles of Austria (the son of Leopold I), and Milan, Naples, and Sicily to the *Grand Dauphin* Louis (the French king's son and heir). This arrangement, while seemingly favorable to Austria, would have put France in control of Italy, thus blocking effective collaboration between the Habsburgs in Austria and in Spain. Leopold and Charles II both indignantly refused these terms, Leopold because for Austria the most important part of the inheritance was Italy, and Charles because he rejected the whole idea of partition. But Louis' agents were busy in Madrid, and they pointed out to Charles's ministers that Spain would need a strong and active protector in order to prevent partition.

Therefore, as the Spanish king sank into his final illness in 1700, he was persuaded to sign a will which stipulated that the Spanish empire had to be kept whole, and which named Louis' grandson Philip of Anjou his sole heir. If Philip declined the Spanish throne, the whole inheritance would pass to Archduke Charles of Austria.

Now Louis faced the most crucial decision of his reign: should he accept his own partition treaty or Charles's will? The will was obviously preferable from the Bourbon perspective, but it precluded any territorial acquisition by France, whereas the treaty gave France direct control of Italy. If Louis violated his treaty, he risked war with England and the United Provinces. If he rejected the will, he alienated Spain. Since Leopold would accept neither treaty nor will, Louis would probably have to fight in any case. Not surprisingly, he quickly accepted the will and endorsed his grandson as Philip V of Spain. Even at this juncture, had Louis exercised exquisite restraint, he might have kept Philip in Spain without war by working out a deal with Leopold and William. But Louis' success put him in a bravura mood. In 1701 he deliberately provoked the Dutch by moving French troops into the Spanish Netherlands; he deliberately provoked the English by recognizing James II's son as king of England; and he deliberately provoked both states by sending French traders into the Spanish colonial empire. Obviously Louis, not Philip, was the effective new ruler of Spain. The Dutch, English, Austrians, and Prussians quickly formed another Grand Alliance against the *Grand Monarque*, and war resumed in 1702.

The War of the Spanish Succession

The second war between Louis XIV and the Grand Alliance, fought between 1702 and 1713, started out as a replay of the Nine Years' War but developed into a much more dramatic and decisive conflict. What tipped the balance was England's enlarged and vigorous participation in the fighting.

In 1702 the English appeared to be totally unready for combat. King William III had had a terrible time rallying English support for the Nine Years' War, and he died just as the new war began. Since William's consort, Mary, had died before him, in 1694, the English crown passed to Mary's sister Anne, the Protestant younger daughter of James II. Queen Anne (ruled 1702–1714) was a much weaker executive than William, and the political situation throughout her reign was extremely stormy and volatile.

The exact character of English politics in the reign of Queen Anne is much disputed, but most historians would agree on two points: English politicians were the only public figures in Europe who addressed themselves to an extensive electorate (some 250,000 persons voted for members of Parliament), and these politicians were far closer to operating under a two-party system than were public leaders elsewhere in Europe. The Tories and the Whigs, ideologically divergent since the 1670's (see p. 192), published propaganda in order to sway public opinion, campaigned in their constituencies in order to win parliamentary elections, and maneuvered at court in order to win the queen's support. These parties were far from tightly organized. Many politicians stayed "above party" or acted for purely personal reasons. But the political scene was far livelier in England than elsewhere because officeholders and office seekers tended to divide openly on basic issues.[1] The Tories had never altogether reconciled themselves to the Glorious Revolution, and they were sharply critical of the enormous expenditures required for the war against Louis XIV. If there must be a French war, they felt, it should be fought at sea and not on land. Because of the partisan pattern of English politics, the Whigs in consequence became violently anti-French and pro-war.

Queen Anne, though temperamentally a Tory, was forced to support the war when Louis recognized her Catholic half brother, the Stuart Pretender, as rightful king of England. Also, she was personally loyal to the chief English general, John Churchill, duke of Marlborough (1650–1722), who wanted to fight the French on land. From 1702 to 1710 Anne's chief ministers were either political neutrals or Whigs, and they endorsed the war wholeheartedly. The Dutch accepted Marlborough as their commander in chief. Marlborough (an ancestor of Winston Churchill) turned out to be the most talented English soldier since Oliver Cromwell. He was a very different sort of soldier from that Puritan warrior, being totally worldly, with an immense appetite for wealth, title, and fame. In order to achieve these goals he spent long years in assiduous personal service to James II, William III, and Anne. In appearance, Marlborough was the perfect gentleman: superbly handsome, magnificently dressed, polished, affable, and correct. He was also the perfect diplomat, receiving the opinions of others while masking his own. He had deserted James II at the last minute in 1688, and was arrested in the 1690's on suspicion of treasonable dealings with the exiled king. But William wanted him to take over the command of the Anglo-Dutch army because Marlborough knew how to win battles. And indeed he did defeat the French in three great battles —at Blenheim, Ramillies, and Oudenarde—fought between 1704 and 1708.

For two campaigns, in 1702–1703, Marlborough searched in vain for a way to overcome the siege mentality of his allies, the Dutch, and his ad-

---

[1]Geoffrey Holmes, *British Politics in the Age of Anne* (New York, 1967), argues that there was essentially a two-party system. Robert Walcott, *English Politics in the Early Eighteenth Century* (Cambridge, Mass., 1956), argues that there was a multi-party system, in which ideology was unimportant.

The Duke of Marborough. *This portrait by John Closterman was painted around 1688, when Marlborough was switching allegiance from James II to William III. National Portrait Gallery, London.*

versaries, the French, so that he could stage a great open field battle. He could pin the French behind their garrison line in the Spanish Netherlands, but every time he maneuvered the opposing armies into combat position, his Dutch colleagues—terrified of losing their troops—refused to attack. Stymied in the Netherlands, Marlborough decided in 1704 to take his army into an altogether different theater—the upper Danube, in southern Germany.

The Danube had become the crucial theater because the French were trying to force Austria out of the war by striking boldly at Vienna. Louis XIV had few allies, but one of them was Max Emmanuel, elector of Bavaria (1662–1726), the most important prince in southern Germany, whose state adjoined Leopold I's Austrian territories. In 1703 Louis sent an army across the Rhine and through the Black Forest to join Max Emmanuel. This Franco-Bavarian force advanced into the Tyrol and Austria, creating panic in Vienna, where the aging emperor, distracted by a major rebellion in Hungary, was unable to mount a counterattack. To meet this emergency, Marlborough staged a daring maneuver that startled his contemporaries. Keeping his destination secret from the Dutch and from his own senior officers, the duke led a column of forty thousand men on a 250-mile trek from the Netherlands up the Rhine and over to the Danube. Two French armies watched in puzzlement as he outflanked them; the French assumed that he would keep close to his magazines and attack either Lorraine or Alsace. Marlborough's red-coated column tramped along rain-soaked, mud-bogged roads, covering about ten miles on an average day's march, able to move even this fast only because the heavy baggage was being shipped by Rhine barges. Logistics for the six-week march were planned so thoroughly that the soldiers found rations ready for them at each campsite, a bridge of boats prepared for them at each river crossing, and forty thousand pairs of new boots waiting for them at Mainz, halfway to Bavaria. In June, 1704, at the Bavarian border, Marlborough rendezvoused with Prince Eugene of Savoy, the brilliant Austrian general. Eugene brought eighteen thousand men, but the French also sent reinforcements into Bavaria, so the allied commanders faced an army larger than their own as they made their plans to force the pitched battle for which they were both eager.

On the evening of August 12, 1704, Marlborough and Eugene climbed the church tower in a Danube village and observed through their telescopes a great open field near the village of Blenheim, five miles distant, where some sixty thousand white-coated French troops were setting up their tents. They saw that attack would be difficult. Their army of English, Dutch, Danes, Prussians, Hessians, Hanoverians, and Austrians numbered fifty-two thousand; they were badly outmatched in artillery; to reach the Franco-Bavarian position they would have to cross a marsh and a brook and climb a high bank beyond; and they could not hope to turn the enemy flank, since one edge of the French encampment was bordered by the Danube, and the other by thickly forested hills. Nonetheless, shortly after midnight the allied forces broke camp and advanced toward Blenheim. At dawn, the French marshal Tallard (1652–1728) was startled to see them so close, but he confidently deployed his men for battle on such advantageous terms.

At noon, after hours of ceremonial cannonading, martial music, and religious services, the slaughter began. For all his loving care of his troops on the march, Marlborough was ready and willing to sacrifice a quarter of them in battle. He sent waves of infantry and cavalry on repeated charges, ordering them to hold their fire until they reached the enemy lines. His men crossed the brook and attacked the stockaded village, pinning much of the French infantry inside its streets and farmyards. Consequently, the allies had superior firepower in the open field, and there Marlborough's well-drilled infantry broke the French cavalry. Marshal Tallard was captured, with nine thousand of his men; at least twenty thousand more were killed or wounded, or deserted. The allied loss at Blenheim was also horrifying—twelve thousand dead and wounded—but the victory was momentous. For the first time in living memory a crack French army had been destroyed in combat; Louis XIV had lost his Bavarian ally, and had lost the chance to take Austria out of the war.

Blenheim was only the most dramatic in a string of allied victories.

Marlborough returned to the Netherlands theater and destroyed another crack French army at Ramillies in 1706. This defeat so demoralized the French that they abandoned most of the Spanish Netherlands to the allies. When Marshal Vendôme (1654–1712) tried to reconquer Flanders in 1708, he was caught by Marlborough and Eugene at Oudenarde and badly beaten. The allies, crossing the French border, captured the great fortress of Lille, and stood poised for an advance on Paris. Meanwhile, on the Italian front the anti-French coalition was equally successful. Louis XIV's sole Italian ally, Victor Amadeus II, duke of Savoy (1666–1732), deserted to the Grand Alliance in 1703. Prince Eugene campaigned for Austria in Lombardy, and outfought a series of French generals. In 1706 he won a smashing victory at Turin; he drove the French across the Alps, and in 1707 set up the Austrian occupation of Naples. In the Spanish theater too the allies appeared to be on the road to success. Portugal joined the Grand Alliance in 1703. The English captured Gibraltar and the island of Minorca, and thus established for the first time an English naval presence in the Mediterranean. In 1705 an Anglo-Dutch force captured Barcelona, and Archduke Charles of Austria set up court as King Charles III of Spain. This proved to be the limit of allied success in Spain. Most Spaniards saw the Bourbon Philip V as their national choice, and Charles III as a foreign usurper. Philip's cause was bolstered when his troops defeated Charles's army at Almanza in 1707.

Though Philip V was surviving in Spain, his grandfather had lost Italy and the Netherlands, and by 1709 was desperate for peace. Not only was Louis XIV's war going badly but—as in 1693–1694—disaster struck on the home front. A bad harvest in 1708 was followed by the coldest January on record, guaranteeing another poor harvest and general famine in 1709. The price of bread quadrupled. Troops were called in to escort grain convoys, to control starving mobs, and to suppress tax revolts. Louis XIV had to swallow his great pride and sue for peace. He was ready to surrender almost all the territories he had conquered since 1661, to accept the Austrian Charles as king of Spain, and to withdraw his military support from Philip V. Unfortunately, because Louis had broken his word in 1700, the allies did not believe his pledge concerning Spain. They wanted even more from him, especially when Marlborough told them that France would collapse completely after another campaign or two. Also, since each of the allied partners had different war goals, they could agree only on the highest possible demands. Accordingly, in May, 1709, they told Louis that if he wanted peace he must expel his grandson from Spain within two months. This the French king refused to do.

So the war continued. Louis XIV called upon his people to defend their country against invasion, and a new army of 80,000 raw recruits under Marshal Villars (1653–1734) faced Marlborough and Eugene with

The Battle of Blenheim. *In this stylized panorama by van Huchtenburgh, Marlborough and Eugene (left center foreground) are savoring their victory, and the French Marshal Tallard (left foreground) is held captive in Marl-*

110,000 men at Malplaquet in September, 1709. It was the biggest and bloodiest of Marlborough's four great battles. The allies forced Villars to retire from the field, but were too exhausted to pursue him. Villars won the moral victory, for there were twenty-four thousand allied as against twelve thousand French casualties. Marlborough's attack was stalled, and the allies began to realize too late that they should have accepted Louis'

borough's coach, while units of the allied army march in drilled precision across the broad plain below. The winding Danube and the village of Blenheim are to the left. The Franco-Bavarian camp is burning in the distance.

peace terms. The campaigns of 1710–1711 brought the allies no closer to victory in either France or Spain.

Then in 1711 the Grand Alliance broke apart. In Austria, Emperor Joseph I (ruled 1705–1711), son of Leopold I, suddenly died, and was succeeded by his brother, the former Archduke Charles and would-be King Charles III of Spain. The accession of Charles VI (ruled 1711–1740) posed a new dynastic threat, for besides being Holy Roman emperor, and ruler of the vast Austrian Habsburg domain in central and eastern Europe, he also held all of the Spanish territory in Italy and the Netherlands which had been seized by allied armies during the war. Immediately, the Dutch and English lost all interest in helping Charles to conquer Spain; his success there would mean revival of the continent-wide monarchy of Charles V.

Nor was this the only blow to the Grand Alliance. In England, Queen Anne had grown sick of the Whigs, who kept the war going interminably. In 1710 she replaced her Whig ministers with Tories, and in parliamentary elections the Tories won a sweeping popular mandate. In 1711 the queen dismissed Marlborough from his military command. The duke was censured by Parliament for alleged corruption, and retired abroad, where he remained until Anne died. Meanwhile, the Tory diplomat Henry St. John, viscount Bolingbroke (1678–1751) opened secret negotiations with France, shamelessly flouting England's treaty obligations to its allies. The Dutch could not carry on alone, and even the stubborn Austrians soon had to drop their unrealistic war goals and accept a peace settlement.

Since the Grand Alliance was hopelessly split, negotiation of a single peace treaty was not feasible. Instead, the combatants concluded a complex series of settlements, the most important being the Peace of Utrecht (1713) between France, England, the United Provinces, Prussia, and Savoy, and the Peace of Rastatt (1714) between France, the Holy Roman Empire, and Austria. Ironically, the settlements of Utrecht and Rastatt were close in spirit to the partition treaties of 1698–1699 that Louis XIV and William III had negotiated in their effort to avoid a major war. All of the participants in the fighting gained something, but most of them also had to make major concessions. Philip V was accepted as king of Spain, but renounced his Bourbon tie to the French throne; his Spanish empire lost three Mediterranean islands, and all territory in the Netherlands and the Italian peninsula. Charles VI of Austria gained Lombardy, Naples, Sardinia, and the Spanish Netherlands, but had to drop his claim to the Spanish crown. Louis XIV secured the Spanish kingship for his grandson, and preserved France's borders as of 1697, losing only some territory in America. Yet the settlement exposed the utter bankruptcy of Louis' expansionist policy, for he had failed to establish a Bourbon Franco-Spanish empire, and in the last thirty-five years of international warfare his only important acquisition was the city of Strasbourg. The United Provinces gained some protection against future French attack when Austria took over the Spanish Netherlands, but the Dutch suffered a commercial defeat when the English made unilateral trade agreements with Spain and Portugal. The English kept their Mediterranean outposts at Gibraltar and Minorca, and took some American territory from France —Newfoundland, Acadia, Hudson Bay, and the Caribbean island of St. Kitts.

The Whigs contended that England should have gained far more than this at Utrecht, but in fact the war had brought substantial benefits to the nation. It had stimulated English business and strengthened the colonial empire; furthermore, during the war, England and Scotland had joined in the parliamentary Union of 1707 to form the kingdom of Great Britain. The British, as they should henceforth be called, were the only major combatants who clearly emerged from the fighting in a much improved position. Among the lesser participants, the duke of Savoy was given Spanish Sicily (soon to be exchanged for Austrian Sardinia); Max Emmanuel, the elector of Bavaria, was restored to the state he had lost at Blenheim; and Frederick III, the elector of Brandenburg, was given Spanish Gelderland and confirmation of his new royal title, king in Prussia.

In one sense the peace of Utrecht and Rastatt was deliberately negative. It rejected Louis XIV's expansionist aims of 1688 and 1701. It rejected the Grand Alliance's vengeful demands of 1709. It rejected the Habsburg effort to restore the empire of Charles V. In another sense, the settlement was positive—an attempt to create a balance of power, in which the chief states of Europe would counterweight one another. This idea was hardly new, for the five leading Italian city-states had worked out just such a diplomatic equilibrium in the fifteenth century. But when the Valois and Habsburgs invaded Italy in the 1490's and destroyed the Italian system, they also rejected the idea of a power balance. The dynastic rivals of the sixteenth and seventeenth centuries punctuated their wars with truces—as when the Valois and Habsburgs made peace in 1559, or the Bourbons and Habsburgs in 1598 and 1659—but these simply provided breathing space; they were not efforts at equipoise. Royal rivals effected reconciliations through royal marriages, and such marriage alliances created new property claims that ignited new wars. At Utrecht and Rastatt, the diplomats endeavored to defuse dynastic rivalries as far as possible. They tried to keep the French, Spanish, and Austrian monarchies separate, to contain powerful France with powerful neighbors, and to bolster a strategically placed small state like Savoy with added territory. The balance-of-power idea which they revived was certainly no cure-all, as modern history has repeatedly demonstrated. But the settlement of 1713–1714 did do much to rationalize international relations. It set up a territorial system tolerable to all of the chief powers, and brought peace and security to western Europe for a full generation, until the 1740's.

THE EAST EUROPEAN WARS OF 1683–1721

While Louis XIV was battling the Grand Alliance, a parallel series of long and bloody wars unfolded east of the Elbe and the Alps. Here the political situation was far more fluid than in western Europe. With no eastern ruler even close to matching the concentrated power of the king of France, six states—Austria, Turkey, Russia, Sweden, Poland, and Brandenburg-Prussia—contended for leadership in the Turkish wars of 1683–1718 and the northern wars of 1700–1721. These states were all highly militaristic, with armies officered by the aristocratic landlords who everywhere dominated the social scene, and foot soldiers enrolled from the servile peasant labor force. The eastern states had far less per-capita wealth than France, England, or the United Provinces; their fighting arena was far larger; their population density was far lower. The style of warfare reflected these political, social, economic, and geographical conditions. Armies were generally smaller (except for the Turkish army) and less professional than in the west, campaigns were more far-flung, generals took more chances, and success or failure frequently hinged on individual heroics—and sometimes luck—rather than on scientific strategy and logistics. Collectively, the Turkish and northern wars proved to be pivotal events. They altered the map extensively. They confirmed the rising strength of some states—notably Austria and Russia—and the declining strength of others—notably Turkey, Sweden, and Poland. And in conjunction with the western wars, they produced a new European balance of power.

Austria Versus Turkey

The Austrian conquest of Hungary, Transylvania, Croatia, and Slavonia, which were taken from the Ottoman Turks in the war of 1683–1699, has already been described (see pp. 96–98). It is instructive to ask why Leopold I's expansionist policy succeeded where Louis XIV's failed. By 1683 Leopold had been Holy Roman emperor, king of Bohemia, archduke of Austria, duke of Silesia, Carinthia, and Carniola, margrave of Moravia and Styria, and count of Tyrol for twenty-five years. His empire was larger than France, and about as populous. No ruler, not even Louis XIV, could excel Leopold in single-minded devotion to the property rights of his royal dynasty. Yet Leopold was a far less potent and aggressive prince than Louis. Bland and phlegmatic in temperament, the emperor was absorbed in his numbing court routine. Habsburg Austria, an atomistic collection of separate provinces, lacked the cohesive community strength of Bourbon France. Leopold's fiscal resources were quite inadequate to his needs. During the wars of the late seventeenth and early eighteenth centuries, despite arduous efforts to expand revenues, Austria's military

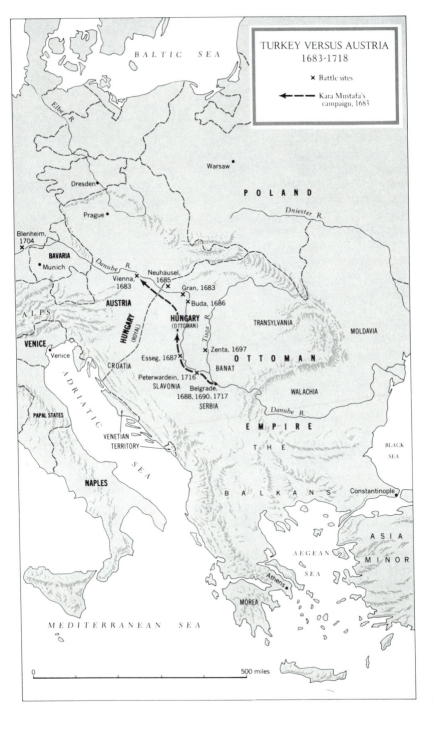

TURKEY VERSUS AUSTRIA
1683-1718

× Battle sites

◄--- Kara Mustafa's
campaign, 1683

BALTIC SEA

Elbe R.

Warsaw

POLAND

Dresden

Prague

Dniester R.

Blenheim,
1704

BAVARIA

Munich

Danube R.

Neuhäusel,
1685

Vienna,
1683

Gran, 1683

Buda, 1686

AUSTRIA

ALPS

HUNGARY
(ROYAL)

HUNGARY
(OTTOMAN)

TRANSYLVANIA

MOLDAVIA

Tisza R.

VENICE

Venice

CROATIA

Esseg, 1687

Zenta, 1697

OTTOMAN

BANAT

Peterwardein, 1716

SLAVONIA

ADRIATIC

Belgrade,
1688, 1690, 1717

SERBIA

WALACHIA

Danube R.

PAPAL STATES

EMPIRE

VENETIAN
TERRITORY

SEA

THE

BLACK
SEA

NAPLES

BALKANS

Constantinople

ASIA

MINOR

AEGEAN

SEA

Athens

MOREA

MEDITERRANEAN SEA

0   500 miles

expenditures were only about one fifth those of France, and one third those of England. Leopold's armies were correspondingly limited: he could field 100,000 soldiers at most, as against Louis' peak force of 440,000. Furthermore, Austria was the only major state forced to face both east and west; hence, in the 1680's and 1690's Leopold had to maintain field armies and garrisons on two fronts, against Turkey and France. How could this monarch, who depended on his allies to do much of his fighting for him, be so successful?

It was the Turks, not the Austrians, who initiated war in 1683. The Ottoman Empire had always been highly militarized, but the army had long been mutinous and corrupt, and for the last thirty years the grand viziers who managed the military machine for Sultan Mehmed IV (ruled 1646–1687) had been able to keep control only by finding constant work for their restless soldiery: the janissaries (professional infantry), the spahis (professional cavalry), and the frontier legions of doubtful loyalty from dependencies in the Balkans and the Crimea. In 1682 the grand vizier Kara Mustafa decided to employ this army in a tremendously bold stroke —the capture of Vienna, capital of the Austrian Habsburg empire. We cannot be sure of Kara Mustafa's motivation, especially since modern scholars have not yet studied the voluminous seventeenth-century Ottoman records in Istanbul. Certainly the grand vizier had supreme contempt for Leopold I and the Christian nonbelievers who inhabited Austria. Certainly he had ready allies in Royal Hungary (the narrow strip held by Leopold), where Magyar patriots were currently rebelling against their Austrian overlord. Probably he reckoned that Austria was weaker (and temptingly richer) than Muscovite Russia, which had recently blocked his efforts to expand into the Ukraine.

The grand vizier's plan was recklessly daring—and he very nearly carried it out. On July 1, 1683, he reached the Turkish-Austrian border in Hungary with a vast army of at least a hundred thousand soldiers (the exact number is not known). Disdaining to besiege the border fortresses, and brushing aside the small Austrian field army that tried to divert him, Kara Mustafa struck directly up the Danube. In two weeks, virtually unopposed, the Turks advanced eighty miles and encircled Vienna. Placing their tents and baggage in a giant crescent around the city walls, they dug a spiderwork of deep trenches and tunnels leading up to and under the Austrian fortifications. Tartar cavalry roamed freely through the Danube valley, looting and burning villages. The emperor and his courtiers fled to the Bavarian border; the Vienna garrison of eleven thousand was greatly outnumbered; and Leopold's field army was far too small to lift the siege. Vienna could be rescued only by massive·external help.

Shocked into action, Leopold's neighbors sent help. King John Sobieski of Poland marched from Warsaw with sixteen thousand men. Elector

The Turkish siege of Vienna. *In this painting Franz Geffels depicts the climactic moment on September 12, 1683, when King John Sobieski's relief army charged down from the heights overlooking the city. The elaborate Turkish siegeworks (center distance) have nearly penetrated the city walls. Ottoman soldiers, tents, and camels can be seen in the foreground. Museen der Stadt, Vienna.*

John George of Saxony marched from Dresden with ten thousand men. Elector Max Emmanuel of Bavaria marched from Munich with eleven thousand men. Count Waldeck brought eight thousand Franconians from the Main River area. To be sure, some imperial princes, among them Elector Frederick William of Brandenburg-Prussia (who had the best army in Germany), pointedly declined to help. And the rescuing forces could not reach Vienna quickly, since they started late and came from far away. King John Sobieski needed six weeks to muster his men and move them four hundred miles—and though the Austrians thought he was dilatory, his pace was faster than that of Marlborough's march to the Danube in 1704. Fortunately for Austria, the Vienna garrison resisted the Turkish siege with the utmost tenacity. Even so, by August 12 the Turks had broken through the outworks of the city defenses, and on September 4 a Turkish mine tore a thirty-foot hole in the inner wall. But Kara Mustafa could not force his way inside the city. His artillery was ineffectual, and his screaming, saber-wielding warriors were stopped by Austrian pikemen and musketeers in close combat. Still, it appears that Kara Mustafa could have speeded up his assault and taken the city by September, had he seen any reason for haste. But it was obvious to him that the Austrians would never dare to counterattack his siege camp. His disorderly Tartar cavalry failed to track the approaching relief armies, let alone stop them at vulnerable river crossings. Even when Kara Mustafa learned that the enemy forces had joined west of Vienna and were advancing to attack him, he did not bother to fortify his camp or post defenders in the hills overlooking his position.

On September 12, 1683, a relief army of sixty thousand deployed on the heights overlooking Vienna. The Polish king, John Sobieski, was in command. Three quarters of the soldiers were non-Austrian. They faced a Turkish cavalry force of only twenty-eight thousand—for Kara Mustafa threw away his numerical advantage by keeping most of his infantry in the siegeworks. As the allies attacked, the Turks resisted as best they could, but Kara Mustafa's recklessness exposed all of the glaring weaknesses in the Ottoman military system. Before nightfall the mighty Turkish army broke and fled, leaving behind ten thousand dead or captured soldiers, and all of the Turkish artillery, powder, wagons, tents, oxen, and camels, as well as an exotic assortment of silks, carpets, jeweled swords, birds in gilded cages, and so many coffee beans that the Viennese shortly opened their first coffeehouse. Thus Kara Mustafa's attack, the boldest maneuver in all of seventeenth-century warfare, had resulted in the most crushing defeat of the century.

The spectacular events of 1683 sent shock waves through the Ottoman system that persisted for years. Kara Mustafa was strangled on the sultan's orders, and Mehmed himself was deposed in 1687. Between 1683 and 1703, five sultans and twelve grand viziers tried unsuccessfully to restore stability. Meanwhile, the Austrian Habsburgs reckoned that the time had come to push back their obnoxious eastern neighbors and reconquer Turkish Hungary, held by the Ottomans since the 1520's. Venice, Poland, and the papacy also hoped to profit from the Turkish collapse. In 1684 they joined the Holy Roman emperor in the War of the Holy League, to expel Islam from Europe. Venice managed to push the Turks out of the Morea peninsula, but Poland accomplished very little. John Sobieski, the savior of Vienna, aimed to conquer Moldavia and establish a Polish outlet on the Black Sea, but the *szlachta* in the Polish Diet gave him no support, and his unpaid troops captured only a few forts on the Dniester River. In contrast, Leopold I accomplished all of his aims. The imperial attack concentrated on the main Turkish fortresses along the middle Danube; Gran was captured in 1683, Neuhäusel in 1685, Buda in 1686, Esseg in 1687, and Belgrade in 1688. By taking this chain of forts, the Habsburgs short-circuited the Turkish frontier-control system, and cleared the Ottomans out of Hungary, Transylvania, Croatia, and Slavonia in only six years of fighting. The imperial armies were largely manned by non-Austrian soldiers, commanded by non-Austrian generals, and paid for by papal revenues, but Leopold was the great personal beneficiary. In 1687 and 1688 he summoned the Hungarian and Transylvanian diets, and they recognized him as their hereditary king.

It was during the Turkish campaigns of the 1680's that Prince Eugene of Savoy (1663–1736) first made his mark. Eugene was the ablest of Leopold I's international brigade of generals. He was the perfect cosmopolite. Paris was his birthplace, his father was a French count, his mother was a Roman beauty who was Mazarin's niece and Louis XIV's mistress, and his cousin was the duke of Savoy. Eugene inherited none of his mother's good looks: he was short, pallid, pockmarked, and slouching. Louis XIV considered him fit only for the priesthood, and rejected Eugene's petition for entry into the French officer corps. So the youth went to Austria to fight in the Turkish wars. He first saw action at the relief of Vienna in 1683. Rising quickly in the Austrian army, he led imperial forces in ten campaigns against the Turks, and (though born a Frenchman) in twenty campaigns against Louis XIV. Eugene fought all over Europe—on the middle Danube, in southern Germany, in northern Italy, in southern France, on the Rhine, and in the Netherlands. He was generally given few troops to work with, and being frequently outmanned, he did lose some battles. But he won many more. No one did more than Eugene of Savoy to build the Austrian Habsburg empire.

After 1688, Austria had to fight on two fronts. When Louis XIV opened the Nine Years' War by invading the Palatinate, most of the imperial troops were hurriedly moved from the Danube to the Rhine. It was fortunate for Leopold that the Turkish campaigns of 1683–1688 had already accomplished so much. The Turks recaptured Belgrade in 1690, but were too disorganized to defeat the small Austrian armies that guarded Hungary and Transylvania. By 1697, with the western war coming to an end, Leopold could spare fifty thousand men, and Eugene of Savoy, for the Danubian front. Late one September afternoon, Eugene caught the sultan and his army in a perfect trap. The Turks were slowly crossing the Tisza River at Zenta, northwest of Belgrade, on a bridge of boats. The sultan and his spahis had reached the far bank, and the janissaries were following them across. By the time Eugene brought his army to the riverbank, only two hours of daylight were left, and his men were exhausted from a ten-hour forced march, but he immediately attacked the janissaries crowded at the bridgehead. The sultan ordered his spahis back across the river to help the janissaries, but this movement clogged the bridge, and lacking an escape route, the janissaries panicked. Thousands dashed into the river and drowned. Others butchered their own officers. The sultan fled, leaving behind all of his supplies. This overwhelming defeat demonstrated to the Turks that they could not recapture their lost provinces. They were forced to accept the Peace of Karlowitz, which was concluded with the Holy League in 1699. Islam was not expelled from Europe, but the Turks had been badly beaten, and Leopold's holdings were twice as large as in 1683.

The Peace of Karlowitz freed Leopold for his dynastic struggle with Louis XIV over the Spanish inheritance. But the War of the Spanish Succession quickly exposed Vienna to two-front problems once again, and showed that Austria was no real match for France. In 1703 Prince Francis Rákóczi (1675–1735) started a Magyar rebellion against Habsburg rule that swept Transylvania and Hungary, while Elector Max Emmanuel of Bavaria—Austria's strongest imperial supporter in the Turkish war—joined forces with the French in southern Germany. As we have seen, Austria was only rescued from this threat by Marlborough's victory at Blenheim. Eugene's subsequent conquest of northern Italy freed enough troops so that the Habsburgs could put down Rákóczi's rebellion in 1708. And Austria's failure to conquer Spain helped to direct Habsburg attention back to the Turks after the Peace of Rastatt. In 1715 the Ottomans declared war on their weakest Christian neighbor, the republic of Venice, and swiftly reconquered the Morea. Austria intervened, and it was apparent that Prince Eugene had not lost his touch. In 1716 he routed a larger Turkish army at Peterwardein, and in 1717—again heavily outnumbered—he retook Belgrade. The Peace of Passarowitz, concluded between Austria and Turkey in 1718, added a further belt of Danubian territory to the Habsburg state: the Banat, northern Serbia, and western Walachia.

In this war, as in the earlier Turkish war, Austria had the rare good fortune to meet an adversary eager to fight and vulnerable to defeat. Furthermore, it turned out that Austria was the only state bordering on Turkish territory which was strong enough to beat the Ottomans. Venice tried but failed to regain its lost possessions in the eastern Mediterranean. Poland and Russia tried but failed to expand toward the Black Sea. Only the Austrian Habsburgs found it possible to profit from Turkish recklessness. It cannot be claimed that Leopold and his sons Joseph I and Charles VI had built a state equal in strength to France or England. Nor indeed was Austria a unitary state on the western model. But the Habsburgs had been marvelously successful at eliminating all alternatives to Austrian rule on the central Danube. They were no longer shadow leaders of an outmoded Holy Roman Empire, but absolute rulers of a new multinational central European dynastic state.

Sweden Versus Russia

In 1700, when the War of the Holy League had just concluded and the War of the Spanish Succession was soon to begin, fighting broke out in quite another quarter—the Baltic region. Here, Sweden was the dominant state, as it had been throughout the seventeenth century. Thanks to the martial exertions of the Vasa kings (most particularly Gustavus Adolphus), the Swedes had built an empire that incorporated Finland, Karelia, Ingria, and Estonia (blocking Russia's access to the Baltic), Livonia (north of Poland), Pomerania (bordering Brandenburg), and Bremen and other small north German territories bordering Denmark.

The apotheosis of Eugene of Savoy. *This huge Baroque statue, which stands in the central hall of Eugene's Belvedere palace in Vienna, commemorates his victories in the Turkish wars. The triumphant general, uplifted by cherubs, tramples the enemy underfoot while modestly covering the horn of Fame with one hand. Oesterreichische Galerie, Vienna.*

Thus the Swedes controlled all of the northern and eastern portions of the Baltic coast, and much of the southern portion. With the Danes they shared control of the Sound, through which all Baltic shipping passed. As in Gustavus Adolphus' day, Sweden had a small population and limited resources, but was very well organized for warfare. A standing army of twenty-three thousand garrisoned ninety forts and castles, and another seventy thousand soldiers and sailors could be mobilized from the peasantry. During the seventeenth century Sweden had repeatedly fought and defeated its Baltic neighbors, who were aching for revenge. When the Swedish king Charles XI (ruled 1660–1697), a tough warrior and autocrat, was succeeded by a fifteen-year-old boy, the time looked right for revenge. In 1698–1699, the kings of Denmark, Poland, and Russia secretly planned a joint attack, and in 1700 they simultaneously assaulted Swedish strong points hundreds of miles apart, in Holstein, Livonia, and Ingria.

Thus began the Great Northern War, which no one in 1700 could imagine would last for twenty-one years. The three allies against Sweden started out with differing war aims. The Danes wanted to regain Scania (lost to Sweden in 1658), across the Sound from Copenhagen, so that they could once again control the entrance to the Baltic. The Poles had little interest in war with Sweden, but their king, Augustus II (ruled 1697–1733), badly needed military conquests. Augustus, who was also elector of Saxony, had just secured the Polish throne in a disputed election after the death of John Sobieski. He was nicknamed "the Strong" because he could bend horseshoes with his bare hands—and also because he was reputedly the father of three hundred illegitimate children. This virile prince wanted to conquer Livonia (lost to Sweden in 1629); he would then either annex this province to Saxony in a dynastic union rivaling Brandenburg-Prussia, or present it to Poland, in an attempt—like that of John Sobieski before him—to strengthen his shaky hold on the Polish crown through his brilliant foreign victory.

The third party in the attack, the Russian tsar, was the most enigmatic. Peter I had not yet earned his sobriquet of Peter the Great; in 1700 he was an untested, half-barbaric figure. He was clearly the most energetic and ferocious Muscovite ruler in a long time, for he had already wrested control of the state from his sister Sophia, and had smashed a rebellion

Charles XII of Sweden. *Note the contrast with preceding portraits of Marlborough and Eugene. Charles looks neither regal nor aristocratic. He has no wig and wears a simple cavalry officer's uniform.* Armémuseum, Stockholm.

of the *streltsy*, or palace guard, through savage torture and wholesale executions. Peter was also clearly intent on opening Russia to western commerce and establishing a Russian navy: he had made a personal tour of Dutch and English shipyards, and had fought the Turks for access to the Black Sea. Now he was hoping to regain Ingria and Estonia (lost to Sweden in the sixteenth century) and sail his navy into the Baltic.

Facing this trio of assailants stood the young Swedish king, a personage of great and disturbing gifts. Charles XII (ruled 1697–1718) had been absorbed from early childhood in shooting and war games. He killed his first deer at age eight, his first wolf at ten, his first bear at eleven. Adept at mathematics, he worked out tactical military problems in the schoolroom. As an adolescent king he amused himself in wintertime by jumping from ice floe to ice floe on horseback, and in springtime by chasing hares around the palace gallery and tossing furniture out the palace windows. But Charles soon developed Spartan, puritanical habits. Scorning the drunken orgies of monarchs like Augustus of Poland and Peter of Russia, he gave up alcohol. Scorning the fopperies of fashion, he refused to wear the great curly wig requisite for a gentleman in this era, and dressed as a man of action in a plain blue uniform with brass buttons. He showed no interest in girls, in court ceremonial, in civil administration. His sole delight was warfare. Thus in 1700 Charles eagerly took to the field with the Swedish army. He never returned to Stockholm during the remaining eighteen years of his reign.

The Swedes first invaded Denmark and closed in on Copenhagen. The Danes hurriedly made peace. Three months later, in November, 1700, Charles XII marched across Estonia with eleven thousand men to relieve the town of Narva, besieged by forty thousand Russians. Tsar Peter, suspecting that a four-to-one advantage was not enough for his untrained peasants, abruptly quit the Russian camp. In a driving snowstorm the Swedes attacked; Peter's soldiers broke almost immediately and surrendered in droves. The Battle of Narva convinced Charles that the Russians did not know how to fight and could be beaten at any time, so he turned to deal with Augustus, of Saxony and Poland. In 1701 he defeated Augustus' Saxon troops at the Livonian border, crossed into Poland, and demanded that the Poles depose their king. By now Charles XII was acting as Kara Mustafa had in 1683, pursuing radical solutions well beyond his military strength. For the next six years he mired himself in Polish politics. Charles could find Lithuanian allies who wanted to break up the Polish state, and Polish allies who wanted a weaker king than Augustus, but most Poles hated the Nordic intruders who plundered their territory. The Swedish army, in these years never larger than thirty thousand men, chased Saxon, Polish, and Russian contingents around the Polish countryside, and occupied each of the chief Polish towns in turn, without ever gaining meaningful control. In 1704 at Warsaw a handful of *szlachta*, attended by Swedish soldiers, were persuaded to "elect" by voice vote Charles's nominee, Stanislas Leszczynski (1677–1766), as the new king of Poland. In 1706, when Charles moved his army into Saxony, Augustus signed a humiliating peace treaty in which he acknowledged his dethronement and even recognized King Stanislas. But nothing lasting had been accomplished; Charles's puppet regime in Poland depended entirely on military force. In 1707 the Swedish king marched his army toward Russia to deal with Tsar Peter.

During the years Charles spent in Poland, Peter had kept working on his plan for a Baltic outlet. Viewing the disgrace at Narva in 1700 as a necessary lesson, he reorganized the Russian army and sent his troops back to fight the Swedish garrisons in Ingria, Estonia, and Livonia. Between 1702 and 1704, while Charles was chasing Augustus, the Russians captured most of the Swedish forts (including Narva) along the southern coast of the Gulf of Finland. These campaigns gave Peter's soldiers much-needed self-confidence and battle experience. In 1703 the tsar started to lay out a new city—St. Petersburg—on the Neva River, at the head of the Gulf of Finland. Russian naval vessels ventured out into the Gulf, while Peter welcomed the first western merchant ships into his new port. He was very eager for peace with Sweden—if Charles XII would relinquish his claim to St. Petersburg. Naturally, the all-victorious Swedish king saw no reason to surrender any Baltic territory to Russia, and Charles was in any case not eager for peace. Like the roving captains in the Thirty Years' War he had become a permanent campaigner. By 1707 the stage was set for a dramatic confrontation between these two manic warrior-kings.

Charles XII marched east toward the Russian border with over forty thousand men, the largest and finest field army he ever assembled. Critics have wondered how he expected to conquer such a vast state as Russia with an army of this size when he had been unable to master Poland. The answer appears to be that Charles's aim was not to conquer Russia, but to catch and destroy Peter's army. An overwhelming military victory might generate a change of regime in Moscow and produce a more compliant new tsar, and it would certainly force the Russians back from the Baltic and thus seal the Swedish king's previous victories over Denmark, Poland, and Saxony. Charles aimed his attack at Moscow, taking the shortest route across Poland to the Dnieper River at Smolensk. Undoubtedly this was a mistake. He should have struck first at St. Petersburg, and if necessary moved from there toward Moscow, keeping open communication lines for supplies and reinforcements from the Swedish Baltic. Unlike western commanders, who stopped campaigning during the winter, Charles moved his troops across the frozen rivers and marshes in the coldest weather. In February, 1708, he almost caught Peter at Grodno, in Lithuania. Thereafter, nothing went well. Peter stayed always just out of reach, systemati-

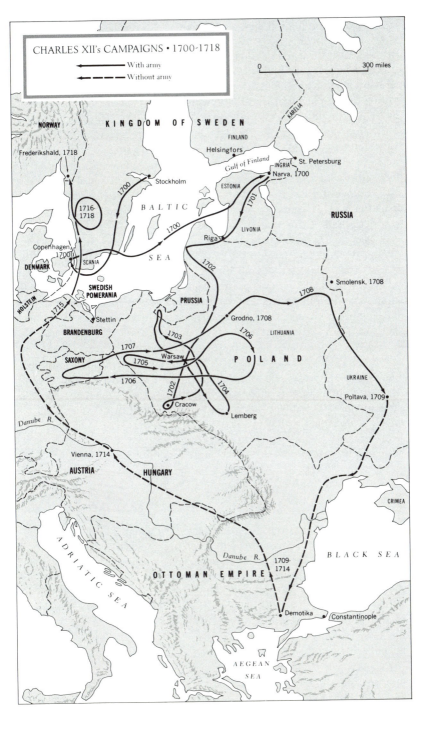

CHARLES XII's CAMPAIGNS • 1700-1718

With army
Without army

0   300 miles

NORWAY

KINGDOM OF SWEDEN

FINLAND

Helsingfors

Frederikshald, 1718

Gulf of Finland   INGRIA   St. Petersburg

KARELIA

1700   Stockholm   Narva, 1700

ESTONIA

1701

BALTIC

1700

RUSSIA

1716-1718

LIVONIA

Copenhagen, 1700   Riga

SCANIA   SEA

DENMARK

1702

Smolensk, 1708

SWEDISH POMERANIA

HOLSTEIN

1715

Stettin

PRUSSIA

Grodno, 1708   1708

BRANDENBURG

1703

1706   LITHUANIA

1707

1705   Warsaw

SAXONY

POLAND

1706

1702   1704

UKRAINE

Cracow

Poltava, 1709

Lemberg

Danube R.

Vienna, 1714

AUSTRIA   HUNGARY

CRIMEA

ADRIATIC SEA

Danube R.   1709-1714

BLACK SEA

OTTOMAN EMPIRE

Demotika   Constantinople

AEGEAN SEA

cally harassing the Swedish column with skirmishes and raids. The Russians ruthlessly laid waste to all surrounding territory, keeping the Swedes perpetually short of food. Charles spent the summer of 1708 near Smolensk, waiting for supplies from the Baltic which never arrived because the Russians cut them off. Now too weak for a direct assault on Moscow, he turned south and joined forces in the Ukraine with a rebel Cossack chieftain, Ivan Mazepa (c. 1644–1709). Charles gained some supplies and reinforcements by this move, but he was more dangerously isolated than ever. In the terrible winter of 1709—which (as we have seen) produced crop failure and famine in France—many Swedish soldiers froze to death. Battle casualties, hunger, disease, and weather inexorably reduced Charles's army to scarcely more than twenty thousand combat troops.

In May, 1709, anxious to establish a base for further operations in the Ukraine, Charles laid siege to the town of Poltava. Peter closed in on him with an army of forty thousand. In late June the Swedish king received a bullet wound in his foot, was prostrated by fever, and could be moved only on a stretcher. Still he refused to retreat. On July 8 the Swedes attacked Peter's encampment, although they had no artillery and were in a poor field position. The Russians outmanned, outshot, and outfought them, and quickly turned the Battle of Poltava into a smashing victory. The Swedes fled toward the Crimea, leaving nearly ten thousand dead or captured. The invalid king, who considered Poltava to be only a temporary reverse, was carried to asylum in Turkey by a small guard. His remaining fourteen thousand troops, trapped on the east bank of the broad river Dnieper, tamely surrendered to Peter.

In practical terms, the Battle of Poltava abruptly ended Sweden's era of great-power status. Between 1709 and 1713 all of Charles XII's military gains were wiped out. Augustus reoccupied the Polish throne, while Stanislas fled into exile. Hanover and Prussia joined the assault upon Sweden, and together with Denmark took over almost all the Swedish holdings on the south Baltic coast. Russia captured the territories bordering the eastern Baltic from Riga to Helsingfors. Charles XII stubbornly—some would say blindly—refused to recognize these losses. From 1709 to 1714 he stayed in Turkey, trying to organize campaigns against Russia and Poland. Then he traveled incognito, disguised by a dark wig and a moustache, through Austria and Germany to his one remaining territory on the Baltic coast, Swedish Pomerania. In 1715 he resumed campaigning against Prussia, Hanover, Saxony, and Denmark. In 1718 he was just starting an invasion of Norway, then under Danish rule, when he was killed by an enemy shot—or possibly murdered by one of his own soldiers.

Judgments of Charles XII differ widely. For some, he is the archetypal individualist who dared to challenge the whole world. Alternatively (and less flatteringly) he is regarded as a Greek tragic hero fatally flawed by hubris. Others see him as a madman who led his devoted followers to destruction. Russian historians have noted the ominous parallels with Napoleon in 1812 and Hitler in 1941–1943. Whatever one's judgment of this warrior-king, the fact remains that he lost his war. Shortly after Charles's death, Sweden formally ceded Bremen to Hanover, Holstein to Denmark, and Stettin to Prussia. More important, at the Peace of Nystad in 1721, Sweden surrendered Livonia, Estonia, Ingria, Karelia, and southeastern Finland to Russia. Thus ended the Great Northern War.

PETER THE GREAT

Peter I, tsar of Russia (ruled 1682–1725), was surely the most remarkable public figure of his day—and an even more controversial leader than Charles XII. Until 1709 his method of rule seemed wildly eccentric to most foreign observers, and absolutely disastrous to most Russians. But Peter's victory over the Swedes at Poltava vindicated his policies, and signaled Russia's belated emergence as a major European power.

Peter was only ten years old when he ascended the Russian throne in 1682. He grew into his job slowly. Even after he overthrew the regency of his sister Sophia in 1689, he spent his time in war games (like the young Charles XII), in building boats, and in making rockets for fireworks displays. Peter grew into a giant of a man—nearly seven feet tall in an era when scarcely anyone was taller than five feet ten. His temper oscillated wildly between knockabout joviality and furious rage, and he had the constitution of an ox, so that he survived innumerable all-night drinking bouts with minimal damage. In the 1690's he scandalized the Muscovites by dressing as a western craftsman or sailor, and carousing with foreign artisans and soldiers in the so-called German suburb of Moscow. He scandalized the aristocrats of the *boyar* class by favoring upstarts like Alexander Menshikov (1672–1729), who rose from hawking pies in the Moscow streets to become the prince of Izhora. Peter broke with tradition most sharply when he traveled to Holland and England in 1697–1698 in order to learn more about shipbuilding, to recruit foreign workers, and to see the sights. His western hosts found Russian housekeeping methods "right nasty"[2] (in London, Peter's entourage broke all fifty chairs in their house in order to stoke the fires), and guardedly described the tsar as a "quite gifted savage." On returning home, Peter greeted his chief nobles scissors in hand, and cut off their long beards and the flowing sleeves of their Muscovite costumes. Next, he eagerly attended the interrogation and torture of hundreds of the *streltsy*, the restless traditional Kremlin guards, who hated his "German" innovations. The tsar even in-

[2]Quoted from *The Diary of John Evelyn*, ed. by E. S. de Beer (Oxford, 1955), Vol. V, p. 284.

Peter cutting a nobleman's beard. A *Russian woodcut, in which the caricaturist shrinks the giant tsar into a child-sized pest.*

vited foreign residents of Moscow to help decapitate those of the *streltsy* found guilty of rebellion.

Not since Ivan the Terrible had the Russians experienced such an overbearing ruler, and Peter was reminiscent of his sixteenth-century predecessor in another way: despite his western innovations, he followed Ivan's traditional Muscovite prescription of autocratic power for the tsar, state service for the elite, and bondage for the masses. His adherence to this formula was especially evident in his reorganization of Russia's armed forces during the Great Northern War. Having destroyed the *streltsy*, Peter discovered at Narva in 1700 that the foreign officers he had recruited made poor commanders, and the raw peasants he had conscripted made poor soldiers. So he set about fashioning a more professional Russian army. Henceforth, Peter kept up-to-date registers of Russia's noble families, and required all noblemen to serve in the army, the navy, or the bureaucracy. Careers in the officer corps were reserved for the elite—men of high birth or exceptional talent. Young cadets received basic training in newly organized artillery or engineering schools, or began as privates in the regiments of the tsar's elite guards (the successors to the *streltsy*). Once commissioned as officers, they advanced in status as they were promoted in military rank. At the same time, Peter created an "immortal" standing army of 100,000 peasant soldiers by conscripting one man from every twenty peasant households, and requiring that each conscript who died or deserted be replaced by a substitute soldier. To pay for this army,

Peter managed to treble government income during the war years—a feat matched only by England among the other European powers—and he accomplished this without contracting foreign or domestic loans; instead, he levied a new poll tax on all male serfs. To supply his army with guns, powder, and uniforms, the tsar set up many new state factories, including fifty-two new ironworks, largely staffed by forced peasant labor. It is estimated that the average Russian peasant household "contributed" the equivalent of 160 days of labor per year to Tsar Peter. Naturally, the landowners disliked the tsar's heavy exactions upon their serfs, but they welcomed his decree that no serf could move from his master's estate without a written passport, which tightened their own control over their labor force. Thus Peter's regime intensified the social and economic polarity between lord and peasant in Russia.

The character of Peter's "westernization" policy has been much debated: was it only window dressing, or did it produce fundamental change? Was it imposed artificially by the tsar, or did it reflect Russia's needs and aspirations? Peter's innovations in foreign policy were certainly more than window dressing. Before the 1690's Russia had never played an important role in European affairs, but Peter campaigned extensively against Sweden

Peter's execution of the *streltsy*, 1698. *This contemporary print shows scores of corpses gibbeted outside the Kremlin walls. Peter kept the rotting bodies on display for months, to edify the Muscovites who passed by in their carriages.*

and Turkey and sent his armies into Poland and Germany. In terms of square miles annexed, Peter's territorial acquisitions do not place him among the chief Russian expansionists. However, his conquests on the Baltic gave Russia direct access to the west; the tsar's creation of the new capital of St. Petersburg—designed to resemble Amsterdam, and located on the western frontier of his state—was a symbolic act at least as meaningful as the construction of Philip II's Escorial or Louis XIV's palace at Versailles. Another break with the past was Peter's decision to imitate western dynastic marriage practices by contracting foreign (especially German) marriages for the Romanovs—a practice continued until 1917. Peter's army reforms were modeled on the Prussian system, and his bureaucratic reforms on the Swedish system. Many of these western borrowings buttressed existing tendencies in Russia; for example, in adopting western dress and speaking German or French the upper classes were bolstering their sense of social superiority over the peasants, who kept their beards and their national costume and language. Peter always wanted Russians to borrow what was useful from the west—mainly technology—with-

Peter the Great's Winter Palace, St. Petersburg. *Engraving by Alexei Zubov. Note how the Tsar has chosen a non-Russian Baroque style of architecture for his new capital.*

out becoming slavish imitators. And he expected two-way contact: in 1697–1698 he went, as a young novice, to see Holland and England; in 1716–1717 he went back to Amsterdam—and to Copenhagen and Paris—to be seen. A giant of a man, with giant control over a giant state, Peter had more confidence in his own ability to deal with the west on an equal footing than most of his countrymen have had, then or since.

Peter's vigorous policy of western expansion was by no means entirely successful. For one thing, he failed to establish a Russian outlet on the Black Sea. In 1696, the Russians captured from the Turks the town of Azov, at the mouth of the Don, which gave Peter access to the Sea of Azov for his navy. In 1711, when the Turks renewed war with Russia, Peter advanced boldly into Moldavia, evidently aiming to establish a Russian base at the mouth of the Danube. He called upon Orthodox Christians living under Turkish rule on the Danube and throughout the Balkans to rise up and join him, but Peter quickly found himself as dangerously isolated as Charles XII had been in Russia. When a large Turkish army encircled Peter's troops at the river Pruth, he hastily made peace, surrendered Azov to the Ottomans, and abandoned his hopes for access to the Black Sea. And though Peter did secure his Baltic outlet from the Swedes, he failed to convert Russia into a naval power. The navy, his favorite project, seemed alien and unnecessary to most Russians, and was dropped by his successors. Nor was Peter able to organize effective alliances with other European states. He could not get Denmark, Prussia, and Hanover to join Russia in an invasion of the Swedish mainland, for these states were thoroughly alarmed by Russia's intrusion into northern Germany and central Scandinavia. On visiting Paris in 1717, Peter baldly told his French hosts, "I, the Tsar, want to take the place of Sweden with you." But the French demurred, for they too preferred to keep their distance from this new "northern Turk."

Peter's style of rule stirred deep opposition within Russia. Many of the clergy hated his regulation of monastic life, his requirement that the church staff schools for the laity, and his decision to keep the patriarchate of Moscow vacant so as to subordinate the church to the state. Orthodox believers were horrified by his tolerance of west European creeds, and his mocking of church ceremonial. The rumor spread that foreigners had killed the true tsar when he went west in 1697 and sent back an impostor in 1698; Old Believers thought they had sent back the Antichrist. Aristocrats had a different set of grievances: they disdained Peter's low-born companions, such as his Livonian peasant wife, Catherine (*c.* 1684–1727), and they resented being forced off their country estates into military or bureaucratic service. Among the downtrodden serfs, Peter was naturally not very popular; thousands of peasants ran away in order to escape his new taxes and ferocious labor requirements. Cossacks in the Don region, always anxious to preserve their traditional liberties, rose against Peter in 1707–1708. Far worse, his own son and heir Alexis (1690–1718) was totally opposed to everything Peter stood for. The more Peter tried to train him, the more Alexis shirked; the more Peter bullied him, the more Alexis feared and loathed his father. By 1716 he was plainly allied with reactionaries among the aristocracy and clergy, who planned to restore the old isolationist foreign policy, the old freedom for priests and landowners, and the old capital in Moscow, as soon as Peter died. Alexis fled to Vienna and then to Naples. Peter hunted him down and had him brought home for interrogation and torture. Alexis received forty strokes of the knout, and died of his wounds before he could be publicly executed.

Seven years later, in 1725, Peter himself died, to the general relief of almost everyone. Today, his memory is still painfully alive. Russians have mixed feelings about the leader who forced foreign manners and standards upon their society. Westerners have mixed feelings about the man who injected Russian power into European politics. Few leaders have displayed such an admixture of brutality and creativity. Few men have done more to shape the course of history. To be sure, Peter did not single-handedly transform Muscovy into Russia, nor did this transformation involve a complete break with the past. But Peter employed his immense personal energy to maximum effect. In a company of powerful kings, Peter was the most dynamic ruler of the day. For better or worse he earned his title: he was indeed Peter the Great.

EUROPE IN 1715

In August, 1715, in a setting far removed from the frontier crudity of Peter's Russia, another great king lay dying, at Versailles. Louis XIV was nearly seventy-seven; he had ascended the throne long ago, in 1643, and had been in personal charge since 1661. He had outlived his younger brother, his son, two of his three grandsons, and two of his five great-grandsons. His heir was a five-year-old great-grandson, who would ascend the throne as Louis XV. The passage of French royal authority from the all-powerful Sun King to a little child marked a symbolic pause in European affairs. Ceremonial throughout his reign, Louis kept to form right to the end. "I am leaving you, but the State will always remain," he told his courtiers. "Try to remain at peace with your neighbors. I loved war too much," he told the young dauphin.[3] This last point was true enough; the wars of 1688–1713 had brought Louis close to disaster. But the old king had no inkling of a deeper problem. The great Bourbon monarchy, his proudest legacy, was too rigidly constructed to meet the changing circum-

[3]John B. Wolf, Louis XIV (New York, 1968), p. 618.

stances of the new century. The French formula for state building, which had provided such impressive internal stability and external power during the seventeenth century, would work significantly less well in the reign of Louis XV. And as the French aristocracy, bourgeoisie, and peasantry all pressed for fundamental changes, the formula would break down completely in 1789.

No prophet in 1715 could have predicted revolution, for never had the European political system been more stable. Everywhere strong rulers presided over centralized governments, domestic strife was minimal, and international rivalry was muted by the new balance-of-power system. To the intelligent contemporary observer, the close of Louis XIV's reign appeared to mark a gratifying stage of fulfillment in European civilization.

How had the people of early eighteenth-century Europe resolved the problems that had precipitated so much turmoil and tension in the sixteenth and seventeenth centuries? First of all, they had redrawn the political map so as to accommodate the chief interests of all the leading states. The territorial boundaries of France, Britain, Austria, Russia, and Prussia had all been significantly enlarged since the mid-sixteenth century. Spain had lost territory, but this reflected its declining status and power. The Dutch republic was still constricted, but this reflected the fact that its prime interest was in commerce, not real estate, and also the fact that the Dutch were beginning to slip in status. Overall, the map of 1715 looks considerably more "modern" than the map of 1559. In the sixteenth century, Europe had been divided into three zones; now the division was simpler—between the commercial, capitalistic, national states of the west and the agricultural, multinational states of the east. The seven leading European powers, in roughly descending order of stature, were France, Britain, Austria, the United Provinces, Russia, Spain, and Prussia—four Atlantic states and three eastern states. The Ottoman Empire, still formidable enough to be ranked fourth or fifth in this hierarchy, remained outside the European system, isolated by religion and culture.

There were still large areas on the map of 1715 which were essentially political vacuums—western Germany, Italy, and Poland in particular. The only west German state to take a leading role in the recent wars, Bavaria, had been badly mauled in the fighting. Poland had also been mauled. Four of the largest Italian states—Lombardy, Naples, Sicily, and Sardinia—had been ignominiously handed over to new rulers at the settlement of 1713–1714. The danger in this situation was that one or several of the leading states might trigger new wars by expanding into the areas of vacuum. But the great powers had had their fill of combat for a while. The warrior-kings Charles XII and Peter the Great were winding up their careers. The other chief monarchs in 1715 were much less bellicose. Louis XV was a child, and George I (of whom more shortly) in Great Britain, Charles VI

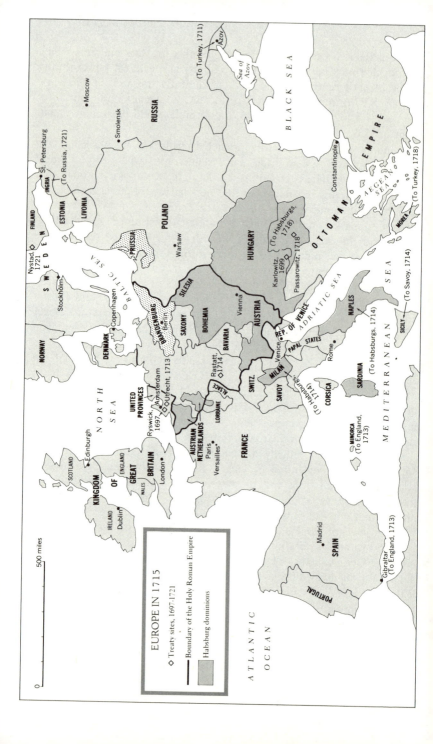

EUROPE IN 1715

◇ Treaty sites, 1697–1721
— Boundary of the Holy Roman Empire
▓ Habsburg dominions

ATLANTIC OCEAN

KINGDOM OF GREAT BRITAIN

SCOTLAND
Edinburgh •
IRELAND
Dublin •
WALES
ENGLAND
London •

NORTH SEA

NORWAY
DENMARK
Copenhagen •
SWEDEN
Stockholm •
BALTIC SEA
Nystad, 1721 ◇
FINLAND
St. Petersburg •
(To Russia, 1721)
INGRIA
ESTONIA
LIVONIA

RUSSIA
Moscow •
Smolensk •

POLAND
Warsaw •

PRUSSIA
BRANDENBURG
Berlin •
SAXONY
SILESIA
BOHEMIA

UNITED PROVINCES
Amsterdam •
Utrecht, 1713 ◇
Ryswick, 1697 ◇
AUSTRIAN NETHERLANDS

FRANCE
Paris •
Versailles •

ALSACE
Rastatt, 1714 ◇
LORRAINE
SWITZ.
SAVOY

BAVARIA
AUSTRIA
Vienna •
HUNGARY
(To Habsburgs, 1718)
Karlowitz, 1699 ◇
Passarowitz, 1718 ◇

MILAN
(To Habsburgs, 1714)
REP. OF VENICE
Venice •
ADRIATIC SEA
PAPAL STATES
Rome •
Sardinia (To Habsburgs, 1714)

CORSICA
SARDINIA

NAPLES
(To Habsburgs, 1714)
SICILY
(To Savoy, 1714)

OTTOMAN EMPIRE
Constantinople •
BLACK SEA
Sea of Azov
Azov (To Turkey, 1711)

AEGEAN SEA
MOREA
(To Turkey, 1718)

MEDITERRANEAN SEA
MINORCA
(To England, 1713)

SPAIN
Madrid •
Gibraltar
(To England, 1713)

PORTUGAL

500 miles
0

in Austria, Philip V in Spain, and Frederick William I in Prussia all kept their dynastic ambitions in check. The treaties of Utrecht and Rastatt, soon to be supplemented by the treaties of 1718 and 1721 which ended the Turkish and northern wars, ratified the power shifts that had taken place since the mid-seventeenth century, created a viable international environment for the first half of the eighteenth century, and set up a state system that has continued, with many revisions, into our own day.

Religion was obviously a more muted issue than in the days of Calvin and Loyola. To be sure, Louis XIV's persecution of the Huguenots rallied outraged Protestant opinion against him, but it did not lead to further conflict between Protestants and Catholics. When they found it necessary to fight Louis, the Protestant English, Dutch, and Prussians did not hesitate to team up with the ultra-Catholic Austrians and Spanish. At the peace settlement, no effort was made to revive Huguenot liberties, nor indeed to alter confessional jurisdictions within any state. The Protestant-Catholic conflict was not merely hopelessly deadlocked; it had become politically irrelevant. The secular authorities were everywhere firmly in charge of organized religion, as they had been during the earliest stage of the Reformation, 1517–1540, before the religious wars began. Europe was covered by a network of territorial churches—some Catholic, some Protestant, but all managed by the state and subservient to the state. In Catholic territory, religious toleration was still considered to be intolerable. In Protestant territory, a measure of diversity was sometimes permitted, but only the Dutch practiced genuine pluralism. Church attendance was a matter of civic duty. Except for their black costumes, the parish clergy were hard to distinguish from other agents of local government, such as tax collectors, constables, and recruiting officers.

If the clergy had changed, so had the nobility, who had been so obstreperous in the era of religious wars. As we have seen, the chief rebellions of the sixteenth and seventeenth centuries had been organized by local magnates hostile to central state authority: the German Protestant princes against Charles V, the Huguenot nobility against the Valois, the Netherlands nobility against Philip II, the Bohemian nobility against Ferdinand II, the English gentry against Charles I, the French *frondeurs* against Mazarin, the Whig and Tory aristocracy against James II, the Russian *streltsy* against Peter I. By 1715 such challenges had run their course. Both in absolutist states like France, Austria, Prussia, and Russia, and in constitutional states like Britain and the Dutch republic, a working partnership—mutually advantageous—had evolved between the local magnates and the central administration. The composition of the "magnate" class differed markedly from place to place. But everywhere the political and social structure was at least as hierarchical and elitist in 1715 as in 1559. The upper orders were richer than ever, with fuller power over the un-

Symbol of a closing era—the elderly Louis XIV directing a military campaign. *In this portrait the king assumes the most grandiloquent pose available to him and dresses as a Roman emperor. The classical costume is far from flattering to Louis' aging physique, but the Roman analogy is appropriate to his aggressive policy of expansion through war.*

privileged lower orders who labored for them. Yet the privileged upper orders were far more domesticated than formerly, and harnessed to state service.

In eastern Europe, the wars of 1683–1721 did much to solidify this new partnership. Leopold I, Frederick III, and Peter the Great entrusted the management of the Austrian, Prussian, and Russian armies to the landed aristocracy. This system worked to the marked advantage of the Austrian *Landgrafs* and Prussian *Junkers*, who gained military promotions, honors, and payments, while escaping from the crushing war taxes. The great Baroque palaces built by the Austrian nobility at Vienna during and immediately after the wars—such as Eugene of Savoy's Winter Palace within the city and his Belvedere in the suburbs—testify that the new Danubian empire was a triumph for the aristocracy as well as for the Habsburgs. The Russian nobility stoutly resisted Peter's reforms, but they too discovered that partnership with the tsar brought more gain than loss. Only the Polish *szlachta* remained intransigent, still wedded to their sixteenth-century centrifugal political pattern. Poland was the classic example of an aristocratic society without the concept of a service nobility— and Poland would soon lose its political independence.

In the capitalistic states of western Europe, the new symbiotic relationship between state power and elite wealth was even more striking. During the wars of 1688–1713, the French, British, and Dutch governments were able to harness the private resources of the chief property holders—merchants, gentry, and nobility—to an unprecedented degree. In each of these states the government raised about a third of the money necessary to pay for the fighting through internal borrowing. The British achievement was particularly impressive. When England entered the war in 1689, it had no machinery for long-term borrowing; it had a past history of royal bankruptcy and default; and it had an annual royal revenue of only £2 million. Nevertheless, through the agency of the Bank of England (established in 1694), the London business community embarked on a massive program of loans to the government and quickly created a national debt, funded through private subscription. Between 1688 and 1714 the British raised £171 million to meet public expenditures, one third of this through loans. By 1714 the national debt stood at £40 million. Since the British government dared not repudiate this debt, it served as an effective deterrent against new wars for many years to come.

The business leaders of London, Amsterdam, and Paris could afford to be fiscal patriots, for the wars of 1688–1713 were highly profitable. Merchants who secured military contracts, opened up new wartime markets, or took advantage of commodity shortages and high prices, built magnificent private fortunes. To be sure, the wartime risks were great, and many traditional commercial patterns were badly dislocated. The Dutch were in the most vulnerable position because their North Sea herring fishery was disrupted by Dunkirk privateers and their Baltic trade in grain, timber, and tar was disrupted by the Swedish-Russian fighting. In 1715 Dutch merchants were still the chief middlemen of Europe, and operated the largest merchant fleet, but the British and French were closing the gap rapidly. During the wars both the British and French built up their long-distance trade, with America, Asia, and Africa, despite heavy shipping losses. This was the biggest boom period to date for the British overseas empire. In 1715 the British Caribbean planters were the world's chief sugar exporters, and the British Chesapeake planters were the world's chief tobacco exporters. To supply these colonial entrepreneurs with labor, the British shipped about 250,000 slaves from Africa to America during the war period—more than had been shipped in the entire English slave traffic up to 1688.

Despite their crucial fiscal power, businessmen played little role in politics, even in Britain and Holland. Politics was a game for leisured gentlemen or professional bureaucrats and lawyers. It is hard for us to conceive of how exclusive the world of politics was in 1715. The officials who managed the great absolute monarchies arrived at their decisions in closed councils and courts, or in palace cabals. Government decisions were transmitted to the man in the street by means of royal proclamations posted in churches and marketplaces. The press was strictly censored, and in any case newspapers were still in their infancy. Private gossip was the substitute for public opinion. Even the Dutch and Venetian republics functioned as closed oligarchies, operated by and for a few thousand men. Only the British could boast a long-established tradition of rough-and-tumble public politics, of strident journalism and street theater. Thus it is particularly interesting to find that the British system at the close of the French wars was becoming more orderly, less divisive, and closer in temper to the private politics of the absolutist states.

In 1714 there was a major political shake-up in Britain. Queen Anne, the last of the Stuart monarchs, died without an heir. In accordance with the terms of Parliament's Act of Succession of 1701, the new king was Anne's distant German cousin the elector of Hanover, who reigned as George I from 1714 to 1727. George came to power because he was a Protestant and because Parliament picked him. Thus the revolutionary settlement of 1689 was firmly ratified in 1714. With George's accession, the stormy two-party ideological combat characteristic of Anne's reign abruptly terminated. The Tories, who had controlled Anne's government from 1710 to 1714, were fatally torn between loyalty to the Church of England and loyalty to the royal house of Stuart. The Tory leader Bolingbroke had wanted to arrange the accession of James II's exiled Catholic son, the so-called Pretender. But Bolingbroke wavered irresolutely, and was deserted in the end by most of the Tories, who would not accept a Catholic king. When George came to England, he looked to the Whigs for support. An uprising in 1715 on behalf of the Pretender was easily smashed. Thereafter Toryism was discredited; criticism of the new Whig establishment could be smeared as political popery. After 1715 the Whigs were so completely dominant that ideology no longer mattered very much. Parliamentary elections were contested less often than they had been formerly. Politics—as elsewhere—became a semiprivate game. After 1715 the operations of the British parliamentary, constitutional system resembled those of the French absolutist system much more than they had during the seventeenth century.

To many observers, Great Britain appeared to have supplanted France as the model society. The British had defeated Louis XIV's armies, and were now overtaking the Dutch merchants. Even the working classes had a rising standard of living. After the 1680's young English men and women, who had been migrating to the American colonies by the thousands every year in search of employment, stayed at home because they found jobs. But the most impressive British achievement was the combination of individual liberty and public order. To be sure, only one adult male in five could vote. The 1689 credo of life, liberty, and property offered no political participation whatsoever to the propertyless lower half of society. Still, the British cultivated more individual diversity and opened more careers to individual talent than their absolutist neighbors. In seventeenth-century Britain the quest for liberty had been more conspicuous than the preservation of order. But the peaceful accession of George I showed that domestic divisions were not so deep after all, that almost everyone now accepted the settlement of 1689, and that awkward decisions could be worked out peaceably by means of representative government.

Britain was also the home of Sir Isaac Newton and John Locke, apostles of the new mathematical science and the new confidence in intellectual progress. Newton was an old man in 1715, and Locke was dead, but their influence was immense and would continue to grow. Working at the close of the seventeenth-century intellectual revolution, Newton and Locke seemed to have reestablished cultural order by harmonizing and reconciling the iconoclastic, disputatious ideas and attitudes that had torn the European intellectual community apart for so long. This was particularly obvious in the case of Newton, who incorporated the discoveries of Copernicus, Kepler, and Galileo into his magisterial concept of the cosmos. But it can be seen also in Locke, who worked out a middle-of-the-road political credo more satisfying to his eighteenth-century audience than the divine-right theory of monarchy which he ridiculed, or the cynical absolutism of Machiavelli and Hobbes, or the visionary radicalism of the Levellers. And Locke's buoyant confidence in the powers of human reason gave hope that Newton's accomplishments in mathematics could be duplicated in other fields of knowledge. Thus Newton and Locke framed a mental outlook stripped of the mystery, poetry, passion, and terror of the sixteenth-century climate of opinion to which Shakespeare, Cervantes, Loyola, and Calvin had responded. The stage was set for the *philosophes* of the eighteenth-century Enlightenment.

Thus the balance stood in 1715. It is essential to remember that in many respects the quality of European life was much the same as it had been in the mid-sixteenth century. The population had scarcely grown. Production methods, based on handicrafts, had scarcely changed. The laboring poor were still downtrodden. Women had no voice. The traditional, elitist structure of society was as firmly fixed as ever. This is why no prophet in 1715 could possibly have foreseen future events. For as Europe's population began to grow in the eighteenth century, as food production increased, industrialization began, and political pressure mounted, the traditional structure of society suddenly became as obsolete as witch-hunting or crusading. At the close of the century, the ordered, stable system of the Old Regime was dissolved by violent revolution. But that is another story.

Suggestions for Further Reading

(Books marked * are available in paperback.)

GENERAL

*J. H. Elliott, *Europe Divided, 1559–1598* (New York, 1968) (Harper Torchbook) provides an excellent survey of late sixteenth-century European politics. *Marvin R. O'Connell, *The Counter Reformation, 1559–1610* (New York, 1974) (Harper Torchbook) covers much the same time span; while not as good as Elliott on politics, O'Connell gives balanced attention to the religious conflict. *A. G. Dickens, *The Counter Reformation* (New York, 1969) (Harcourt Brace Jovanovich) and H. Outram Evennett, *The Spirit of the Counter-Reformation* (Cambridge, Eng., 1968) offer attractive surveys of the Catholic reform movement in the late sixteenth century. For the Calvinist side, R. H. Tawney, *Religion and the Rise of Capitalism* (New York, 1926) is a classic effort to correlate religious with economic developments. *Michael Walzer, *The Revolution of the Saints* (Cambridge, Mass., 1965) (Atheneum) is a parallel effort to correlate religion with politics. Both Tawney and Walzer deal mainly, though not exclusively, with English Puritanism.

General surveys of seventeenth-century history are rather less satisfactory. Carl J. Friedrich, *The Age of the Baroque, 1610–1660* (New York, 1952) makes extreme claims for the pervasiveness of the Baroque style. F. L. Nussbaum, *The Triumph of Science and Reason, 1660–1685* (New York, 1953) is another eccentric book, strongest on intellectual developments. John Stoye, *Europe Unfolding, 1648–1688* (New York, 1970) devotes more attention than Nussbaum to events in central and eastern Europe. John B. Wolf, *The Emergence of the Great Powers, 1685–1715* (New York, 1951), is one of the few general surveys of events at the close of our period.

While the late seventeenth century has attracted little attention, a number of historians have worked out interpretations of the hundred-year span from the mid-sixteenth to the mid-seventeenth century. Henry Kamen, *The Iron Century: Social Change in Europe, 1550–1660* (New York, 1971); Charles Wilson, *The Transformation of Europe, 1558–1648* (Berkeley, Calif., 1976); and *The Age of Expansion: Europe and the World, 1559–1660*, ed. by Hugh Trevor-Roper (London, 1968) are three recent examples. Kamen's book is particularly suggestive and interesting, though he perhaps unduly stresses the bleak side of life in this period. Trevor-Roper's collection of essays is a coffee-table book, superbly illustrated. *Crisis in Europe, 1560–1660*, ed. by Trevor Aston (New York, 1965), another collection of essays dealing with this time span, focuses on the question of whether there was a "general crisis" in seventeenth-century Europe. *Theodore K. Rabb, *The Struggle for Stability in Early Modern Europe* (New York, 1975) (Oxford) wrestles further with this "general crisis" proposition.

Four volumes in the *New Cambridge Modern History* (Cambridge, Eng.) survey the events of 1559–1715: Vol. III, *The Counter-Reformation and Price Revolution, 1559–1610*, ed. by R. B. Wernham (1968); Vol. IV, *The Decline of Spain and the Thirty Years War, 1609–48/59*, ed. by J. P. Cooper (1970); Vol. V, *The Ascendancy of France, 1648–88*, ed. by F. L. Carsten (1961); and Vol. VI, *The Rise of Great Britain and Russia, 1688–1715/25*, ed. by J. S. Bromley (1970). These are reference manuals, with contributions, prevailingly technical in character, by an assortment of British, European, and American scholars. In each volume some chapters are excellent and some are very dreary. The Bromley volume is perhaps the most valuable of the four, because it deals with a time span much in need of fresh investigation.

POLITICAL HISTORY

There are a number of first-class recent books on Habsburg Spain. *J. H. Elliott, *Imperial Spain, 1469–1716* (New York, 1964) (Penguin) and John Lynch, *Spain under the Hapsburgs, 1516–1700*, 2 vols. (Oxford, 1964–1969) are both outstanding. R. Trevor Davies, *The Golden Century of Spain, 1501–1621* (London, 1937) is partisan (pro-Philip II) and rather outdated, but highly readable. H. G. Koenigsberger, *The Practice of Empire* (Ithaca, N.Y., 1969) is a study of Sicilian institutions under Philip II's rule. *Charles Gibson, *Spain in America* (New York, 1966) (Harper Torchbook) is a model survey of the Spanish colonial system, and J. H. Parry, *The Spanish Seaborne Empire* (New York, 1966) is almost as good. Peter Pierson, *Philip II of Spain* (London, 1975), the best biography of Philip in English, puts emphasis on his administrative system. *Geoffrey Parker, *The Army of Flanders and the Spanish Road, 1567–1659* (New York, 1972) (Cambridge), despite its forbidding title, is an exceptionally interesting account of the strength and limitations of the Spanish military machine. *Garrett Mattingly, *The Armada* (Boston, 1959) (Houghton Mifflin Sentry) is a dramatic narrative of the Spanish-English confrontation in 1588. J. H. Elliott, *The Revolt of the Catalans* (Cambridge, Eng., 1963) is an important analysis of the internal Spanish crisis in 1640. Henry Kamen, *The War of Succession in Spain, 1700–1715* (London, 1969) focuses on efforts at internal reform by the new Bourbon monarchy at the close of our period.

For France, though a number of fine historians are developing a general reinterpretation of the sixteenth and seventeenth centuries, much of the new scholarship is as yet highly specialized, and some of the best recent work is not available in English. For the sixteenth century, the book to start with is J. H. M. Salmon, *Society in Crisis* (New York, 1975), which focuses on the impact of the religious wars. J. R. Major, *The Estates General of 1560* (Princeton, N.J., 1951); N. M. Sutherland, *The Massacre of St. Bartholomew* and the European Conflict, 1559–1572 (New York, 1973); and *Sir John Neale, *The Age of Catherine de Medici* (New York, 1943) (Harper Torchbook) offer three approaches to the late sixteenth-century Valois collapse. Robert M. Kingdon, *Geneva and the Consolidation of the French Protestant Movement, 1564–1572* (Geneva, 1967) and A. Lynn Martin, *Henry III and the Jesuit Politicians* (Geneva, 1973) focus on the religious protagonists in the sixteenth-century wars. Davis Bitton, *The French Nobility in Crisis, 1560–1640* (Stanford, Calif., 1969) is a slim treatment of a big subject. David J. Buisseret, *Sully and the Growth of Centralized Government in France* (London, 1968); A. D. Lublinskaya, *French Absolutism: The Crucial Phase, 1620–1629* (New York, 1968); Orest Ranum, *Richelieu and the Councillors of Louis XIII* (Oxford, 1963); and Georges Dethan, *The Young Mazarin* (London, 1977) discuss the early evolution of the Bourbon monarchy in the seventeenth century. P. R. Doolin, *The Fronde* (Cambridge, Mass., 1935) treats the abortive protest of 1648–1653. *C. V. Wedgwood, *Richelieu and the French Monarchy* (New York, 1950) (Macmillan) is a useful short biography. Roland Mousnier has written a number of important books that correlate social with institutional developments, including *La vénalitié des offices sous Henri IV et Louis XIII*, second ed. (Paris, 1971); *The Assassination of Henry IV* (London, 1973); and *Les Institutions de la France, 1598–1789* (Paris, 1974). For the Sun King's reign, the place to start is Pierre Goubert's provocative survey, *Louis XIV and the Twenty Million Frenchmen* (New York, 1972) (Random). *John B. Wolf, *Louis XIV* (New York, 1968) (Norton) is a detailed biography. Lionel Rothkrug, *Opposition to Louis XIV* (Princeton, N.J., 1965) discusses internal criticism of French absolutism. *W. H. Lewis, *The Splendid Century: Life in the France of Louis XIV* (New York, 1953) (Morrow) is an entertaining account of court life during Louis' reign.

On England, only a few of the many good books can be listed here. G. R. Elton, *England under the Tudors*, second ed. (New York, 1974) is an excellent, though strongly biased, survey of the sixteenth century; Elton stresses the conservative character of Elizabeth I's reign. *Wallace T. MacCaffrey, *The Shaping of the Elizabethan Regime* (Princeton, N.J., 1968) (Princeton) and Sir John Neale, *The Elizabethan House of Commons* (London, 1949) analyze political developments lucidly. Patrick Collinson, *The Elizabethan Puritan Movement* (Berkeley, Calif., 1967) is a thorough account of the opening phase of Puritanism. *A. L. Rowse, *The England of Elizabeth* (New York, 1950) (Macmillan) is an affectionate, effusive portrait of the age. Lacey Baldwin Smith, *Elizabeth Tudor* (Boston, 1975) is the best of many recent biographies of the queen; *Sir John Neale, *Queen Elizabeth I* (New York, 1934) (Doubleday Anchor) is also very readable. D. H. Willson, *King James VI and I* (London, 1956) effectively probes the weak points in the first Stuart king. *Christopher Hill, *The Century of Revolution, 1603–1714* (London, 1961) (Norton) and *Lawrence Stone, *The Causes of the English Revolution, 1529–1642* (New York, 1972) (Harper Torchbook) argue for the fundamental depth and vigor of the revolutionary upheaval in seventeenth-century England. By contrast, *Conrad Russell, *The Crisis of Parliaments* (New York, 1971) (Oxford) and *Perez Zagorin, *The Court and the Country* (New York, 1969)

(Atheneum) see the challenge to the Stuarts as much more limited and transitory. *William Haller, *The Rise of Puritanism* (New York, 1938) (U. of Pennsylvania); *A. E. Barker, *Milton and the Puritan Dilemma* (Toronto, 1942) (Toronto); and *G. E. Aylmer, *The Levellers in the English Revolution* (Ithaca, N.Y., 1975) (Cornell) illuminate various aspects of the Puritan movement in the seventeenth century. C. V. Wedgwood, in her trilogy *The King's Peace* (London, 1955) (Macmillan), *The King's War* (London, 1958), and *A Coffin for King Charles* (New York, 1964), presents the revolution of 1640 as a royal tragedy. Christopher Hill, in his trilogy *God's Englishman: Oliver Cromwell and the English Revolution* (New York, 1970) (Harper Torchbook), *Antichrist in Seventeenth-Century England* (New York, 1971), and *The World Turned Upside Down* (New York, 1972) (Penguin), presents the revolution as a victory—unfortunately short-lived—for radical attitudes. For the closing years of our period, Sir George Clark, *The Later Stuarts, 1660–1714*, second ed. (Oxford, 1955) is a good survey. David Ogg, *England in the Reigns of Charles II, James II and William III*, 3 vols. (Oxford, 1955) covers most of the same terrain at a more leisurely pace. *J. R. Jones, *The Revolution of 1688 in England* (New York, 1973) (Norton) is perhaps the best recent treatment of this event. *J. H. Plumb, *The Growth of Political Stability in England, 1675–1725* (London, 1967) (Humanities); Robert Walcott, *English Politics in the Early Eighteenth Century* (Cambridge, Mass., 1956); and Geoffrey Holmes, *British Politics in the Age of Anne* (New York, 1967) offer sharply differing interpretations of post-revolutionary politics. Winston Churchill's six-volume biography of his ancestor, *Marlborough* (New York, 1933–1938), has been abridged into one large volume by Henry Steele Commager (New York, 1968).

For the Netherlands, one should start with Peter Geyl's two books: *The Revolt of the Netherlands, 1555–1609*, second ed. (New York, 1958) and *The Netherlands in the Seventeenth Century*, 2 vols. (London, 1961–1964). Charles Wilson, *Queen Elizabeth and the Revolt of the Netherlands* (Berkeley, Calif., 1970) argues that Elizabeth should have supported the Dutch more vigorously. Wilson has also written a more general account, *The Dutch Republic* (New York, 1968) (McGraw-Hill). K. H. D. Haley, *The Dutch in the Seventeenth Century* (London, 1972) is another attractive survey. Two members of the house of Orange have admiring biographies in English: *C. V. Wedgwood, *William the Silent* (London, 1944) (Norton) and S. B. Baxter, *William III* (New York, 1966). Herbert Rowen, *John de Witt* (Princeton, N.J., 1977) is a massive study of Holland's leading mid-seventeenth-century statesman. For a broader view, C. R. Boxer, *The Dutch Seaborne Empire, 1600–1800* (New York, 1965) is especially interesting and informative.

The literature on post-Renaissance Italy is very uneven. There are a number of excellent books on the Venetian republic in the late sixteenth and seventeenth centuries. These include William Bouwsma, *Venice and the Defense of Republican Liberty* (Berkeley, Calif., 1968); *Crisis and Change in the Venetian Economy*, ed. by Brian S. Pullan (London, 1968); Brian S. Pullan, *Rich and Poor in Renaissance Venice* (Cambridge, Mass., 1971); and James C. Davis, *The Decline of the Venetian Nobility as a Ruling Class* (Baltimore, 1962). The history of the other Italian city-states in this period has generally received scant attention. For an interesting survey of post-Renaissance Florence, see *Eric Cochrane, *Florence in the Forgotten Centuries, 1527–1800* (Chicago, 1973) (Chicago).

On the Holy Roman Empire, the best introduction is supplied by the first two volumes of Hajo Holborn's *History of Modern Germany;* these are *The Reformation* (New York, 1959) and *The Age of Absolutism* (New York, 1964). H. G. Koenigsberger discusses the role of the imperial family in *The Habsburgs and Europe, 1516–1660* (Ithaca, N.Y., 1971). R. J. W. Evans, *Rudolf II and His World* (Oxford, 1973) looks at the exotic cultural tastes of one of the Habsburg emperors. F. L. Carsten studies the institutional development of local representative estates within the Empire in *Princes and Parliaments in Germany* (Oxford, 1959). *C. V. Wedgwood, *The Thirty Years War* (London, 1938) (Doubleday Anchor) is a detailed narrative without much analysis. Georges Pagès, *The Thirty Years War* (London, 1970) presents the diplomatic history of the war. Gunther Franz, *Der Dreissigjährige Krieg und das deutsche Volk* (Stuttgart, 1961) discusses the social and economic impact of the war. *S. H. Steinberg, *The Thirty Years' War* (New York, 1967) (Norton) claims that the destructiveness of this war has been much exaggerated. For the post-1648 rise of the Habsburg Danubian monarchy, John Spielman's biography *Leopold I of Austria* (New Brunswick, N.J., 1977) is interesting and informative. For a fuller account of the rise of the Danubian empire, see Oswald Redlich, *Weltmach des Barock: Osterreich in der Zeit Kaiser Leopolds I* (Vienna, 1961). John Stoye, *The Siege of Vienna* (London, 1964) recreates the dramatic crisis of 1683. Derek McKay, *Prince Eugene of Savoy* (London, 1977) is the best account in English of Austria's leading general. For the rise of Brandenburg-Prussia, the two best accounts in English are F. L. Carsten, *The Origins of Prussia* (Oxford, 1954) and *Hans Rosenberg, *Bureaucracy, Aristocracy and Autocracy: The Prussian Experience, 1660–1815* (Cambridge, Mass., 1958) (Beacon).

On eastern Europe, *W. H. McNeill, *Europe's Steppe Frontier, 1500–1800* (Chicago, 1964) (Chicago) is a suggestive new look at Slavic developments. Halil Inalcik, *The Ottoman Empire: The Classical Age, 1300–1600* (London, 1973) and L. S. Stavrianos, *The Balkans since 1453* (New York, 1958) are good on Ottoman Turkey. *Pursuit of Power*, ed. by James C. Davis (New York, 1970) is an attractive anthology of Venetian ambassadors' reports, including several on Turkey. *The Cambridge History of Poland*, ed. by W. F. Reddaway, 2 vols. (Cambridge, Eng., 1941–1950) is the best introduction—though very far from a perfect one—to that state. M. T. Florinsky, *Russia*, 2 vols. (New York, 1953) and George Vernadsky, *The Tsardom of Moscow, 1547–1682*, 2 vols. (New Haven, Conn., 1969) offer surveys—neither of them very readable, unfortunately—of pre-Petrine Russia. *Jerome Blum, *Lord and Peasant in Russia* (Princeton, N.J., 1961) (Atheneum) and Roland Mousnier, *Peasant Uprisings in Seventeenth-Century France, Russia and China* (New York, 1970) provide interesting analyses of Russia's system of deep social stratification. *B. H. Sumner, *Peter the Great and the Emergence of Russia* (New York, 1951) (Macmillan) is a good short biography. M. S. Anderson, *Peter the Great* (London, 1978) is also good. See also *L. Jay Oliva, *Russia in the Era of Peter the Great* (New York, 1969) (Prentice-Hall). For Sweden,

Michael Roberts, *Gustavus Adolphus, 1611–1632*, 2 vols. (London, 1953–1958) is a splendid biography with much background data. Roberts has also written a briefer book on the same subject: *Gustavus Adolphus and the Rise of Sweden* (Mystic, Conn., 1973). For Sweden's second great warrior-king, R. N. Hatton, *Charles XII of Sweden* (London, 1968) is a richly detailed, if somewhat uncritical, biography.

ECONOMIC HISTORY

*Ralph Davis, *The Rise of the Atlantic Economies* (Ithaca, N.Y., 1972) (Cornell) provides a good survey of sixteenth- and seventeenth-century economic developments in western Europe. *Fernand Braudel, *Capitalism and Material Life, 1400–1800* (New York, 1973) (Harper Colophon) is much broader in scope. *The Cambridge Economic History of Europe*, Vols. IV–V, ed. by E. E. Rich and C. H. Wilson (New York, 1967–1977) covers our period, with technical chapters on population and prices, among other topics. Immanuel Wallerstein, *The Modern World-System*, Vol. I (New York, 1974) is a programmatic statement about the process of modernization in Europe between 1450 and 1640.

Economic surveys of individual states include *Violet Barbour, *Capitalism in Amsterdam* (Baltimore, 1950) (Ann Arbor); Charles Wilson, *England's Apprenticeship, 1603–1763* (London, 1965); P. M. G. Dickson, *The Financial Revolution in England* (London, 1967); Jaime Vicens Vives, *An Economic History of Spain* (Princeton, N.J., 1969); Martin Wolfe, *The Fiscal System of Renaissance France* (New Haven, 1972); and Charles W. Cole, *Colbert and a Century of French Mercantilism*, 2 vols. (New York, 1939).

Population in History, ed. by D. V. Glass and D. E. C. Eversley (New York, 1965) and *Household and Family in Past Time*, ed. by Peter Laslett and Richard Wall (New York, 1972) (Cambridge) are collective works with a number of good chapters concerning the demography of our period. Earl J. Hamilton, *American Treasure and the Price Revolution in Spain* (Cambridge, Mass., 1934); *J. U. Nef, *Industry and Government in France and England, 1540–1640* (Oxford, 1940) (Cornell); and W. K. Jordan, *Philanthropy in England, 1480–1660* (London, 1959) are three pioneering works whose conclusions are now widely challenged. B. H. Slicher van Bath, *The Agrarian History of Western Europe, 500–1850* (London, 1963) is a broad survey of farming practices. Eric Kerridge, *The Agricultural Revolution* (London, 1967) is a more narrowly focused book, arguing that the British transformed their farming techniques in the sixteenth and seventeenth centuries rather than in the eighteenth century as traditionally maintained. Eli Heckscher, *Mercantilism*, second ed. (New York, 1955) and Charles Wilson, *Profit and Power* (London, 1957) present contrasting approaches to mercantilism. The controversy over the Weber thesis is conveniently summarized in *Protestantism and Capitalism and Social Science*, ed. by R. W. Green, second ed. (Boston, 1973) (Heath).

*J. H. Elliott, *The Old World and the New* (New York, 1971) (Cambridge) discusses the impact of America upon Europe in the 150 years after Columbus. *Philip D. Curtin, *The Atlantic Slave Trade* (Madison, Wis.,

1969) (U. of Wisconsin) is a path-breaking work that reinterprets the dimensions of the trade of African slaves to America. *D. B. Davis, *The Problem of Slavery in Western Culture* (Ithaca, N.Y., 1966) (Cornell) and *Winthrop Jordan, *White over Black* (Chapel Hill, N.C., 1968) (Norton) examine why early modern Europeans were so ready to enslave Negroes. Both of these books are first-rate. *Richard S. Dunn, *Sugar and Slaves* (Chapel Hill, N.C., 1972) (Norton) describes the slave-based society in the seventeenth-century West Indies.

SOCIAL HISTORY

In the years since World War II, a number of talented French historians have created a distinctly new and very stimulating approach to the social history of the early modern period. Some of them work on the largest possible scale: Fernand Braudel, *The Mediterranean and the Mediterranean World in the Age of Philip II*, 2 vols. (New York, 1972–1974), which was originally published in Paris in 1949, is a massive, richly suggestive evocation of the subsurface quality of life in all of the sixteenth-century societies bordering the Mediterranean. Others do intensive case studies: Pierre Goubert, *Beauvais et le Beauvaisis de 1600 à 1730*, 2 vols. (Paris, 1960) is a penetrating analysis of peasant and town life in one district of northern France. *Emmanuel Le Roy Ladurie, *The Peasants of Languedoc* (Urbana, Ill., 1977) (U. of Illinois) is a parallel investigation into peasant life in southern France during our period. Ladurie's *Times of Feast, Times of Famine: A History of Climate since the Year 1000* (London, 1972) is a very inventive study of changes in the European climate. Robert Mandrou, *Introduction to Modern France, 1500–1640* (London, 1975), by a psychohistorian, is a broadly gauged portrait of the mental world of the early modern Frenchman. *Philippe Aries, *Centuries of Childhood* (New York, 1965) (Random) is another impressionistic work which looks at changes in child rearing. Aries has also written *Western Attitudes towards Death* (Baltimore, 1974).

The "new social history" is flourishing also in England. W. G. Hoskins, *The Midland Peasant* (London, 1957) and Margaret Spufford, *Contrasting Communities* (New York, 1974) are close examinations of life in particular English villages during the sixteenth and seventeenth centuries, somewhat comparable to Goubert's work on French community life. Two books by Peter Laslett, *The World We Have Lost* (London, 1965) and *Family Life and Illicit Love in Earlier Generations* (New York, 1977) (Cambridge) are stimulating explorations into English family life in our period. Lawrence Stone, *The Family, Sex, and Marriage in England, 1500–1800* (New York, 1977) covers the same terrain as Laslett, but differs from him in methodology and interpretation. *Alan Macfarlane, *The Family Life of Ralph Josselin* (New York, 1970) (Norton) is an interesting reconstruction of one seventeenth-century Englishman's life style through close examination of his diary. One of the most seminal recent books by an English historian is *Lawrence Stone, *The Crisis of the Aristocracy, 1558–1641* (Oxford, 1967) (abridged, Oxford Galaxy), a probing analysis of the declining power and prestige of the English peerage. A follow-up study on the post-1660 revival of the English aristocracy is much needed.

There are a number of good recent studies of towns and cities in sixteenth- and seventeenth-century Europe, including Ruth Pike, *Aristocrats and Traders* (Ithaca, N.Y., 1972) on Seville; E. William Monter, *Calvin's Geneva* (New York, 1967); *Gerald Strauss, *Nuremberg in the Sixteenth Century* (New York, 1966) (Indiana U.); Orest Ranum, *Paris in the Age of Absolutism* (New York, 1968); and *Crisis and Order in English Towns, 1500–1700,* ed. by Peter Clark and Paul Slack (Toronto, 1972). Peter Burke, *Venice and Amsterdam* (New York, 1975) compares the members of the elite in charge of these two cities during the seventeenth century. Natalie Z. Davis' stimulating collection of essays, *Society and Culture in Early Modern France* (Stanford, Calif., 1975) gives special attention to the city of Lyons, as well as to the social role of women.

There are a number of good recent books on witchcraft and witch-hunting in the sixteenth and seventeenth centuries. *Keith Thomas, *Religion and the Decline of Magic* (New York, 1971) (Scribner) is a richly detailed work of fundamental importance. Thomas' book exposes the shortcomings in *H. R. Trevor-Roper, *The European Witch-Craze of the Sixteenth and Seventeenth Centuries* (New York, 1967) (Harper Torchbook), a provocative but distorted view of the subject. For studies of witchcraft in particular places, see Alan Macfarlane, *Witchcraft in Tudor and Stuart England* (New York, 1970); E. William Monter, *Witchcraft in France and Switzerland* (Ithaca, N.Y., 1976); H. C. Erik Midelfort, *Witch Hunting in Southwestern Germany, 1562–1684* (Stanford, Calif., 1972); *J. C. Baroja, *The World of the Witches* (Chicago, 1965) (Chicago) for Spain; and Robert Mandrou, *Magistrats et sorciers en France au xviie siècle* (Paris, 1968).

INTELLECTUAL HISTORY

The following four books are very helpful studies of the scientific revolution: *A. R. Hall, *The Scientific Revolution, 1500–1800,* second ed. (London, 1956) (Beacon); *Herbert Butterfield, *The Origins of Modern Science, 1300–1800* (London, 1949) (Free Press); Hugh Kearney, *Science and Change, 1500–1700* (New York, 1971); and *E. A. Burtt, *The Metaphysical Foundations of Modern Physical Science* (London, 1925) (Doubleday Anchor). For Copernicus, see *Thomas S. Kuhn, *The Copernican Revolution* (Cambridge, Mass., 1955) (Harvard). For Galileo, see Giorgio de Santillana, *The Crime of Galileo* (Chicago, 1955). For Newton, see Frank Manuel, *A Portrait of Isaac Newton* (Cambridge, Mass., 1968). R. K. Merton, *Science, Technology and Society in Seventeenth-Century England* (New York, 1970) argues for a symbiotic relationship between the new science and Puritanism—a proposition attacked by several contributors to *The Intellectual Revolution of the Seventeenth Century,* ed. by Charles Webster (London, 1974). The intellectual and psychological impact of the new science can be demonstrated by comparing the pre-Copernican view of nature described by *E. M. W. Tillyard, *The Elizabethan World Picture* (New York, 1944) (Random) with the environment of

Newton and Locke described by *Paul Hazard, *The European Mind, 1680–1715* (London, 1953) (New American Library).

For an excellent survey of musical developments in our period, see Manfred F. Bukofzer, *Music in the Baroque Era* (New York, 1947). The art and architecture of the period are best surveyed through the splendid *Pelican History of Art (London, 1953–   ), which includes the following pertinent volumes, all well illustrated: Jakob Rosenberg, *Dutch Art and Architecture, 1600–1800* (1966); Sir Anthony Blunt, *France, 1500–1700* (1954); Rudolf Wittkower, *Italy, 1600–1750* (1958); H. K. Gerson and E. H. ter Kuile, *Belgium, 1600–1800* (1960); George Kubler and Martin Soria, *Spain and Portugal, 1500–1800* (1959); Eberhard Hempel, *Central Europe, 1600–1800* (1965); and J. H. Summerson, *Britain, 1530–1830* (1953).

The best way to study the philosophers and dramatists is to read their works. E. A. Burtt, *The English Philosophers from Bacon to Mill* (New York, 1939) conveniently assembles generous selections from Bacon, Hobbes, and Locke. Descartes' *Discourse on Method,* Montaigne's *Essays,* Pascal's *Pensées,* Spinoza's *Ethics,* and representative plays by Lope de Vega, Calderón, Corneille, Racine, and Molière are all available in paperback in modern translations. The plays of Marlowe, Shakespeare, and Jonson are available in myriad editions.

Index